1 MONTH OF
FREE
READING

at

www.ForgottenBooks.com

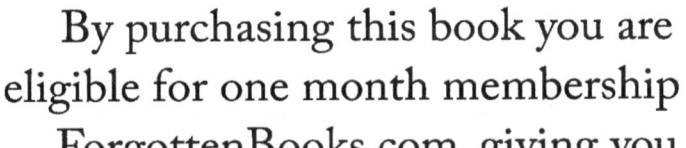

By purchasing this book you are eligible for one month membership to ForgottenBooks.com, giving you unlimited access to our entire collection of over 1,000,000 titles via our web site and mobile apps.

To claim your free month visit:

www.forgottenbooks.com/free188613

ISBN 978-0-266-19101-8
PIBN 10188613

Technical and Bibliographic Notes / Notes tech

The Institute has attempted to obtain the best original copy available for filming. Features of this copy which may be bibliographically unique, which may alter any of the images in the reproduction, or which may significantly change the usual method of filming are checked below.

☑ Coloured covers /
Couverture de couleur

☐ Covers damaged /
Couverture endommagée

☐ Covers restored and/or laminated /
Couverture restaurée et/ou pelliculée

☐ Cover title missing / Le titre de couverture manque

☑ Coloured maps / Cartes géographiques en couleur

☑ Coloured ink (i.e. other than blue or black) /
Encre de couleur (i.e. autre que bleue ou noire)

☑ Coloured plates and/or illustrations /
Planches et/ou illustrations en couleur

☐ Bound with other material /
Relié avec d'autres documents

☐ Only edition available /
Seule édition disponible

☐ Tight binding may cause shadows or distortion along interior margin / La reliure serrée peut causer de l'ombre ou de la distorsion le long de la marge intérieure.

☐ Blank leaves added during restorations may appear within the text. Whenever possible, these have been omitted from filming / Il se peut que certaines pages blanches ajoutées lors d'une restauration apparaissent dans le texte, mais, lorsque cela était possible, ces pages n'ont pas été filmées.

Additional comments /

L'Institut a
été possibl
plaire qui
ographique
ou qui peu
de normale

☐ Colo

☐ Page

☐ Page
Page

☑ Page
Page

☐ Page

☑ Sho

☑ Quali
Quali

☐ Inclu
Com

☐ Page
tissu
poss
parti
pelu
obtei

☐ Opp
disco
possi
color
film
possi

L'exemplaire filmé fut reproduit grâce à la générosité de:

Bibliothèque nationale du Canada

Les images suivantes ont été reproduites avec le plus grand soin, compte tenu de la condition et de la netteté de l'exemplaire filmé, et en conformité avec les conditions du contrat de filmage.

Les exemplaires originaux dont la couverture en papier est imprimée sont filmés en commençant par le premier plat et en terminant soit par la dernière page qui comporte une empreinte d'impression ou d'illustration, soit par le second plat, selon le cas. Tous les autres exemplaires originaux sont filmés en commençant par la première page qui comporte une empreinte d'impression ou d'illustration et en terminant par la dernière page qui comporte une telle empreinte.

Un des symboles suivants apparaîtra sur la dernière image de chaque microfiche, selon le cas: le symbole ⟶ signifie "A SUIVRE", le symbole ▽ signifie "FIN".

Les cartes, planches, tableaux, etc., peuvent être filmés à des taux de réduction différents. Lorsque le document est trop grand pour être reproduit en un seul cliché, il est filmé à partir de l'angle supérieur gauche, de gauche à droite, et de haut en bas, en prenant le nombre d'images nécessaire. Les diagrammes suivants illustrent la méthode.

3

1

2

MICROCOPY RESOLUTION TEST CHART

(ANSI and ISO TEST CHART No. 2)

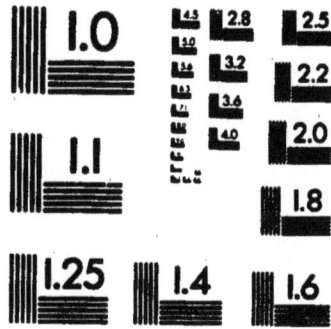

APPLIED IMAGE Inc

1653 East Main Street
Rochester, New York   14609   USA
(716) 482 - 0300 - Phone
(716) 288 - 5989 - Fax

Commission of Conservation
CANADA

COMMITTEE ON FISHERIES, GAME
AND FUR-BEARING ANIMALS

—

FUR-FARMING IN CANADA

Second Edition, Revised and Enlarged

—

By

J. WALTER JONES, B.A., B.S.A.

Ottawa:
The Mortimer Co., Ltd.
1914

Committee on Fisheries, Game and Fur-bearing Animals

Chairman:
DR. CECIL C. JONES

Members:
HON. O. T. DANIELS
HON. J. K. FLEMMING
HON. W. H. HEARST
HON. J. H. HOWDEN
HON. J. A. MATHIESON
DR. HOWARD MURRAY
DR. J. W. ROBERTSON
HON. W. R. ROSS

To Field Marshal His Royal Highness Prince Arthur William
Patrick Albert, Duke of Connaught and of Strathearn,
K.G., K.T., K.P., &c., &c., Governor-General of Canada

May it Please Your Royal Highness:

The undersigned has the honour to lay before Your Royal Highness
the report on Fur-farming in Canada, new edition, corrected and
revised.

Respectfully submitted,

CLIFFORD SIFTON,
Chairman

Ottawa, February 4, 1914

OTTAWA, FEBRUARY 3, 1914

Sir:

I have the honour to transmit herewith the report on Fur-farming in Canada, new edition, corrected and revised.

Your obedient servant,

JAMES WHITE,

Assistant to Chairman

HON. CLIFFORD SIFTON,
  Chairman
    Commission of Conservation

Contents

ILLUSTRATIONS

Preface to Second Edition

Rapid progress has marked the fur-farming industry since the publication of the Commission's first report on the subject a year ago. From all parts of Canada requests have been received for information and for copies of the report. To meet this demand it was deemed advisable to issue a revised and enlarged edition, so as to make the report as up-to-date as possible.

Assistance in the preparation of the original report, as well as the revision, has been received from various sources, many of which it is impossible to acknowledge here. It seems fitting, however, that special mention should be made of the courtesy and assistance rendered by Mr. Ernest Thompson Seton for helpful suggestions, as well as for permission to reproduce from his "Life Histories of Northern Animals," the maps showing the ranges in Canada of the Red Fox, Raccoon, Mink, American Marten, Skunk, Muskrat, and Beaver. Valuable statistics of fur production and sales were furnished by the Hudson's Bay Co., through the office of the Canadian High Commissioner, by Messrs. C. M. Lampson & Co., Messrs. A. and W. Nesbitt, Mr. Emil Brass, Mr. J. D. Whelpley and others. Messrs. Henry and Ernest Poland, of P. R. Poland & Sons, London, England, courteously revised a number of tables of statistics, in addition to providing considerable new material. Mr. R. H. Campbell supplied a short article on the Reindeer, Mr. Johann Beetz on the conservation of game in Quebec, and reports of the American Breeders' Association, and the Fur News Magazine have been freely quoted.

Mention should also be made of the kindness shown by Provincial game authorities and others who furnished the names and addresses of fur farmers and fur-farming companies given in Appendix XI.

SITTING ON THE BOX IN WHICH HE MADE A RAILWAY JOURNEY. SEPTEMBER FUR

FUR-FARMING IN CANADA

I. Introduction

UR-FARMING is a new industry in Canada, but its development has been rapid. A particular investigation conducted in the latter half of 1912 and further inquiries made during 1913 revealed numerous instances where animals of various species were being bred in captivity for their fur. Foxes of two species and of all colour varieties, skunk, mink, raccoon, fisher, beaver and muskrat were found upon fur-farms. The marten and otter are likewise being domesticated for their fur. During the past two years the number of fur-farms has multiplied exceedingly. In the province of Prince Edward Island, which may be considered the centre from which the fur-farming interest has chiefly radiated, probably six hundred ranches exist where one species or another is kept in confinement. In Nova Scotia, New Brunswick and Newfoundland the industry is extending with great rapidity and at this date— November, 1913—practically every trapper is trying to capture foxes, mink, marten, otter and skunk for purposes of domestication. A great and rapidly extending interest is manifested in Quebec, Ontario, Western Canada and the New England states. Russia has realized her advantageous position for the prosecution of this industry and has passed an enactment prohibiting the export of her karakule sheep. An extensive development of sable, silver and polar fox farms is also taking place in that country.

The great interest manifested in fur-farming is to be ascribed to the remarkable success attained in breeding silver and other colour phases of the fox common to Eastern Canada. The black and dark silver prime skins from foxes produced on Prince Edward Island ranches have rarely brought less than $500.00 each, and frequently bring over $2,000.00 at London auction sales. The pioneer fox breeders have acquired wealth in the business and their success has inspired their neighbours to engage in a similar line of work. Naturally the price of breeding stock, responding to the increased demand, has risen to many times the fur value, so that the ownership of even a pair of silver foxes is impossible to the average farmer.

Corporations and partnerships with a total capitalisation of $10,000,000 or $12,000,000 have been established for farming the silver fox. A large proportion of the inhabitants of Prince Edward Island and a smaller proportion of those of New Brunswick and Nova Scotia have invested their money, sometimes even mortgaging their property, to buy stock in these enterprises. Others have attempted to breed fur-bearing animals which require less capital for foundation stock.

Thus, in 1912 and 1913, upwards of 6,000 red and 1,000 cross or patch foxes were captured and made inmates of ranches in Eastern Canada. Probably more than 1,000 animals of various other species fared similarly. The industry has spread into Russia, where fur-bearing animals such as the Russian sable and the polar and the silver fox are now extensively farmed. Sables from the vicinity of Irkutsk and karakule sheep from Bokhara have, at great expense to the importers, been brought to America.

The great enthusiasm for fur-farming in Eastern Canada has resulted in high prices for breeding animals and seems to have created in the popular mind the impression that the soil and the climatic conditions of that region are favourable to the production of the best fur. It is true that splendid fox and mink are produced there, but it should not necessarily be assumed that polar fox, Labrador marten and Russian sable will thrive and fur up as well as in their own habitat. But, whatever the outcome of these experiments, the fact is that the reputed skill of its fur-farmers in caring for the animals has led to a centralisation of the fur-producing industry on Prince Edward Island. It is probably true that at least 85 per cent of the silver foxes in captivity are to be found in the Island province.

The high prices for furs prevailing during recent years explain why fur-farming has made such rapid progress in such a short time. This is particularly true of the black fox industry. The *fur-value* of a high-grade prime black fox skin ranges from about $500 to about $2,500; but the demand for breeding animals has been so great that the price has risen to $35,000 a pair for the best quality of breeding stock. Moreover, the promoter has entered the field and companies are being floated whose capitalizations are based on these high prices for pelts and on very rosy expectations of profits. It cannot be predicted with certainty what the price will be when even a few thousand more skins are marketed yearly. The price will certainly decline eventually in conformity with the increase in supply, but will probably always remain high on account of the fur's extreme beauty. Although there is ample basis for a sound industry fox-farming, it is necessary that the general public should realize that the industry is a highly speculative one, and that the individual who puts his money in companies capitalised at from five to ten times the fur value of the animals assumes a great risk.

Since the fur-farming industry is so intimately connected with the present high prices of furs, it will be worth while to enquire into the causes of these high prices and endeavour to forecast to what extent they will continue to operate.

DEMAND AND SUPPLY

Increasing Demand for Furs Stated in general terms, fur has become scarce because less is produced and more is used than ever before. The remarkable increase in the demand for costly furs in the past twenty years is due to a combination of causes. The population is growing. The relative number of people in the wealthy classes is increasing. The habits of travelling extensively and of living in metropolitan centres are rapidly increasing. Commerce and more efficient salesmanship have introduced furs all over the world, so that their admirers and users are multiplied. Dame Fashion, whose influence is predominant everywhere, is responsible for a very heavy demand for certain kinds, and only the best and scarcest are in high favour with her. Then, too, our growing cities, which multiply the opportunities for gatherings and concourses, especially of the well-to-do classes, engender competitive habits in choosing personal adornments.

The growing use of the automobile and the more general habit of living out-of-doors have made furs almost a necessity. In America alone, the valuation of automobiles is now about $2,000,000,000, and a proper equipment for the luxurious vehicles and their occupants necessitates the use of many millions of dollars worth of furs and leather. Better roads, more extensive travel, and cheaper automobiles are important factors in determining the growing demands for fur and pelts generally.

Lessening Supply of Fur If the keenness of the hunt is maintained, some species of animals must soon be exterminated. When dead-falls, snares and the bow and arrow were used in hunting there was a chance for the game to escape; but with modern guns, smokeless powder, improved traps and the most alluring baits and scents that modern chemists can compound or trappers can invent, there are fewer opportunities. Coupled with increased efficiency of destructive gear is the general diffusion by railways, steamship lines and hunting and trapping magazines, of knowledge respecting game resorts and the hunter's art. Railways and steamship lines are tapping new territory, corps of guides are organised, canned food and better camping equipment make the hunter's life more enjoyable, and as a result, the uttermost sanctuaries of the fur-bearers are invaded. Their last retreats have been made and they must now slowly diminish in numbers year by year. The musk-ox, for instance, has figured in the London sales only for the past forty years because, prior to that time, Arctic hunters were unable to reach its habitat. Continued invasion of its territory may lead to its extinction. The usual method employed to prevent the complete extinction of a species is to establish a close season. Recently, a close season of three years was declared for the Russian sable to allow it to recuperate in numbers in Siberia. The chinchilla has similar protection in Bolivia, and the Canadian beaver is frequently protected in a similar way. Perhaps the most concerted effort on the part of nations to prevent the extinction of a species by establishing a close season is to be found in the case of the Alaska fur-seal. In July, 1911, the United States, Great Britain, Russia and Japan entered into a treaty which provides for the prohibition of pelagic or open sea sealing for a period of fifteen years. In the same year the United States enacted a provision prohibiting land-killing of seals on the Pribilof islands for a period of ten years. The general decrease in the number of fur-bearers during the past twenty years indicates how ineffectual are the preventive methods employed.

Destruction of Haunts   The ever-expanding areas of human settlements have caused some kinds of fur-bearers to retreat farther into the woods. The clearing away of the forests and the grazing of the natural covers by domestic animals have destroyed their haunts and exposed them to their enemies. Draining swampy areas has destroyed the homes of the muskrat or musquash, the mink, the otter and the beaver. The fisher and the marten never seem to exist long near man's habitation. Even the fox, which appears to increase near human settlements, will decrease if the forests are wholly removed or burned.

DECREASING NUMBER OF PELTS

Statement, based on the London Sales of C. M. Lampson & Co. By Alfred Fraser, New York)

KIND OF SKIN	DECREASE IN NUMBERS, PERCENTAGE		
	1892-1901 over 1882-1891	1902-1911 over 1892-1901	1892-1911 over 1882-1891
Fox, silver............	10	45	50
" cross.............	5	65	70
" red..............	53	2	55
" blue.............	34†	40	23
" white............	750†	25	510†
Marten, pine..........	65†	55	20
Fisher or pekan.......	5†	95	95
Mink.................	75†	55	20
Skunk................	30†	55†	110†
Muskrat..............	250†	10	215†
Lynx.................	3800†	80	700†
Otter, land..........	45†	30	5†
" sea.............	65	50	85

† Increase

INCREASING PRICES OF PELTS

(Statement based on the London Sales of C. M. Lampson & Co. By Alfred Fraser, New York)

KIND OF SKIN	INCREASE IN PRICES, PERCENTAGE		
	1892-1901 over 1882-1891	1902-1911 over 1892-1901	1892-1911 over 1882-1891
Fox, silver............	155	55	300
" cross.............	10	100	125
" red..............	85	85	245
" blue.............	20*	145	100
" white............	120	100	350
Marten, pine..........	470	15	580
Fisher or pekan.......	0	430	430
Mink.................	60	150	300
Skunk................	20	110	150
Muskrat..............	0	230	230
Lynx.................	25	130	200
Otter, land..........	30*	170	80
" sea.............	110	65	240

* Decrease

NOTES.—1. The increase in the price of pelts during the past twenty years has been general averaging about 25 per cent for the staple fur-bearers of Canada.

2. All pelts, except those of skunk, have decreased in numbers during the past ten years.

3. Pelts considered of little value twenty years ago are being hunted to the verge of extinction; e.g., fisher, lynx, marten, mink, cross fox and even muskrat, show signs of failing.

4. The increase in numbers of pelts fifteen years ago was caused by keener hunting. This was inspired by the rising values.

The extent to which these influences have diminished the number of furs marketed is well put in the *Fur News Magazine*, for November, 1912, which says:—

"We present elsewhere in this issue a record of the collection of all fur skins centring at London, and the majority are sent there, for the years 1911 and 1912, both secured under the terrific pressure of a strong demand and record-breaking prices which induced strenuous and persistent trapping to the limit—and past good business judgment.

"The figures are remarkably interesting, and definitely serious as showing the marked decrease in quantity straight down the column with rare and insignificant exceptions; in most instances the declines are very great and invite careful attention, particularly as it is perfectly true that every possible effort was made the country over to effect the opposite result, and which surely would have been noted if the fur-bearers were present in usual numbers in their customary haunts or new and unusual retreats. The few exceptions, where there is an increase instead of a decrease, include cross fox and fisher, both of which were so high in value that it paid better to catch one a week rather than waste time catching other animals twice a day every day; but the total increase for both is only thirty-two hundred for the entire year and country; wolf is the only other fur of moment showing an increase in catch over 1911, and the difference is due to a general impulse to effect extermination, and not to the fact that there were more wolves than in the preceding year. Not a few 1911 skins were held back and came forward in this year's sales.

"A study of the figures further shows the same general decrease in collections of Russian, German, Japanese and Australian skins. Every fur skin caught *anywhere* this year will have a value and not a skin should be sacrificed."

SUPPLYING THE DEMAND

Confronted with this condition of a decreasing supply and an increasing demand, the fur trade has sought to prevent high prices by popularizing the use of furs which were formerly considered of slight value. A large part of this work now devolves on the fur-dressers and dyers who can render stiff pelts more supple and change the colour of the fur to resemble that of other more valuable animals. The use of furs pro-

Popularizing less costly and Domestic Furs

duced under domestic conditions has also been enormously extended. Ponies, kids, lambs and even pups are killed in large numbers to supply the increasing demands for fur. The great vogue of Russian lamb skins of which about three millions are used yearly, emphasizes the importance of achieving production of fur from domestic animals. The costly baby lamb or broadtail, the Persian lamb, the astrakhan and krimmer furs are the skins of the karakule sheep. The various names have been supplied by the furriers and have no geographical significance at the present time. If the marten and mink had been domesticated a score or more years ago, they might now be supplying fur in the same way as the karakule sheep, and, with the modern addition of the fox, would have served as a counterpoise in Canada to the monopoly now enjoyed by Russia—particularly Bokhara—in the production of domestic fur. When the perennially fashionable sable, ermine, chinchilla and silver fox did not supply the demand, the Persians, broadtail and seal became more costly. Gradually, too, from its plebeian rank of coat-lining at fifty cents a skin, mink was adopted into the select family of valuable furs, closely preceded by marten and, latterly, followed by fisher and cross fox. To take the place of mink as a coat-lining, muskrat or musquash was chosen, sharing this promotion with the less valuable marmot and hamster of Europe. To supply the demand for a medium-priced black fur of beauty, a common animal, the skunk, has been chosen and named Alaska sable. The black domestic cat, known to the trade as 'genet,' is also utilized to meet the demand for black furs, while northern hares and conies are extensively manufactured into 'Baltic fox' or 'white fox' or 'black lynx' or 'electric seal.'

Renaming Furs When the fur dressers and dyers produced a clipped and dyed muskrat skin that resembled sealskin almost perfectly, it was found that it would not sell under its real name because it was a common fur, used largely by the poorer classes. Consequently a name was invented for it and this popular and high-priced fur is now sold as 'Hudson Bay seal'. The fur of the coney, a very cheap and common animal in France, is the raw product in producing 'electric sealskin', 'clipped seal' and 'Baltic seal'. Raccoon, when first introduced, was cheap and was in little demand, but when given the name 'Alaska bear' and 'silver bear' it immediately came into favour. Skunk, which is an excellent fur of a dark hue, though beautiful and durable, could not be sold as skunk, but, as 'black marten', and 'Alaska sable', it is in high favour and likely to remain in the class of the medium and higher priced furs. It is worth remarking that, since the prejudice against the muskrat, skunk and other cheap furs has been overcome, they can be sold under their real names. Muskrat backs are now sold as 'rat' fur at almost as high figures as the dyed product.

Imitations and Misnaming

The pressure of increasing demand has brought into common use the fur of animals with harsh, brittle hair of any colour, which is sold under names which mislead the unwary public. Thus, the pelts of animals from the warmer zones such as Chinese goat, Thibet lamb, Manchurian dog, hamster, marmot, Tartar pony, opossum, raccoon, weasel, jackal fox, monkey, antelope, otter and many others are now worked up by dressers and dyers into very respectable-looking furs. They are inferior, however, to the furs from colder climates in suppleness of leather, closeness of underwool, fullness of overhair and silkiness of hair and, because they are dyed, they are less durable and less prized.

Misnaming and Deceptions

The misnaming of furs has caused the London Chamber of Commerce to give notice that misleading terms are not to be used and that offenders are liable to prosecution under the Merchandise Marks Act, 1887. Even in the early days when misnaming was in its infancy, the manufactured furs were frequently misnamed as follows:

Muskrat or musquash, pulled and dyed......................Seal
Nutria, pulled and dyed....................................Seal
Nutria, pulled and natural ....Beaver
Rabbit, sheared and dyed..................................Seal
Otter, pulled and dyed. .   ...Seal
Marmot, dyed............ ....Mink or sable
Fitch, dyed...,..Sable
Rabbit, dyed..............................Sable or French sable
Hare, dyed....................................Sable, fox or lynx
Muskrat, dyed...................................Mink or sable
Wallaby, dyed..Skunk
White rabbit..Ermine
White rabbit, dyed...................................Chinchilla
White hare, dyed or natural........................Fox, foxaline
Goat, dyed....................................Bear or leopard

But, if laws were necessary twenty-five years ago to protect the public from frauds, what must be the necessity at the present time, when two hares reared by the same mother may pose on the same counter as 'white fox' and 'black lynx', respectively?

The following is a list of common misdescriptions:

VARIETY	SOLD AS—
American sable	Real Russian sable
Fitch, dyed	Sable
Goat, dyed	Bear
Hare, dyed	Sable or fox
Kid	Lamb or broadtail
Marmot, dyed	Mink, sable or skunk
Mink, dyed	Sable
Musquash (muskrat), dyed	Mink or sable
Musquash, pulled and dyed	Seal, electric seal, Red River seal or Hudson Bay seal
Nutria, pulled and dyed	Seal, electric seal, Red River seal or Hudson Bay seal
Nutria, pulled, natural	Beaver and otter
Opossum, sheared and dyed	Beaver
Otter, pulled and dyed	Seal
Rabbit, dyed	Sable or French sable
Rabbit, sheared and dyed	Seal, electric seal, Red River seal, Hudson Bay seal and seal musquash
Rabbit, white	Ermine
Rabbit, white, dyed	Chinchilla
Wallaby, dyed	Skunk
White hare	Fox and other similar names
Dyed furs of all kinds	Natural
White hairs inserted in foxes and sables	Real or natural furs

The following list has been published by the London Chamber of Commerce as permissible descriptions:

NAME OF FUR	PERMISSIBLE DESCRIPTION
American sable	Canadian sable or real sable
Fitch, dyed	Sable fitch
Goat, dyed	Bear goat
Hare, dyed	Sable hare or fox hare
Kids	Karakule kids
Marmot, dyed	Sable marmot, mink marmot or skunk marmot
Mink, dyed	Sable mink
Musquash (muskrat), pulled and dyed	Seal musquash
Nutria, pulled and dyed	Seal nutria
Nutria, pulled, natural	Beaver nutria or otter nutria
Opossum, sheared and dyed	Beaver opossum
Otter, pulled and dyed	Seal otter
Rabbit, dyed	Sable coney
Rabbit, sheared and dyed	Seal coney or musquash coney
Rabbit, white	Mock ermine
Rabbit, white, dyed	Chinchilla coney
Wallaby, sheared and dyed	Skunk wallaby
White hare	Imitation fox or mock fox
White hairs inserted in foxes or sables	Pointed fox or sable

Frauds in Selling Furs Reliable furriers, however, do not use the misdescriptive names mentioned above. Many of the smaller furriers are doubtless ignorant of the real names of their stock; but cheap advertisers are frequently guilty of misnaming. Many advertisers giving private addresses mislead the public; when a lady who is 'going South' offers her 'new $150 Russian lynx set for $25', the conclusion may readily be reached that it is 'doctored' rabbit. However, the enterprise of furriers should not be wholly discouraged, as, otherwise, owing to the scarcity of really good fur, many ladies would have to appear in worsted scarfs and mitts for six months of the year. The pride they take in their 'ermines', 'foxes', 'minks' and 'chinchillas' and in their bargain 'fishers' and black 'marten' would probably be diminished if they knew they were only 'doctored' rabbit, marmot, opossum and wallaby.

Hunter-trapper Age Passing — All the artifices of the fur-dressers and dyers in preparing the skins and of the furriers and jobbers in supplying fancy names for inferior stock have failed to compensate for the decreasing supply of fur of good quality. It is quite possible that the supply of all domestic animal skins like rabbit, lamb, and kid can be indefinitely and rapidly increased to the limit of demand, but it is not possible under present methods of breeding, to secure an increasing supply of really good fur such as comes from the carnivorous animals—notably the *mustelidœ* or weasel family— unless they are domesticated. This one fact stands out prominently: the hunting and trapping of wild fur-bearing animals must be supplemented by their domestication if the demand for furs is to be satisfied.

The hunter-trapper age has passed its zenith. With the demand exceeding the possible supply, more economical methods must be introduced and the supply must be increased. The tearing up of trapped animals by carnivorous mammals before the trapper can reach the traps is common and represents a great loss. The killing of animals whose pelts are not in prime condition represents a large annual loss of valuable fur. These and other wastes are eliminated when fur-bearers are domesticated.

Cruelty of Trapping — Apart from economic considerations the cruelty involved in trapping wild animals affords a powerful argument against the continuation of the practice. Trapping is notoriously cruel and tends to destroy the finer feelings of those engaged in the business. Trappers visit their lines only two or three times a week, and in the interval the captured animals, in most cases suffering excruciating pain, are exposed to frost, hunger, their natural enemies and, finally, their arch-enemy—man. Elliott Coues in his monograph on the North American *mustelidœ*, aptly describes the actions of a mink when caught in a trap:

"The tenacity of life of the mink is something remarkable. It lives for many hours—in cases I have known, for more than a day and night—under the pressure of a heavy log, sufficient to hold it like a vice, and when the middle of the body was pressed perfectly flat. Nay, under one such circumstance which I recall, the animal showed good fight on approach. When caught by the leg in a steel trap, the mink usually gnaws and tears the captive member, sometimes lacerating it in a manner painful to witness; but, singular to say, it bites the part beyond the jaws of the trap . . . The violence and persistence of the poor, tortured animal endeavouring to escape are witnessed in the frequent breaking of its teeth against the iron—this is the rule rather than the exception. One who has not taken the mink in a steel trap can scarcely form an idea of the terrible expression the animal's face assumes as the captor approaches. It has always struck me as the most nearly diabolical of anything in animal physiognomy. A sullen stare from the crouched, motionless form gives way to a new look of surprise and fear accompanied by the most violent contortions of the body, with renewed champing of the iron, till, breathless, with heaving flanks, and open mouth dribbling saliva, the animal settles again, and watches with a look of concentrated hatred, mingled with impotent rage and frightful despair."

When it is remembered that millions of animals are captured yearly in traps the sum total of their sufferings must be so great that the cruelty practiced on dumb domestic creatures, which so greatly concerns the Society for the Prevention of Cruelty to Animals, must seem slight in comparison. The methods of killing domestic animals are humane and painless, and it would seem that humane considerations alone present a sufficient argument for the domestication of fur-bearing animals.

Domestic Fur-bearers The first step towards raising animals for their fur was taken years ago when karakule sheep—a domestic animal from which the Persian lamb and broadtail are obtained—began to be bred for its pelt. Up to recent years this animal was the only example of a valuable fur-bearer in captivity. It is a domestic animal merely, but, because of the difficulties in travelling, in language, in religious prejudices of the people who breed them, in knowledge of good stock, in quarantine laws and in remoteness of the district in which they flourish, it has been very difficult to secure specimens for breeding purposes. Latterly, exceedingly optimistic reports of success in karakule 'crosses' in the United States have been reported. If the Persian lamb can be economically produced in America, millions of dollars will be saved annually, as the use of this lasting and handsome fur is increasing steadily. That the business is regarded in

Russia as an important one, is indicated by the calling of a convention of breeders at Moscow in October, 1912, at the special request of the Czar. As a possible source of future fur supply, the karakule crossed with lustrous woolled sheep like Lincolns and Cotswolds appears to be one of the most promising. Experiments made recently have produced lamb skins of magnificent gloss and curl. Because, however, of a recently-enacted prohibition of export of fur-bearing sheep, from Bokhara and Russia, it is feared that the animals already brought to America cannot be augmented in number by new blood from Asia. Enough sheep have been imported to prove the practicability of producing on this continent the best grades of Persian lamb fur, and, if too much in-breeding can be avoided, it is possible that the industry may become established.

Despite the progress that has been made in breeding
Domesticating karakule sheep, it must be acknowledged that domestica-
Fur-bearers tion of fur-bearing animals has, thus far, failed to supply the demand for pelts which are highly valued for fur. The increasing demand and the ever-decreasing supply of desirable fur pelts is producing a state of trade that would be alarming were it not for the possibilities of domesticating and breeding other fur-bearers. The time has come when, on account of the high range of prices, every effort should be made to domesticate all wild fur-bearing animals of considerable value.

There is a broad field for activity in this direction. According to Lantz' estimate, there are about five thousand species of mammals at present inhabiting the earth. About twenty-three of these are in a state of domestication, serving man as beasts of burden or furnishing food, clothing, or companionship.

The hoofed animals (*ungulata*) comprise:

The Asiatic elephant, horse, ass, hog, camel, dromedary, reindeer, goat, sheep, yak, buffalo (two species), ox (two species), and llama (possibly four species).

The flesh-eating animals (*carnivora*) comprise:

The cat, dog, ferret and cheetah or hunting leopard of India.

The rodent animals (*rodentia*) comprise:

The rabbit and the guinea pig.

The Arctic fox (*vulpes lagopus*) and the common fox (*vulpes vulpes*) may be classed as domestic, as for twenty years they have been nurtured under man's care, and the rising prices of fur will probably make the industry permanent. The marten is said to have been domesticated by the Romans and even to-day the mink is sometimes crossed with the domestic ferret to produce a more desirable disposition in the off-spring.

THREE ORDERS OF WILD CANADIAN MAMMALS AND THEIR ECONOMIC USES

Order	Family	Species	Parts of Economic Use
Hoofed Animals (*hoofed; large*)	Deer	Elk	Flesh, hide, trophies
		Deer	" " "
		Moose	" " "
		Caribou	" " "
	Cattle	Bison (Buffalo)	" " "
Rodent (*no canine teeth; 4 incisors only, except in rabbit*)	Squirrel	Squirrel	Pelt, flesh
		Chipmunk	Pelt
		Woodchuck	"
	Beaver	Canadian Beaver	Pelt, flesh, castors
	Mouse	Mice	
		Voles	
		Lemming	
		Muskrat	Pelt, flesh
	Hare	Hare	Flesh, pelt, hair
Carnivora (*12 incisors; 4 large canines; shearing premolars*)	Cat	Lynx	Pelt
	"	Cat (*domestic*)	"
	"	Wild cat	"
	Dog	Fox	"
	"	Wolf	"
	"	Coyote	"
	Weasel (*mustelidæ*)	Otter	"
	"	Weasel	"
	"	Mink	"
	"	Marten	"
	"	Fisher	"
	"	Wolverene	"
	"	Skunk	Pelt, oil and galls
	"	Badger	Pelt, hair
	Raccoon	Raccoon	Pelt, flesh
	Bear	Bear	Pelt, flesh
	Seal	Fur-seal	Pelt, oil, flesh
		Hair-seal	Pelt, oil

The Precious Fur-bearers It is desirable to breed the species producing the most valuable fur rather than those whose fur does not bring such a high price. The sea-otter, the silver fox, the Russian sable and the chinchilla are the precious fur-bearers of modern times.

Baby lamb and Alaska seal are among the highest priced furs. Of the above named, Russian sables, Alaska seal, chinchilla and sea-otter are under close season restrictions for several years to permit them to recuperate in numbers. The silver fox and baby lamb are being bred successfully under domestic conditions and the others are being strenuously experimented with. The Alaska seal may almost be said to be under domestic conditions of breeding as the herd is properly husbanded at the breeding season by United States Government agents.

The sea-otter, which probably brings the highest average price of any fur animal on the market and yields the most durable fur known, can hardly be domesticated. Little is known of its history or even of its domestic habits. Its extreme scarcity and remote habitations will probably prevent extensive experiments in domesticating it.

The Russian sable is now kept in ranches, but Mr. Vladimir Generosoff, who furnished information and photographs of Russian sable farms and who has done excellent work in Russia for the encouragement of the domestic production of fur, did not state whether they have yet bred in captivity. The best sable skins bring over $500.00 but the majority fetch less than $50.00 each—the price usually depending on the colour—a bluish black being highest priced. They are found in remote parts of Siberia.

It is evident that only the Russian authorities can secure a sufficient number of excellent wild specimens to conduct a practical experiment. In the meantime, in preparation for the time when the Russian sable will be available for breeding in Canada, experiments should be conducted with the Canadian sable, which is very closely related to the Russian and very similar in habit.

Because of its ubiquitous character and its fondness for living near human habitations, the silver fox has been subjected to more domesticating experiments than any other valuable fur-bearer. When it became known that it was simply a pelage colour of the common red fox, experiments were multiplied with the cheaper red foxes to gain experience in breeding the species. The breeding of the fox in captivity is proceeding on an increasingly large scale and no doubt exists now regarding the possibility of domesticating it.

A FULL-FURRED FOX   DECEMBER FUR

A FULL-FURRED BLACK FOX, DECEMBER FUR

II. Early Attempts to Domesticate the Fox

IT would be futile to record all the early attempts to rear foxes in captivity and note has, therefore, been made of the experiences of only a few breeders at widely separated points. The experimenters, in most cases, were wholly unacquainted with the experience of others.

It has been customary for trapper-farmers to keep aliv., foxes caught in warm weather until the fur is prime. Thus, young foxes captured in July are kept until December before being killed. The earliest authentic record obtained of producing young from foxes kept in captivity on Prince Edward Island, comes from Tignish, where Benjamin Haywood reared several litters some thirty-five years ago; but they were destroyed by the parent foxes because they were not kept in seclusion and quiet.

Doubtless there had been, in earlier years, numerous cases that were as successful as Mr. Haywood's, but it is interesting to record this experiment because he was a near neighbour of the men who finally achieved the greatest success in the commercial fox-breeding industry.

Several furriers in Quebec have been connected with breeding experiments. Messrs. Paquet Bros. had a small ranch at one time at St. Joseph-d'Alma near the head of the Saguenay, which they finally sold. Revillon Frères were interested in a ranch on the north shore of the gulf of St. Lawrence a dozen years ago, but finally abandoned the experiment believing that fox raising was destined to fail. Holt, Renfrew & Co. have a ranch near Quebec the foundation stock of which was a litter of silver foxes from . pair of exhibition foxes in their menagerie at Montmorency Falls.

In Ontario, Rev. George Clark, of St. Catharines, an experienced breeder of pheasants, bred a litter of reds from a pet pair of wild foxes in 1905. Two ranches were started about 1906, near North Sydney, and on the Lingan road near Sydney, N.S., respectively; but, after several years, they failed to maintain the foxes in breeding condition. These were later sold to Bruce, Cummings, McConnell, and others, who have proved to be successful ranchers.

Quebec Breeders Excellent success in breeding the fox has been achieved by Mr. Johann Beets, at Piastre Baie, North shore, gulf of St. Lawrence, and Mr. T. L. Burrowman, of Wyoming, Ontario. The former is the scion of a wealthy Brussels family, and his roving spirit led him to Labrador and Alaska on hunting expeditions. He finally settled at Piastre Baie, about 1898, and attempted fox ranching with a pair of silver foxes brought from Alaska. There were trees at

several points in the neighbourhood, and at some ten or twelve wooded
spots, a hundred or more rods from his dwelling, he kept his pens,
having two females and one male at each point. He adopted the system
of double mating. Large quantities of salmon, lobsters and game were
caught for food for the foxes, while horse-meat was occasionally brought
from Quebec city. He augmented his stock with native Quebec wild
foxes and conducted feeding experiments with red foxes. Careful
selection has improved his strain until they grade dark silver throughout.*

Authentic reports state that the late M. Menier, who owned Anticosti island, attempted to breed foxes there, and set at liberty silver
and patched foxes to grade up the colour of the wild fox.

An Ontario Experimenter   Mr. Burrowman is a fur-buyer who, at an early date,
recognized the possibilities of domesticating fur-bearers.
He kept foxes in captivity twenty-two years, but did not
successfully rear young to maturity until about ten years ago, because,
prior to that time, he kept more than one pair in a single pen. He
may be called the father of the Ontario fox-ranching business. The
only assistance he obtained was from the late Dr. Robertson of Fox-
croft, Me.

Oulton and Dalton   The placing of the fox-raising industry on a commercial
basis is due to the efforts of Robert T. Oulton, formerly
of Alberton, P.E.I., but now of Little Shemogue, N.B.,
and his former partner, Charles Dalton, now of Tignish, P.E.I. Dalton
began experimenting about 1887, with red foxes, which he kept in a
shed at Nail Pond. Later, he bought silver foxes from neighbouring
districts and from Anticosti island and continued his experiments with
indifferent success for about ten years. During that time, Oulton was
also experimenting with foxes, having bought silver foxes at various
points in P.E.I., Anticosti and elsewhere, and working somewhat in
conjunction with Dalton. All Anticosti foxes were subsequently
slaughtered because they did not come up to the requisite standard
of quality.

One of their chief concerns was keeping prying neighbours
from their ranch premises. While Beetz had little difficulty with
neighbours, the obtaining of a sufficient food supply was a matter that
gave no little trouble. Dalton and Oulton were more fortunate in
their food supply as the thickly settled farming country all about them
supplied horse-flesh and other cheap meat in abundance. Tallow, corn-
meal, fish, oat-meal, flour and butcher's waste were available in plenty
and a very small outlay in cash procured a large supply.

*See memorandum by Mr. J. Beetz, Appendix VIII.

Oulton pursued his work on Savage Cherry island, or as it is commonly called, Oulton island, of which he was the sole inhabitant. He managed to impress the public with the necessity of keeping away from his ranch, and his pens, constructed within an outside enclosure a quarter acre in area, were the models for the pr _nt system of ranching. Dalton joined interests with Oulton in 1896 or thereabouts, and, together, they used the present forms of wire enclosures which were first constructed by Oulton. In 1898, Dalton built a ranch at Tignish, still retaining a half interest in the Oulton ranch. He bought and sold skins and generally conducted the fur sales for the district. All Oulton's foxes were sold in Dalton's name. Dalton also conducted a general correspondence with the fur trade, and imported stock which proved of value for crossing.

Up to this time—1898—no very high prices were realized for skins. The prices paid for silver fox were not as high as at the present time and probably did not average more than thirty or forty per cent of present day prices. Moreover, the foxes of those days had not the advantage of good breeding and selection like the foxes of the present time. They were simply captured wild foxes or else, probably, not more than one or two generations removed from the wild state. The first high prices recorded were in London in the year 1899 or 1900— when it is said about $1,800.00 were paid for a silver fox skin. This price of course gave a new vision to Messrs. Oulton and Dalton who up to this time had been operating with but meagre capital, and the expectation of only moderate prices for their skins.

The neighbours of Dalton and Oulton, who were their companions on hunting expeditions in Cascumpeque bay, naturally chafed at not being able to participate in this profitable but carefully guarded fox-farming business. One of the most alert, Captain James Gordon, was able to purchase from Mr. Oulton, in 1898, a pair of silver foxes, which he ranched at the remote and secluded farm of his friend, Robert Tuplin, of Black Banks. It is said that this pair were purchased for $340, which demonstrates the value of the fur at that date. In the following spring, high prices were received at the London sales, and Dalton and Oulton attempted to buy back their former stock at a price $100.00 higher, but Gordon and Tuplin would not sell. For several years Gordon and Tuplin lost their litters on account of not providing small well-insulated nests for the young, but they finally achieved success with a nest constructed of small barrels within larger ones, the intervening space between being packed with dry, insulating material. To Captain Gordon must be given the credit of inventing the modern form of nest, while Oulton must be credited with designing the form of pen. Frank Tuplin of Summerside obtained the foundation

2

stock for his la.... .....c.: f.... his uncle, Robert Tuplin.   Other neighbours were able to secure sto... at various points, and as the years went
by purchased fr.... h.... .der ranchmen, an animal or two for
crossing.   In this manner Silas Rayner, Harry Lowis and John
Champion started their ranches.   A large number of neighbours secured
red and cross foxes and began breeding them for the purpose of per-
fecting themselves in the art of rearing the silver foxes which, in after
years, they were able to obtain.   By the year 1909, a dozen or more
farmers in the vicinity of Alberton, P.E.I., were engaged in fox-farming.
Two ranches were in operation near Summerside, P.E.I., several in
Maine, two in Ontario and one in Quebec.   Selling foundation stock
became general in the following year and enhanced prices for breeders
soon put a stop to the slaughter of animals for fur, the last sales of pelts
being recorded in 1910 of animals slaughtered in 1909.   Since that
time only the pelts of old, accidentally killed, and diseased animals
have been marketed.

Most of the early attempts to rear foxes failed because:

Causes of Early Failure

1. No good fencing material, such as the woven wire used at the present time, was available.

2. Warm, dry quarters for the young litters were not provided, the principle of having a small well-insulated nest which
would be sufficiently warmed by the mother's body heat not being
recognized sufficiently.

3. The monogamous nature of foxes was not recognized and
being quartered in one pen in large numbers, the young were
killed.

4. The price of fur was not high enough to induce breeders
to risk large amounts of capital in experiments, and those who
had the aptitude for the business usually possessed but little
capital.

The rising prices of fur in the "nineties," the availability of woven
wire fencing material, and the invention of a suitable nest and the
persistence of men like Oulton, Gordon, Dalton, Beetz and Burrowman
are responsible for the successful methods of ranching evolved.   General
details of feeding and management are still kept from the public and new
ranchmen frequently pay considerable sums of money to older ranchmen for advice which, they, in turn, seek to retail to others.   Other
ex....anced ranchmen demand large salaries for their services as care-
takers.   A large proportion of the newer ranchmen have been less
successful than the older and more experienced, for it is obvious that

the care and feeding of a wild animal in confinement is much more difficult than feeding and attending domestic animals. Yet results have been such that stringency in the money market and failures to rear any young whatsoever in some ranches, does not prevent an increasing enthusiasm for investment in the industry. The price of a pair of five months' old silver fox pups of the best Prince Edward Island stock has risen as follows:

September, 1909........................$3,000
September, 1910........................ 4,000
September, 1911........................ 6,000
September, 1912........................10,000
September, 1913........................16,000

The price of old, proved breeders is more variable. Usually few are sold as it is considered somewhat unsafe to remove them from the pens in which they have bred. When old stock of proved fecundity are sold they fetch from $25,000 to $35,000 per pair.

III. Manual of Fur-farming

COMMON RED FOX

THE fox is found on every continent and comprises a number of species. The common red fox, which exists in the greatest numbers, has a range which "extends across Europe and northern and central Asia to Japan, while, to the south, it embraces northern Africa and Arabia, Persia, Baluchistan and the northwestern districts of India and the Himalayas." In North America, its range extends south to Virginia and includes all Canada (except some northern regions), and the northeasternmost portion of the United States. Its wide geographical range accounts for many distinct local phases or geographical varieties. These phases, or sub-species, differ from one another in form, in size and, to some extent, in colouring; but the differences are often not apparent to the untrained observer. It is easy to distinguish the four species of foxes commonly seen in America, viz., the common red with its white tipped tail, the arctic or polar fox with its short ears and blue or white pelt, the kit-fox with its black tail and small size, and the gray fox with its gray and red colour and erectile hairs down the tail; but it is more difficult to distinguish the sub-species of the common red fox.

The popular classification is by colour, as follows:

COMMON RED FOX (*Vulpes*), found in some districts in several colours, viz.:
  Red Fox—When red or yellow over sides and back.
  Silver Fox—When no red is present.
  Cross or Patch Fox—When the sides and neck are red and the back, shoulders and hips are silver. An intermediate between silver and red.
  The red, silver and cross foxes are not distinct species and not even distinct breeds. Silver foxes usually breed true to colour, and continued selection will insure the distinctive colour markings of each colour variety.

Scientists, of course, follow the universal rule of measuring the skulls and teeth for classification purposes. The colour is not a consideration with them. Merriam classified the North American red foxes as follows:

  V. fulvus—Ontario, Quebec, Eastern United States.
  V. bangsi—Labrador and North shore of gulf of St. Lawrence.
  V. deletrix—Newfoundland.
  V. rubricosa—Nova Scotia, New Brunswick, Gaspe, Prince Edward Island.*

---

* As it has been segregated for ages, the Prince Edward Island fox is, possibly, a distinct variety.

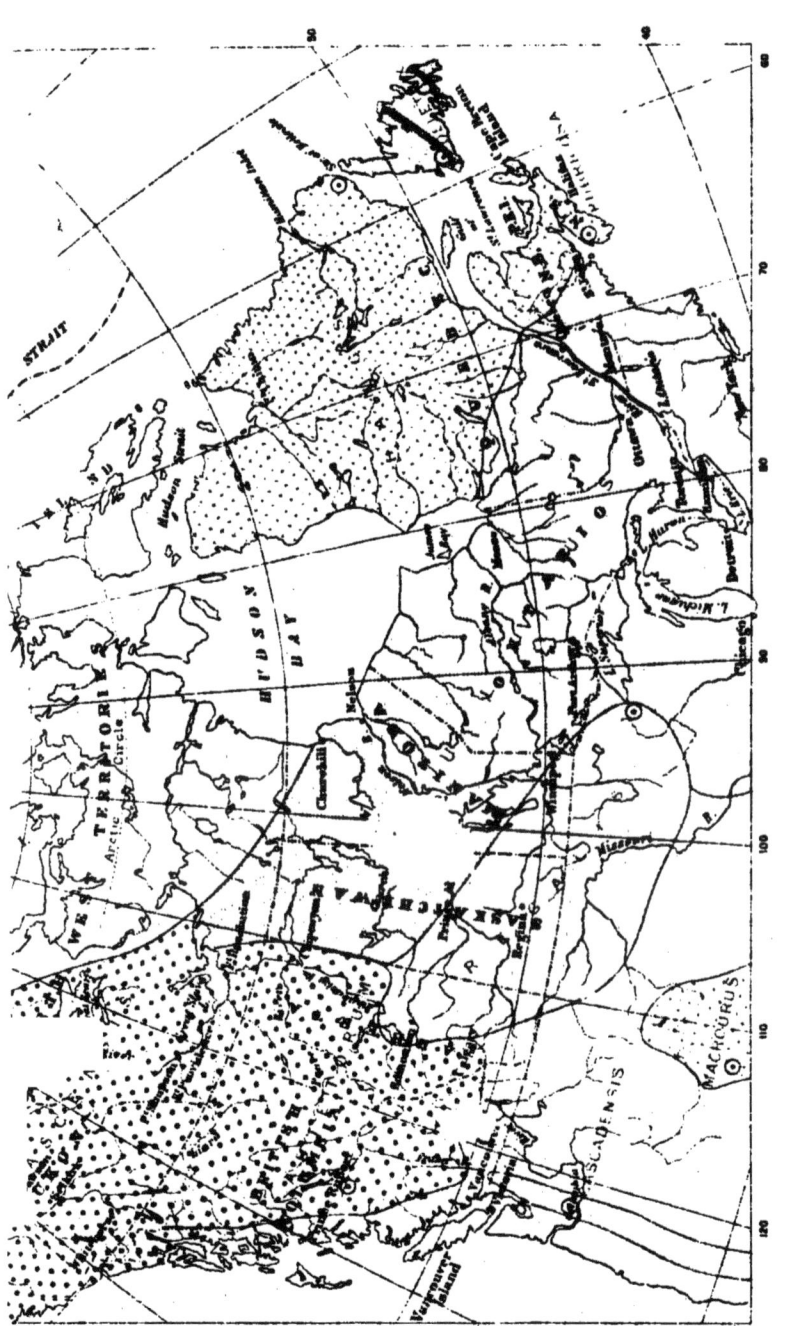

MAP 1.—RANGE OF THE NORTH AMERICAN RED FOXES IN CANADA

Reproduced by courtesy of Charles Scribner's Sons from Ernest Thompson Seton's "Life-Histories of Northern Animals." Copyrighted 1909 in the United States, by Ernest Thompson Seton.

This map is diagrammatic and must be greatly modified by further work, especially in the west. It is founded chiefly on C. Hart Merriam's revision with additional records by E. W. Nelson, S. F. Baird, J. Fannin, R. MacFarlane, Audubon and Bachman, A. P. Low, V. Bailey, E. A. Preble, O. Bangs, A. E. Verrill.

The following are the species:

Vulpes fulvus (Desmarest),	Vulpes kenaiensis (Merriam)
Vulpes macrourus (Baird).	Vulpes harrimani (Merriam).
Vulpes rubricosa (Bangs) with 2 races,	
Vulpes deletrix (Bangs)	

V. regalis—Manitoba, Dakota, Montana, Alberta.

V. macrourus—Wyoming, Nevada.

V. abietorum—British Columbia, Alberta, North West Territories.

V. alascensis—Alaska, Yukon.

V. harrimani—Kadiak islands.

V. kenaiensis—Kenai peninsula.

V. cascadensis—Washington, Oregon, California.

V. mecator—California.

Colour Phases Investigation of the debated question of the colour phases of foxes has produced definite information regarding its occurrence. The fact that the cross, silver, black and red colours are all colour phases of the common red fox is of too common knowledge to warrant the citing of the many cases examined for evidence. The colours all exist and why they exist may be left to the discussion of biologists, some of whom say that ages ago foxes were originally dark coloured and that the silver is atavistic. It will be more useful in this discussion to describe how the costlier, darker colour is produced from cheaper, red parents.

A summary of the facts may be given as follows:

1. Silver parents always produce silver pups—never red or cross pups. (See possible exception below.)

2. Red parents mostly produce red, but, occasionally, some cross or patch pups and even a small proportion of silver pups is produced.

3. Usually cross or patch parents produce cross or patch pups.

4. When a silver and a pure red are bred, they produce red pups with blacker markings on the belly, neck and points than the red parent. The pups are about of the colour known to furriers as 'bastard'.

5. When a bastard red fox and a silver are mated often the litter is on the average 50 per cent silver and 50 per cent red.

6. Bastard red parents often produce a black or silver pup in a litter—the proportion of silver being about one out of four.

7. The exceptions to the above rules are that sometimes the colours do not segregate, but rather blend, as in roan cattle when red and white hairs are intermixed and not separated into distinct patches. Cross foxes are produced by mating a red and a silver and, sometimes, an intermediate colour is secured in the pups. Thus, in some districts, every combination of the red, white and black colours of foxes is found. There are foxes which are:

RED

    Red.—Red above and white below, with dark points.

    Bastard.—Red above and dark below and on the neck, with darker points.

CROSS
or
PATCH

    Poor Cross.—Mostly red and dark as above with a silver patch down the back and over the shoulders and hips.

    Good Cross or *Rusty Silver.*—Slightly red on the sides, neck and ears, dark below and silvery over the back, shoulders and rump.

SILVER

    Silver or *Light Silver.*—Silvery all over, except possibly the neck; dark below and white only on the tip of the tail.

    Silver Black or *Dark Silver.*—Black all over, except the tip of the tail and the silvery hairs on the hips and forehead.

    Black.—Pure black all over, except the tip of the tail, with, perhaps, dark silvery hairs only discernible on close examination.

No two foxes are exactly alike in colour unless they be black. Three silver foxes examined had no white tips on their tails and others had only a half dozen white hairs—yet the white tip is one of the marks of identification for the species. Others had white patches on the legs or breast, while the rest of the colouring was almost pure black.

A silver fox when mated with a pure red usually produces silver pups in two crosses. If the first cross produces all red pups, two methods of breeding may be adopted:

(a) A male and a female pup may be crossbred, producing, on the average, one silver pup to three reds.

(b) A red pup may be bred to the silver parent, producing, on the average, 50 per cent red pups.

It is a more unusual occurrence to secure a blend or intermediate colour from crossing a silver and a red. By breeding the pups for four generations to a silver, the red colour is eliminated from the pelage markings. The segregation of the red and silver colour appears to be very common in many localities, but, in others, the roan or intermediate form of colour is produced quite frequently, the parent characters blending and the hybrid usually breeding true.

In this connection it will be of interest to quote from a letter dated August 2, 1912, received from Professor W. Bateson of Cambridge

University, England, a naturalist of high repute and an authority on hair pigmentation. In the early stages of the investigation the usual opinion of naturalists and breeders was accepted and it was thus stated to Professor Bateson that silver parent foxes would produce an occasional red pup. This popular opinion has since been found to be usually incorrect. Professor Bateson's opinion has, therefore, been proved correct in every detail by subsequent development.

Professor Bateson says:

"At first sight I should suppose silver to be a recessive to red and that it would always breed true. This, however, you say, is not the case. If silvers, really, when mated together, throw reds, there must be some complication which we cannot yet represent. Provisionally, I should doubt the statement until incontrovertible evidence is produced.

"I am not perfectly clear what a silver is, but I take it that a silver fox is to a red fox what a silver tabby is to a common tabby, viz., the same thing devoid of the red or yellow element. It may be difficult to disentangle the relations of the colour when there is a series of gradational forms* and, in the first instance, I should try to get a family in which the distinction between the reds and the silvers was sharp. Then I should breed the silvers together—brother and sister if need be.

"From what you say, I infer that two silvers of opposite sexes cannot be gotten to sta:., from. That being so, you must mate together the silvers produced which you will raise from the reds produced by mating red and silver—if only reds come. But, if silvers come, then mate them together or back with the silver parent.

"Apart from the great practical difficulties which there are in breeding foxes in domestication, I think you will easily fix a strain of silvers."

Professor Bateson outlined perfectly the fox-breeding experiences of ranchers. Those who have spent their time working with gradational forms like the cross or patched foxes do not know what they will get until mating tests are made. Those who have chosen two distinct colour types are able to breed out to the pure recessive type in two generations.

* Such as cross foxes.

Mendel's Law of Hybrids Dr. Eugene Davenport makes an explanation of the action of Mendel's Law of Hybrids that will prove instructive to many breeders. He says:

"When diverse characters are thus brought together two very different results may follow. They may blend into a single new character, in which case our figures show the *proportions within the blood*, or they may remain distinct as two independent characters within the same individual. Stature and size as well as many colours blend freely, but not all characters behave in that simple way. For example, white and black blend freely in the human race, and the offspring of white and negro are mulattoes of various shades, according to the respective infusions; but colours do not blend in pigs, which are either black, white, or spotted, never roan or mulatto. Some colours blend in horses (roan); some do not. Some breeds of cattle have blended colours (Shorthorns); in others, the colours remain distinct (Holstein-Friesian.)

"And so with characters generally. Many will blend and many others will not. When they will not blend, then the appearance is still less a guide to the real hereditary qualities, and under these circumstances it is little or no index to what will happen when the mixture is bred. This fact was long a great stumbling-block to breeders, involving the business of improvement in unfortunate and as we now know, unnecessary mystery."

Silver Colour Mendelian Recessive to Red Suppose that a breeder has a silver fox, which, being recessive, always breeds true, and he chooses a pure type of red fox for a mate, being careful in order to secure pureness of type to obtain the red fox from a district where no melanism exists. Let the red fox be denoted by R. R. and the black or silver fox by B. B. (As to results, the sexes are equal in influence.)

R.R.	+	B.B.	
R.B	R.B	R.B	R.B
(red)	(red)	(red)	(red)

All pups are red, but of the bastard type mentioned above, with blacker points,—legs, muzzles and ears. They are really half black, but the colour is hidden or recessive in the first generation, red being dominant.

1. A RED FOX TWO MONTHS OLD, SHOWING A DARK LINE OF BLOOD
2. A CROSS FOX, RED ON SIDES, NECK AND EARS, SEPTEMBER FUR
3. A DARK SILVER FOX WITH A WHITE PATCH ON HIS BREAST
4. A BLACK FEMALE IN OCTOBER

There are now two methods by which he can proceed to secure the black colour or pure B.B.

When diverse colours are mated in foxes the hybrid sometimes only, has the *proportions within the blood* and does not demonstrate its parentage by its colour until the second generation. When the crossing acts thus it is said to follow Mendel's law of hybrids. But often the result is a blend giving a hybrid which has a proportion of silver fur, i. e. a cross or patch fox. And it is not strange that foxes in different districts breed thus for colour, as there are various examples of the same phenomenon in different breeds of animals. Holstein cattle segregate the colours; Shorthorns blend in some cases.

First method:

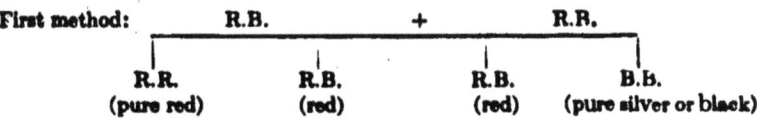

R.B. + R.B.

| R.R. | R.B. | R.B. | B.B. |
| (pure red) | (red) | (red) | (pure silver or black) |

Results: One-quarter of the litter is pure red
One-half of the litter is red of the bastard type
One-quarter of the litter is black or silver

Second method:

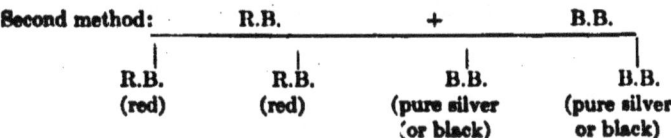

R.B. + B.B.

R.B.	R.B.	B.B.	B.B.
(red)	(red)	(pure silver	(pure silver
		(or black)	or black)

Results: One-half of the litter is red of the bastard type
One-half of the litter is pure black or silver

Thus, it may be concluded that, in a district where melanism occurs, o ' re black and cross foxes occur, or either, there are very few foxes pure as to colour.

If the unit of union be regarded as of gametes which are produced by each parent in the proportion of its ancestors—red and silver— the results may be forecasted by a simple mathematical calculation, the law of probabilities governing the mating of the gametes.

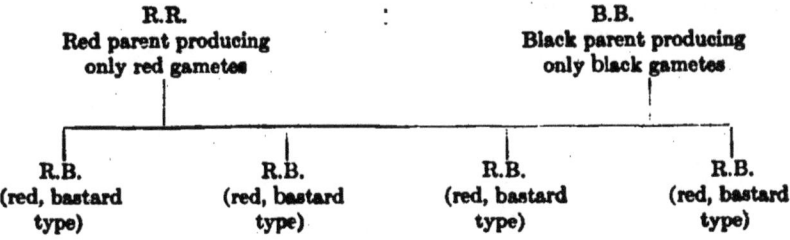

R.R.   :   B.B.
Red parent producing   Black parent producing
only red gametes   only black gametes

R.B.	R.B.	R.B.	R.B.
(red, bastard	(red, bastard	(red, bastard	(red, bastard
type)	type)	type)	type)

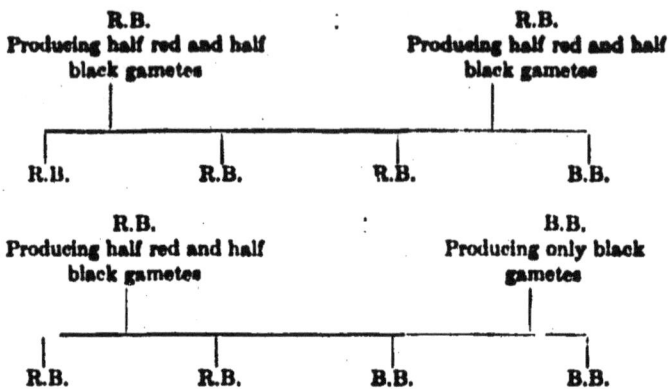

It will be noticed that when the black colour (B.B) appears the animal is always pure, while, R.R. is pure red and R.B. is also red with darker points.

It is well to bring out clearly the average results to be expected, as considerable speculation is indulged in as to whether or not certain foxes when bred to a silver will produce some silver pups. As much as $500.00 each has been paid for red pups that have one silver parent, because it is expected that, if the pup is mated to a silver, the resulting litter will be composed of silver and red foxes in about equal numbers. The hopes are realised in most instances; but many chances of securing silver pups are lost because the breeder gets only red pups the first generation and becomes discouraged.

Rearing Silver Foxes from Reds   There is a wide-spread belief that the silver descendants of red foxes are rusty black in colour and are not as pure a type as those bred pure for generations in the fox ranches. Professor W. E. Castle, of Harvard University, says that only experiments will prove what quality will be obtained in the silver young of a red parent.* The results noted in this investi-

---

* Professor Castle, replying to an inquiry, says:

"The several facts stated in your letter of November 14th, 1912, which I assume you have sufficiently verified, show clearly that black (or silver) coat character in foxes is a Mendelian recessive in relation to the common red coat and may be recovered in the second generation from a cross with red. Whether it would be improved or deteriorated as a consequence, experiment alone could show. I should think that the 'patch' or 'cross' foxes occasionally obtained in the F_1 generation might be well worth experimenting with, as indicating in that particular strain a tendency for the dominance to be reversed. If this tendency could be strengthened by judicious selection, a more potent strain of silvers might result. If, by this means, a strain potent enough to dominate F_1 could be secured, it is evident that silver foxes could be produced much more readily."

gation indicate that some of the best skins ever produced are those of silvers having a red parent. There was difficulty in obtaining information on this important point, as breeders were extremely reticent in giving information concerning their experiences in cross-breeding with reds, because of a great prejudice against such breeding on Prince Edward Island. The prejudice, no doubt, results from an ignorance of Mendelian principles in segregating types.

It is interesting to note that Rev. George Clark, of St. Catharines, Ont., has in his possession a black dog fox obtained from near York Factory, Hudson bay, which, he asserts, has sired none but silver pups, when mated with any vixen. Of course, the five or six litters sired by one dog does not provide sufficient data from which to form a general conclusion. It may be that many of the six thousand or more red foxes kept in captivity will yet be crossed so as to produce a proportion of silver stock. As the red foxes were generally purchased from districts which produce very ordinary pelts, it is quite probable that, in many cases, the resulting silver will not be of good quality. The climatic conditions of Canada, however, which are very favourable to the production of good pelts, may improve exotic sub-species.

If a prepotent race of silver foxes can be developed which will produce silver young by mating to red, thus reversing the supposed dominance of the red colour, the silver colour could be more readily produced: but the red colour would appear in the second generation. No record of such behaviour, other than the case mentioned above, was obtained, so that it is probable that breeders cannot get possession of prime silver foxes by breeding them from red ones · other than by the usual method of mating a silver male of polygamic tendencies with red females.

Cross Foxes as Breeders Breeders are generally better pleased if cross foxes are produced the first generation; but, as a rule, if cross foxes are bred out, the tendency to produce an occasional red pup will never be wholly eliminated. Having cross foxes in the ancestry of silver foxes means that a proportion of red gametes are thrown and, at any time, a red fox may appear among the other silvers in a litter. Some cases of red or cross pups bred out of silver parents were recorded, but general experience, together with some evidence produced, favours the opinion that the parent foxes were animals captured in the wilds and probably had cross or patch parentage. It may be declared generally, that the silver colour is easily fixed and will practically always breed true after one or two generations of silver colour. Silver foxes can be produced of good silver colour by top-crossing cross foxes with silver for several generations and, if the silver foxes used in the crossing had ancestors of cross foxes, the probability is that a proportion of red, bastard, and cross foxes would appear among their offspring. All evidence tends to show, however, that very few, if any, with red colour on them are produced, and it clearly demonstrates that the blackness of foxes can be made practically permanent by top-crossing to silvers. After mixing red, cross and silver foxes for several generations, it is practically impossible to estimate the kind of pups that will come. Litters were seen that had red pups, cross pups and silver pups in them.

The Best Furred Foxes Beyond a doubt, the finest foxes in captivity at the present time are the descendants of foxes captured in Prince Edward Island. The best foxes, therefore, belong to the geographical species, *vulpes rubricosa;* or, what is affirmed —and is not impossible—the Prince Edward Island fox, because it has been cut off from the mainland, is a distinct sub-species or geographical race. No cranial and other measurements have yet been secured. If scientists admit the fact of its difference from the mainland species, a new name *vulpes abegweit,* could be chosen—Abegweit being the Micmac Indian name for Prince Edward Island.

As London sales show that silver and red foxes from Prince Edward Island have been sold for the highest prices, the evidence seems to bear out the assumption of its superiority. Red foxes have, in some cases, sold for 80 shillings. Twenty-three red fox skins from Prince Edward Island, marketed in London in 1910, by one man, were sold for £68 sterling, or an average of $14.39 each. Other vendors claimed to have received as much as 88 shillings each, but no documentary proof was produced.

When black colour phases of such animals are captured, they are usually of excellent quality in fineness and colour of coat. As a general rule, the ancestors of the highest priced foxes were dug out of dens, situated on Prince Edward Island.

One instance of the capturing of wild foxes may be quoted, as the silver blood procured on this occasion flows strong in the highest priced animals of the present time. Two residents of Bedeque, P.E.I., had seen a red vixen in that locality, and it was reported one winter that a silver fox was seen running with her. The following July (1900), Louis Holland and Louis Spence found the den and proceeded to dig the young foxes out. They found four blacks and three reds, which they sold to Charles Dalton for $300.00.

Many other instances show that litters frequently occur in nature as described above—half of the litter silver and half of it red. One red female ranched in Nova Scotia and mated to a silver fox has produced fourteen pups in the years 1910, 1911 and 1912. Seven of the pups are red and seven silver.

Most of the fox-breeders in other provinces have sold silver and dark silver stock to Prince Edward Island, where the demand has been greatest. Probably in all the dozen or more ranches in Ontario there are not three score silver foxes. The stock kept is bastard and cross foxes that produce litters with a proportion of silver pups. As their experience in selling fur has not led them to believe the present high prices for breeders in the Maritime Provinces were warranted by the pelt value of the animals, the attitude of Ontario ranchers has, in general, been to sell out at the high prices offered.

The Best Localities for Ranches Fur experts who have given special study to the fauna of Canada say that the red and silver foxes found on the Athabaska river and in the Yukon and Alaska are often of great value. These regions should produce a weighty pelt and, if good quality were secured in foundation stock, conditions for fox ranching should be ideal—especially if venison and fish could be easily secured for food. The rapidly rising price of meats may finally necessitate the removal of the fox industry to remote points where cheaper meat can be obtained. Newfoundland and Labrador would provide sites where meat and fish could be cheaply secured and preserved for long periods by inexpensive refrigeration. The foxes of these regions are often of considerable value especially in size and strength though the fur is usually coarse. The cost of feeding a pair of foxes on Prince Edward Island, where the price of the offal and cheaper grades of meat has risen, is about $50.00 a year, cash outlay, in addition to considerable labour in collecting the great variety of foods seemingly required. When the industry finally settles down to the production of pelts for fur, it is probable that foundation stock for new ranches will be obtained on Prince Edward Island at high prices and that the fur will be produced on ranches situated at distant and remote points.

"Imported" or "Foreign" Stock On account of a lack of sufficient data it is practically impossible to discuss intelligently the vexed question of the relative merits of "imported" and "domestic" stock. As many animals—in fact the large majority of the animals caught in the wilds—are of poor quality, they will need to be subjected to methods of rigid selection for many generations to come, if fur of good quality is to be produced. Only a few of the domestic stock are as poorly furred as the average wild stock. The chief deficiency noted in fur quality of the domestic stock was in the thin coat of fur. Among the wild stock the poor colour and the coarseness of fur are notable. There are exceptional individuals of excellent quality among the wild foxes, but none yet examined is the equal of the selected domestic animals in silkiness and sheen of coat. Those who favour the wild class of stock contend that wild foxes are stronger and will produce as good fur as domestic foxes after they have been penned up and fed properly. They argue that the lower average for pelts of wild animals is caused by the fact that they are killed out of season; that they are shot, are poorly skinned and carelessly handled before marketing and are not especially prepared for market like the domestic animals; and that the average price is thus lowered several hundred dollars a skin. The exponents of the domestic stock say that selection practised for eight or ten generations—when at least 50 per cent of the animals have been culled out and slaughtered—has produced a type of animal that will bring upwards of one thousand dollars each or five times as much as the wild animal.

There is much to be said on both sides. In our opinion, however, the prime killing of the wild stock after careful fattening would probably increase the value of the pelts 100 per cent but they would still be less than half as valuable as the best grade of selected Island stock. Excellent foundation stock, improved through several generations by selection and feeding, has done its work in a fashion similar to the development of our breeds of domestic stock.

The owners of selected stock will do well, however, to bear in mind that their animals can be still further improved and that it may require a Labrador, Alaskan, Newfoundland or Hudson Bay fox to grade up their stock in some particular quality. It is not probable, however, that improvement of stock can be effected by importations from Kansas, New Jersey and other southern states. To protect the character and reputation of their established strain of stock, all true fox breeders should discourage the practice of importing southern foxes for speculative purposes merely.

The Capture of Live Fur-bearers   When the great success of the Prince Edward Island fox ranchmen was disclosed several years ago, a general search was made for wild silver fox by trappers and others acquainted with the situation. Until 1912, the business was not generally known. Up to that year, probably a hundred or more foxes had been imported and at least half the Island stock had "imported blood" in them. In the year 1913, hunting for wild silver foxes became a veritable craze. The digging out of dens and nests proceeded throughout summer, and in November, when the trapping season opened, the search was prosecuted with

A MATED PAIR, VERY DARK SILVER MALE AND HALF SILVER FEMALE, OCTOBER FUR

PEN IN THE MAPLE WOODS—SUNNY IN WINTER AND SHADED IN SUMMER

greater zeal than ever because trappers hoped to receive larger prices for the live animals than they could obtain for the pelts. The business of the trapper has changed from that of securing pelts to the capturing of the animals alive and the fur buyers of the district have simply transformed themselves into live stock salesmen. An estimate of the number of wild animals shipped to Prince Edward Island in 1912 and in 1913 (till November) is as follows:

Year	Red Fox	Cross Fox	Silver Fox	Mink	Skunk	Marten	Polar Fox	Beaver	Fisher	Russian Sable
1912	500	100	20	50	20	2	30	5	3	0
1913	1000	250	50	250	50	20	30	8	3	2

Inasmuch as Prince Edward Island protested against the importation of foreign stock in July 1913 and induced the Federal government to establish a quarantine on all importations, many animals imported to Eastern Canada remained in New Brunswick and Nova Scotia. Probably more "imported" stock is held there than on the Island.

RANCHING PRACTICE

While it is legal to keep fur-bearers in ··. ·ity in those provinces in Canada where there is no close season provi· ı for them, it is unlawful in most provinces to keep protected fur-bearers during the close season. In the close season, in all provinces except Prince Edward Island, it is also unlawful to catch fur-bearers for ranching purposes. Apparently it is lawful in Saskatchewan and Quebec to hold the animals during the close season, provided, they have been caught in the open season, or brought from a point outside the province. In all the other provinces, no ranching can be legally done without a permit from the provincial department charged with the care of game and fur-bearing animals.

The various provincial authorities should encourage fur-farming by amending their game laws so as to allow the issue to residents of permits to catch fur-bearers at any season and to hold them in captivity for breeding purposes. Requiring annual returns of production would prevent any abuse of this privilege.

Location of the Ranch   If foundation stock of excellent quality has been secured, the next most important question to be considered is the selection of a site for the ranch where the quality of the stock can be maintained from generation to generation. Climatic influences are largely responsible for the value of the coat of fur. If an abundance of good food can be secured, an animal produces the heaviest coat where the climate is coldest. Humidity of atmosphere must also be considered. Poland* says that open waters, such as lakes and seas, render the fur thicker, probably owing to the high percentage of humidity in the atmosphere. Exposed sea coasts and exposed prairies, he says, render fur coarse, while woods and forests cause it to be finer. For instance, the timber or forest wolves have finer fur than those living on the exposed prairie. Mr. Wesley Frost, United States consul at Charlottetown, in a report to his government, September, 1912, says: "The temperature and humidity on the island [Prince Edward] are a happy mean between the intense cold and the moist, dull weather of Newfoundland, Labrador and Alaska, and the warmer, drier weather of regions farther south. The far northern furs are said to be coarse and shaggy, while the furs produced in the northern states of our own country are light and thin." It is also said that the absence of limestone in Prince Edward Island and Westmorland county, New Brunswick, gives a perfect soil for foxes to burrow in and is beneficial to the fur covering. As some excellent foxes do not burrow, the ranchers carefully stopping up the holes whenever a start is made, there cannot be much ground for this assumption.

The following is a summary of the best conditions for fox-ranching operations:

1. Foxes should be ranched in woodland areas with good drainage in a climate cold enough to produce a heavy fur and overhair and which is cool in summer.

2. The value of the pelt depends on good health as well as on climatic conditions. Wholesome, varied food is a necessary condition for health and can be best secured in a thickly-settled rural district.

3. Foundation stock should be the best obtainable. The best foxes are those in captivity in ranches, and they have the additional advantage of being half-domesticated.

There are some advantages to be gained by conducting extensive ranching operations in one locality, particularly because breeding animals may be easily exchanged and the dangers of close, or in-breeding, prevented. Neighbours can also impart to one another more freely what their experience has taught them. These advantages, however, may be offset by the difficulties of securing food for the foxes. In every rural township there is enough cheap meat and offal to supply

*Fur-Bearing Animals in Nature and Commerce, p. xvi. By Henry Poland, F.Z.S.

THE BEST LOCATION FOR A RANCH IS A WOODLOT

flesh diet to scores of foxes, but not to hundreds. Several hundred foxes, therefore, ' i one neighbourhood, would necessitate the purchase of costly meat. An ordinary farm has enough waste meat scrap, dripping, bread, biscuits and game to support several animals.

A Woodland Site   A wooded area, not subject to flooding, and where the snow does not pile up in deep drifts in winter, is best adapted for the site of the ranch. The subsoil should be a hardpan to prevent deep burrowing and escape under the fences. Areas which produce a growth of birch, spruce, fir and cedar, with heath plants and blueberries in the open areas, have usually a good turfy cover and a hardpan subsoil near the surface. In such a situation it is easy to erect pens as the fences have only to be extended down to hardpan to prevent the foxes from burrowing under and es :aping. A sandy soil and subsoil, on the other hand, while providing good drainage, entails an additional expense, as foxes can burrow to depths of six feet or more. A family of foxes working one behind the other will relay earth out of a sandy hole in a veritable shower. In ordinary loam, the fence is not considered safe unless it extends down a depth of over three feet or is founded on a subsoil of considerable hardness.

Proximity to the dwelling of the keeper is also an important consideration. This is usually accomplished by building the ranch in a woodland lot a few hundred yards distant from the house, or, if the ranch is a considerable distance from the owner's dwelling, by building a house for the keeper. It is not advisable to keep fox pens nearer than ten rods to a dwelling as, particularly during muggy weather, the peculiar and somewhat disagreeable 'foxy' smell is strong and unpleasant.

The advantages of a large woodland ranch may be summed up as follows:

1. The outer fence and bush cover protect the foxes from curious sightseers, dogs, cattle and thieves, and give them a sense of being hidden from enemies.

2. The bush cover is especially valuable for nervous foxes to hide in and to provide shade for the fur. They will also sleep contentedly all day under a bush, where it is more healthful than in a nest or a burrow.

3. The outer fence is an additional insurance against escape to the woods. If a fox escapes from the paddock, he can be easily caught in the outer enclosure, or, if the door is left open, he may, of his own accord, go back to his pen at feeding time.

4. The snow does not pile in drifts, but lies level, on wooded areas. Huge drifts necessitate higher fences, or wiring over, to prevent escape. Fences do not need to be more than six or seven feet high if the snow never lies more than one or two feet deep.

5. A ranch in the woods has more equable climatic conditions. It is cooler in summer, less windy in winter, and is warmer for young foxes in the spring. There is less thawing and freezing up of snow to injure the fur. It also affords protection from rain and sleet.

6. The foxes can hide from thieves and could not be captured by a stranger unless the house were broken into when they were shut in their nest. So much noise, however, would be sure to rouse the dog and the watchman.

7. The outer enclosure permits of protective measures being taken. The keeper sleeps in a house there. Dogs are kept chained. Traps for thieves are laid, as, *e.g.*, bear traps, burglar alarms, electric shocking devices; and some ranches are lighted with lanterns or electric lights and are equipped with telephones.

8. Large ranches seem to be more successful than smaller ones, because foxes in contiguous pens are company for each other.

Other Sites Chosen If a wood-lot is not available, the ranch may be built in cleared ground and quick-growing trees planted. The Carolina poplar, soft maple, Manitoba maple (*Acer negundo*), black locust and willow are among the fastest growers. One rancher living in an Ontario city in a grape-growing district has planted grapes vines about the paddocks and will train them over his pens. The predilection of the fox for grapes is well known since the time of Æsop, but life in a vineyard may not be more beneficial to reynard's health than life elsewhere. The vines provide a dense shade in summer no shelter in winter, fresh fruit in season, and exercise in securing food. The whole ranch is surrounded by a concrete wall. Such a ranch is impossible in a district where there is a heavier snowfall. The lack of ventilation through the pens is objectionable and the cost is considerable. It shows, however, that an experienced breeder can establish the industry on city lots in a populous neighbourhood.

Sometimes an orchard serves as a suitable situation for a ranch. For instance, Mr. T. L. Burrowman of Wyoming, Ont., has placed his pens in a four-acre orchard, the foxes being kept out of the trees by trunk shields.

Barnyards, open fields about the houses, hill-tops where snow drifts off and many other situations are frequently chosen, but the

DETAIL OF FENCE CONSTRUCTION WITH SHEET IRON

DETAIL OF FENCE CONSTRUCTION. MANY BREEDERS PREFER AN ALLEY
SURROUNDING EACH PEN

ranchman, as a rule, regards such sites as temporary only. They usually contemplate larger ranching operations on better sites when sufficient capital can be raised.

An Island as a Site
Sometimes a small island has been chosen as a site for a ranch. When such is the case, visitors can be kept out of the vicinity more easily. Also a fox that has escaped is not apt to swim to the mainland away from the place where he has been fed. Prince Edward Island has an advantage over mainland areas as a ranching centre because a fox that has escaped can usually be traced and captured, whereas on the mainland, he could roam for hundreds of miles and get into uninhabited territory.

Fences and Fencing
When the site of the ranch is chosen, the bush surrounding the selected area is cleared for a width of four feet and the ground levelled for the erection of an exterior fence. The trees are trimmed or cut so that foxes may not climb over the fence by means of them. Post-holes three to four feet deep, depending on the depth the frost penetrates, are dug from 10 to 16 feet apart, cedar posts being used if it is possible to secure them. If cedar, locust or other durable wood cannot be obtained, the ground end of the post may be charred or treated with hot petroleum or creosote to render it more lasting. Posts from 10 to 15 feet long are used according to the usual snowfall of the locality and should be sharpened at the end to prevent heaving by the frost. A post four inches in diameter at the small end and 12 feet long will cost from 30 cents in some districts, up to 75 cents in others.

The corner posts need not be anchored when a purline is used. The latter is made of one-inch boards, five inches wide, or of straight poles. These are nailed to the posts to brace them and support the meshed wire on the upper side. They also support the overhang wire.

The overhang wire is usually from 18 to 24 inches wide and is laid on brackets nailed at right angles to the posts and purline and then stapled to them. It is usually made of No. 16 galvanized wire having a two-inch mesh.

The fence is composed of two-inch diamond meshed wire fastened to the purline with staples and hung on the outside of the post. If several rolls of wire are used, the selvedges are laced with a soft No. 16 wire. No. 16 galvanized wire is strong enough for the upper part of the fence and No. 15 for the lower part and No. 14 for the underground part of the fence. The wire is stretched at each corner with second class levers passed through the meshes, the post being used as a fulcrum. All corner posts must be perpendicular and when the whole area is not perfectly level, care must be taken to pleat the wire or gore it when a change from one level to another is made; otherwise it 'buckles.' This occurs at corner posts on sloping land, and at changes of slope in the fence.

The exterior fence is frequently built of boards 6 feet, or even 10 feet, high. The upper four feet are usually of wire with an overhang to prevent the foxes from escaping. On the ground, inside, is a carpet wire 30 inches wide, made of No. 14 wire having a two-inch mesh. It is laid on the ground and laced to the selvedge of the fence at the ground level, or stapled, if the fence is of boards. The other selvedge of the carpet wire is stapled to stakes driven in the ground. As a fox almost always begins to burrow close to the fence, the carpet wire will prevent him from burrowing under it.

Wire Used
The most durable wire yet used has been imported from Great Britain. It is specially woven with an extra twist, and has a selvedge of three wires on the ends as well as the sides. In the smaller sizes a triple turn is made. The galvanising, which is done after weaving, practically solders the joints. It comes in bales of 150 feet length and is of various widths. The best wire will last only from eight to twelve years underground. Figures submitted by a hardware firm which has made a specialty of handling wire netting for ranches, prove that they alone, sold wire enough to build more than sixty miles of fox-proof fence.

The following table shows the comparative cost of the various meshed wires manufactured. The Canadian price can be determined by discounting the list price for all sizes under gauge No. 14 by about 15 per cent. On account of a lower rate of duty, the list price of gauge No. 14 and larger gauges may be discounted by about 22 per cent.

The following list gives the prevailing prices of British-made diamond mesh ranch wire.   They are from 10 to 20 per cent lower than the prices of ranch wire of United States manufacture:

PRICE LIST OF RANCH WIRE

Width	Mesh	Gauge No.	Price per 150 lineal feet
18	2	16	$ 2.65
24	2	16	3.50
30	2	16	4.25
36	2	16	4.85
48	2	16	6.40
60	2	16	8.00
72	2	16	9.65
36	2	15	6.10
48	2	15	8.15
60	2	15	10.15
24	2	14	5.20
30	2	14	6.20
36	2	14	7.25
48	2	14	9.40
60	2	14	11.85
36	1	17	8.50
48	1	17	11.00
72	1	17	16.50
24	1	16	7.25
36	1	16	10.25

DETAILED PRICE LIST OF RANCH WIRE

(Gross prices per roll of 50 yards; galvanized after manufacture)

Mesh	Gauge	12 inches wide	18 inches wide	24 inches wide	30 inches wide	36 inches wide	42 inches wide	48 inches wide	60 inches wide	72 inches wide	108 inches wide
½ inch	22	3.53	5.10	6.61	8.07	9.67	11.30	12.90	16.15	19.35	
"	20	4.29	6.15	8.00	9.75	11.70	13.65	15.60	19.50	23.30	
"	19	5.73	8.18	10.65	12.96	15.60	18.20	20.80	25.95	31.20	
⅝ inch	22	2.85	3.84	4.99	6.09	7.20	8.40	9.60	12.00	15.40	
"	20	3.33	4.77	8.17	7.54	9.05	10.55	12.06	15.10	18.10	
"	19	4.61	6.52	8.49	10.35	12.40	14.50	16.55	20.70	24.80	
¾ inch	20	2.26	3.21	4.11	5.00	5.84	6.82	7.80	9.74	11.68	
"	19	2.87	4.15	5.23	6.40	7.48	8.74	10.00	12.50	15.00	
"	18	3.92	5.62	7.16	8.73	10.20	11.90	13.60	17.00	20.40	
1 inch	20	1.81	2.58	3.27	4.00	4.66	5.44	6.21	7.76	9.32	
"	9	2.15	3.09	3.92	4.78	5.60	6.53	7.46	9.32	11.20	
"	18	2.62	3.76	4.77	5.82	6.82	7.95	9.10	11.36	13.62	
"	17	3.52	5.03	6.38	7.80	9.12	10.65	12.15	15.20	18.25	
"	16	4.70	6.74	8.56	10.32	12.33	14.27	15.90	20.37	24.45	
1¼ inch	19	1.73	2.48	3.15	3.79	4.40	5.12	5.85	7.32	8.78	13.15
"	18	2.11	3.03	3.84	4.64	5.36	6.25	7.15	8.95	10.63	16.10
"	17	2.76	3.98	5.04	6.08	7.05	8.25	0.42	11.80	14.15	21.20
"	16	3.72	5.34	6.80	8.22	9.50	11.10	12.68	15.85	19.10	10.40
1½ inch	19	1.36	1.97	2.50	3.00	3.45	4.05	4.63	5.80	6.95	13.15
"	18	1.73	2.48	3.15	3.80	4.40	5.12	5.85	7.32	8.80	17.20
"	17	2.26	3.23	4.11	4.93	5.75	6.70	7.60	9.55	11.45	19.20
"	16	2.87	4.13	5.20	6.30	6.40	7.45	8.50	10.65	12.80	
1¾ inch	19	1.26	1.81	2.27	2.78	3.20	3.75	4.27	5.35	6.42	9.60
"	18	1.55	2.22	2.80	3.40	3.95	4.60	5.20	6.55	7.90	11.80
"	17	2.11	2.87	3.65	4.40	5.11	5.96	6.83	8.52	10.22	15.33
"	16	2.32	3.61	4.60	5.53	6.39	7.46	8.52	10.64	12.77	19.16

Notes (right-hand mesh groupings):
- ½ inch, ⅝ inch — Made up to 96 inches wide
- ¾ inch, 1 inch — Made up to 84 inches wide
- 1¼ inch, 1½ inch, 1¾ inch — Made up to 120 inches wide

DETAILED PRICE LIST OF RANCH WIRE (cont'd)

(Gross prices per roll of 50 yards; galvanized after manufacture)

Mesh	Gauge	12 inches wide	18 inches wide	24 inches wide	30 inches wide	36 inches wide	42 inches wide	48 inches wide	60 inches wide	72 inches wide	108 inches wide	Gauge	Mesh	
2 inch	19	1.08	1.55	1.97	2.35	2.68	3.12	2.57	4.46	5.35	8.00	19	2 inch	Made up to 120 inches wide
"	18	1.36	1.97	2.52	2.98	2.40	4.00	4.55	5.68	6.80	10.20	18	"	
"	17	1.77	2.54	3.25	3.84	4.38	5.12	5.84	7.30	8.76	13.10	17	"	
"	16	2.30	3.29	4.20	5.00	5.72	6.67	7.62	9.53	10.63	17.15	16	"	
"	15	2.89	4.15	5.26	6.28	7.38	8.37	9.57	11.77	14.34	21.54	15	"	
"	14	3.72	5.31	6.80	8.10	9.25	10.82	12.35	15.45	18.54	.....	14	"	
2½ inch	19	.92	1.34	1.70	2.02	2.30	2.70	3.08	3.85	4.66	.....	19	2½ inch	Made up to 96 inches wide
"	18	1.14	1.63	2.07	2.30	2.84	3.26	3.80	4.75	4.68	.....	18	"	
"	17	1.50	2.16	2.76	3.30	3.77	4.40	5.02	6.30	7.55	.....	17	"	
"	16	1.89	2.74	3.49	4.14	4.75	5.55	6.35	7.90	9.50	.....	16	"	
"	15	2.34	3.35	4.28	5.10	5.84	6.80	7.80	9.75	11.70	.....	15	"	
3 inch	19	.85	1.22	1.54	1.84	2.10	2.45	2.80	3.50	4.20	6.30	19	3 inch	Made up to 120 inches wide
"	18	1.00	1.43	1.80	2.17	2.47	2.92	3.30	4.12	4.93	7.40	18	"	
"	17	1.38	1.85	2.38	2.82	3.20	3.70	4.25	5.35	6.40	9.60	17	"	
"	16	1.69	2.32	2.94	3.50	4.00	4.68	5.35	6.68	8.00	12.05	16	"	
"	15	.....	2.74	3.49	4.15	4.75	5.55	6.35	7.90	9.50	14.20	15	"	
"	14	.....	3.33	4.22	5.05	5.76	6.70	7.63	9.58	11.50	17.25	14	"	
4 inch	18	.85	1.22	1.54	1.84	2.10	2.45	2.80	3.50	4.20	6.30	18	4 inch	Made up to 120 inches wide
"	17	1.34	1.43	1.81	2.17	2.47	2.88	3.29	4.12	4.95	7.42	17	"	
"	16	1.50	1.69	2.15	2.55	2.92	3.40	3.90	4.86	5.84	8.76	16	"	
"	15	.....	2.19	2.83	3.36	3.83	3.48	5.10	6.40	7.66	11.50	15	"	
"	14	.....	2.64	3.35	4.00	4.56	5.33	6.08	7.60	9.13	13.68	14	"	

Construction of Pens The requirements of an ideal pen may be summarized as follows:

1. It should be large enough for foxes to run in at full speed when playing.

2. Part of it should be shaded overhead and it should provide good hiding cover.

3. It should have warm, well-drained, sunny areas in which the young pups may play.

4. Turfy or mossy ground cover is desirable. Leaves, or spruce or pine needles, make a good ground cover. Sand is good, but mud is objectionable.

The smallest pens used by the best ranchers enclose an area of at least 9,000 square feet. One rancher has a highly-valued pair in an enclosure of over 4,000 square feet. The usual size is a pen enclosed by one bale of wire, which is 150 feet long. Thus the area is 37 feet by 37 feet, or 30 feet by 42 feet, or 25 feet by 50 feet. In some cases the last-named dimensions are adopted and a cross fence is used, so that the male is shut in one end and the female in the other during the latter part of the period of gestation and while the pups are young.

Inasmuch as they must be extended into the ground to prevent the foxes from burrowing under them, the paddock fences are harder to build than the exterior. When a solid hardpan exists, the fence may be laid on it, even if it is only one foot from the surface. If the subsoil is light and open, paddocks are not fox-proof unless the fence is buried over four feet. In light soil, additional precautions may be taken by digging the trench wide and by rough-concreting the base a couple of feet inwards from the fence. One rancher, on a sandy area, planned to concrete the whole floor area of his paddocks and cover it with a foot of sand. When it interferes with the drainage, this use of concrete is objectionable.

The carpet wire should be used on the paddock fence as well as on the exterior. It prevents the fox from burrowing alongside the fence where digging out is always attempted.

The following material is necessary for the construction of a paddock fence 9 feet high and extending three feet into the ground.

12 posts, each 13 feet long.
150 lineal feet of 1-inch board, 5 inches wide.
150 lineal feet of overhang wire, 24 inches wide, 2-inch mesh, gauge No. 16.
150 lineal feet of fence wire, 5 feet wide, 2-inch mesh, gauge No. 16.
150 lineal feet of fence wire, 4 feet wide, 2-inch mesh, gauge No. 15.

USUAL TYPE OF KENNEL AND PEN

CHEAP KENNEL CONSTRUCTED FROM A PACKING BOX

150 lineal feet of ground wire, 2½ or 3 feet wide or even more, 2-inch mesh, gauge No. 14.

150 lineal feet of carpet wire, 30 inches wide, 2-inch mesh, gauge No. 14.

Nails, spikes, staples, hinges, locks for door and No. 16 soft lacing wire.

It is not customary to use a smaller meshed wire at the ground level, but cases are known of the death of fox pups caused by having their heads caught in the two-inch mesh. A smaller mesh, therefore, if it could be procured in No. 15 gauge, furnishes an additional precaution against the death of the valuable animals.

A new type of paddock fence, which is evidently an improvement, is being put up in some of the newest ranches. Instead of the two-inch mesh No. 16 wire, a strip of galvanised sheet iron three feet wide is fastened at a height of four or five feet from the ground. Joist pieces 2 inches by 4 inches are placed from post to post to nail to. The advantage of the sheet iron is that foxes cannot climb to the top of the fence and fall, breaking their legs or producing a rupture or an abortion. One pen was seen where the sheet iron was placed at the top of the posts and no overhang was required. Foxes climb fences only when badly frightened. Such a state of fear is to be avoided, but with some animals, may be impossible to control. Sharp sticks and stumps near the fence should be taken out lest the falling fox be ruptured or otherwise hurt. The middle toe nails of the fox may be cut off every few months to prevent climbing, or the sheet iron used as described above. It should not be placed near the ground as it would interfere with the circulation of air in the paddock. The objection to the iron is that the reflected heat makes the pens warmer in summer.

Paddock Door The door into the paddock should be placed from eighteen to twenty-four inches above the ground level and should be provided with good hinges and a good lock. If no exterior fence is used, make a double door entrance, so that one door is closed and locked before the other is opened. If foxes have the run of two pens, a door between the pens set up two feet high and with a sloping platform on each side from the sill to the ground, should be provided. Doors should be about 2 feet by 4 feet in dimensions. Many ranchers have a small passageway between pens, which foxes are obliged to crawl through. When playing, they do this so often that they wear off the guard hair over the hips and shoulders.

Construction of the Kennel In the earlier days, the houses were of logs, which were buried in the soil to simulate fox burrows. Later, a small box was placed within a larger one and the intervening space packed with sawdust or chaff. An entrance was provided by a passageway constructed of boards. The roof was made water-tight by a piece of sheet iron. Such houses are still in use, but have the disadvantage of being easily robbed.

Mr. Burrowman, and some other Ontario ranchers, attempt to imitate nature more closely by constructing solid one-piece cement dens built mostly underground and in well drained spots. They can be made quite thief-proof and, indeed, there is apparently no way for the keeper to get access to the nest. In the case of one den, it was only possible to crawl in by shovelling out the small entrance used by the fox.

The most generally approved houses are wooden constructions, placed in the centre of each paddock. The interior consists of an inner and an outer kennel, and the entrance for the foxes is through a passageway of rectangular cross-section constructed with four boards. The interior dimensions of this passageway should be about 7½ in. by 10 in., and it should slope from the building down to within 6 inches of the ground or even less, in order that very young foxes may be able to climb in easily. The entrance for the keeper is through a door in the end, or else by means of a hinged roof. The door or hinged roof is, of course, always kept locked. The house is usually made with a floor area 3 feet by 4½ feet, or slightly larger. The posts are about 3 feet high; the walls are boarded, papered and shingled; the floors are double boarded with paper between; the roof is boarded, papered and shingled and ventilation is provided by openings in both gables. All parts that the foxes rub against are smoothed and sand-papered so as not to injure the overhair. The building should be set on skids a foot off the ground so that the foxes cannot hide under it.

Construction of the Nest The inner kennel, or nest is to be the home of the young foxes and must be large enough to prevent crowding and small enough to be warmed by the body heat of the animals. The usual size of the nest is about 18 in. long by 18 in. wide by 20 in. in height, but some prefer to make them with floor dimensions 16 in. by 18 in. or 20 in. The entrance, 8 in. in diameter, is centred on one side; the floor corners are filled up with a triangular piece of moulding; three or four half-inch holes are bored in the roof to provide a slight ventilation and the roof or cover of the nest can be lifted off so that the manager can see into the nest when necessary. The nest is kept warm by being packed about on all sides with some material of low thermal conductivity. The best yet discovered are the ground cork in which the Spanish Malaga grapes are packed, dry seaweed, sawdust, chaff and leaves. A space of four or five inches

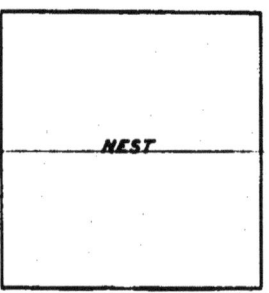

GROUND PLAN
Scale 1 inch = 1 foot

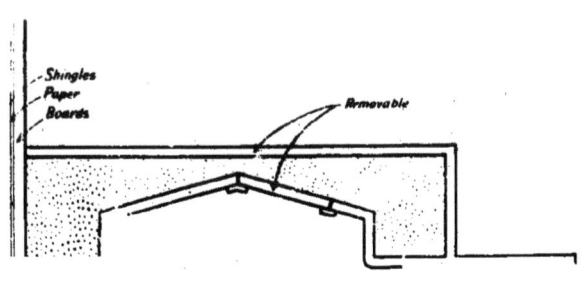

Shingles
Paper
Boards

Removable

NEST

Fox
Entrance

SECTION on AB

all about the six sides of the box, if packed with insulating material, will retain the heat sufficiently and will absorb dampness. In some cases, a light bedding of earth, leaves, seaweed or marshgrass is given in the winter.

Arrangement of Pens and Kennels It is usual to place pens side by side on both sides of an alley about six or eight feet wide,* the fences at the ends of the alley being an additional safeguard against escape. The dog (or male) pen, according to one plan, consists of one end of the common pen and the male is segregated by simply closing the door. According to another plan, the pen for the male is several feet distant and segregation is effected by simply closing the slide door in the passageway. The kennel provided for the dog fox may be a box or barrel with a chute entrance. The dog pen is becoming less used year by year. It should be constructed near the other pen and arrangements should be made so that the pairs can be separated quietly. No confusion or excitement whatever in effecting a separation of the male and female at this critical period should be permitted.

Food and Feeding The food of foxes in the wild state does not consist wholly of flesh as many suppose; for, to a certain extent, the fox is omnivorous, and will eat grass and berries. If flesh only were fed to a ranch fox the probability is that, after a time, digestion would be greatly impaired and the whole intestinal tract would become infested with worms.

The food varies so much in each locality that it is impossible to do more than state the principles which should govern the feeding of foxes. The very fact that success is achieved with so many kinds of dieting proves that the fox, like the dog, can live well on almost any kind of food. A prospectus of a ranch at Copper River, Alaska, says that the pelts of their foxes have a magnificent sheen because the animals are fed on oily salmon. Ontario ranchers have many excuses to hunt rabbits and groundhogs, because they are 'natural' food for the foxes. J. Beetz of Piastre Baie, Que., finds fish and lobster good, and his success in catching foxes is largely due to the fact that they come down from the interior each winter to seek just such food on the shore of the gulf of St. Lawrence. And who could tell an old Prince Edward Island rancher how to feed his foxes? 'The best in the house is none too good,' he says, and he will feed them almost everything he would eat himself, and some grass, minnows, mice, crickets and berries besides.

*See diagram facing this page.

Meat Diet

The flesh diet of foxes is horse meat, cheap beef, calves, butcher scraps (livers, hearts, heads, etc.), fish (both cured and fresh), rabbits, groundhogs, mice, rats, birds, squirrels, lobster bodies and old cattle and sheep. The flesh is usually fed raw but some feeders parboil it. It is salted slightly when parboiled, only a small amount of salt being used. Frequently carcasses are salted down in casks, and, when required for food, a portion is freshened by placing it in running water for a day or two. Some of the finest foxes seen were fed with this kind of food and seemed to be in very thrifty condition, possibly because of being free from worms. Some ranches have cold storage plants, and keep the meat packed with ice. No storage houses similar to bait-fressers are used as yet, but the bait-freezer at Rustico, P.E.I., might serve as a model for such a house. Neither has any mechanical refrigeration of any kind been attempted on any ranch although local cold storage plants are extensively used.

Old cattle and horses are kept on the hoof and slaughtered from time to time as required. As foxes have been known to die of tuberculosis, cattle should be subjected to the tuberculin test or, at least, examined for tubercules after killing. The amount of meat fed should be about one-fourth pound a day and, if any of it is buried by the fox, this amount should be decreased.

Non-flesh Diet

The non-flesh food consists of biscuits, yeast bread, hoe bread, vegetables, porridge, grass, berries, apples, milk and eggs. Patent dog biscuits are fed with good results, one ranch using only Spratt's biscuits, with milk and water, as food. The best ordinary biscuit is the plain hardtack. It is probable that hard-baked non-yeast bread is better than leavened bread. Bread is more relished if grease drippings are poured upon it. Tallow has been used with good success as a butter on hoe bread.

Any rations are liable to fail unless the food is served properly. The dishes should be frequently scalded and scrubbed and kept scrupulously clean. The water vessel should be fastened to the fence with wire hooks so that the foxes cannot climb over it. The food must be withheld when foxes are observed to bury or hide it. In frosty weather in April or May, as frozen meat would kill the young foxes, it is necessary to feed it warm or parboiled in such weather. If one fox dominates the other and takes too large a share of the food, a large quantity must be supplied at night and removed when both have had enough, *e.g.*, a cow's head may be left in a pen for several days to furnish the flesh diet.

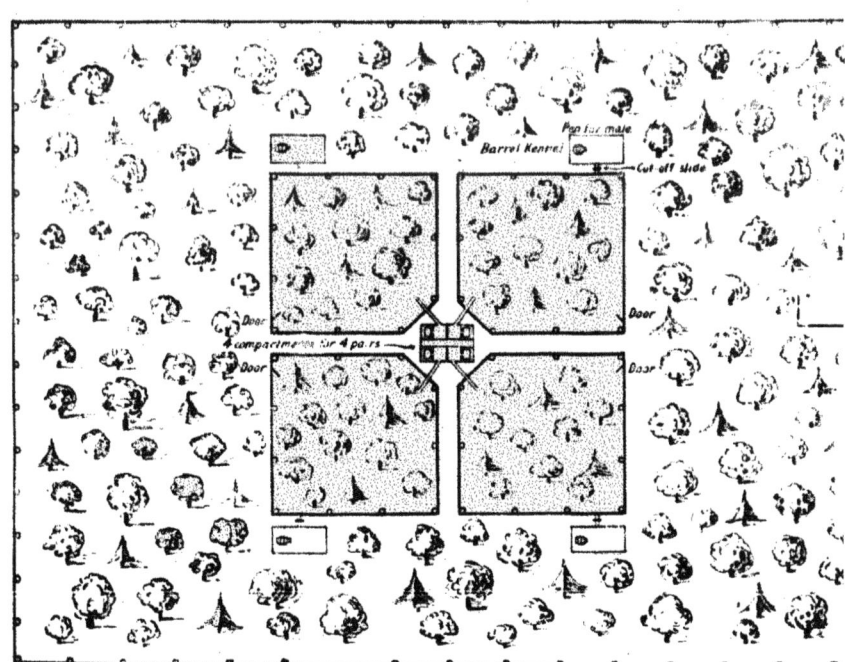

THE BEST TYPE OF FOX RANCH
Scale 1 inch . 50 feet

Fox Biscuits

A perfect fox diet can be secured in the patent dog biscuits. These are made with various kinds of food content, so that balanced rations can be provided. The biscuit medicines have also been proved excellent, and are easy to administer. It is possible that the manufacture of biscuit with meat or fish fibre will be an industry that will develop contemporaneously with fur-farming. The meat can probably be best preserved in this way and feeding made easier and pleasanter.

General Directions for Feeding

Broken bone should not be fed lest some of it be swallowed. Bone should be fed, especially to young foxes, to assist in building up bone and in removing the milk teeth. Some do not feed bony fish, *e.g.*, perch, lest the bones rupture the delicate linings of the throat and intestines. Observation, however, leads to the belief that such injury is not likely to happen, as foxes are dainty feeders, and, unlike dogs, do not devour their food greedily. In addition to bones, growing foxes are fed a quantity of lime-water—about one teaspoonful a day—with their milk. This food gives a substance to the bone and insures stronger limbs. The pregnant mother should also be fed bone broth and limy foods to insure strong limbs for her offspring.

Neither of the foxes should be allowed to become too fat for breeding. When the foxes are less than a year old, they can be fed almost as much as they will eat; after they are older, a full diet may make them too fat for good breeding condition. An average size fox should weigh from ten to fifteen pounds. Some feeders stint foxes in food in November and December and January, to get them into breeding condition; others endeavour to keep them normal always. In the mating season, foxes are very active, and fat pork is fed and a full supply of food is given to keep them in condition. Some roll the meat in sand and soil, claiming that soil is nature's medicine for worms. Some feeders throw food into the pen over the fence; others, in order to tame them, try to coax them to receive it from between the meshes of the wire. A skilful feeder can do more to tame his foxes through feeding them than in any other way. If the food is always delivered at the same place, the tendency will be for the animal to approach nearer and nearer at each feeding. The science of foods is of less importance than a knowledge of the art of feeding.

The mother should be well fed on an attractive and strengthening diet for several weeks before the young are born. Milk, eggs and bone broth are good for the purpose . When the young are expected, a large meal is provided, preferably of game, such as a newly-killed rabbit; a live hen put into the pen is a standard feed on such on occasion. It is said that a fox which eats the fresh brains and blood will never destroy her young.

When the mother appears two or three days after the young are born she should be fed well several times a day with meat, eggs, fresh new milk, meat broth, well-cooked oatmeal and other appetizing and varied foods, while a supply of clean, wholesome water in a clean trough should be constantly available. Live rabbits and poultry, squirrel and other game may be used to give variety to her ration.

Failure in Management   Despite the assertions of many experienced breeders that feeding is the most difficult of all operations in fox ranching, very little evidence was found to confirm this opinion. Few cases of failure due to bad dieting were noted. It is not difficult to keep foxes alive in captivity and, usually, the cause of nearly every loss can be traced. Occasionally mature foxes die suddenly and no satisfactory cause of death can be found, even though post-morten examinations have been carefully performed by qualified operators. The proportion of deaths, however, is low, only four being reported in Prince Edward Island in 1912, and a like proportion in 1913 though probably more took place.

In most cases, lack of success may be attributed to an inexperienced keeper. When men who have never fed even a horse or cow, attempt to rear foxes, they may keep them alive, and may rear a few young, but the probability of failure is great. The failures are usually made in feeding to maintain good breeding condition, and in the care and feeding at the critical period of whelping and rearing the young. The keeper's own character and disposition will have much to do with the success with shy and nervous foxes at this period. A good manager is always studying his animals at the breeding season and he carefully notes the dates of mating and whelping. He treats each pair according to their dispositions. In some cases, he separates the male and female before whelping and, in other cases, he leaves them together. He must be observant, resourceful and faithful, for he is dealing with animals which have had only several generations of domestic breeding or possibly none at all.

Mating and Gestation   The critical period of each year in breeding foxes is between the dates January 1 and June 30. At this time, as the wild nature of some of the foxes renders them exceedingly sensitive to strange sights, noises and smells, all ranches are closed to every one but the keepers. All domestic animals are kept at a distance from even the outer fence. Strangers are warned

1. Fox Kittens Two Weeks Old
    2. A Three-quarters Black Fox Badly Frightened; No Hiding
        Cover to Retreat Into
    3. Keeping Watch on the Strangers
        4. A North Shore (Que.) Fox in August

not to approach the ranch premises on pain of being fined for trespass. In New Brunswick, Prince Edward Island and Quebec, laws have been passed making it an offence punishable by a heavy fine to approach near a fur ranch.*

The keeper should move cautiously and quietly about the pens when feeding. He should have a post of observation from which he can see the pens and yet not be seen. A dark chamber with a hidden approach and a small window to look through may serve. From this post an experienced breeder can ascertain when mating occurs. At the earliest, whelping will take place fifty days after mating, though it may be fifty-two days, or, in rare instances, fifty-three or fifty-four days, especially with the first litter. Fifty-one days is the usual period of gestation.

Removing the Male If the keeper plans to remove the male, he should have the pens built in such a manner that the male may be shut out (away from the female, though with only a fence or double wired fence intervening) without a suspicion on the part of the foxes of design in such a removal. The action of some breeders in entering the pen and catching the dog with tongs or catching box is universally condemned as very dangerous at this period. If the male is kept close by, he will watch and warn whenever he fears danger and, moreover, he takes an interest in the rearing of the young—frequently carrying his food along the fence, apparently with the intention of giving it to the female and the young.

Calming Excited Mothers It is not usual for parent foxes to kill the young intentionally, but, when they become nervous, they sometimes remove the pups to another place. A mother will frequently become greatly excited and, dashing into her nest, will carry out the pups one by one and bury them in the snow or mud. This frequently occurs and is the great fear of ranchers in the spring months. It is difficult to tell what to do in such an emergency, except to see that the foregoing preventive measures are taken. The measures suggested in the following paragraph have been successfully carried out in more than one instance.

A crate of chickens or rabbits should be kept near at hand so that if a mother carries her young about, a live chicken or rabbit may be put into the pen to attract her attention and turn her from her impulse of hiding the young elsewhere. One breeder says that he stopped one mother with an egg which he threw in front of her from outside the fence when she was carrying out her pups.

*See Appendix VII.

Some ranchers, during the whelping season, always keep posted regarding the whereabouts of at least one cat with young kittens. If the mother fox, for any reason, proves to be incapable of rearing her young they are taken from her and reared on the cat until four or five weeks old, when the cat will usually desert them. They are then able to lap milk. Young foxes have been found stiff and cold, but by warming them in hot cotton wool and providing them with a feline wet-nurse, have finally grown to maturity. A nursing bottle and a medicine dropper also might be kept on hand to feed milk.

Data for Breeders The young are blind for fourteen to eighteen days and do not leave the nest, but, when they are about four weeks old, they venture out into the pen often in answer to the decoy call of the keeper. They soon learn to lap milk and eat. When less than three months old, the mother weans them and they may go to quarters of their own.

Foxes have only one litter a year, each litter consisting of from one to nine pups. The earliest noted litter came on March 12; the latest, on June 4. No instances are yet recorded of two litters in one year, but it is believed that it may occur within a few years when the animals are more domestic in habit.

According to the best authorities, foxes in the wild state are monogamous. In captivity, they are usually paired for life, and in many instances re-mating is said to be impossible. In some cases, however, foxes can be re-mated yearly. Some males will mate with several females during the same winter. Two systems of double mating are practised. Under one system, a male and two females of the same litter are given the run of three pens. After mating they are all separated into their respective pens. The other system also requires the use of three pens, the male spending alternate days with each of the two females. When mating is effected in these ways, success is not as certain as with single mating.

The fox continues prolific until about ten or eleven years of age. If a pair fail to produce young after the eighth year, they are usually slaughtered. In the majority of cases foxes mate before they are a year old. Some breeders endeavour to mate a young female with a male a year older.

Hygiene and Diseases No serious diseases were observed in foxes on Canadian ranches. No sick fox was seen, except one that had produced no overhair and appeared to be in very poor condition generally. It was probably the type known to hunters as the Samson fox. Evidence furnished by R. E. Hamilton of Grand

Valley, Ont., who once had one in similar condition in his possession, indicates that the lack of fur and the poor condition is caused by a tapeworm. Mr. Hamilton cured it by administering a violent vermifuge, using a biscuit vermifuge, puppy doses.

Writers report that rabies and canker of the ear have been known, but no evidence of these diseases was found during the present investigation. Two cases of mango were reported in 1913. The usual remedies applied in the case of dogs seem to be effective wherever used and they are usually put up in a form easy to administer.

The following quotation from a letter from Spratt's Patent, Ltd., who manufacture dog biscuits and medicines, contains a number of useful suggestions for the rancher:

"In our pamphlet on dog culture, you will find chapters on all the diseases mentioned in your letter. If foxes, also, are subject to these diseases special precautions will have to be taken. Besides being wild animals, we presume they live in artificial or natural earths, and you can readily understand that, when an animal is suffering from ophthalmia, special precautions will have to be taken.

"The same applies to mange; otherwise, all the animals will soon contract the disease.

"When the animals are from four to six weeks old, they start changing their milk for permanent teeth and bone is a useful article to give, as this helps the shedding of the milk teeth. Sometimes, of course, they are so firmly imbedded in the gums that forceps must be used, and should you find an animal's head swelling, we strongly advise you to examine the mouth and remove the milk, especially the canine, or eye, teeth."

Dr. Alexander Ross, of Charlottetown, formerly of Alberton, P.E.I., who has given much attention to fox diseases and their treatment and has acquired a rare experience in treating foxes on the numerous ranches situated within his practising territory at Alberton, has written the following article on fox diseases and surgery for this report:

"Foxes bred in captivity are more liable to disease than those which roam the wilds. In confinement they are shut off from various foods they seek in the wild state, particularly when they are not well. They are also limited as to exercise, so their muscular tone is usually below par. They often show malformation in the bones of their limbs (rickets) which, I think, is due principally to their food being deficient in bone salts and to restricted exercise. On the whole, however, I have found, in an experience extending over fifteen years, that the colonies of foxes in Prince Edward Island are remarkably free from diseases.

4

Care of Pup Foxes "As young foxes when born have but little fur to protect them from cold, the chief object among breeders was to make the pens warm enough. The provisions for ventilation seemed adequate enough for the usual weather conditions that obtain in Prince Edward Island during the time the young foxes remain in their dens. Last April, however, during a period of exceptionally hot weather a number of pups were smothered owing to insufficient ventilation. Now, many ranchers have a two-inch pipe leading horizontally from the inner den to the outer kennel. Although it is usually inadvisable to enter the kennel and open the nest about the time of whelping, yet, if the mother runs about the enclosure in an excited manner, the nest should be examined. During the examination the mother fox should be shut out. When the young foxes die, the mother usually eats them, and, as is the case with pigs, the mothers sometimes actually destroy and eat their young. Foxmen assign various reasons for this practice. It may be due to a craving for some ingredient lacking in the food supplied during gestation. The mother often destroys them if she is disturbed and apparently fears she and her young are attacked by enemies, or that her hiding place is discovered. It may also be due to an inverted maternal instinct and is then a vice. This vice is liable to occur in all animals that devour their placenta. When the pups come out of the nest about four weeks after birth and any one of them looks unthrifty it should be caught and examined for vermin. If lice are found, it should be washed with an infusion of quassia chips, made by pouring two quarts of boiling water on a half pound of quassia chips and letting the mixture stand for twelve hours. This infusion is non-poisonous. If fleas are found, the pups should be washed in a creoline bath—(one ounce to a gallon of water). The kennel and the den should also be washed with a stronger creoline solution and the mother should be washed with the infusion of quassia. Sometimes a pup is unthrifty owing to his being abused by the others. He should then be placed in a pen and fed by himself.

Diseases of Malnutrition, Rickets, etc. "Quite a few show rickets which is due largely to deficiency in bone and tissue forming food. In those ranches where proper care is taken, very few of them have this disease. Where they are bred simply for quality of fur without due regard to physique, where they are in-bred, and especially when they are not properly fed, they are apt to develop rickets. The disease is characterized by deformities in the bony structures or by lack of growth. The legs are the parts principally affected. The animal cannot stand straight although otherwise it seems active and hardy enough. Ground bone, lime-water or cod liver oil and hypophosphites of lime and soda administered with their food will help to arrest the disease at its beginning. Abundance of fresh air and sunshine should also be provided.

Disorders of Digestion "Foxes in confinement are prone to suffer especially from disorders of digestion due to lack of knowledge in feeding them. The following are a number of the more common of the diseases of the digestive organs, together with directions for treating them.:

"*Diarrhoea.*—Diarrhoea is caused by abuse of purgatives, prolonged vegetable diet, feeding too much liver, exposure and specific causes *e.g.* germs, distemper, etc.

Treatment: First ascertain the cause. If severe, give a purge of castor oil with a few drops of spirits of turpentine, followed by 10 to 20 grains of bismuth every two hours till the animal is better. The castor oil dose may be repeated more than once in smaller doses if the diarrhoea persists. At the same time, the food should also receive attention. Meats should be restricted, and milk, biscuits and eggs given. No food should be left in the feeding-pans more than a few hours and the pans should be scalded out frequently. If the animal seems weak, liberal doses of brandy should be given frequently. If the pups are young, artificial heat must be provided by the use of hot water bottles, or some other efficient means. If the enclosures are dark and damp, they must be removed to a dry, sunny place or indoors.

"*Constipation.*—They do not suffer much from this disease. It can be overcome largely by means of dieting. A dose of cascara acts well, and, when needed, injections of soap suds may be given. The diet should be of a laxative mixture and sloppy. Feed liver.

"*Inflamation of the bowels.*—This is one of the commonest and most fatal diseases that affect the fox. Causes: Improper feeding, unhygienic surroundings, worms, irritant poisons, specific agencies, e.g. germs, distemper, etc. The symptoms are,—loss of appetite, diarrhoea, excreta often blood-stained, mucus, fever, listlessness, loss of flesh, coat dry, staring eyes, dull, pulse rapid. When the foxes show the above symptoms a qualified veterinary surgeon should be immediately summoned. A short delay may prove fatal. When a fox is taken in hand early much can be done, but, if the disease has made much headway, it almost invariably proves fatal. In pups it is apt to cause fits. The young ones will not eat; their coats lose sleekness and they become listless. If not promptly treated, they die quickly. Give castor oil and turpentine and feed judiciously. This can only be done by separating the ill from the well. After death the bowel is found to be dark red or black and gangrenous and, in some sections, a thin bloody fluid is found. As the disease is infectious, the diseased animal should be separated from those that are well, and the enclosures should be disinfected. I am of the opinion that nearly all the half grown and fully grown foxes that have died on Prince Edward Island, died from either this disease or from intestinal parasites.

"*Round Worms.*—The commonest round worm is the *acaris marginata*. It is present in a large proportion of foxes. It is a very frequent cause of convulsions in puppies and, if abundant, causes obstruction or inflammation of the bowels. In fact, in young foxes, this is the principal cause of that disease. These worms are from half an inch to several inches in length. They are cream coloured and tapering. Castor oil with a few drops of spirits of turpentine is a good and safe remedy. Santonin in doses of about ½ grain for a pup, given every day or two is also good; no food should be given and the santonine should be followed in three hours with a purge. Areca nut, in two grain doses is also fairly safe to puppies.

"It is well to remember that all worm medicines are poisonous and should be followed with a purge. It is claimed that the feeding of mollassine dog biscuits will prevent intestinal parasites.

"*Tape Worm.*—Foxes may be infected with several varieties of tape worm. They come from eating meat or fish infected by the worm in the larval stage. In this respect, they differ from the round worm which grows directly from the egg. There is the marginated tape-worm, the serrated tape worm, the *tinea coenuris* (larval stage in the brain of the sheep) and *tinea cucumerina* (larval stage in the hare). These worms are flat and in sections. They vary in length from several inches to several feet. It is rather difficult to rid foxes of these pests and a good veterinary surgeon should be called in. Many drugs have been recommended but they are all dangerous. Doses vary with the condition of the animal.

Skin Diseases   "Sarcoptic and follicular mange, are caused by minute animal organisms that invade the skin structure. They can be seen only with a magnifying glass. The sarcoptic mite has an oval body and four pairs of legs while the follicular mite has a lobster-shaped body. The sarcoptic mite lives near the surface of the skin and, for this reason, spreads much more rapidly over the animal and is much more easily communicated from one animal to another than the follicular. Sarcoptic mange if allowed to run its course, will, in a short time, denude the animal of hair and the skin becomes thickened and spongy. Follicular mange spreads very slowly and occurs in patches, usually about the head and along the back. Sarcoptic mange if taken in hand early, yields to treatment much more readily than follicular mange which can only be eradicated with difficulty.

"Owing to the highly contagious nature of these diseases, particularly the sarcoptic variety, the animal should be isolated and no communication allowed with healthy animals. The keeper of healthy foxes, if exposed to the disease, should disinfect himself and his clothes. If an animal is badly affected, it should be killed and buried deep in quick-lime or burned. The kennel should be burned and the enclosure left unused for a long time. The treatment of these diseases should not be undertaken by an untrained person. I have seen two cases of sarcoptic mange in foxes; both in a very advanced state. They occured in a batch that were imported into Prince Edward Island. Since the disease was discovered in July, 1913, all foxes, when imported, must remain three weeks in quarantine and be twice inspected more particularly for mange and distemper.

Ringworm "This contagious disease is caused by a vegetable parasite. There are two forms: the circular or tonsurate and the honeycomb. Foxes will take this disease from cattle. A circular patch covered with branny scales and stubby hairs, appears over parts infected with the circular form. The name 'honey-comb' describe the appearance of the other. Keep the fox isolated; anoint the sore with an ointment of oleate of mercury. Painting with tincture of iodine is also good treatment.

Ophthalmia or Inflammation of the Eyes "There is a specific or recurrent form of ophthalmia that foxes are subject to and may cause total blindness. It usually attacks puppies 6 to 8 weeks old and is not accompanied by any of the signs of distemper. Cold, draughts, dirt, distemper or any irritating substance introduced in the eye may cause ophthalmia. Bathe the eye frequently with a hot saturated solution of boracic acid. Several times daily instil drops of sulphate of zinc solution (4 grs. to the ounce) into the eye. Between the lids insert night and morning, Ung. Hydrarg. ox. Flav. (4 grs. to the ounce lanolin) the size of a split pea.

Distemper "Although no case of this disease has occurred among foxes in Prince Edward Island, it has been reported in other localities among dogs and foxes and has almost decimated them. It is so highly contagious and so fatal that the below note has been added that fox-breeders may detect the initial symptoms and take it in time. Fortunately the quarantine adopted last July will be of the greatest service in excluding it from the colonies of foxes in captivity here. As dogs readily communicate it directly, or indirectly, to foxes they should not be allowed near ranches. The young are more

MICROCOPY RESOLUTION TEST CHART

(ANSI and ISO TEST CHART No. 2)

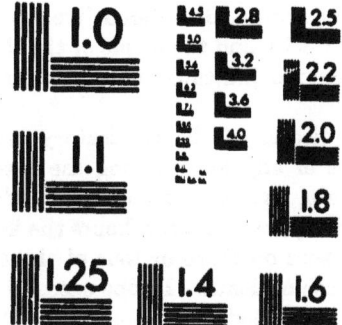

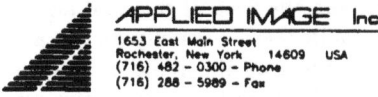

APPLIED IMAGE Inc

1653 East Main Street
Rochester, New York   14609   USA
(716) 482 - 0300 - Phone
(716) 288 - 5989 - Fax

easily infected. Feeding utensils, hands and clothing of attendants, bedding, water vessels, contact of diseased with the healthy, wind carrying dried up discharges, etc., are the usual media of communication. The preliminary symptoms are dullness, loss of appetite, sneezing, redness and heaviness of the eyes, slight husky cough, vomiting, constipation if the animal is young, or diarrhoea. Temperature in vagina or rectum 103°F or 104°F. Following these symptoms is a profuse discharge from the eyes and nose,—first watery, then creamy. The disease may go no further than this, but it is frequently followed by bronchitis, pneumonia, pleurisy, pericarditis, disordered liver, a fetid breath, and pustular eruption on the belly and the inside of the thighs. These symptoms should be sufficient to indicate the character and gravity of this dreaded disease.

"I have met with no case of disease of the respiratory organs.

"There have been no epidemics of any kind among the foxes of Prince Edward Island. Now and again, a grown fox has died suddenly. Usually the fox seemed to be quite lively, and in a few hours the keeper found him dead. I performed autopsies on three or four of these and could in no case be certain of the cause of death. In one case, I found some congestion of the lung, which I regarded as post-mortem. In another, the gall bladder was abnormally distended. Most of them showed some redness of the alimentary tract. I am of opinion that death was due to some food poisons—ptomaine. In one animal that died there was a jelly-like fluid between the pelt and the flesh of the hind legs.

"When pups are shedding their milk teeth—usually at the age of three months—abscesses are liable to form at the roots of the tusks. The fox then swells around the snout. In such cases the tusks, which are quite loose, should be extracted. Give them large bones to gnaw so they can knock out these teeth. This will usually prevent the formation of these abscesses.

Fox Surgery "I have had more to do with foxes in a surgical than in a medical way. They frequently break their limbs in fighting among themselves or in an effort to escape by climbing their enclosures. These fractures are usually compound and necessitate the amputation of the limb. The flesh is stripped back and the protruding bone is snipped off with bone forceps. The wound is dressed antiseptically and the flesh is stitched over the bone. The whole part is well dusted with iodoform, and wrapped in gauze bound on with surgeon's adhesive plaster. The fox will not touch the dressing when dusted with iodoform. The operation is simple, no anæsthetic is needed and there is no danger from bleeding, because, as a rule, no arteries have to be tied. In fact, it is dangerous to give an anæsthetic.

"When the fracture is not compound, the limb may be set in splints of any light wood; maple saplings make good splints. Bind the splint on with adhesive plaster and with rabbit wire; the fur makes sufficient padding for it. Dust with iodoform to keep the fox from tearing the splint off. In winter, care must be taken that the leg does not freeze.

Directions for Feeding
".Judicious feeding can only be learned by experience. Grass and other green food and fresh earth should be placed in the enclosures at frequent intervals, as the animals require something of that nature to keep them healthy. Their kennels should be kept as clean as possible and should be washed out once or twice a year with a hot solution of creolin, two drams to the pint. One breeder dips all his foxes, after the pups are weaned, in a weak solution of creolin to rid them of fleas and other vermin.

"In general, it is far better to take good hygienic precautions before the foxes get sick, than to invite disease by permitting them to live in filth in small enclosures."

Dangerous Fox Diseases
In 1912, vague reports were circulated among the breeders of Prince Edward Island that a contagious parasitic disease was being introduced by blue foxes imported from Alaska. A definite warning was furnished the Commission of Conservation by an eminent United States authority that such a dangerous disease exists and would prove fatal to the fox industry if introduced; but few details of the disease were presented. A letter of inquiry was sent to Mr. George M. Bowers, Commissioner of Fisheries, Department of Commerce and Labour, who has charge of the conservation of foxes and seals at certain points in Alaska. The reply under date of November 25, 1912, is as follows:

"The Bureau has not been informed of any particular parasitic disease as existing among the foxes of Alaska. So far as known, fatal disease has been so rare as to be negligible in the consideration of fox raising. Improper feeding, accidental poisoning and tuberculosis have been known to cause the death of individual foxes, but nothing in the nature of an epidemic has been reported."

Where in the cases reported, two ranches—one in Labrador and the other in Maine—lost all, or nearly all their foxes, it is very probable that the trouble was distemper.

Capturing Escaped Foxes
As already stated, the capturing of escaped foxes presents little difficulty provided they do not get outside the exterior fence. They will often, of their own accord, return through

the open door after a few hours. Or, in the cases where escape has been over snow banks, they will usually return when hungry. They may be driven into the alleys from the outer enclosure when a temporary fence of meshed wire is stretched across from the pen to the outer fence. They can also be caught in the box traps, or in steel traps which have the jaws wrapped with muslin so that the limbs will not be injured. A live hen or rabbit makes excellent bait. The latter method will often prove effective when the fox has escaped to the woods, as they are likely, especially if ranch-bred, to remain in the vicinity of the ranch.

The ownership of an escaped fox is a disputed point. Many people contend that a fox roaming at large is game for anyone, but, if the ranchman can identify the live fox or the skin, he can recover it as his personal property.

Marking for Identification   Ranchmen have given serious study to the question of marking for identification. A numbered aluminum tag, which may be seen at a considerable distance, is often fastened into the ear. In some way, however, the fox manages to get it off. Marking the teeth by filing or tattooing them is also resorted to, and has, at least, proved practicable. But the disadvantage of not marking the skin is obvious. Tattooing the skin with the owner's number or brand, could be done on the hide where it is least valuable; or, the ear could be marked as with sheep and cattle. The brand could be registered and the skin or the live animal thus identified. If such a method were practised, it would have the additional advantage of being undiscovered by thieves and of rendering it possible to identify the skin on the open market. Branding on the flank is also a possible method.

Catching and Handling   The catching and handling of foxes in their pens present little difficulty. Expert ranchers will catch and handle them without gloves or instruments, but the ordinary rancher provides himself with a pair of tongs the jaws of which will close to a diameter of two and a half inches. The fox is shut into his nest and when the cover is lifted, is grasped about the neck with the tongs. The fox may then be carried away on the arm and the rancher be in no-danger of getting bitten. A catching box is also useful. It is made just large enough to admit the fox and has a slide door at each end. When it is placed at the end of the entrance to a house with one slide door opened, the fox may be driven out of the nest into it. The slide door is closed and the fox is thus trapped in the box. If the catching box be made of stiff wire-mesh sides and top, the fur can be closely examined. In the case of the latter type of construction, however, the fox might not readily enter it unless a blanket was placed over the box to darken it. The usual method of handling them is with gloved hands and no instruments.

When foxes are transported, they are put into a box which is lined with meshed wire so that they cannot escape by gnawing their way out. They can be kept without water or food for days, but are generally fed water biscuits or a bone and are watered, a can being nailed on the interior for that purpose. Express companies are obliged to feed them if food is provided.

When foxes are brought to their pens for the first time, they should be liberated by making a small opening in the box and holding it up to the entrance of the kennel. They will then enter their nest and, after a minute's inspection, will come out into the pen. By this time, the keeper can be away out of sight, and none, or very few, will attempt to climb the wire or rush against it. If pens are provided with cover and built in secluded woodland, the wildest foxes will not climb the wire if the keeper is competent and no strangers are admitted.

Slaughtering for Fur No foxes except a few old ones and culls were killed in Prince Edward Island for their pelts in 1910, 1911, 1912 or 1913. The pelt of a fox becomes prime in November, but is not as heavy then as in December. They are killed on Prince Edward Island in the last week of December. A fox eight months old is said to have as full and large a skin as an older one. Some breeders, however, disagree with this common opinion and say that one year and eight months is the proper age for killing.

The fox when young, has less silver than in the later years and this is an advantage in the present market, silver skins being more common than pure black. It is hardly necessary to remark that no fox should be slaughtered without a careful examination of his coat, and, if it be light and thin and the fox only a pup, he should be spared for a year in order to improve his condition if possible.

Considerable care should be taken against injury to the coat during the months previous to killing. They should not be allowed to lie on damp places and thus have the guard hair frozen into the ground or snow and broken. Smooth, large passage ways should be provided. Fleas or mange or other skin affections or parasites should be prevented as they would induce scratching and thus wear off the hair on the shoulders and hips.

It is claimed that heavy feeding of nutritious laxative food like molasses, patent food preparations, boiled barley or oats, will fatten the fox and improve the gloss of its coat. Some of the costliest skins marketed were taken off foxes with one quarter of an inch of fat over their ribs. This is contrary to a popular, but incorrect, impression that starving makes the hair longer and improves the coat.

Foxes are killed by crushing the chest walls. They are placed on their sides, and the slaughterer places the sole of his foot immediately behind the foreleg and bears down with his full weight. They are also killed by forcing the head back until the neck breaks. There is a danger that the sheen of the overhair—especially the silver hairs—may be somewhat injured with blood and dirt so that clean quarters and methods of killing are essential.

The information available indicates that the adoption of some more humane method of killing, such as the use of chloroform or ether, would not injure the fur and, at the same time, be far more merciful. A small padded box with a wad of cotton batting in one of the upper corners upon which chloroform could be dropped from a hole in the corner of the box would be all that would be required. As soon as it is dead, the animal should be removed from the chamber. In the case of such a valuable animal as this, it is not too much to expect of ranchers that they provide one of these inexpensive lethal chambers.

Poisons that are available are: cyanide of potassium, prussic acid, strychnine and white arsenic. A very small quantity of cyanide or of prussic acid will kill the fox instantly, but, as these drugs are excessively poisonous, it is dangerous to have them in one's possession unless securely locked up. Strychnine and white arsenic do not kill immediately, and, if another animal ate the flesh of an animal poisoned by them, it would be poisoned in turn.

The cased method of skinning, described elsewhere, is used.* The only difficulty will be with the forelegs and tail. The forelegs become stiff and hard in a short time and should be turned fur side out after a day or two. If the tail bone is not wholly removed in the first attempt, the tail may be slit down the under side. The skins are marketed fur side out and are sewed up in muslin and packed flat in a box.

Judging a
Silver Fox Skin
The condition of the pelt in respect to primeness, proper killing, skinning, drying and shipping is important. Skins may be blue or unprime; springy, when the hips and shoulders are worn and the hair loose; dirty, shot, chewed, heated, or greasy. In such cases their value is largely decreased.

The skin value of the live animal may be judged from the following standards:

Colour.—Glossy black on neck, and wherever no silver hairs are found. The black must be of a bluish cast all over the body

*See page 119.

rather than a reddish. The underfur must also be dark-coloured. The fur of silver and black foxes is a dark slate next to the skin.

Silver hairs.—Pure silver bands—not w' :te nor very prominent. In the costliest skins there are only a few silver hairs, which are well scattered over the pelt. Flakiness, which is the appearance of whitish silver hairs placed close together in patches, is objectionable.

Texture.—Buyers pass judgment on the skins by drawing the hand over the fur. The softest fur is the most valuable. The quality of softness is referred to as "silkiness".

Gloss.—The sheen must be evident. It is caused by the perfect health of the animal and the fineness of the hair, as well as by hereditary influences. Woods and humid atmosphere also favour this important quality.

Weight.—A good fox skin will weigh at least one pound, the weight usually varying from ten to nineteen ounces. The thick, long fur makes the weight. This is a very important point, as heavy fur is more irable and handsome.

Size.—The value of silver fox pelts increases with the size.

FINANCIAL ASPECTS

The amount of capital required to finance a ranch containing even three or four pairs of foxes, involves the organization of companies or extensive partnerships among people of experience and in a situation suitable for fox ranching. In the autumn of 1912, at least $50,000 was required to build, equip, and stock a ranch in Prince Edward Island with five pairs of first-class stock, and, in 1913, this amount of money would hardly suffice to provide three pairs. Many ranches have been equipped for less money, but either cheaper wild or unselected stock from Newfoundland, western Canada or elsewhere was purchased, or options had been taken at an earlier date on pups for delivery at that time.

Options on Stock

Because of the keen demand for breeding stock, it has been customary to sell options for future delivery. Usually the options are taken on the unborn pups, and 10 per cent of the price agreed upon is paid when the options are taken. Time of delivery is made the essence of the contract and, if the rancher has not as many pups as he has sold options for, the orders are filled consecutively, *i.e.*, the earliest orders are filled first. In case delivery cannot be made, the agreement provides that the deposit must be returned with 6 per cent interest per annum. In 1913, as in 1912, options were sold on

more pups than could be delivered because of the unexpectedly small
number of young born. At the present time (December, 1913), many
options on 1914 stock at an average price of about $12,000 per pair have
been sold. As large ranchers carefully number the options, the holder of
the first option has the best chance of securing the choice of pups when
the deliveries are made.

All over North America, wherever the common red fox is found,
agreements are being made with lumbermen, miners, missionaries,
fur traders, trappers, government officials and others for future
delivery of wild animals captured in their respective districts.
The supply of fur will be appreciably diminished by the capture of
wild fur-bearers alive, in 1913 and probably in succeeding years. More
trappers are working than ever before and practically all of them are
seeking to capture live animals.

Sales for Breeding Stock In 1911, 1912 and 1913, all available foxes were sold for
breeders. The first general sales were made in 1910,
at prices not far above the fur-value, viz. about $3,000
to $4,000 a pair. In 1911 the price rose to $5,000 a pair, and, about
littering time in 1912, one pair was sold for $20,000. This, however,
was for a pair of excellent proved breeders, which, a few weeks later,
produced five whelps which were sold for $20,000 in August, 1912. By
September 1, when the deliveries of stock began, the price was $8,000
a pair for pups and a month later, $11,000. By December, 1912, $12,000
and $13,000 was the ruling price, with few sales. Old proved breeders
of good quality were valued during the last months of 1912 at from
$18,000 to $35,000 a pair. In September, 1913, prices of pairs of young
silver foxes ranged from $12,000 to $17,000 and advanced but slightly
until December when all exchanges of animals from one ranch to another
must cease. Options on deliveries for 1914 were selling at from $10,000
to $12,500 a pair.

It can thus be readily understood how highly speculative fox trading is at the present time. The tendency towards inflation is encour-
aged and fostered by many of the older breeders. Their optimism is
accounted for by the fact that they have become wealthy in the last
three years, whereas six or eight years ago, some of them possessed only
mortgaged farms and a few foxes. All but three or four have made
their fortunes by selling breeding stock and, with the exception of,
possibly, $200,000, obtained for pelts, all of the million or more dollars
received by ranchers have been made in this way.

Futures The present system of buying for future delivery is another
indication of the optimism of investors. In December, 1912,
many of the unborn pups of 1913 were purchased and partly

paid for, delivery to be made in the first week of September, 1913. The difference between purchasing futures in foxes and gambling in futures in May wheat or October cotton is more apparent than real. Fox exchanges were opened at various centres for trading in stocks and futures.

Craze for Ownership* Naturally, the rapid rise of such an industry has unsettled the peaceful rural conditions in a country like Prince Edward Island. Farmers are using the credit of their farms to purchase shares in silver foxes, or to buy outright cross foxes, red foxes, blue foxes, minks and any other fur-bearer likely to prove profitable. The banks report a serious withdrawal of deposits and realisation upon outside investments, while the lawyers of the little town of Summerside, P.E.I., are reported to have recorded about $300,000 in farm mortgages in 1912. A goodly share of the savings banks deposits made by these prosperous islanders has also been withdrawn.

Remarking on the great craze for shares of stock in fox ranches and for fox ownership, Wesley Frost, the United States consul at Charlottetown, wrote to his government in January 1913:

"In adjudging the soundness of the present position of the fox industry in Prince Edward Island it should be borne in mind that the community is an intensely conservative one, composed of Scottish and English farmers, intelligent and fairly educated, and with a per capita savings deposit figure to compare with almost any portion of the civilized world................

"It is true that a large number of the foremost citizens of the Island refuse to participate in the fox boom to any degree whatsoever. Every large •·le by one of the big ranches is hailed as an effort to unload ·‹·· · ₁₁ · 'ide turns. Investment at the present time is regarded ·. ···· · · tive speculation—but with the speculative element too ·₍₎· us. Granting nearly all that the fox men say, the scе₁ ·ᵣ that, in the readjustments involved in getting back to the pelt basis, the industry will injure many of its followers."

Pro and Con It is maintained by some that the present craze is similar to the Belgian hare craze in America and the tulip craze in Europe, both of which collapsed with a heavy slump. It is contended that fox fur is only a poor quality; that silver fox has never been bought in large quantities and that, if production is increased, it

---

*Appendix XI of this report gives a list of the fur-farming companies and licensees operating in each of the provinces. Practically all of the companies named have been incorporated since the beginning of 1912, which shows that the development of the industry has been decidedly phenomenal.

will become as cheap as rabbit; that wild foxes do not decrease in numbers when a country is settled; that investments usually yield from 2 to 10 per cent per annum and that, therefore, the large profits made by fox ranchers during the season of 1912 were abnormal. A smaller proportion state that the fox boom was promoted by exaggerated statements respecting the prices received for pelts and by other misrepresentations. They assert that many of the skins marketed have not brought over $50.00 or $100.00 each and that a large proportion of the foxes now in captivity is of little more value than red foxes. They also state that the demand for silver fox has been supplied and that the Russian nobility and some other Europeans are the only ones who will pay a high figure. It is also maintained that skins of ranch-bred foxes have not the gloss and quality of the product of the wilds.

On the other hand, it is stated that the supply of valuable wild silver foxes captured is decreasing, that the demand for costly natural furs is rapidly increasing; that only a few hundred silver foxes are in captivity and that there is ample time for readjustment of values before enough are reared to warrant marketing for fur. The fact is also pointed to that the domestication of fur-bearers has been predicted and attempted for centuries and that those who achieved the work are entitled to reward. Furthermore, it is claimed that when fur is so valuable no animals will be sold unless enormous prices are paid; that it is proved that the fur is better in all respects than the wild product and that the best foxes have not yet been sold and will bring higher prices than the present high record, viz. $2,900.00. In addition, the best customers are millionaires and not the nobility.

A general comment is all that can be made on the arguments advanced. Some of the points are discussed elsewhere in this report, notably those respecting the prices obtained for ranch-produced furs as compared with the wild, the decline in numbers of the natural wild supply, and the general excellent quality of ranch-bred stock as compared with the wild stock.

The increased demand and its causes have already been discussed and little remains to be said on that subject. It is possible that silver fox will become even more fashionable than at present and that the demand will thus be increased, but no one can forecast definitely what fashion will do. It should also be noted that the Russian sable, chinchilla, sea-otter and seal will be off the market for several years and, on this account, an increased demand for the fur of the silver fox may be created.

The imitation of silver fox is also impossible because of the colours of the silver-banded black overhairs. The nearest imitation is the German-dyed pointed fox, made from a common red fox dyed black, which has white hairs from the badger or other animals sowed into it or fastened in by adhesives. It is easily distinguished from the silver fox fur and is not favoured except as a medium-priced article. It is not nearly so beautiful as silver fox. The silver band in a genuine skin is not white, but silvery, and the whole skin possesses a gloss not equalled by a dyed product. The dyeing process, also, has the disadvantage of rendering the fur less durable.

With regard to the statement that much of the stock is of poor quality and low-priced, it must be admitted that this is true. While statistics of the low prices obtained for pelts obviously could not be secured, it is quite probable that at least 30 per cent of the silver foxes would bring a price of from $50.00 to $500.00. At the present quotations, probably another 30 per cent, would be priced between $500.00 and $1,000.00 and the other 40 per cent would bring from $1,000.00 to $4,000.00* each. The ability to recognize a cheap grade of fur instantly is essential in the present state of the business as traders represent a silver fox as such regardless of quality; and, usually, only a short and distant examination of the animal is possible. Besides, the sales are made at a season when the fur is not in prime condition.

If wild foxes do not decrease when a country is settled, it is not recorded that they increase. The number in unsettled regions, however, is diminishing.

Thus far, profits in the industry have been large, but, except from the point of view of the individual, the dividend on the money invested is not the main consideration. From the social and economic viewpoint, the discovery of how to breed high-grade foxes is what is important. It is akin to an invention; but, as it cannot be patented, the neighbours of the inventors have become the promoters of a new method of producing a remarkable commodity. No huge factories can be built in a few months to manufacture the article to the limit of demand; only the natural law of increase of fox which is not much over 100 per cent per annum can be utilized. Thus, it will be several years before the supply will meet the demand, as it is sure to do eventually. If the investing public can be made to believe that future profits are assured, it is human nature to ask as large a premium on the shares of fox-ranching companies as can be obtained.

The stories of the predilection of the nobility of Russia and of other countries for expensive furs like silver fox, sea-otter and sable are mostly drawn from the imagination. The current story that gold is tipped on silver fox overhair was unknown to any of the furriers interviewed, some of whom have been purchasing furs in Europe and

---

*Inasmuch as Mr. Jones states (p. 62) that the record price of a skin is $2,900, the upper limit—$4,000—seems too high.—*Ed.*

America for many years. The story of the Royal Russian furs is doubtless derived from the fact that certain sable and other costly furs were formerly given as tribute to royalty. Ermine happens to be a royal fur and is demanded at coronations and great court ceremonies, yet it is stated that much of the so-called 'ermine' at the coronation of King George V was really rabbit. The best customers of silver fox will be fashionable ladies who will use it in trimmings, stoles and muffs.

Number of Foxes in Captivity Because of the removal of foxes to new ranches in September. October and November while this investigation was proceeding, no very exact data could be procured regarding the number of silver foxes. The following is an estimate of the number in captivity in each province in October, 1912:

FOXES IN CAPTIVITY IN CANADA IN 1912

	Silver	Cross	Bastard and Red	No. of Ranches
P. E. Island.....................	650	150	1,000	200
Nova Scotia...................	32	30	150	13
New Brunswick..................	30	10	50	8
Quebec........................	40	10	50	6
Ontario.......................	30	40	150	14
Other provinces and territories.....	18	10	50	..
Total.....................	800	250	1,450	241

The silver fox industry is centred about the following points: Alberton, Summerside, Charlottetown and Montague in Prince Edward Island; Port Elgin in New Brunswick; Piastre Baie on the north shore of the gulf of St. Lawrence, Quebec city in Quebec, and Wyoming in Ontario. In November, 1913, the number of silver foxes within driving distance of each point was approximately as follows: Alberton, 500; Summerside, 300; Charlottetown, 300; Montague, 50; Murray Harbour, 40; Port Elgin, N.B., 60; Quebec city, 30; Piastre Baie, 20; Wyoming, 20. In the United States there are several ranches in Maine, one in New Hampshire and one in Minnesota. In Russia, a number of fox and sable farms have been established since M. Vladimir Generosoff aroused interest by his report on Canadian fox farms.

The Increase in Numbers Since, under present ranching conditions, silver foxes increase in numbers approximately 100 per cent each year, it seems evident that the present [...] for foundation stock must decline to near the pelt value before many years. The price of the scrub stock and of specimens with the poorer grade of skins will decline first. It is likely that this inferior stock will be used for mating with red and cross foxes which, by the year 1916, should be producing a large number of silvers, mostly of poor quality, however.

Final Value of Silver Fox With regard to statements frequently made that silver fox will be as cheap as rabbit if produced as numerously, the point is not worth discussing, since production will not increase beyond the point where a profit can be made. The London importation of rabbits is now over 80,000,000 skins annually and Australia uses thousands more weekly in her great felting industries. An attempt was made to secure export opinions from qualified furriers as to the final value of silver fox pelts when they are produced in as large numbers as those of red foxes are now. The concensus of opinion was that, because of its greater beauty and more favoured colour, silver fox fur would be three times as valuable as red fox, natural black furs not occurring commonly in nature. In this connection, it must be remembered that all ranch silver foxes are killed when the fur is prime and no injury whatever is done to the pelt, so that their pelts would be worth from $40.00 to $80.00 each for No. 1 skins, at the present valuation of the pelts of red foxes from Northeast Canada. But it will be a long time before the production of silver foxes will approach to the number of even high-grade red foxes marketed yearly. The total number of skins, according to the estimates of E. Brass is 1,337,000 yearly for the common fox. Even if the pelts fell to $30.00, foxes could be raised profitably by a farmer who maintained other live stock. In many districts the annual cash outlay per fox for food need not exceed $5.00, and attending to twenty foxes would not involve so much labour as attending to ten cattle. If fox ranch fences cost more, the land and houses cost much less. The fox, moreover, reproduces rapidly and comes to maturity in eight months.

Because the silver fox has never been produced in considerable numbers, it has been impossible for furriers to carry a stock large enough to warrant advertising it and featuring its sale. It has been difficult to obtain even two matched skins at one sale. Under the new conditions, when thousands of skins may come to the market season after season, matching will be easy, and the best fur stores can carry in stock enough silver fox to warrant the featuring of it.

Organizations Among Producers An opportunity is now presented to the ranchmen to unite into a strong co-operative association to protect and promote the industry. Frauds could be exposed, breeding records kept, thieves arrested and prosecuted, legislation secured, the product advertised and the whole market situation studied. The publication of inexact and fanciful statements by promoters of stock companies is also injurious to the industry's future. The better protection of the stock from thieves could be achieved by

5

amending the provincial trespass laws so as to increase the fine for trespassing near fox ranch property.*

Because of the mixing of various strains of foxes, it is difficult to secure reliable "performance" records of stock. The only "performances" worth noting in foxes are the prices of the pelts of the ancestors, and such features as fecundity, beauty, size and weight of the pelt. Well-organized provincial associations could keep performance records, and the various provincial organizations could co-operate with the Federal Department of Agriculture for registration.

Quarantine is a question that may, at any time, become of prime importance. Thus, if disease breaks out in any district, the Federal Department of Agriculture, if requested by a strong association of breeders, might be induced to undertake a quarantine.

The whole problem of the protection of wild animals and the possibility of propagating them in captivity are broad questions that require more attention than has been given them in the past. A Dominion Furriers and Fur-farming Association organized along lines similar to the Canadian Forestry Association, and like the latter, publishing its own journal, could do much to promote a healthy interest in protecting and propagating wild life. The organization of provincial associations would be the first logical step in such a movement. To establish a permanent national organization, representatives of the fur trade, the fur farms, the game wardens and commissioners, and the government experts could be called together.

POLAR OR ARCTIC FOX

(Vulpes lagopus)

The polar fox is found in the high latitudes. It is of two colour phases—white, and the so-called blue, which is really a drab gray resembling somewhat in colour a maltese cat. The white fox is brown in summer with the under parts lighter or drab. The white winter coat has a pure white long overfur with an underwool of a darker colour. The blue phase is of a gray-brown colour all the year round and is found more abundantly in the southern portion of the range of these foxes. It is said to exist in Greenland and Iceland. The number of blue-fox pelts sold annually is about one-tenth of the number of white-fox, and they sell for several times as much, bringing, at present market prices, from $20 to $75 each, and even higher for choice pelts.

---

*See Appendix VII.

POLAR FOX (WHITE) RANCHED IN RUSSIA. THIS ANIMAL IS OF THE SAME SPECIES
AS THE BLUE FOX WHICH IS RANCHED IN ALASKA AND CANADA.
THE FOX IS IN SUMMER COAT

A RUSSIAN RED FOX

A considerable number of blue foxes were imported into Canada during the season of 1912. Possibly a hundred or more were brought into the Maritime Provinces from Alaska, where feeding is now difficult because the killing of seals is not permitted. One consignment numbered thirty-two and arrived in very fair condition.

As no increase whatever was obtained from those imported in 1912, not more than 40 or 50 blue foxes had been imported into Prince Edward Island up to December 1, 1913. No authenticated instances of whelps of blue foxes being raised to maturity are recorded. Statements were made that a number of litters had been born, but investigation proved that very few, if any, of the young were seen by the ranchmen and they simply surmised that birth had taken place because of the actions of the vixen. It is difficult to understand why blue foxes have not produced young in the Maritime Provinces. This failure can hardly be ascribed to the removal of the animals to more southern latitudes as, in many instances, common red foxes imported from Alaska have bred in Prince Edward Island. The southern latitudes would hardly affect their fecundity, though it might lessen their fur-value—particularly in weight of fur. The probability is that the facts concerning the feed, care, and general management of blue foxes are not yet known. In Alaska they are rarely, if ever, ranched in pens, but roam wild over the islands. It is probable that those now ranching blue foxes, who have spent considerable time studying their habits in Alaska will succeed in rearing young in the spring of 1914.

The blue fox is a better climber than the red and an overhang wire of 36 inches is required. Otherwise, the pens are built similarly to those of the common fox.

Blue Fox Farming The following account of blue fox farming is taken from "Fur Farming for Profit," published by the Fur News Publishing Co., of New York.

"For some years past the blue fox has been successfully raised in rather large numbers on several small islands off the coast of Alaska, and for a shorter period on the mainland. The blue fox thrives and multiplies in captivity, and can be raised with rather more satisfaction than the other members of the fox family, as it is more tractable and easily managed. An island makes an excellent blue fox farm for various reasons: there is no large outlay in cash for fencing; as the islands are surrounded by the sea, the water does not freeze over in winter and the foxes cannot leave the farm; no danger is to be apprehended from the intrusion of other animals; a considerable supply of food may be obtained from the sea, which is to a considerable extent self-supplied; crabs are found along the shore, fish are washed up on the beach from time to time, and other food is found on the islands. While a number of the islands are now occupied by blue fox farmers, there are many more that are available for the purpose, and which can be leased from the United States government on reasonable terms. Farms on the mainland may be enclosed with wire fencing, and need not be larger than 50 feet by 50 feet. For raising the foxes on a larger scale than would be possible in an enclosure of the above-mentioned area, several little farms, adjoining each other, may be fenced off.

"Blue foxes breed once a year, mating about February 1, and the young are born near the end of May, the litter comprising from three to seven. Artificial dens or hiding places in which the foxes may remain secluded at will are provided.

"Food for the blue fox includes fresh, dried and cured fish, crabs, fresh meats obtainable in the vicinity of the farms, cooked corn-meal cakes made of a mixture of corn-meal and chopped dried fish, and meal, tallow and fish preserved in oil.

"Food should be supplied to the animals most abundantly from the first of July to August, as, at that period, the care of the young foxes makes it necessary for the old foxes to be better fed than at other times.

"The price of blue fox skins is about $30.00 each, and even more is paid for well-coloured, full-furred and properly handled pelts.

"Stock for beginning may be procured from persons raising blue foxes on the islands at a cost of somewhere near $200.00 per pair.

"The Secretary of Commerce and Labor has authority to lease for the purpose of propagating foxes, such islands in the waters of Alaska, excepting the Pribilof group, as have been so leased by the Secretary of the Treasury prior to May, 1898. The rental in the past has been one hundred dollars per annum for each island."

Rate of Increase   The rate of increase of blue foxes is said by Ernest Thompson Seton to be good index to the increase of red foxes. He says: "St. George island, about 36 square miles, has about 270 pairs of foxes, and although they are fed and protected and the species has 5 to 12 in a litter, not more than 400 to 500 can be marketed each year without reducing the stock." The figures are about correct for the annual increase of the silver fox, despite the claims of some ranchers of an average annual increase of from 200 to 300 per cent.

Maj. Gen. A. Greely, in his Handbook of Alaska, published in 1909, writes:

Additional Details   "Unwise exploitation has very greatly reduced the fur-bearing productivity of the land animals of the Aleutian islands, as well as of the interior of Alaska. With the early extermination of foxes in prospect, there was organized about 1894 the Semidi Propagation Company, to domesticate and raise foxes on uninhabited islands. The original fox farm was stocked from the Pribilof group and was situated on North Semidi island, whence the industry has extended to thirty or more islands to the eastward, far the greater number being situated in Prince William sound, though there are seven in the Kodiak group. Most of the islands are occupied under lease from the United States, and, under the law, are not open for homesteading. The companies and several individuals have followed this industry, which has been only moderately successful from the financial standpoint. Considerable investment is necessary, it takes at least four years before any revenue is obtained, the life is most isolated, and skins are not very productive, usually varying in value from $10 to $20, according to quality and demand. In some instances natives have become fox breeders and, where private parties are so engaged, they have supplemented their fox breeding by fishing, farming, or lumbering.

"The largest fox farm is at Long island, near Kodiak, where there are nearly 1,000 blue foxes. The largest number of skins comes, however, from the Pribilof group, where about 700 foxes are annually taken by the natives, supplementary to the fur-seal catch. These foxes are not domesticated.

"The very valuable silver-gray fox is too thoroughly savage to accept conditions necessary for profitable fox breeding and, in consequence, fox farming is confined almost entirely to the blue fox. The fox is monogamous, and an average of four foxes come to maturity from each litter. It is necessary to feed them the greater part of the year, and careful supervision is essential to their successful raising.

"The blue fox thrives wild on the extreme easterly isle of Attu, and from that point several of the Shumagin islands, Chernabura, Simeonof, etc., have been stocked with moderate success. The extension and development of this industry is desirable as one of the much needed means to enable the Aleuts the more successfully to meet changed conditions of Alaskan life."

BLUE FOX BREEDERS IN ALASKA*

Island	Locality	Name of Breeder	Post-office Address
Little Naked...	Pr. William sound.	Walter Story.......	C/o Alaska Packers Assoc., San Francisco, Cal.
" ...	"	Olaf Carlson.........	....
" ..	"	Louis Carlson.......	....
" ..	"	Fred Lilyogren......	Ellamar, Alaska.
Big Naked.....	"	James McPherson....	" "
" ...	"	Edward Elk........	" "
Fairmount.....	"	William Byers......	" "
Bligh.........	"	Pres. Cloudman......	" "
"	"	William Busby......	" "
Goose........	"	George Donaldson....	" "
"	"	Louis Thorstensen...	" "
Greene.......	"	Peterson & Brower..	" "
Long.........	"	George Fleming.....	" "
Gage.........	"	George Fleming.....	" "
Pond.........	"	A. W. Lind........	" "
Smith	"	James Bettles......	" "
Squirrel......	"	John L. Johnson.....	Orca, Alaska.
Perry........	"	Kendall & Stering....	Ellamar, Alaska.
Small, near Perry.......	"	Christ Christensen....	" "
Glacier........	"	Peter Jackson.......	
An island (no name).......	Resurrection bay...	Alfred Law.........	" "
Yukon........	Kachemak bay....	A. R. Ritchie........	Homer, Alaska.
Cape Elizabeth.	....	M. F. Wright........	Seattle, Wash.
Chirikof........	Southwest of Kodiak........	Semidi Propagating Co..............	Kodiak, Alaska.
North Semidi...	"	"	" "
South Semidi...	"	"	" "
Chernobura....	Near Unga.......	"	" "
Little Konuigi..	"	"	" "
Simeonof......	"	"	" "
Marmot........	"	"	" "
Whale.........	Near Kodiak......	"	" "
Andronica.....	Near Unga........	W. L. Washburn..... (administrator)	San Francisco, Cal.
Long.........	Near Kodiak......	Semidi Propagating Co..............	Kodiak, Alaska.
Pearl.........	Near Cape Elizabeth.......	Alaska Fox Co......	" "
Dry	Near Kodiak......	Semidi Propagating Co..........	" "
Samalga........	West of Unalaska,.	Not occupied.	
Peak..........	Pr. William sound.	McPherson & Elk....	Ellamar, Alaska.

There are also two small islands near Prince of Wales sound not now occupied. The following islands, also, are no longer occupied: Demidof, Eastern Chugatz, Praznik and Near islands.

*From Report of U. S. Department of the Interior, Public Lands Section, House Documents, 58th Congress, 2nd Session.

Additional light is thrown on the breeding of blue foxes by the following article on "The Blue Foxes of the Pribilof Islands," by James Judge:

THE BLUE FOXES OF THE PRIBILOF ISLANDS

"The Pribilof islands have many natural advantages as a home for foxes. The innumerable caves and subterranean passages afford the best protection possible against the elements or natural enemies, while the bird, seal, and sea-lion life, with what may be picked up on the beach, have, in the past, afforded a supply of food rarely found elsewhere. At the present time foxes are about extinct on St. Paul and Otter islands and have been preserved on St. George only through a system of artificial feeding adopted several years ago. This paper deals with St. George foxes only.

Former Food Supply "In former times the annual quota of seals killed on St. George island varied between 20,000 and 25,000. Hundreds of sea-lions also were killed annually. With the exception of what the natives took for food, these vast quantities of meat were left on the ground where the animals were killed, and, during the long period from September to May, these seal and sea-lion fields furnished the foxes with food, when other and more palatable food was not obtainable. Frequently dead whales, walruses, sea-lions, or fish were washed ashore and, when this occurred, the killing fields were abandoned by the foxes, and only resorted to again when this temporary food supply was exhausted. These were practically the conditions under which the St. George foxes lived from the time of Russian occupancy of the island down to 1890. During this long interval, no attention was paid to the animals, except that trapping was indulged in by the native residents, from one to two months each winter when the skins were prime.

Present Food Supply "During the summer of 1896, I had the natives salt 500 seal carcasses, the meat being preserved in an old silo formerly used by the sealing company. During the following winter, these carcasses were taken out, a few at a time, freshened, and thrown out for fox food. The rapidity with which the foxes learned that food would be set out daily at a certain place and time, and the numbers in which they came for it, surprised everyone on the island. They not only ate the meat but nearly all the bones as well. For an hour before feeding time they could be seen coming from all directions to participate in the feast. While waiting, they prowled around the village picking up everything of an edible nature and many things not edible. They came in greatest numbers when the weather was clear and cold.

"Since that time all seal meat on St. George, not used by the natives, has been salted within two or three days of the killing, and fed to the foxes during the succeeding winter. When taken from the silo it is half rotten, most of the brine having escaped, but the foxes prefer it to fresh beef, mutton, or fish of any kind, as has been learned by experiment. With the exception of three seasons, the catch of seals has been under 2,500 and, as fully half the meat is required by the natives, it has been necessary to supplement the amount allowed the foxes with other food.

"In the spring and summer, thousands of sea birds make the islands their home. This is the time the foxes enjoy life to the utmost. The birds are very numerous and, in the early part of the season, many meet death or injury accidentally and, of course, fall a ready prey to the foxes. During the month of May, hundreds of small auklets or 'choochkies' in flying to and from the sea, strike the telephone wire and are killed or injured. No sooner do they reach the ground, however, than the foxes are there to pick them up. For the first few days, reynard will eat the entire bird, but, later on, as he becomes surfeited, he eats only the head and leaves the body untouched. The eggs of birds are a delicacy enjoyed by the foxes. The 'arrie' or murre and other large birds lay their eggs on shelving rocks on the cliffs; and it is astonishing to see a fox climb around an almost inaccessible place, secure an egg and carry it away for its young, to return shortly and repeat the operation.

"By September 1, the birds, their breeding season being over, have mostly left the island, the deaths among seals on the rookeries are few, and marine food is not abundant, so it behooves the foxes to seek food in other quarters.

"One season a mush of either corn-meal or middlings was used; but, while readily eaten by the foxes, it was not good for them. Dried fish was tried and found excellent food, and, during the last two years, salt fish has been in use. Salt itself is deadly to the foxes, so that in feeding salted food, care must be taken to thoroughly freshen it.

"Seal killing begins in June and, as the carcasses are left on the ground, a good supply of food becomes available. It appears, however, that, at that season, the eggs and meat of birds are preferred to seal meat, as the latter is seldom touched, while bird feathers and egg shells are to be found along the trails and at the mouth of every fox warren. With the departure of the birds in the fall the foxes follow the shore line in search of food thrown up by the sea, and pay particular attention to seal rookeries, on the lookout for dead pups, which seem to be relished, and are dragged off for the young.

"While the animals eat a great deal of grass and other land and marine vegetation, it is evident that they cannot long survive on a diet that does not include animal food.

Modern Conditions "The year 1890 may be considered the turning point in fox life on the Pribilof islands, which, of course, include St. George. At that time, or soon after, a scarcity of foxes was everywhere apparent, and the government agents in charge, wrongly attributing the diminution to over-trapping, forbade all trapping for three different winters in the early nineties, with the result that the total catch for the seven years ending with 1897 was only 2,198. The real trouble was a shortage of substantial food, such as the foxes had always been accustomed to, but this was not then understood, or at least no steps were taken to supply the deficiency.

"The slaughter of seals upon the ocean by pelagic hunters had so decimated the seal herd, that, in 1890, only 6,139 were secured on St. George island, instead of the regular quota of 25,000. In 1891, 1892 and 1893, owing to the *modus vivendi*, the number of seals killed on this island was further reduced to 2,500. The sea-lion herd of the island had likewise been greatly depleted, so that but few of those animals were killed, and, consequently, there was little or none of that meat for the foxes.

"With the departure of the birds in the fall, the foxes, as usual, scoured the beach for food, and that source proving insufficient, recourse to the seal fields, where formerly they were sure of something when driven to extremities, proved unavailing. The limited amount of seal meat was soon cleaned up. After that, there was nothing for them but starvation, and those that succumbed were quickly devoured by the survivors.

Modern Trapping "Coincident with the regular feeding of foxes, the experiment of catching them in small box traps was made. This was successful from the beginning, as the foxes did not hesitate to enter for the bait, and sometimes two would get in before the trap was sprung, although it was intended only for one. The foxes came in such numbers that at least 50 box traps would be needed to accommodate them. This suggested the erection of a house trap, and accordingly a rough corral or house trap 8 by 14 feet was constructed beside the coal house. Three or four seal carcasses were placed in the trap for bait. The foxes entered with little hesitation and soon

40 or more would be inside. The man operating the trap stood inside the coal house, and by pulling a rope, caused the door to drop, and the foxes were prisoners. Subsequently a wire-mesh trap or cage 14 by 10 by 8 feet was procured and placed at one end of a house especially for the fox business. This house is divided into three rooms, in the larger of which is a vat for freshening salt meat or fish. The other rooms are designated as trapping and examination rooms, respectively. The cage adjoins the trapping room. All food set out for foxes is placed in the cage, the door b'ing always open. Week after week before trapping begins the foxes fe..d in this trap, and of course have no fear of it.

"When trapping time arrives, food is placed in the trap as usual and 8 or 10 men repair to the fox house. The door of the wire cage is adjusted and the man who operates it is stationed in the trapping room, in a position to observe what is going on in the cage; and when a sufficient number of foxes have entered, he closes the door by pulling a small rope. He then goes into the cage and drives the animals into the trapping room, where two men with large leather mittens pick the foxes up and pass them, one at a time, into the hands of others waiting in the examination room.

"When the foxes are numerous in the trapping room, they run between the legs of the men attempting to catch them, climb up their bodies and jump from their shoulders, but very seldom bite except when they are taken hold of. If they get a good hold of a man's hand they hang on with bull-dog tenacity until their jaws are pried apart. They seem to realize their inability to bite through the mittens, and with few exceptions are easily handled. Major Clark reports one last year as lying inert in the native's arms, making no struggle whatever, and apparently enjoying the smoothing it received.

Selecting the Breeders
"The Government Agent is stationed in the examination room, and when a fox is passed in he decides whether it shall be killed, or branded and dismissed as a breeder. The elements on which his decision is based are the colour and quality of the fur, the age, length of brush, and live weight of the animal. All white foxes, runts, those off colour, crippled, bob-tailed, in poor condition physically, suffering from mange, or otherwise unfit to be left as breeders, are despatched at once. All animals left as breeders must be in good physical condition, of good colour, and either young or in the prime of life; males must weigh at least 10 pounds, and females at least 7½ pounds.

"The age is determined by a dental examine   which is made by opening the animal's mouth with a soft gag, and inspecting the teeth.

"In taking the live weight, a strap two inches wide is looped around the animal's tail and the other end of the strap attached to a spring balance suspended from the ceiling of the room. When the animal becomes quiet the weight is ascertained and entered.

"If the beast is to be left as a breeder, a ring one inch wide is cut in the fur of the tail with a pair of scissors after which it is dropped into a hopper and finds itself out of doors. Males are branded near the end of the tail, females near the rump. About four-fifths of those dismissed as breeders are caught the second time, and some of them are re-caught ten times or more in the course of the season. Recently, Mr. Chichester installed several automatic traps, auxiliary to the regular traps, which have done good work.

"When the animal is to be killed, the man who has it in hand bends the head backwards until the neck is broken. The dead animal is then thrown into the adjoining room, where other men remove the pelt This is done by running a sharp knife up the inside of the legs, and down the length of the tail, and drawing the pelt off, leaving the fur side in. After the breeding quota is secured, all unbranded foxes entering the trap are killed. All trapping is done at night with light from lanterns. The next day the skins are cleansed and stretched on frames to dry. Later on they are whipped and combed, and, the following summer, barrelled and shipped to London.

"The skins are prime from November 15 to January 15, approximately. About the latter date the fur begins changing colour, and the skin shows signs of 'staginess.'

"As indicated, the animals' ages are ascertained by dental examination. In this work no pretense to absolute accuracy is made. Dental examination of a hundred or more dead foxes of both sexes showed a division of the animals into three classes, which classification has since been followed in making the annual census. These are: first, yearling or approximately one year old; second, middle-aged or approximately two years or three years old; third, over three years old. The young and the advanced in life are easily distinguished, but the intervening ages are more difficult to determine. It is doubtful if the life of St. George foxes ordinarily exceeds five years.

Contents of Stomachs

"On examination of 334 stomachs, seal meat formed the entire contents of 64, and the partial contents of 100 others. This meat of course was gotten in traps, and was what the animals came for. The contents of 17 full stomachs varied in weight between 14 and 20 ounces. These animals were still feeding when trapped and how much more they would have eaten if unmolested, cannot be determined. The stomach, when empty, weighs from 1½ to 2 ounces, but its capacity of distention for the reception of food is astonishing. It is doubtful if an animal after gorging with so much meat would feed the next day, but it is known that certain foxes living in the vicinity of the village do come for food daily.

"Grass was found in 88 stomachs, feathers in 57, wild parsnip in 12, fish bones in 8, bird or seal bones in 28, dirt or sand in 22, tunicates in 00, sea eggs in 4, and fox fur in 8. Seven stomachs contained only water, and 14 were empty.

Contents of Intestines . "The intestines varied in length from 0½ to 10 feet, no difference being found in this particular between the sexes. On examination of the intestines of 240 foxes killed in trapping, grass was found in 62, feathers in 20, wild parsnip in 16, tunicates in 5. Neither of these things undergoes any apparent chemical change in the stomach or intestines, and can be identified upon evacuation in the excrement. Those small circular tunicates are swallowed without mastication and passed without digestion. Dirt was found in 24 intestines, gravel in 11, bones in 12, fox fur in 10. Two varieties of intestinal worms were found in the intestines of 26. Specimens sent to Dr. Stiles were identified as species that affect domestic animals, and not particularly harmful. The distribution of the worms was general, all ages and sexes containing them. Excepting lice in the fur, these worms were the only parasites discovered.

Physical Characteristics "The live weights of 198 males left for breeders varied between 10 to 20 pounds each. Of this number 180 weighed between 10 and 13½ pounds.

"The live weights of 225 females varied between 7½ and 11½ pounds. Of this number, 18 weighed less than 8 pounds and 13 over 10½ pounds. Of 180 males killed, 101 weighed 10 pounds and under, while 17 weighed over 13 pounds, the heaviest weighing 19½ pounds.

"Of 86 females killed, 55 weighed 8 pounds and under, and 9 weighed 11 pounds, and over. The heaviest female killed weighed 13½ pounds, the lightest 4½.

"The average length of 180 male skins, after being dried and ready for shipment, was 30 inches plus; average breadth, 11 inches plus; average length of tail, 15 inches plus.

"When the skins of male and female are placed side by side and compared, the fur of the former is generally found to be superior to that of the latter. As a rule, the fur of the two and three year old males is the choice of all.

"Assuming that the sexes are equal in number at birth, the evidence at my command tends to the conclusion that the males are more vigorous and better able to survive adverse climatic or other conditions than the females.

Breeding "Except for a few cases, mating, according to my observation, is confined to the month of March and the first half of April. The earliest birth of pups noted by me was May 17, the latest June 6. Altogether I have seen 22 litters of new born foxes. The largest of these consisted of 11, the smallest of 5 members. Three litters contained 1 white each; three, 2 dead each; and six, 1 dead each. These discoveries were made shortly after the young were born and before some of them were dry. In all these cases the mother made no preparation, but gave birth in slight depressions on the surface of the ground. In every case the mother was much concerned by my presence, and immediately transferred her young to some subterranean spot in the neighbourhood. She removed the dead as well as the living. The male consort was not present at any of these births. I am inclined to think the mother always gives birth on the surface of the ground, and within a day or so transfers the young underground for protection and security.

"As a general thing, the young are not observed until about the middle of June. They are then of pretty good size and play or feed about the mouths of their burrows, on food brought by their parents. When the young are thus playing or feeding, one and occasionally two old foxes are in the vicinity. These are supposed to be parents when two are present; but genera" only one, presumably the mother, is about and the approach of a person causes the emission of a shrill note from her which sends the young scampering under the ground.

"The number of young seen at the mouths of their burrows varies between 1 and 4, according to my observation. Major Clark saw 12 at the mouth of one warren, but he was under the impression that more than one family was represented. During the summer of 1906, Mr. Chichester observed daily for many weeks a family of eleven, all of which were eventually brought up by the mother. I am inclined to consider this litter a very exceptional one. If it were not, we would have a great many more foxes at trapping time.

"The infant mortality, which is very great, takes place shortly after birth and is probably attributable to want of nourishment, cold, and inclement weather. As soon as the young can eat meat, they thrive rapidly and, under ordinary conditions, reach maturity.

"On one occasion a native found a family of 12 young that had just been born. One he thought was dead and brought it to me, but after being in the house ten minutes the little thing showed signs of life. It was placed on a hot water bottle, where it soon revived and began to squeal. Mrs. Judge administered milk with a medicine dropper and it soon settled down and went into a healthy sleep. When it awoke, the medicine dropper was again brought into use; and, later on, it learned to nurse one end of a bunch of cotton, the other end of which was immersed in milk. It improved steadily on a milk diet until it was three weeks old. It then grew less ravenous, probably as a result of overfeeding, and, at times, refused to nurse. At the age of four weeks it died. Its eyes opened on the 15th day. When brought in, it weighed 2½ ounces; when three weeks old, it weighed six ounces.

Reduced Number of White Foxes "White foxes are occasionally found in litters of blue. There is no record of a litter of white foxes. As the white skins are of comparatively little value, continued effort to exterminate white foxes has been pursued since 1897. Every white fox entering the trap since that time has been killed at once and, in addition, the natives are permitted to shoot them any time during the winter. The total number killed in 1897 was 40, in 1898 it was 18, and, since that time, the number killed per year has varied between 6 and 12, with the exception of the winter of 1903-1904, when 15 were killed. Last winter 8 white skins were secured, but Major Clark, who was then in charge of St. George, says that only three of these were pure white, the others being either marred or mottled with faint blue spots. During the summer of 1906, Mr. Chichester observed a number of foxes that were part blue and part white. After September, he saw but one of these and therefore concluded that as winter approached the parti-coloured coats became white.

Diseases "Evidence of disease among foxes on the island is scanty. Foxes found dead at any season are always autopsied, the local physician assisting, but it is seldom that the cause of death can be definitely ascertained. Dr. Mills and I found a fox in spasms, which on post mortem was found to have been suffering from uræmic poisoning. One death was due to hemorrhage of the kidney, and another to tuberculosis. This latter case was found by us on May 28, 1905. The animal was a female, 3 years old, carrying one brand. She was void of fat and weighed not more than 4 pounds. The loss of flesh had occurred since the time of trapping, a few months previous. Tubercular nodules were found in both lungs. Death, on one occasion, resulted from a sac of pus which had formed on the intestine. Another dead fox showed all the organs normal except one of the kidneys, which was atrophied.

"Mr. Chichester reports three dying of kidney disease and one of tuberculosis in 1906, and one of perforation of the stomach caused by an ulcer in 1907. In that year, he killed four that were suffering from mange, and in 1908, Major Clark killed nine that he found afflicted with the same disease.

"An unusual number of dead on St. Paul island the winter of 1902-03, taken in connection with symptoms of mania noticed by Mr. Lembkey, led him to believe that an epidemic of some sort affected the foxes that year.

"When foxes starve to death a dark discharge issues from the anus.

Yield of Fox Skins — "Statistics of the catches prior to 1840 are not available. For the 19 years ending with 1860, the average annual catch for St. George island was 1,278.

"For the 19 years ending with 1889, according to figures kindly furnished me by the Alaska Commercial Company—the former lessees of the sealing privileges—the average annual yield was 1,074.

"The following table shows concisely the entire trapping since steel traps were abandoned, which is coincident with the inauguration of regular feeding.

BLUE FOXES TRAPPED

	NUMBER OF TRAPPINGS		Killed, inc. white	RELEASED AS BREEDERS		*Total trapped
	Fox-house	Elsewhere		Male	Female	
1897–98....	11	1	346	102	324	772
1898–99....	7		386	110	389	885
1899–00,...	9		418	65	498	981
1900–01....	24	7	441	204	690	1,335
1901–02....	24	9	246	202	650	1,098
1902–03....	28	21	511	250	250	1,011
1903–04....	28	21	491	284	286	1,061
1904–05....	38	37	272	244	250	766
1905–06....	43	22	481	279	302	1,062
1906–07....	36	31	380	232	270	882
1907–08....			446	267	272	1,005

"During the first three years shown in the above table, the work was under the supervision of the government agents, the next five under that of the company agents, and, since 1906, again under the government agents. The ebb and flow in fox life as shown by the trapping is capable of explanation, but the details cannot here be considered.

*Occasionally the column "Total trapped" includes skins of animals found dead.

Summary   "Females were immune from killing during the first six years; since then, approximately an equal number of males and females have been released for breeding purposes, and the remainder killed, regardless of sex. It was thought, in the first instance, that, by saving all females and a small number of males, polygamy would become general among the foxes as is the case with domestic animals. Results not meeting with expectations, the scheme of leaving a number of pairs and saving them for breeders was adopted.

"Evidence of promiscuous sexual intercourse among the foxes is confined to a very few cases, none of which appear in the printed reports of the agents of the Department of Commerce and Labor. Only one case has come under my observation. The different method of branding males and females is reported by Mr. Chichester as showing that pairs of foxes often seen playing together in the spring are not always male and female. He also observed a female fox bring up a litter of young alone and unaided. Later on, however, the same gentleman found the first authentic case of paired foxes jointly engaged in feeding and guarding the same litter of young.

"It is possible that some of the females do not mate or become impregnated, and there is evidence that others abort; so, on the whole, it would seem wise to leave a surplus of healthy vigorous females, instead of adhering rigidly to the rules now in vogue.

"At present the business is carried on under a contract, by which the North American Commercial Co. gets all the skins taken, compensates the natives for their labour, and furnishes a certain amount of fox food; but the feeding, trapping and entire conduct of fox affairs is in the hands of the government agents.

"While the regular annual catch of fox skins on St. George island since the present methods were adopted is less than half what it was from 1870 to 1890, as herein shown, it is evident that the herd, and with it the annual catch of skins, can be indefinitely increased. The fact that on St. Paul island, where nothing was done to perpetuate fox life, the species is about extinct, justifies the opinion that the measures taken on St. George island have preserved the foxes thereon. Summing it up, it may be stated that the preservation and increase of the foxes on St. George island depend, primarily, upon the bountiful feeding of proper food for about eight months every year; and secondarily, upon the careful and methodical selection of the animals reserved for breeding purposes."

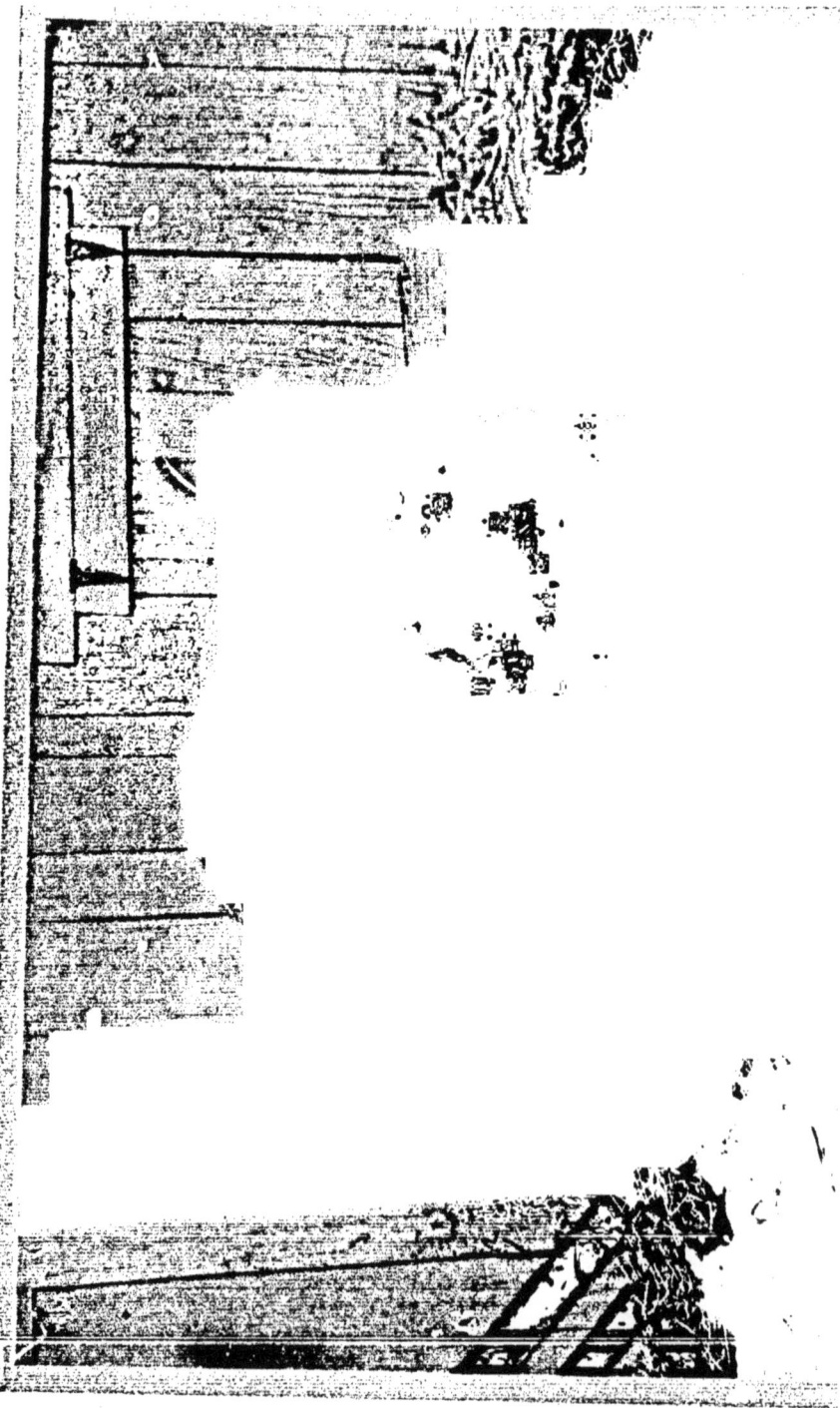

KARAKUL SHEEP

(Of the *Ovis platyura* or broadtail class)

THE information respecting the breeding of karakul sheep for Persian lamb and astrakhan fur production has been, in large part, extracted from a Russian Government bulletin by Mr. M. Karpov, published in 1912 and entitled "Facts concerning Karakul Breeding"; from the United States Department of Agriculture which experimented for two years with karakul sheep supplied by Dr. C. C. Young; from Dr. Young himself; from the article of Prof. Wallace of Edinborough University in the Pastoralist magazine published in 1909; from Herr Carl Thorer of Leipzig, the largest importer of karakul sheep fur in the world; from Mr. Vladimir Generosoff, Russian Agricultural Commissioner in America; from Consul Emil Brass' book "Aus dem Reiche der Pelze"; from the American Breeders Association; from daily personal observation of the karakul sheep recently imported to Charlottetown, P.E.I., and from the examination of skins produced on the ranch of the Middlewater Cattle Co. of Middlewater, Texas, whose herd was recently imported into Prince Edward Island.

Habitat of Karakuls The khanate of Bokhara, West Turkestan, Central Asia —especially the districts of Karakul, Karshi, Kerki, and Tcharjui on the Amu-Darya river—is the original home of the karakul breeds of sheep which produce the furs known to commerce as Persian lamb, astrakhan, baby lamb, or broadtail and gray krimmer. From these centres the industry has, in recent years, extended to the khanate of Khiva, lying immediately north of Bokhara; southerly to Northern Persia and Afghanistan, westerly to Transcaspia, the Caucasus, and the Crimea, and to the eastern provinces of West Turkestan, Syr-Darya, Ferghana, and Semiryetchensk. A few small outlying herds have very recently been established in southern Russia, Germany, Hungary, Africa, and America.

Breeds of Karakuls The karakul consists of six classes which may be roughly referred to as distinct breeds. These, Dr. Young asserts, are all descended from the 'danadar'—now practically extinct—and from which they have derived their black colour, lustre of wool, and tendencies to produce tightly-curled lambs. The breeds that produce the most highly valued fur are:

1. The small arabi—a small sheep with coarse, long, gray wool when mature; small head, with small, erect ears and straight nose line;

6

thin feet, long, broad tail of 18 or 20 vertebræ; at birth, jet black, with lustrous, close, tight curls, which, soon after, open out on all parts of the body and become gray except on the face, neck, legs, abdomen, and end of tail; rams are horned.

2. The 'large arabi,' or 'doozbai'—a larger sheep than any common breeds in America and Great Britain; same coarse, gray wool as the small arabi or somewhat coarser; large head with long, drooping ears and convex nose line; strong, thick feet; enormous broad tail of about 16 vertebræ. The wool characteristics at birth and at maturity, are similar to those of the small arabi, except that an occasional specimen is fawn-coloured at birth gradually changing to white and whitish-gray at maturity; rams often horned.

3. The 'intermediate class' is a cross between the small arabi and the doozbai and possesses one or the other characteristics of each breed.

4. and 5. The 'gray shiras' and the 'zigai' are too few in number to merit description.

6. The 'karakul Afghan' (also known as the 'karakul finewool') comprises probably 98 per cent of all karakul sheep in Bokhara. They are characterized by the presence of fine, short, lustreless, merino-like wool often completely hidden by the longer, coarse, gray arabi over-wool. At birth, the skins have open, lustreless, curls, due to the presence of the fine wool, and are practically worthless if a large quantity of fine wool is present. It is this class of sheep that is usually sold to the unsuspecting foreigner by the crafty natives who care little how they treat the 'giaours,' or 'infidel dogs,' as they term Christians.

When, in 1908, Dr. Young made his first importation of fifteen head to America, he found, after three years of breeding, that twelve of the fifteen were karakul Afghans and produced almost worthless skins when bred to one another. However, when they were crossed with one good doozbai ram, the skins brought an average price, in whole-sale lots, of $6.50 according to valuation furnished by United States Government furriers. This mistake was avoided in the second importa-tion from Bokhara in May, 1912, and the nine lambs born in transit, none of which were slaughtered or died, possessed skins of magnificent tight curls and gloss. It is not probable that any profit can be made by breeding the karakul Afghan type of sheep, though, because of the mistake made in the choice of the first importation, they are in the large majority even in America. Dr. Young largely retrieved himself in the choice of his second importation, but unsuspecting fur farmers will almost certainly be disappointed if they depend on the fine-wool karakul strains of his first purchase in Bokhara. Descendants of the first karakul Afghan sheep imported are in the possession of several

American breeders who, themselves, may be in ignorance of the inability of their sheep to produce lambs with valuable skins.

Persian Lamb and Astrakhan   When the vogue for black Russian furs arose one or two score years ago the first traders to secure the raw furs and market them were the Persians, hence the trade name of the karakul sheep lambs became 'Persian lamb.' Their proximity to Bokhara, because they were Mohammedans and because they could enter a land, at that time, closed to Christians, enabled the Persians to monopolise this trade. The skins were brought out by caravans through Transcaspia to Asun-da on the Caspian sea and were shipped by water to Astrakhan. Hence the trade name of 'astrakhan' was also attached to these pelts by the European merchants who traded there. Thus, for a time, the terms 'astrakhan' and 'Persian lamb' were used indiscriminately to describe all lamb pelts used as fur, except gray ones, which were called shiraz and, later, krimmer. In the last dozen years, the term 'Persian lamb' is applied to all black, lustrous, tight-curled skins; 'astrakhan' or 'karakul' has been applied to open-curled skins or skins with no curl whatever, of any colour except gray, and includes the skins of fawn-coloured kids and kalmuck, khirgiz, mongol, tshuntuk, Persian or other fat-rump sheep as well as to the skins of karakul Afghan or karakul sheep with fine underwool. All gray lambskins with tight curls are named 'krimmer' by the furriers; the gray skins with only slight curl or no curl are 'astrakhan.' It should be distinctly borne in mind that the terms 'Persian lamb,' 'astrakhan,' and 'krimmer' are trade names used by furriers and tradesmen. These names are never applied to the live animals, but to the skins only.

Tartar Names and Their Meanings   According to Karpov, "kara-kul" is a Tartar term, signifying "black rose" or "black lake" to which the native in his enthusiasm likens the black tight-curled skin known as 'Persian lamb'. 'Arabi' is a Tadjik word meaning 'black' and should not be confounded etymologically with Arabia, which country, according to Consul Emil Brass, possesses no fur-bearing sheep. 'Koordiuk' in Tartar, signifies 'fat rump' and is applied by the Russians to some thirty different breeds of fat-rump, coarse-wool sheep (*ovis steotopyga*) whose lambs are not killed for fur purposes. The skins of the still-born and young lambs which have unavoidably died are styled 'astrakhan' and are practically valueless outside of the country of their origin. As the fur is of the poorest class, it is referred to as 'peasant fur,' and is, generally, fawn-coloured.

Native Sheep as Fur Producers   It was noted above that the presence of fine wool in the karakul Afghan sheep destroyed their value for the production of the costlier skins. This suggested the possibility that our long and coarse-woolled sheep, *e.g.*, the Lincoln, Cotswold, and the Highland black-face might produce lambs with tight curls of considerable gloss. These skins could then be dyed and sold as 'Persian lamb.' But experiments have shown that the curl is rather open—not possessing enough horny substance in the wool fibre to produce and maintain a close, tight curl. If a karakul ram with an entire absence of fine-wool blood, be bred to coarse-woolled native sheep, the lamb-skin produced is the equal of the best skins produced in Bokhara from full blood karakuls. This has been well proven in America and is certified by officials of the United States Department of Agriculture, who had such skins valued by New York furriers. It has also been proven that the half-blood karakul rams, produced by the above cross, will, if mated with the coarsest-woolled native sheep, again produce the same character of fur. A karakul of the requisite quality, when crossed with any coarse-woolled breed of Asia, Africa or elsewhere, always produces valuable lambs. The most valuable skins yet produced in America (wholesale value $12.00) were from a cross of a coarse-woolled karakul ram with coarse-woolled, fawn, Persian fat-rump ewes, which themselves possess no inherent fur qualities. The successful production of Persian lamb fur of high quality seems to depend on both parents possessing (1) practically no fine underwool, (2) very coarse wool, (3) the proper strain of karakul blood.

Preparing and Marketing Skins The lambs designed for killing are slaughtered before they are two weeks old. If a fine, close curl is demanded by the market, killing should take place within three days of birth; if open curl is desired, the lambs may run for six weeks but, when size is increased, the price decreases greatly. The half-blood and quarter-blood karakul-Lincoln and karakul-Cotswold crosses produced in the United States, which were bred from coarse-woolled parents with an almost entire absence of fine wool, and which were killed at the proper time, were priced at from $8.00 to $12.00 each in bale lots of two hundred or less. A considerable number of cheaper skins were produced bringing from $5.00 down. These low prices are due to fine wool in the parents, to killing too late or too early, to improper salting of skins, to deaths of lambs out of season and to tearing of skins. Experience will probably correct these errors and raise the average price. If sheep raising will pay in a district where six months' old lambs are sold for $3.00 each, it is obvious that a profit can be made if only $5.00 each were obtained for three-day-old lambs, but the average price for Persian lamb fur would probably be much higher than $5.00. M. Karpov states that: "In the last 15 years the increase in price of these furs in Asia and Southern Russia was

KARAKUL RAM. THE FLEECE IS GRAY, COARSE, LONG AND FREE FROM FINE WOOL.
THE FACE AND LEGS ARE COVERED WITH BLACK, STIFF, LUSTRIOUS HAIR
WITH NO WOOL, INTERMIXED

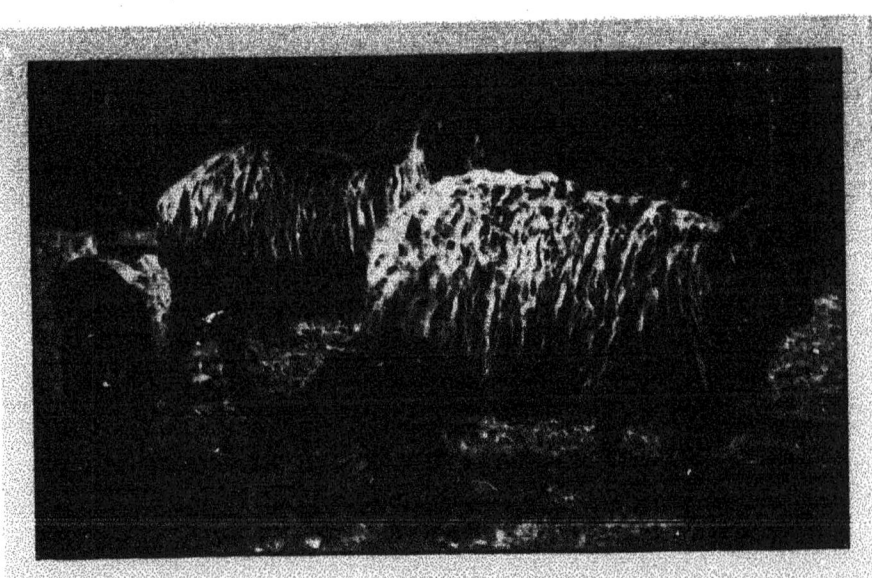

FULL BLOOD, COARSE-WOOL KARAKUL EWES AND LAMBS AT FOOT

140 per cent," which increase, if maintained, will soon leave even a larger margin of profit.

An appreciable profit over ordinary sheep raising is also secured because the 'slinks' or still-born lambs, as well as the lambs that die soon after birth, produce skins often valuable, and sometimes more valuable, than those of lambs born healthy and killed afterwards. The 'baby lamb' or 'broadtail' fur, which is made from the still-born lambs is one of the costliest furs on the market, ranking among the precious furs. It is by far the costliest fur produced by a herbivorous animal.

The wool of the karakul is used in Bokhara for the manufacture of valuable rugs—an industry in which Bokharans excel.

Importing Karakul Sheep When the large margin of profit obtained in rearing lambs which will fetch from $5.00 to $12.00 each at birth, as compared with ordinary sheep farming, is considered, the importation and rearing of karakul sheep would appear to be a profitable industry. Unfortunately for America, the difficulties of securing these animals are practically insurmountable. The Bokharans are Mohammedans who do not hesitate to cheat, or even to kill, a Christian. A passport and permits from the Russian Minister of War and from the Vice-Emir of Bokhara are required before entering the khanate, and the djigits, or Bokharan police, will accompany the foreigner only a short distance from the military posts. Caravans to remote oases are necessary. The health of the foreigner is liable to break down because of the absence of pure water, the unspeakable filth in which the natives live, and because of dangerous diseases such as reshta, bubonic plague, Asiatic cholera and pendinka. In his bulletin, Karpov says: "The natives, especially the Tenkintze and Sarts, are greatly averse to selling any sheep, and, if they do, they will try to dispose of those known to them as not producing the best of fur. Sometimes, after covering great distances on camels, one finally meets the herd owner, and, he is informed that the sheep are not for sale at all, or is asked prohibitive prices. I do not deem it best to describe the sale of sheep when they are commanded to do so by the Emir's higher officials . . The cost of delivery of the sheep to the railroad station when bought, for instance, in the interior of the Kerki desert, is enormous, even though they cost only $60.00 each at the ranch. Several sheep have been exported to Germany, also to Hungary and Africa. The fifteen head taken to Texas by Dr. C. C. Young, assisted by the Poltava Agricultural Society, are especially noteworthy. The success obtained in America is a movement that may in future give tremendous competition and disrupt the industry in Bokhara. It may be a little early as yet to make these predictions. To overcome this pending danger, the most stringent measures must be taken immediately. Already, the Emir has taken steps prohibiting the exportation of karakuls from Bokhara into countries other than Russia. Already, Persia and Afghanistan have some karakuls and these brought to America were secured by a third (Russian) party who acted as a go-between to overcome these laws of the Emir. This proves that they are somewhat ineffective. There are taken out of Bokhara 1,500,000 skins yearly."

The laws of European Russia now prohibit the exportation of karakuls and the quarantine laws of Canada, England and the United States provide very strict regulations, guarding against the possible introduction of Asiatic sheep diseases.

These facts, together with the difficult language, demonstrate the seeming hopelessness of securing more sheep for America.

If the Persian lamb fur can be economically produced in America, it will lessen the importations and would ensure a very important industry supplying a market capable of absorbing about a million skins yearly. Only six known distinct blood lines of Bokharan karakul sheep are in America and a number of these are represented in the Prince Edward Island herd. If success can be achieved with them, Canada will be an important distributing point for these animals. The successful production of Persian lamb would also supply the market with breeding stock at high prices.

The following circular on karakul sheep has been issued by the United States Department of Agriculture.*

KARAKUL OR ARABI SHEEP

"The numerous inquiries directed to the Department of Agriculture concerning the Persian lamb industry have led to the compilation of the following information.

"Persian lamb skins are the product of the young of the karakul or arabi sheep and not of the Persian breed of sheep. These sheep are native of Bokhara, in Russian Turkestan, and are not found in Arabia, and only to a small extent in Persia. A number of other terms have been used in connection with the industry some of these being used interchangeably with Persian lamb. Among these are 'broadtail,' 'astrakhan,' and 'krimmer.' The term 'broadtail' is applied to skins of lambs of karakul blood born before the close of the regular gestation period. Astrakhan and krimmer skins are supposed to come from sheep of somewhat different breeding.

*In the letter accompanying the karakul sheep circular, it is stated that: "We have not felt justified in publishing a bulletin upon karakul sheep raising. Inquiries have been so numerous, however, that we prepared a circular, copy of which is enclosed, embodying what little we feel safe in saying at the present time."

"The demand for Persian lamb skins has increased wonderfully during the past fifteen or twenty years and is still expanding. A member of the largest importing firm in America is of the opinion that there is no immediate indication that the supply will exceed the demand. The higher prices paid for skins, has led to a great deal of crossing for the purpose of procuring a greater supply of skins, and it is held by some authorities that the very existence of the breed in Bokhara is threatened.

"The skins imported to this country come over in the raw state in bales containing about 100 skins each. They are unsorted and some of them are not worth more than twenty-five cents each, but most of them range in value between $3.50 and $15.00. It has been estimated that $14,000,000.00* are spent abroad annually for skins and this may indeed be possible, for one New York house alone handles from 200,000 to 250,000 skins per season.

"The possibility of establishing the industry in America led to two importations being made in 1908 and 1912, respectively. These sheep were brought over by Dr. C. C. Young of Belen, Texas. The first lot consisted of five rams and twelve ewes and the second of twelve rams and seven ewes. From this stock and its offspring, flocks have been established in Texas, New Mexico, Kansas, Maryland and Prince Edward Island.

"The karakul is a hardy, broad-tailed, medium sized sheep of considerable length. The rump is characteristically rounded and usually steep. The rams are horned but the ewes are usually hornless. The ears are small and pendulous. The face is narrow and much rounded and together with the legs is covered with short, glossy hair. The body of the adult bears a coarse, long, hair-like wool, varying in colour from light gray to black. The absence of soft under-wool is said to be an indication of purity of blood. The mutton of the karakul is said to be of a very high quality.

"The lambs, when dropped, are usually a glossy black but, rarely, golden brown ones occur. The wool of the lamb is tightly curled over the body and well over the head and down over the legs. The qualities that determine the value of a skin are tightness and size of curl, the lustre, and size of the skin. The lustre is improved by the dyeing process which is essential in preparing the skin for use. The curls rapidly lose character and the lamb should be killed when not older than ten days, though there is much variation in the age at which the skins are of greater value.

*Foreign Commerce and Navigation of the United States, 1912, states that, in the year ending June 30th, 1912, furs, with a total value of $25,438,834, were imported into the United States. Deducting seal-skins imported, gives a total for all other furs of $25,000,000. It seems improbable that Persian lamb skins account for 56 per cent of this sum.

"The industry is at"; in its infancy in America and much is yet to be learned concerning it. Present indications point out a gradual progress which is most desirable.

"The U. S. Department of Agriculture, in its work at the Experimental Farm at Beltsville, Maryland, found that the karakul cross upon the American merino was unsatisfactory from a fur standpoint. Results from private flocks confirm this finding. This crossing has extended to include more of the breeds, and indications are that none of the close-wool sheep give satisfactory results, especially in the first crosses. Good results have been reported from breeding karakul rams to coarser woolled ewes of the Lincoln and Cotswold breeds. What can be developed from higher crosses containing a higher percentage of karakul blood remains to be seen. The karakul-barbado cross was also tried at Beltsville. The barbado is called the woolless sheep and the first cross resulted in a failure so far as curl was concerned, although the lustre was all that could be desired. In November, 1913, the skins of eight lambs sired by a karakul ram, and out of first cross karakul-barbado ewes, were sent to New York for valuation. One skin was appraised at fifty cents and one at $10.00. The average value of the eight skins was $4.75. The work is being continued and the higher karakul crosses are being produced. If the high fecundity of the barbado can be maintained in these crosses and the fur improved by continually using pure bred karakul sires, this may prove the means of increasing the amount of karakul blood in America. Some Cotswold and Lincoln ewes are now being bred to a karakul ram.

"The method of removal and treatment of the lamb skin should be as follows:—Cut a straight line down the belly, and also cut down on the inside of the legs to meet the centre line. Do not cut off any portion of the skin, leave on the ears, nose and tail to the tip. Be careful not to make unnecessary cuts. Stretch skin evenly on a board, fur side down, and dry in a cool place. Do not salt the skin or double it up for shipment purposes. The principal object is to avoid cracking the skin. See that it is properly shaped when nailed down to the board and thoroughly dried before shipping. Do not sun-dry the skin.

"The high price of breeding stock is, at the present time, a deterrent influence upon the industry. Such pure bred rams as are available have sold at from $500.00 to $1,000.00 each. Ewes are somewhat cheaper. When buying breeding rams be careful to get pure bred animals. Some breeders claim that as good results can be obtained by the use of half-blood stock, but this has not yet been established. It is advisable to buy only such rams as have already demonstrated their ability to sire skins of value."

MAP 2.—RANGE OF THE NORTH AMERICAN RACCOONS IN CANADA

This map is founded chiefly on papers by Messrs. D. G. Elliot, V. Bailey, R. MacFarlane, W. H. Osgood, C. Hart Merriam, John Richardson, R. Kennicott, L. Adams, J. A. Rowley, J. A. Allen, G. S. Miller, S. F. Baird, E. A. Mearns, and E. T. Seton.

In the north and east the lines are tolerably accurate, but in the Rocky Mountain and Pacific Coast regions, must be modified by future work.

Two species of Raccoon are recognized:

Procyon lotor (Linnaeus), with its 2 races.
Procyon psora (Gray), with its 2 races.

RACCOON

(*Procyon lotor*)

THE raccoon belongs to the *Carnivora* and is closely related to the bears. It weighs from 10 to 25 pounds, is of a brownish-gray colour with black tipped hairs over the back and dark rings on the tail, and, when captured as a cub, is easily tamed. It does not appear to have the fighting characteristics peculiar to the *mustelidæ* and, therefore, might, possibly, be easily kept in a wooded area where numerous dens and hollow trees are found. Its habits are somewhat similar to those of the bear. It hibernates in winter, so that mating probably takes place in the fall, and the young are born about May 1. It will eat meat of all kinds, frogs, corn and vegetables. One breeder said that he had fed his pair almost wholly on wheat shorts supplemented with table scraps.

A heavily-wooded area, several acres in extent, with a creek running through, affords a favourable site for a raccoon ranch. The fence enclosing it should be of No. 14 galvanized woven wire, 2-inch mesh, with a substantially constructed overhang. A sheet of iron around the top of the fence would also help to prevent escape. It is probable that a pen for each pair is unnecessary.

Brass estimates the yearly production of pelts at 600,000—all from America. The northern pelts are best and No. 1 large northern are now quoted at $4.50 each, with price   ncing sharply. Near large cities the flesh also may be sold for fi   or more.

If the rich mahogany-coloured racc   uld be secured and bred true to colour, and if present prices were maintained, a profitable industry could probably be built up in northern districts after the necessary experience had been acquired.

The fact that raccoons are found in only a few portions of Canada does not mean that they cannot be successfully raised in more northern regions if food is provided. In general, it is safer to move a fur-bearer from a warmer to a colder home than to reverse the process.

WEASEL FAMILY

(Mustelidæ)

THE weasel family includes the mink, marten, otter, weasel, fisher, wolverene, sea-otter, skunk and badger, all of which are very valuable for their fur. The Russian sable, sea-otter, Hudson Bay sable, ermine, black marten, fisher, Alaska sable, otter and mink furs are derived from the animals mentioned above and are among the most expensive skins. Russian sable skins are frequently sold at $500.00 or more. As some sable skins are only about eight inches long, exclusive of the five-inch tail, they cost more than silver fox, area for area. The pelt of the wild sea-otter brings a higher price, on the average, than the wild silver fox. The Hudson Bay, or American marten, sometimes has almost as beautiful fur as the poorer Russian sable, but the finest pelts sell for less than $100.00. The Canadian weasel, or ermine, is usually inferior to the Russian, often having a yellowish white or gray colour. The most expensive mink pelts are those from the Laurentian plateau and the Maritime Provinces. The price of fisher skins has recently advanced greatly and prime skins sell for as much as $75.00 each. The price of skunk pelts has also advanced and black skins from northern districts now bring from $8 to $12 for the finest specimens.

If the domestication of the marten, fisher otter, mink and skunk, or, in other words, the family of the mustelidæ, were accomplished, there is no doubt that a market for more than $10,000,000 worth of raw fur annually could be found. The annual production of all American pelts is between $25,000,000 and $50,000,000, and the above-mentioned family, with the Russian sable included, would supply a large proportion of the demand for high-priced furs—probably well over one half. It is worth noting in this connection that the recently established fur-farming experiment stations in the United States will experiment first with this family of animals. They will probably keep the marten and the mink, these two being considered, by experts, among the most desirable for domestication.

MINK

(Putorius Vison)

There are two well-known species which resemble each other closely, the European mink or marsh otter of Europe (P. lutreola) and the American mink (P. vison). The latter is found over a large portion

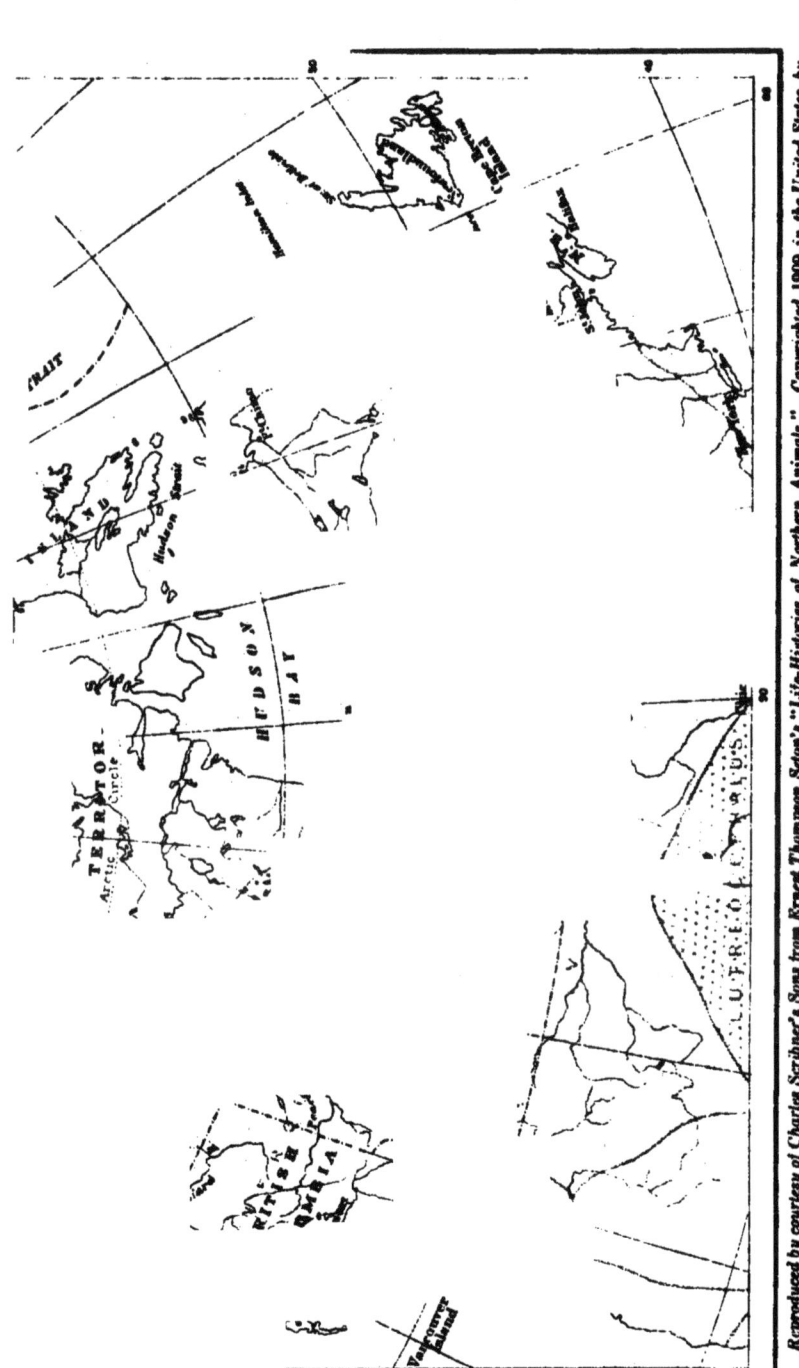

MAP 3.—RANGE OF THE NORTH AMERICAN MINKS IN CANADA.

Reproduced by courtesy of Charles Scribner's Sons from Ernest Thompson Seton's "Life-Histories of Northern Animals." Copyrighted 1909 in the United States, by Ernest Thompson Seton.

The map is founded chiefly on records by J. Richardson, Audubon and Bachman, R. Kennicott, E. W. Nelson, J. Fannin, C. H. Townsend, C. Hart Merriam, O. Bangs, W. H. Osgood, E. A. Preble, S. N. Rhoads, D. G. Elliot, V. Bailey.

The following are recognized:
　　Putorius vison (Brisson) with 5 races.

of North America, the finest and darkest being the small minks of Quebec and the Maritime Provinces of Canada. While it lives on the water a large part of its time and makes its home near streams, it can live on the land away from the water and has even been found in trees.

The fur is dense and soft and the over hair is of stiff, lustrous water hairs. The darkest colour extends down the back and tail. The dyers usually accentuate the dark colour by brush dyeing or tipping the fur.

Brass estimates the world's yearly supply as follows: America, 600,000 skins; Europe, 20,000; and Asia, 20,000. They do not seem to be decreasing rapidly, but the price is advancing and, owing to the excellent quality and durability of the fur, is likely to remain high. Some fancy ranch skins have been sold for $13.00 and the best skins bring about $10.00 each wholesale. Some conception of the extra value of north-eastern mink can be formed when it is known that Quebec furriers sold their mink to New York in 1911 at $9 each, and purchased mink of the same quality mixed with the best eastern United States skins at $8 each.

MINX-FARMING

The farming of the mink is still in the experimental stage. It has been demonstrated that mink can be kept in captivity and its young reared successfully. As for the quality of pelt, only a few statements could be secured. All attempts to rear this animal in Canada are too recent to furnish data for a general conclusion, or else were made over thirty years ago when mink was high-priced, and accurate records were not kept. The statements of sales of skins received were highly satisfactory, and indicate that pelts from stock bred in ranches are, under certain conditions, better than the wild stock. It was also demonstrated that rapid improvement in the stock is possible because of the opportunity for selection of sires—an opportunity not possible in fox rearing at the present time because of the latter animal's monogamous habits. Thus, one male out of every four or five can be chosen for his size, beauty of colour or quiet disposition, and a rapid improvement towards a good stock made.

There have been hundreds of mink ranches in America and there are probably about fifty in Canada at the present time. None of them are very pretentious except, possibly, that of La Compagnie Zootechnique de Labelle, Ltd., the head office of which is in Montreal and the ranch at Lac Chaud, in the Laurentian highlands of Quebec. The capital of the company is $49,000.00. As soon as the success of mink-ranching is assured, it is proposed to proceed with the breeding of the otter along similar lines.

The whole question of mink-ranching is one that needs more thorough investigation and probably the establishment of experimental farms under experienced ranchmen.   A somewhat vague classification into three types of farming can be made from the information gathered:

1.   The Natural Plan.—The minks are given an extensive range and the conditions under which they live differ from the natural conditions only in that the animals are fed and occasional nests provided.   All catching is by trapping.

2.   The Colony Method.—The families are kept in colony houses with a runway to a creek.

3.   The Pen System.—Each mink is kept in a separate pen.

The Natural Plan   The ranch of La Compagnie Zootechnique de Labelle was the only one of this type visited; and the examination was made in 1912 when the ranch had been in operation only one year.   In 1911, some two dozen mink were placed in the area shown in the illustration, comprising about one-quarter acre. They increased about 100 per cent in number in 1912.   The manager explained the small increase as being due to the limited quarters with which they were provided.   Another possible explanation is that 1912 appeared to be a poor year for both mink and fox.   It is also possible that the old wild animals captured did not take kindly to their new location or to the artificial nests.   The last cause will disappear, particularly as soon as ranch-bred mink are available.

As stated, the total area enclosed in the ranch in 1911 was about one-quarter acre.   In 1912, work was under way to enclose an area 2,000 feet long and 1,500 feet wide at the widest point.   The larger range will probably insure considerable success.

The situation of the ranch is on an island in Lac Chaud in an uninhabited section of country in the Laurentians.   It is high and rocky and covered with birch and spruce.   The ranch is enclosed with one continuous fence about 12 feet high, set on solid rock on land, and on sunken piers in the water.   The chief difficulty is in the construction of the water fence as ice breaks the wire in spring.   It is proposed to prevent this by dropping a plank fence three feet wide into the piers to protect the wire during the icy season.   In spring the planks will be removed.   Not more than a dozen feet of the margin of Lac Chaud are included within the fence.   To prevent the escape of the mink under the fence, a wide carpet wire is turned in on the lake bottom.   To prevent high climbing, a strip of sheet iron a foot wide is fastened half way up the fence.   There is also an overhang of iron.

KEY TO MINKERY

1. Outside pen 12ft. x 4ft. by 5ft. high
2. Inside pen 2ft. 3in. x 4ft. by 2ft. high
3. Passage holes 3½in. x 3½in.
4. Inside nests are 12in. x 11in., with litter
5. Outside nests are 15in. x 12in., no litter
6. Elevated feed platform 11in. x 11in. by 18in high
7. Tin can for feed dish
8. Feed platform which can be drawn out to facilitate feeding

The pen walls are constructed of 1in. mesh, No. 17 wire, except the dividing walls, which are of wood for the lower two feet and are buried a foot deep. There is a cellar under each pen to which the minks have access. There is water in the trough at the end of the pen, but in winter only snow is given.

END ELEVATION OF MINKERY
Scale 1 inch – 4 feet
Adapted from plan of ranch, built by Austin Scales

Dark cellar

Inside pen

nclosed with 1" mesh, Nº 17 wire

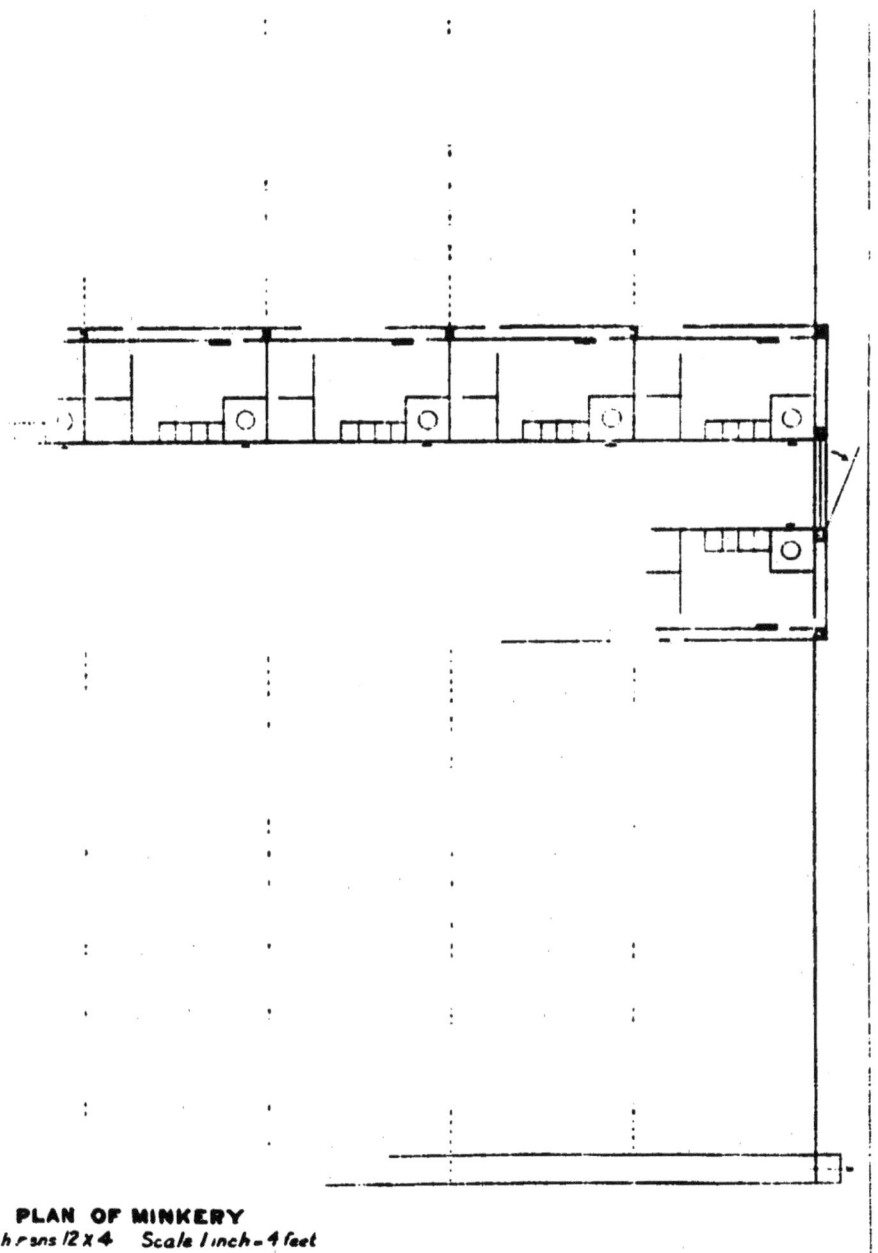

PLAN OF MINKERY
h r sns 12 x 4   Scale 1 inch = 4 feet

Nest of the Female The nests are made about 16 inches by 16 inches and 6 inches high, and are pushed into a large box (similarly to a drawer in a chest of drawers), which is placed in a bank of earth and covered up. Thus, if it is necessary to examine the nest, it may be drawn out. A piece of meshed wire over the inner box will permit a view of the whole interior. The entrances should be a foot or more long and from three to four inches in diameter. Mr. Desormeau, the manager at Lac Chaud, reported that, once a female took possession of a nest, no other mink was allowed to enter, always being met at the entrance to the passageway and beaten back. The food is always carried to the entrance and is taken from the hand as quickly as offered. As many nests as there are females in the ranch, and probably a few more, are required to prevent fighting for possession or the making of nests in burrows.

Home of the Male The males are provided with large caves roofed over with planks or concrete. Food is thrown in through a hatch in the roof. In summer the mink obtains a considerable quantity of food in the water, as small fish can get through the meshed fence. Because of the free range, only flesh food is fed.

It could not be ascertained how the mother and young are cared for during the several months when the latter are dependent on their mother for food and protection. It is the intention of Mr. Desormeau to separate the young from the old each year and place them in one end of his fenced area, having a fence crossing the island to divide them. It is likely that when they are about two months old, or about July 1, the separation of the young from the mother could be easily effected by simply carrying them away in their box. They would be old enough at that time to live on solid food and would be tamer and gentler than if left with their mother.

The food is almost wholly fish, supplied from the lake. Permission has been received from the Quebec authorities to capture the fish by any method. It is proposed to restock the lake with fry.

It is estimated that six men can manage the ranch and that about two thousand females and one quarter as many males can be accommodated as breeding stock.

The Colony Plan No ranches of this type were examined, but proof that such exist was furnished by owners who did not wish to reveal to the public the methods they used. The promoters of this method claim to be highly successful and have given considerable study to the habits of the mink, a fact which is proved by their intelligent discussions of mink-ranching problems.

The chief difficulties appear to be in securing the first litter from the wild animals and in getting suitable food. The wild mink is usually wholly unsusceptible to domestication or even semi-domestication. They frequently kill themselves by hanging, cutting their throats, or beating their heads against a wall. Most of them will commit suicide or die of fear on the near approach of a dog. These facts have been corroborated in the experience of 1912, a large proportion of wild minks having died while being shipped and a large number of those caught for ranching purposes being found dead, sometimes badly cut or lacerated.

If the young are taken from the mother as early as possible—say six weeks or seven weeks old—in Eastern Canada about June 15—they become very tame and according to the advocates of this new method of ranching, can be reared in family colonies afterwards. A colony house, or large box, can be provided and a considerable runway or paddock may extend in front to include a portion of a stream.

The usual food is bread and milk, meat twice the size of an egg, fish and dog biscuit. One experienced breeder who feeds rabbits the whole year round recommended a meat diet of one quarter pound a day. He also states that milk should be fed to mother minks twice a day. Fish, he considers unsuitable for a steady diet, and pork should not be fed at all. The young are fed new milk. The English sparrow is a great favourite for mink food and frogs and eels are also supplied. It is noteworthy that minks will frequently eat food with avidity when thrown into the water, whereas they might refuse to eat it if placed in a feeding trough. Food should be given twice a day.

The Single Pen System The method of ranching mink which has been used almost exclusively in America is one which employs a small pen for each animal. The two largest establishments visited in 1912 consisted of an ordinary barn about 20 feet wide and 30 feet long. The walls were open under the eaves to make the interior as airy as possible. On either side of a central alley were pens about 4 feet wide and 8 feet long, provided with a nest box on a slight elevation, and having a crooked passage for entrance. Water ran through troughs at the ends of the pen, or was pumped in daily. The partitions were of wire above and boards near the floor. If wire is used for the walls, an overhang is necessary to prevent climbing out, or the wire might be made to extend over the pens completely. Very little light is required, as the mink usually sleeps during the day.

Mink can be reared in such pens, but there are grave doubts of the permanency of the good health of the animals. In a Nova Scotia ranch there was no difficulty in rearing an average of three and a half to

MINK RANCH AT LAC CHAUD ONE QUARTER OF AN ACRE IN AREA

MINK'S DEN, ARTIFICIAL

a litter. The young minks had litters of from two to four and the older breeders sometimes had six. With such satisfactory results, when every pair raised could be sold for $40.00 and food could be procured freely, it is inconceivable why development of the business did not proceed. The managers were continually selling off their stock and capturing more wild ones. They also admitted that they would not again use board floors for mink, but would have pens enclosing a large area of ground. From these facts, it may readily be concluded that there were considerable difficulties of some kind.

Proper Site for Pens A study of the literature available leads to the conclusion that it will be possible to rear mink in secluded wooded areas on the banks of a ᴧᴧam or pond. The method adopted at Lac Chaud is sure to be, at l . pᵃ ᴧlly successful and may prove to be profitable. The cost of bᵤ... ᴧ-proof fence in the water is high, compared with the cost of building on land. For this reason a site on an island is not considered as good as a site on a pond; for the whole pond or lake can be enclosed with a land fence. Thus a small lake, a dam, or a stream can be utilised for a ranch of any of the above-mentioned types. A shed could be built on the banks of a stream and the pens extended outside the walls of the building across the stream. The pens need not be wider than 3 or 4 feet nor longer than 5 or 6 feet inside the building, but should be twice as long outside. To prevent burrowing, the outside walls should be sunk in the ground about 18 inches, except where in the water. If the natural method of ranching is used, two water areas would be necessary to provide two fenced areas.

It is advisable to double fence a mink ranch, similarly to a fox ranch, in order to prevent their escape and to keep off intruders, especially dogs and other wild animals, the smell or sight of which seems to inspire the mink with great fear.

In the natural method of ranching, the sexes seek each other out, but, when one animal is placed in each pen, the keeper has to be very watchful during the latter part of February and up to the middle of March. The male mink can be admitted through chutes or by a box trap and has to be withdrawn at once if the two begin to quarrel and returned at intervals of two days. If no quarrelling occurs, the male is not withdrawn for two days. When as many males as females are kept they are placed in the same pen about the last of February and left together until about April 15th. Single mating is preferable. Mating usually takes place in March, and constant watchfulness has to be exercised to prevent fights when the male is admitted at the wrong time. Some males are very vicious and will fight other animals of either sex which come near them. They should be slaughtered. In one case the canine teeth of a vicious male were cut off and he became quite docile. Mink may be safely handled if two pairs of woollen mitts are worn or one pair of heavy leather gloves.

The period of gestation is about six weeks. The litters are from two to nine and average five. The tiny young, which are blind for about five weeks, should not be handled. Before they are six weeks old, the mother leads them out and they begin eating solid food. At eight or ten weeks of age they should be taken from the mother, unless she is of a very quiet and gentle temperament. They should be weaned at about 3 months of age. At first take out all but one.

Practical Hints on Mink-farming The following practical hints on mink-farming have been recently published in circular form by the Biological Survey of the United States Department of Agriculture:

(1) Minks should be kept in the proportion of one male to five or six females.

(2) Each breeding female should have a separate pen. The male should be kept by himself except at mating time. The females begin to rut about the middle of February. The male should be admitted to the female for about one day. The young are born about the middle of April.

(3) The females must be kept alone or they will be likely to kill each other's young. The male would also kill them if he had an opportunity.

(4) *Food:* The best steady food for minks is bread and sweet milk, corn-mush and milk, or corn-mush cooked with bits of meat in it. The animals should have meat or fish about twice a week. The meat may be a very cheap kind. Keep pans clean and feed only as much as the mink will eat up clean at each feeding. Feed once a day, except females that are suckling young. These should be fed twice. Provide fresh wo' regularly. Do not salt the food.

(5) *Pens:* Pens should be 5 or 6 feet square, the sides of smooth, wide boards cut 4 feet long and set up with the lower end resting on a footing of stone or concrete 18 inches in the ground. The floor of the pen should be the bare ground. The pens can be built economically in groups of four or more. The sides can be of heavy wire netting instead of boards, but, in that case, the top would need to be netted or the animals would climb out.

(6) *Boxes:* Boxes about 2 feet by 1½ foot by 1½ foot in size should be provided for nests. They should have hinged lids so as to allow

A Successful Mink Ranch of the type shown in the Drawing at page 93

their being opened and examined.   Fine straw or hay should be provided.   The boxes may be outside the pens, bolted to the fence; a hole in the fence and box admits the animals, the box to be 3 or 4 inches above the ground.   The boxes should be as dark as possible, with a hole 4 inches in diameter for the entrance of the minks.

In 1913, continued reports of success in breeding minks, were circulated and prices rose until they ruled at from $80.00 to $200.00 r pair according to quality and disposition.   Ranch-bred minks are reputed to be more tractable than old wild ones and bring double prices. The rapidly growing interest in mink-ranching might, at first blush, be described to the enthusiasm in Eastern Canada for fox-farming and to the successes achieved in that industry.   A visit to one or two ranches however, furnished conclusive evidence that, when the initial difficulties have been overcome, mink-ranching will become an important industry.

MARTEN OR AMERICAN SABLE
(Mustela Americana)

No marten farms were found in operation in 1912 although ranchmen were attempting to secure specimens, but, in 1913, a number of farms were stocked.

The experience of only one person in breeding marten was obtainable, that of A. H. Cocks, of Henley-on-Thames, England.* Mr. Cocks, who has raised five litters of marten in captivity, states that the principal difficulty is to ascertain when the female is in season. If a pair are put together when the female is not in season, it is very apt to end in the death of the female from a sudden snap through her brain by the male.

Habits of the Marten The wild marten is one of the most blood-thirsty of animals, being inferior only to the weasel and possibly the fisher, in this respect. In captivity, however, it becomes quite docile and may even become a pet. It mates promiscuously like the rest of the weasel family and, because of its savage nature, two wild marten can not safely be placed in one pen. The pens should be similar to the mink pens, but constructed of No. 14 or not lighter than No. 16, one-inch mesh wire, but higher and wired all over. The g und may be covered with wire to prevent burrowing or the fence may be sunk into the ground at least three feet and should have an inhang of one foot. Mr. E. T. Seton says: "I prefer a carpet wire and have carpet wire or concrete floor in all my marten pens." Trees and brush may be placed in the pen, or the pen placed in the woods. They are ac-

*An account of his experiences has been published in *The Zoologist* for 1883, p. 203; and in the *Proceedings of the Zoological Society of London* for 1900, p. 836. Further notes on the young of the species are to be found in *The Zoologist*, 1881, 1897, etc.

7

customed to an exceedingly active life in the trees and must have an opportunity provided for exercise or they will not remain long in breeding condition. The nest should be about the size of that advised for the mink, or, possibly, slightly larger.

Mating — The difficulty with the marten, as with the mink, comes at mating time; only it is much harder to control the difficulties in the marten's case, as mating takes place at night, whereas minks mate at any time. The placing of crossed straws about the pens by the females gives the keeper his clue to the time for the admittance of the male. He should be left in several days. The litter of ranch-bred marten, if removed from the mother when about two months old, will be much tamer. The marten was domesticated by the ancient Romans and used for the same purposes as a ferret.

Mating takes place in January or February. The period of gestation is a little more than three months. The young are seen outside the nest when about eight weeks of age. They are full grown at six months and breed when a year old. The number of young in a litter ranges from one to five.

Directions for feeding are the same as for mink, but it is well to remember that one-half of the marten's food is fruit and vegetable matter. Two meals a day reduced at times to one meal are sufficient for either in order to keep them in good breeding condition.

Marten should be transported in metal-lined boxes, because they will eat their way through a sound inch board. If the Hudson Bay marten can be bred as a domestic animal, there will be no difficulty in finding a market for the skins. At the present time, Asia produces 75,000 sable skins annually, and North America 120,000. The experience of rearing the Hudson Bay marten would probably lead to the domestication of the Siberian marten or Russian sable, which is a smaller animal, but whose fur is much more valuable. As the fur would be more generally favoured and fashionable, besides being more durable. there can be no doubt that the total trade possible in marten skins would be as great as in all kinds of fox skins combined.

Mr. Ernest Thompson Seton says: "Of all the animals in my fur ranch, which include mink, marten, skunk, otter and wild-cats, none has responded more quickly to attempts at taming than has the marten. I have great expectations of developing a most manageable strain."

FISHER, PEKAN, OR PENNANT MARTEN
(*Mustela Pennanti*)

Only two ranches were found in which the fisher, or pekan, or pennant marten, was kept. The experiments at one of these appeared

MAP 4.—RANGE OF THE NORTH AMERICAN MARTENS IN CANADA

This map is founded chiefly on records by J. Richardson, S. F. Baird, R. MacFarlane, E. W. Nelson, R. Bell, H. C. Yarrow, A. P. Low, C. Hart Merriam, O. Bangs, E. A. Preble, J. Macoun, W. H. Osgood, C. B. Bagster, D. G. Elliot, J. Fannin, J. D. Figgins, E. T. Seton, B. N. Rhoads, A. K. Verrill, and E. R. Warren.

The following are recognised:

Mustela americana(Turton,) with its 8 races.
Mustela abieta(Bangs.) The Newfoundland species.
Mustela caurina(Merriam) in 2 races, caurina and origenes.
Mustela nesophila(Osgood,) in Queen Charlotte Islands.

to be quite successful as far as conducted, the animals being quite tractable and in good condition. The owners are confident of final success, but no young have yet been produced.

The fisher is about two feet long and has a large bushy tail. At first sight, it resembles a black cat, and hence has received that name locally. It is the swiftest and fiercest of the weasel family and can catch a marten in an open chase, jumping from limbs even 30 or 40 feet high to the ground. When it is known that the marten can catch the squirrel, the significance of this feat can be appreciated.

Ranching methods should be the same as for marten, but on a scale of twice the dimensions. Mating takes place about March 1. Young, numbering from one to five, are born about May I. It is believed by many that they pair in the wild state, but it is probable that one male will serve for several females in ranches.

The rapidly rising-prices of fisher pelts make the possibility of rearing this valuable fur-bearer the more interesting. In March, 1914, best dark Northern Canada skins sold at from $20.00 to $40.00.

CANADIAN OTTER

(*Lutra Canadensis*)

The otter is very easily tamed and may even be given the run of the premises without deserting its owner. The natural method of ranching described for mink, where a whole pond is enclosed and kept stocked with fish, would certainly succeed with otter, especially if arrangements were made to care for the female and the young.

About the time the young are expected, the mother could be caught in a box-trap with a meshed-wire bottom and examined. If she is found to be about to give birth to young, she could be placed in a pen similar to that used for mink, and the young reared successfully. The quiet disposition of the otter and skunk will allow of such treatment. No otter ranches were examined, but the docility and good health of those kept in zoological gardens make it quite evident that it will be 'easy to rear them when we only know how.'

Though the otter is found almost everywhere, the Canadian otter is most valuable. The *Fur News Magazine* for March, 1914, quotes large No. 1 otter from Eastern United States and Canada at $20.00; medium at $15.00 any small at $10.00. In January, 1913, large No. 1 otter from Eastern Canada was quoted at $25.00.

A large, easily available supply of fish is necessary for success with these animals if profits are to be made at the above-mentioned prices. As there is undoubtedly a strong demand for live animals for parks and for foundation stock for ranches, the breeding of otter can probably be prosecuted with profit.

The following article on the otter, by Vernon Bailey, was published in the report of the American Breeders' Association Vol. 5:

THE OTTER AS A FUR BEARER

"Next to silver and blue foxes, otters seem to promise the best results in fur-farming. They combine coat of real and permanent value with habits easily controlled and well adapted to domestication. They have cheerful dispositions, are playful affectionate, and intelligent, and though, in their wild state, great wanderers, they are contented and thrive when confined in very limited quarters. Under ordinary conditions they do not breed in captivity, but it is believed that this failing can be overcome by giving them sufficiently normal conditions. In their wild state they are in no danger of extermination. Man is their only enemy worth considering and, owing to their swimming habits and keen intelligence, they have little to fear from any but the most experienced trapper. They have held their own over thickly settled parts of the United States better than any other animal of equal fur value. They still inhabit most of their original range over the country, never in abundance, but scattered one or two in a stream or lake. They are apparently as common around the suburbs of Washington and in settled sections generally, as in most of the wilder but more trapped forest areas of the country.

General Characteristics "Full-grown Canadian otters are about 4 feet in total length and weigh approximately 20 to 30 pounds. Their striking characteristics are long, lithe bodies, tapering into long, muscular, flattened tails; very short legs, fully webbed hind feet; short ears, keen little eyes and a beautiful coat of dense, dark brown fur. They are weasel-like in their quickness, extremely muscular and, for their size, fearless and savage fighters.

Distribution and Variation "Many kinds of otter occur in different parts of the world, but the largest and most valuable for fur are those of North America, *Lutra Canadensis*, and its several closely related sub-species or geographic varieties. Considering their wide range from Labrador to Alaska and from near the Arctic coast to Florida and Arizona, they show surprisingly little variation in size or in colour or quality of fur. This is, of course, owing to their aquatic habits and to the nearly uniform temperature of water in winter over almost the whole continent. The average lower price of southern otter skins may be due largely to the fact that most are caught before the midwinter cold has brought them up to prime con-

MINK SITTING ON HIS HOUSE, THE COVER OF WHICH HAS BEEN REMOVED

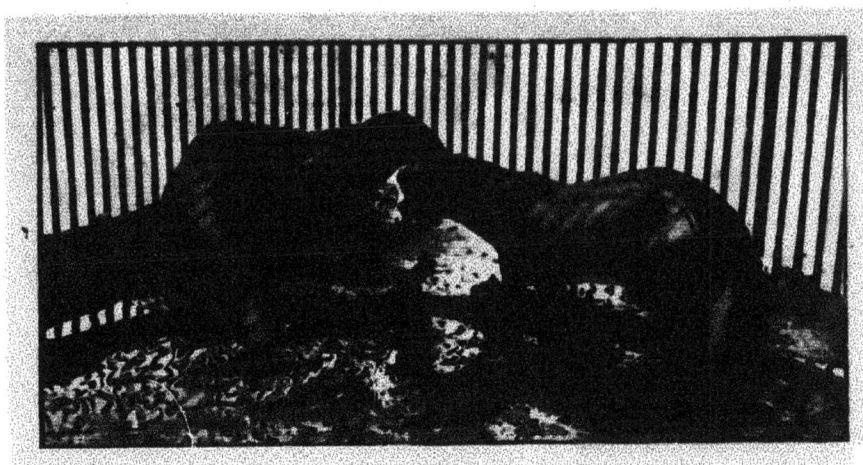

OTTER

dition.   It seems not improbable that, with dark otters from eastern
Canada to breed from, a high grade of fur might be produced over most
of the southern states where no other high-priced fur could be successfully raised.   The abundance of fish and crustaceans in many of the
southern streams would be a distinct advantage in the way of food
supply, and ideal situations for otter farms could be found on hundreds
of streams where a few of the animals now live in the wild state.

"For breeding purposes otters with the most valuable coats should
be selected, preferably the very dark individuals from eastern Canada,
Labrador, Newfoundland or Maine.   Considerable individual variation
is shown and the grade of fur could doubtless be steadily improved by
selective breeding.   The largest individuals are from Alaska and the
Northwest, but the skins of these are less valuable than those of the
smaller and darker animals of the Northeast.   The highest quotations
are always for skins from Canada and the Eastern United States.

"The *Fur Trade Review* for December, 1908, and January, 1909,
quotes No. 1 otter skins as follows:

Canada and eastern............................$18 to $20
Northwestern and Pacific coast..................$12 to $14
Western and southwestern......................$10 to $12
Western Pennsylvania and West Virginia.........$10 to $12

"Otter fur in the north is at its best in December, but keeps in
prime condition until March.   In the southern states it probably does
not reach its best condition before January.

General
Habits

"The prime requisite for success in raising any fur-bearing
animals is a thorough knowledge of their habits, especially
breeding and food habits.   The following notes are offered
as suggestions in conducting experiments with otters:

"Otters are semi-aquatic, are powerful and rapid swimmers, able to
stay under water for a considerable time in pursuit of prey or in escaping
from enemies, but they are also well adapted to dry land.   They make
long journeys overland from one stream to another and especially delight in travelling over soft snow, on which they run and slide on their
silky bellies with apparent enjoyment.   On freshly fallen or wet snow
they often prefer this method of travelling and will follow the banks
of a stream for miles; but the greater part of their travelling is in the
water where most of their food is procured.   The long flattened tail
is a powerful propeller and the large webbed hind feet give additional
paddle surface for easy and rapid progress through the water.   While
on dry land their motions are comparatively slow and awkward; in
the water, they are rapid, lithe and seal-like, almost as easy and graceful

and even more rapid than those of many fish. Fish are pursued and caught, apparently in fair chase and with great ease, though it is perhaps not safe to say that all kinds are an easy prey. Otters seem to be about equally active night or day, but most so in the morning and evening hours.

Food Habits   "Live fish, caught in the water and eaten on the banks or on the ice seem to be the favourite food for otters, though it is doubtful if they are more extensively eaten than crayfish. Otter sign is more often composed largely of fish scales and bones and crustacean shells than of any other food remains; but frogs, water fowl, and small mammals or any fresh meats are eagerly eaten. Otters will soon clear a pond or stream of muskrats, especially in winter when, under the ice, they readily enter the houses and bank burrows. In confinement they are usually fed on fish and fresh meat, about two pounds each per day as an ordinary allowance. This is usually thrown into the water and the animals seem to enjoy fishing it out.

"To raise otters at a profit, a locality should be selected where an abundant supply of fish can be procured at small cost.

Breeding Habits   "Otters are polygamous and, during the early spring months, the males travel widely in search of mates, apparently remaining with each female no longer than the nuptial period requires. They are soon off in search of new mates and circumstantial evidence indicates that a male is successively paired with as many females as he can find in condition to accept his attentions during the season. The female finds or makes her den alone in burrows or hollow banks, and raises, guards and feeds her family until the young are large enough to hunt and fight for themselves. They follow her until nearly full grown, but, by the time the first snow and ice have come, they have usually scattered and each is living a mainly solitary life. However often their paths may cross or friendly visits may occur, their hunting grounds are selected so far as possible on different streams or lakes; their wanderings are apparently determined by scarcity or abundance of food, and they have no definite home. In confinement they are usually not unfriendly. Two females in a small enclosure in the National Zoological Park have been on good terms for eight years, but a male put in the inclosure with them some years ago was soon killed. For the past 18 months another female and a large male have been in the pen with them and while the three females are usually romping and playing together in the best spirits, one or all often pounce on the male and bite him savagely. Although much larger than any of the females he merely defends himself as best he can and backs away, refusing to either fight or run. It is evident that the males should be kept separate from the females except during the mating season, and it would almost certainly be necessary to isolate the females before the young were born and until they were well grown.

"The number of young in a litter is usually given as two or three, but there are also records indicating four or five, and it seems probable that the smaller numbers are those of the first year of breeding. Data are extremely meagre on this point; but a number of records of families of five or six otters seen together in summer would indicate four or five young, while the uniform number of five mammae of the females would further indicate four as the normal number.

"Whether females breed when a year old remains to be tested, but it seems probable that they do.

"The fact that otters do not breed in zoological parks, where kept on exhibition and under constant excitement and nervous strain, is not surprising and probably does not mean that under more normal conditions they would fail to reproduce at their usual rate.

Suitable Location "A large spring or section of a small stream, preferably in the woods, should be selected for an otter yard. A pool at least six feet deep and 20 or 30 feet across should be formed. Steep banks down which the otter can slide into the water are an advantage in furnishing exercise as are also a few old logs reaching into the water. If the banks are firm and stony the otter will be less inclined to burrow, and clear, cold, running water tends to keep them in good health. A series of yards along a suitable stream could be separated economically into family enclosures with inexpensive partition fences. A yard 50 feet square is ample for a family of otters if plenty of food is provided.

"Small houses, hollow logs, shallow caves or artificial burrows should be provided for sleeping quarters where a cool, dark retreat can be had at any time.

Fencing "Otter yards should be inclosed with a fence four feet high, made of heavy woven wire of one-inch mesh and with a 16-inch curved tin overhang on the inside. The fence should be carried on iron uprights four feet apart, curved in at the top for the tin overhang. These iron uprights should be set in a stone or concrete wall, laid one foot deep in the ground and carried across the stream as dams above and below the otter pool. In place of the wall an additional foot of the woven wire can be bedded in the ground, but, as it rusts out, it will have to be renewed every few years. In the National Zoological Park a welded wire fence with rectangular mesh one inch wide and four inches high, of No. 11 wire is used. This is not easily climbed and is very strong and secure. The iron uprights are double straps one inch wide by $\frac{1}{4}$ inch thick, one on each side of the netting and riveted together.

"Otters do not dig extensively and are not inclined to burrow under a fence. They do not usually climb trees, but can climb up a rough barked or leaning tree to above the top of a fence.

Conclusions   "It seems highly probable that, under favourable conditions, otter can be raised for fur at a profit, and that, in course of time, a breed can be established combining in the same animals quiet and domestic dispositions with fur of great beauty and value. But the actual test has yet to be made and carried over a term of several years before a decision can be reached as to the degree of success and the profit to be expected. Many facts of vital importance, such as methods of insuring breeding, the rate and dates of breeding, the most satisfactory and economical food supply, improvement of fur by selection of breeders, and age and date when fur reaches its greatest perfection, remain to be worked out. If the necessary experiments can be carried to a successful conclusion, a valuable industry will be added to our national resources."

SKUNK

(Mephitis)

No skunk-farms that were examined could be regarded as commercial ventures, but two or three ranchers purposed building larger pens when the animals increased in numbers sufficiently. In 1913 reports of numerous successful skunk-ranches were received. The increase in all cases examined was an average of five to six young for each female kept. One male was kept for each half dozen females.

The question always asked when skunk-farming is mentioned, is concerning the difficulty of conducting such a business in any reputable neighbourhood on account of scenting. Contrary to popular expectation the skunk appears to be least objectionable of all ranched animals, the fox being the most objectionable. One might pass alongside a hundred skunks and not observe any odour. They can be easily handled as the accompanying photograph shows. Concerning the practice of cutting into the scent glands, Mr. Ernest Thompson Seton says: "Skunks are commonly deodorized or disarmed when from one to two months old, and the operation consists of cutting out entirely the two scent glands. An expert can disarm twenty skunks in an hour."*

Skunks are graded according to the proportion of white hair on the
*Letter from Mr. E. T. Seton, April 9, 1914.

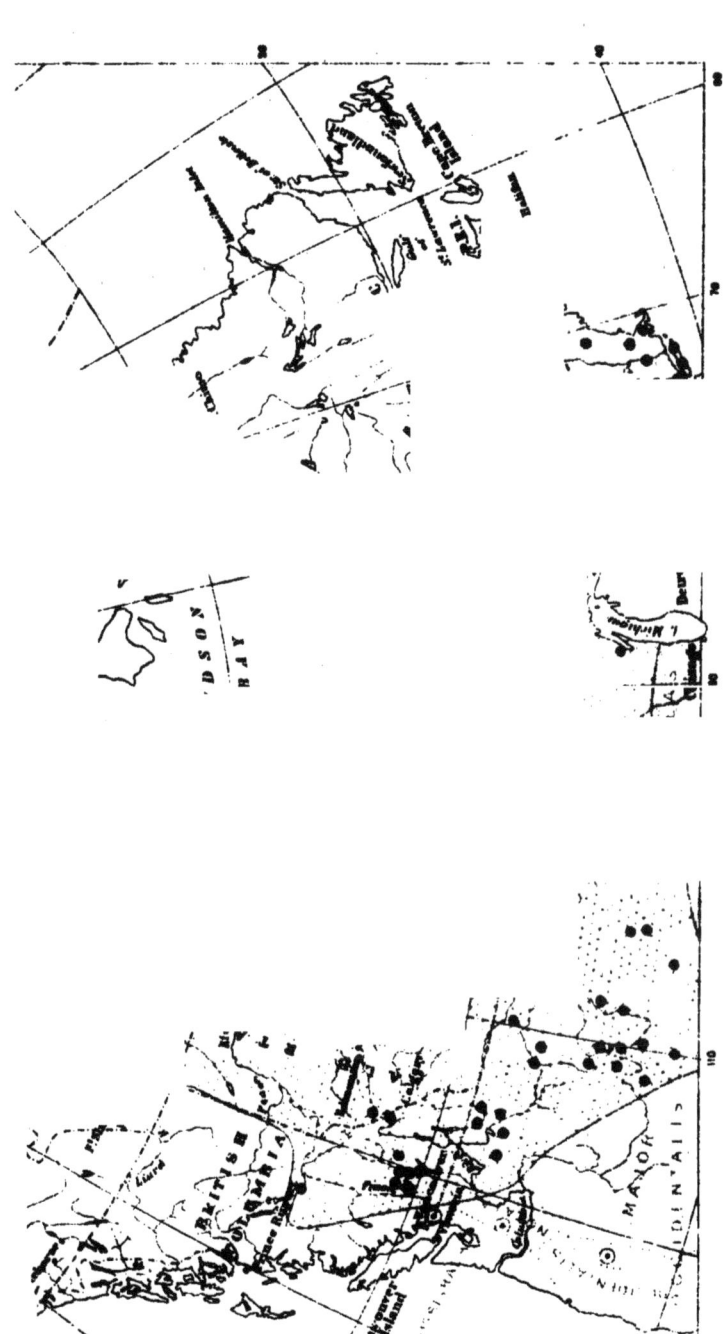

Reproduced by courtesy of Charles Scribner's Sons from Ernest Thompson Seton's "Life-Histories of Northern Animals." Copyrighted 1909 in the United States, by Ernest Thompson Seton.

MAP 5.—RANGE OF THE LARGE SKUNKS OF THE GENUS MEPHITIS IN CANADA

This map is founded chiefly on A. H. Howell's revision, N. A. Fauna No. 20, 1901. Spotted on it are all the records he gives for the species found in Canada, except *occidentalis* which barely enters British Columbia. Additional records by E. A. Preble, J. Alden Loring, and E. T. Seton are marked.

Mephitis mephitis (Shaw) with 2 races,
Mephitis hudsonica (Richardson),
Mephitis putida (Boitard.)
Mephitis mesomelas (Licht.) with 3 races,
Mephitis occidentalis (Baird) with 4 races.

skin, as: No. 1 with no stripes or very short ones; No. 2, with more white hair, and No. 3 when the white hair extends the full length of the body. The white part is cut off the pelts and only the black fur is used so that there is a larger area of good fur on No. 1 pelts than on the whiter ones.

It is probable that the rapid advance in price of skunk in 1912 and 1913 will give an impetus to the skunk-raising industry. If the present high prices—$8.00 to $12.00 for finest black northern—continue, there is a large profit to be made in skunk-farming.

Skunks can be kept in captivity under conditions similar to those recommended for mink. On account, however, of the lower value of the pelts and the less vicious and even harmless nature of the animal, it is better to allow them a large run together. The males will not injure the females, but the females will kill the males after mating if they are kept enclosed with them. The females might be kept in pens, before littering and while rearing the young. The young are weaned when from 5 to 7 weeks old.

Skunks should have a considerable area to roam over in order that they may secure varied food and exercise. Well insulated nests about a cubic foot in size should be used so that the young may not be chilled in very cold weather or heated in very warm weather. Nests should be constructed in a bush. The outside fence can be effectively built with galvanised roofing 4 feet wide, set one foot into the ground. It is better to shut out all strange sights by a fence, especially during the breeding season.

The methods used in skunk-raising are completely outlined in the following extracts from letters written to the *Hunter-Trader-Trapper Magazine* by Mr. Brae:

SKUNK-RAISING

"Skunk-raising is a failure if on a small scale, while on a large scale it would be a paying business, giving from 50 to 100 per cent profit. I will give you my experience on a small scale. The first season, I had 12 females and 3 males, all black; the average litter of young was from 3 to 6; the average grade, about 85 per cent black, the balance being Nos. 2, 3 and 4.

"Naturally, skunks live in holes in the ground, rocks, trees, stumps, etc. Their food consists of mice, birds, bugs, crickets, grasshoppers, bees, wasps, yellow jackets, angle worms, seeds, berries, ground roots and bark. My pen was 14 feet by 36 feet, and 4 feet high with ½-inch mesh wire floor and 1-inch mesh wire top and covering. I had a number of boxes for harbours. My pen is secure against escape but entirely too small for the purpose intended.

"In the first place, I wish to discuss the disadvantages of starting on a small scale. Having a large number in a small place, will cause them to crowd and fight and kill one another, while to have a separate pen for each female is expensive. After the rutting season the female will kill the male, apparently to protect her young. Skunks are liable to a fatal disease, similar to sore throat or diphtheria. I have known females that had no young ones to take the young of other mothers to their boxes and fight the real mothers away until the kidnapped young starve to death. Others that had young would steal the young of two or three others and then, having more than they could care for, some would starve.

"Another disadvantage in a small enclosure is this, that they get so tame they come out in the daytime to feed and the exposure to sunlight fades the fur to a certain extent. As it is also almost impossible to supply a lot of skunks with the kind of food they get in the wild state, it becomes necessary to substitute some other kind of food, such as dead horses, cows, chickens, corn and various other things which a man with a small lot cannot always have. If not fed properly, they become cannibalistic.

"Like every other business, skunk-raising requires capital; and with some one who has capital, together with the experience and practical knowledge, I venture to say there is 50 to 100 per cent profit in the business. To make a success, a man should have at least $2,500 to start with. At least one acre of ground should be enclosed with a 3-foot concrete wall in the ground, and about a 6-foot board fence on top. This would probably cost $1,500. One should then secure at least 100 females and 25 males. These would probably cost $300. The remaining $700 would be needed to pay for feed and for a man to take care of them.

"The necessary attention would be to feed and water them and, in the season of maternity, to see that the females do not steal one another's young and crowd one another in the boxes. The males and females should, of course, be separated. With good care 90 per cent of the young should be raised.

"Thirty years ago black skunk pelts sold at from 50 to 75 cents. To-day they are one of the leading furs on the market, although they are not known by their own names, but by various assumed ones. At the present time, it is profitable to raise skunks for their fur. The demand is now greater than the supply and is increasing because of the heaviness of the fur, its fine texture, its good wearing qualities and strength. On the other hand, the supply is decreasing for various reasons. The large forest and prairie fires, devasting large sections so that neither bug, snake, nor fur-bearing animal can exist, and the high price which

BEAVER

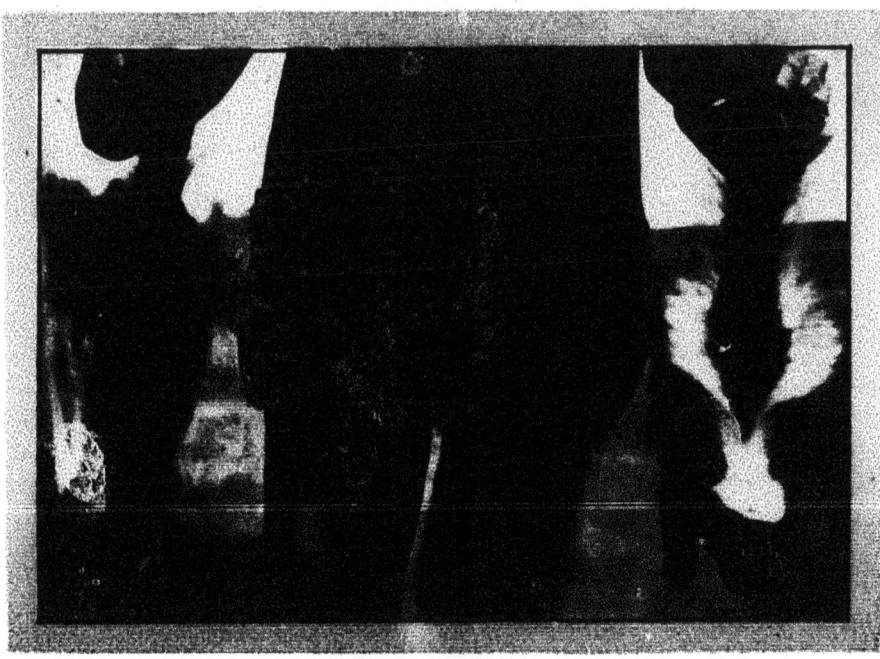

LIVE SKUNKS—LONG-STRIPED

spurs every hunter and trapper to his utmost effort, are the principal reasons. Then coon hunters coming from the city with a pack of hounds to hunt for sport, destroy a good many. In fact, they usually get one coon and kill six or eight skunks. You can follow their trail by the smell and the dead bodies of skunks which they have wantonly destroyed.

"Skunks can be raised as easily as house cats, provided you have an enclosure where they cannot dig out or climb over. For every hundred mature skunks, you should have an acre of ground enclosed.

"I experimented for three years on a small scale. The first year, I had one male and three females. They brought forth fifteen young. One of the young ones died, leaving eighteen—eleven females and seven males. Five of the young graded as No. 2, the balance star black.

"The second year, I started with twelve females and two males, which brought forth forty-three young. Three of the young ones died, so I had fifty-four in all—fourteen old ones and forty young ones. I disposed of seventeen males and five No. 2 females, leaving a balance of thirty-two black ones.

"The third year the females had from three to six young. Unfortunately, I could not attend them myself and had to entrust them to a man who had no interest in them except the pay he received from me for his work. About the first of August, the skunks dug a hole in the pen and made their escape. That veritably settled my skunk-raising, but, in the fall and winter, I do considerable night hunting with dogs, which I have trained not to take hold of them. I catch them alive and use the pen I have to keep them in until their fur is prime. In that way I have live skunks from the first of November to about the first of January."

The following notes are summarised from the accounts of Ernest Thompson Seton, who has kept these animals in captivity:

Gestation is about six weeks. The young run from 4 to 9 in a litter. The young come out to eat when two months old and can be admitted to the general run when four months old. They should be fed heavily in autumn in order to produce the fat on which they mostly exist in winter. The colder the weather, the better the fur. Not more than 50 or 60 can be kept on an acre. A diet of all meat will kill every skunk. Feed once a day in the evening. If the bodies of the skinned animals are fed, they should be thoroughly boiled with vegetables. The oil rendered from the skunk fat is valuable.

Habits of the Skunk The skunk is a burrowing animal and, therefore, like the fox, requires a sunken fence around the enclosure in which he is kept. Woven wire is best for all underground fences as it does not interfere with the drainage and is cheapest. To stop a skunk the fence need not extend more than a few feet above ground, but it should be built at least six feet high with an overhang in order to provide for snow banks and to keep other animals out. In northern

• regions, where the best fur can be produced, a wooded area will be found the best because it is secluded, provides shade and because the snow there lies level. The nest should be a warm insulated box with a passageway entrance similar to that of the mink nest. All nests should be only barely large enough for a mother to move about in without trampling her young and should not be more than 6 or 7 inches high. Thus the interior will be sufficiently warmed by the body heat.

A method of killing skunks by drowning is mentioned elsewhere. They can also be dispatched easily and painlessly in a poison box, using carbon bi-sulphide gas or prussic acid. The latter is a deadly poison and is very dangerous in the hands of an inexperienced person. They can also be killed by a blow over the back, which paralyses the muscles and destroys the power to scent. They are skinned by the case method. The skins should be carefully cleaned of fat to prevent heating and should be packed separately for shipping.

Practical Hints on Skunk-farming   The following practical hints on skunk-farming have been recently published in circular form by the Biological Survey, United States Department of Agriculture:

In General:—Many attempts have been made to raise skunks for their fur, but the enterprises have usually been given up as unprofitable. The chief causes of failure have been: cost of fencing inclosures, cost of maintenance, or lack of experience, leading to overcrowding and over-feeding the animals. In many cases, where the animals were successfully reared, it was found that the expense of feeding them to maturity exceeded the value of the fur, while in other instances, the antipathy of neighbours led to the abandonment of the experiments. At present the value of the best black skins would probably allow a margin of profit in rearing this class of skunks.

Food:—The chief aim is to supply a suitable and sufficient diet at reasonable cost. A certain proportion of meat is necessary, but the animals eat also bread, green corn, clover, tomatoes, and many other vegetable substances. Butcher and table scraps given when fresh are the main reliance. The food should not be salted, and fresh water should be supplied regularly. Skunks are especially fond of insects, and, if the pens are large enough and favourably placed, the animals will forage for a part of their food.

Pens.—At least an acre of ground should be enclosed for each 50 skunks, and, even then, there is danger of cannibalism unless there are plenty of separate dens for the females. The fence should be made of poultry netting 1½-inch mesh. The posts should be set in ditches 18 inches or more in depth, which should be filled with broken stone or concrete. Another plan is to extend the wire netting underground. The fence should be three or four feet high and have an overhang at the top to keep the animals from climbing over.

Skunks breed once a year and produce from 6 to 8 young. They are born in May or June, and mature by December.

RODENTS

THE order of mammals known as rodents are nearly all small-sized and are generally not valuable for their fur. They are distinguished by their chisel-edged teeth, of which they possess two in each jaw. There are no canine teeth and a wide vacant space divides the incisors from the grinders. The rabbit is an exception, having four incisors in the upper jaw.

For furs, the most useful animals of this order are the beaver of the beaver family, the muskrat of the mouse family and the rabbit of the hare family. None except the rabbit can be domesticated, but they can be kept under control to a certain extent, especially the muskrat.

MUSKRAT*

(*Fiber Zibethicus*)

While muskrat is one of the lowest priced pelts, it has risen rapidly in value in recent years. In 1911, the best northern muskrat cost the furrier about 80 or 85 cents each, and, in 1912, the price of the best skins was approaching $1.25 each. The price paid the trapper is, of course, considerably less, being about 50 cents at the present time. The demand has been increased by the new uses found for this fur. The handsome and popular 'Hudson Bay seal,' which is made from the muskrat, even in our own dressing and dyeing establishments, has given the fur much of its present value. About ten millions of pelts are used annually and the high prices are sure to spur trappers and hunters to greater efforts and, if the fur continues fashionable, may result in the depletion of the species in some sections.

Because of the ease of stocking a marsh and feeding the rat, it is feasible for owners to take charge of their marshes, control the number killed, improve the housing and nesting conditions and supply food by planting suitable crops and feeding vegetables and fruits.

In the salt marshes around Delaware and Chesapeake bays, on the Atlantic coast of the United States, a good quality of rat is produced and the marshes are protected by the owners. The 'ratting' privileges are rented, usually for one half of the catch. Use is made of the fur, the flesh and the musk bags. The flesh, known as marsh hare or marsh rabbit, is sold in large quantities on the Baltimore, Philadelphia, Norfolk and Washington markets and is said to be very agreeable in the fall and early winter, but to be unfit for food in the spring because of the musky flavour. The Indians consider it a splendid dish. In the

*For further information with respect to the muskrat see Appendix VI.

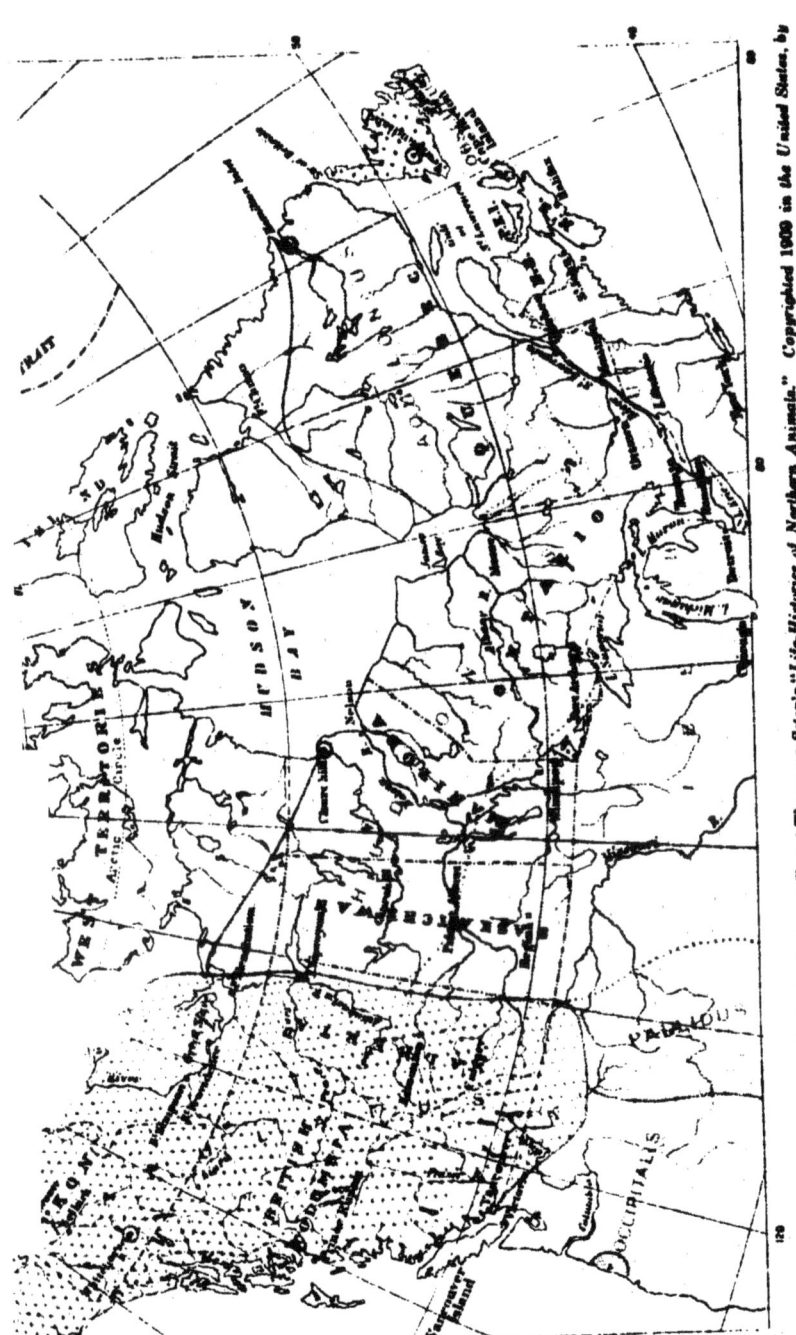

MAP 6.—RANGE OF THE MUSKRATS IN CANADA

Reproduced by courtesy of Charles Scribner's Sons from Ernest Thompson Seton's "Life-Histories of Northern Animals." Copyrighted 1909 in the United States, by Ernest Thompson Seton.

Founded on records by J. Richardson, Audubon and Bachman, D. G. Elliot, C. Hart Merriam, E. A. Mearns, E. A. Preble, R. MacFarlane, E. W. Nelson, E. R. Warren, Vernon Bailey, J. Fannin, O. Bangs, R. Bell, W. H. Osgood and E. T. Seton.

The map must be considered provisional and diagrammatic.

The following are recognized:

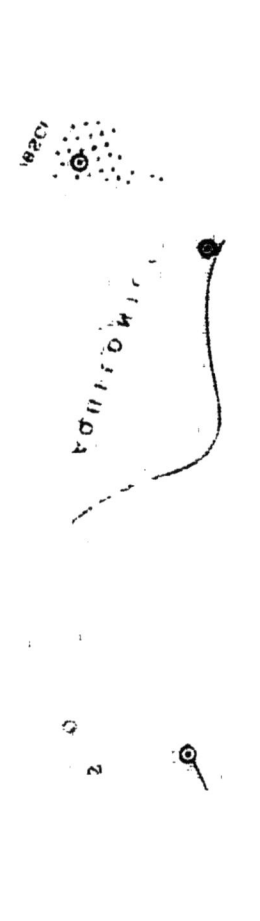

proper season, canning companies will purchase as much as can be put up.

It is said that the best salt marshes will furnish 50 rats a year per acre. They may be fenced with 1½-inch mesh wire, 5 feet wide, by burying it a foot on dry land and deeper near water area. Not more than 50 rat houses, or pairs, should be kept on an acre. It is necessary to have an area of water which does not freeze to the bottom. This, in many cases, could be secured by dredging and the mud thrown up would be used by the rats for making homes. Wild rice, water lilies, cat-tails, and various roots, are their natural food. Carrots, beets, turnips, apples, pumpkins and other cheap vegetables and fruits may be grown in nearby fields for summer food, or stored in pits for winter. A small quantity of meat may also be fed.

The muskrat probably has two litters the first, and three each succeeding season, and the first litters bear young in the autumn. The first are born about the middle of May and each litter numbers from four to nine, although as many as twelve have been reported.

BEAVER

(Castor Canadensis)

The beaver formerly existed over nearly all the continent of North America. It was also found in Europe and the greater part of Asia and Northern Africa, but, in most of these, became extinct centuries ago. There are only a few colonies in Europe at the present time and these are preserved carefully by the government authorities. It is rapidly becoming extinct in America. The homes of the greatest numbers, at the present time, are in the country between the Great lakes and the St. Lawrence river northward to Hudson bay, and in northern British Columbia.

No animal did more than the beaver to effect the colonization of America. It lured men into the most remote wildernesses, furnished him food and clothing, and was one of the chief articles of commerce with Europe. So universal an article of trade did it become that, in northern Canada, beaver skin became the unit of currency.

Brass estimates the world's production as follows: America, 80,000 skins; Asia, 1,000; Europe, a few. Besides the skins, the castoreum, or dry beaver castor, is traded in, bringing from $12 to $15 a pound at the present time.

Uses of the Beaver Because of its interesting habits, every schoolboy is well acquainted with most phases of the life of the beaver. Its flesh, skins and castors are valuable, the latter being used as a base in perfume manufacture. The flesh is excellent and the tail is considered a delicacy. The skin was formerly used in the manufacture of beaver hats, but, later, this use declined owing to the advent of the silk hat. At the present time, the fur is mostly plucked in dressing and sold for use in coats, stoles and muffs. The largest and finest skins are not worth more than $15 to $20, large No. 1 skins being quoted at $12.

The beaver cannot be farmed because of the wide extent of territory required to furnish food and also because it usually makes trouble for all neighbours in the same water area, whose lands have aspen, poplar, willow or other trees that furnish food. The only possible method is to enclose a large tract for both the forest and beavers that could be produced on it. Patrolling would be necessary and a certain number of beaver would have to be taken each year to maintain the proper supply. Possibly the range of the animals might be limited by fencing across the valleys. Trappers have said that the beaver will eat cultivated crops (e.g., turnips) but no proof of this statement could be found. If it eats such crops, ranching the beaver is feasible.

National Game Preserves The logical method to perpetuate the beaver is to create national game preserves under constant patrol. This plan has proved successful in the Algonquin Provincial Park, Ontario, where a considerable revenue is now derived from the sale of their skins. A system of national parks where the beaver and muskrat would be efficiently protected and where other wild life would be propagated, as well as protected, is advisable. Protective laws, particularly in the case of the beaver, do not protect. During the years when the beaver was contraband in Ontario and Quebec, bales of furs frequently contained a number of beaver skins. The bale was sold as it was packed, or another customer was sought. Thus, many Montreal furriers testified that they purchased beaver skins continually and could not avoid it, if they wished to continue to buy raw pelts.

For the information of those who desire to keep a few pairs of these interesting animals, it may be stated that when two years old, the beaver mates for life, mating taking place in February. The period of gestation is about three months. The litter usually consists of two or three, but may be larger. The young are weaned before they are two months old and taught to eat tender shoots of the raspberry and other plants. They accompany their mother the whole season. Foundation stock may be obtained from the Department of Lands, Forests and Mines, Toronto, Ont., at about $50 a pair. Success is easily achieved where water and the proper food are available.

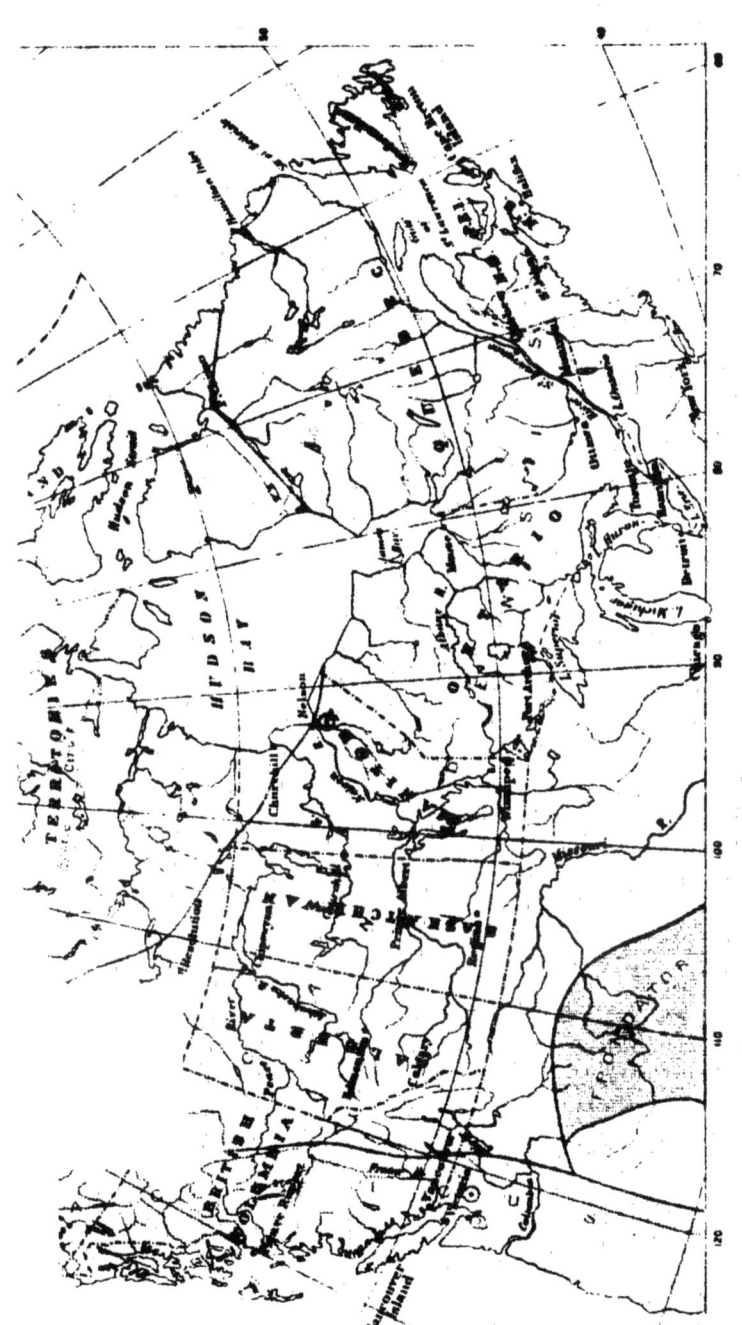

Reproduced by courtesy of Charles Scribner's Sons from Ernest Thompson Seton's "Life-Histories of Northern Animals." (Copyrighted 1909 in the United States, by Ernest Thompson Seton.)

MAP 7.—RANGE OF THE AMERICAN BEAVER IN CANADA

Castor Canadensis(Kuhl)3 races.

Founded chiefly on records by S. Hearne, J. Richardson, L. H. Morgan, Audubon and Bachman, R. Bell, D. G. Elliot, H. Y. Hind, S. N. Rhoads, J. Fannin, E. W. Nelson, O. Bangs, V. Bailey, E. A. Mearns, E. A. Preble, V. Bailey, F. M. Chapman and E. T. Seton.

This map must be considered provisional and diagrammatic; the north boundary only, is well established.

THE United States Congress, in 1892, at the instance of Dr. Sheldon Jackson, appropriated $240,500 to establish herds of reindeer (*Rangifer tarandus*) in Alaska. Twelve hundred and eighty reindeer were imported before 1902, when the Russian government withdrew its permission to make shipments from its territory. More lately, Dr. Grenfell has established herds in Labrador. Both herds are entirely successful in providing labour, transportation, skins* and food for the more primitive people of Canada and Alaska. The native reindeer of Canada, comprising the woodland caribou (*Rangifer caribou*) and the barren-ground caribou (*Rangifer arcticus*) might produce a domestic animal of a type superior to its European cousin. In any event, the European reindeer might possibly be improved by crossing with the woodland caribou, which is stronger and larger.

The following interesting account of the introduction of reindeer to Canada was contributed by R. H. Campbell, Director of the Forestry Branch, Department of the Interior:

THE REINDEER IN CANADA

"The earliest recorded attempt to domesticate reindeer on this continent is that of the United States government which, about 1892, imported a herd of Siberian deer to Alaska for that purpose. Several small herds have since been imported and, as the result of careful and intelligent handling, there are now some 15,000 domesticated reindeer in Alaska. The deer are used for practically all the purposes for which domestic cattle may be used and are, in addition, very useful for transportation purposes.

Transportation in the Arctic "The problem of transportation is, aside from the severity of the weather, the most serious with which dwellers in the arctic regions have to deal. The cost of grain and hay, neither of which is grown in any considerable quantity, precludes the use of horses or cattle for transportation purposes and, prior to the introduction of reindeer, dogs were used almost entirely. While Eskimo dogs make excellent beasts of burden, their usefulness is seriously impaired by the necessity of hauling with them sufficient fish or other food for their own subsistence. As on long trips they can haul little, if any, load beyond their own food supply, this seriously limits the sphere of a dog's usefulness. Reindeer, on the other hand, while quite as hardy as the best train dogs and able to haul somewhat larger loads, find their own subsistence in the moss which

---

*Concerning the price of buckskin, see page 154.

8

covers practically all of the sub-arctic region. No matter how cold the weather, or how deep the snow, the deer can paw their way down to the moss and thus keep themselves in good condition on the longest and roughest trips. Another point in favour of deer is that, should misfortune overtake a party of Arctic travellers and it become necessary to kill the transport animals for food, the flesh of the deer is palatable and nourishing, while only dire necessity would impel anyone to use dogs for food.

"It seems to have been the idea of the United States government that the establishment of large herds of domesticated reindeer in Alaska would be a long step in the direction of solving the transportation problem of that district and, in addition, would, to a considerable extent, provide a food supply for the natives who otherwise would, from time to time, become charges upon the public treasury.

"This experiment by the United States government was followed with great interest by many Canadians who were interested in the development of our northern territories, and particularly by Dr. Wilfred Grenfell, who, in connection with his medical missionary work on the Labrador coast, found himself confronted by practically the same conditions that obtained in Alaska, viz.: severe climate, absence of means of winter transportation other than dogs, and scarcity of food supply for natives and fishermen during periods of unusually severe weather.

"At Dr. Grenfell's request, the Dominion Government, in
The Reindeer 1907, purchased a herd of some 300 Norwegian reindeer.
in Labrador These were handed over to Dr. Grenfell to be used by him in connection with his work. It was originally intended that the herd should be established on the North shore of the gulf of St. Lawrence, but he finally decided that his mission station at St. Anthony, on the northeast coast of Newfoundland, was a more suitable place for the experiment. There is an abundance of reindeer moss at, or near, St. Anthony, the climate is in all respects suitable and, should occasion require it, the deer can readily be shipped from there to any desired point on the Labrador coast as conveniently as from the point first selected.

"Dr. Grenfell's experiment proved successful from the start and his herd of reindeer now numbers over 1,200. A considerable number of stags and barren does have been killed for food and there have been the usual unavoidable losses by death and accident. He reported in May, 1911, that the meat is excellent and the skins valuable and that, in his opinion, reindeer will, in the future, be as valuable in Labrador as in Alaska and will afford an export industry of meat from a district where it is not probable that wheat, corn or other cereals can ever be profitably produced.

"During the summer of 1910, His Excellency the Governor-General, Earl Grey, visited Dr. Grenfell's mission station on his return journey from Hudson bay. His Excellency was greatly interested in the reindeer experiment, and having just seen a considerable part of sub-arctic Canada, was impressed with the desirability of further extending the experiment by the establishment of herds in portions of the Northwest territories. He subsequently discussed the question with Hon. Frank Oliver, then Minister of the Interior, with the result that an arrangement was made with Dr. Grenfell to supply fifty reindeer to the Dominion Government at what the animals had actually cost him. It was decided that the reindeer should be sent to a suitable place near Fort Smith, on the Slave river, practically on the northern boundary of Alberta. In addition to the reindeer, Dr. Grenfell was to supply two herders and one apprentice to look after the herd, three trained dogs and a supply of moss sufficient for the journey from Newfoundland to our Northwest.

Reindeer in the North-west

"There was no choice as to the time of year when the reindeer were to be shipped. They could be not taken across the continent in summer weather as they could not stand the heat. They could not be taken across in winter unless provision were made for a supply of reindeer moss near Edmonton, as the rivers are frozen and they could not be transported beyond that point. They could not be moved in the spring as that is the fawning season. There was, therefore, only the short season left between the close of summer and the 'freeze-up' of the northern rivers.

"It was arranged with the Department of Marine and Fisheries that one of their steamers should call at St. Anthony for the reindeer early in September, 1911, and take them to Quebec, from which point they would be sent by train to Edmonton. If the boat had proceeded direct to Quebec, it is probable that there would have been very small loss of deer, but the steamer had to stop on the way to take on board a cargo of powdered gypsum, and the effect on the reindeer was serious. Four deer died before the steamer reached Quebec and five more on the train after leaving Quebec; and, from the symptoms it is practically certain that death was caused by inhalation of gypsum dust.

"It was a somewhat difficult matter to transfer the reindeer from the boats to the cars awaiting them at Quebec, but this was finally accomplished and the trip to Edmonton and from there, sixty miles further on to the end of the steel, was made expeditiously, most of the reindeer reaching this point in good condition.

"From the end of the steel to Athabaska Landing, something over fifty miles, the deer were conveyed in waggons and were then loaded on scows for the trip down to Fort Smith. This turned out to be the most difficult part of the trip. The scows were hard to manage and a great deal of ice was encountered which hindered progress. In the end it was found impossible to get as far as Fort Smith, and it was decided to remain at a point seventy miles from the fort, where reindeer moss was plentiful, until such time as the deer could be driven to their destination, or until the spring, when they could be conveyed down the river. The herd was kept here very comfortably until the spring, and on the 20th May, 1912, reached Fort Smith, the total loss of deer *en route* being nineteen.

"The herd wintered satisfactorily and was in good condition in the spring. The chief herder had selected a suitable place for them west of Fort Smith on a point jutting out into a lake lying south of Great Slave lake.   There is plenty of reindeer moss in this locality and it seemed in every way suitable for the keeping of the herd.   However, the flies became so troublesome to the herd in the summer that they stampeded.

"Early in 1913, a new range for the deer was selected on an island in Great Slave lake. Attempts were made to move the herd thence in the spring of 1913, but owing to flies, they stampeded, and the attempt ended in failure. In the fall, all but three of the reindeer died, probably owing to too close confinement. A larger range was provided and the remaining three are healthy. It is planned to move them to the island in the spring of 1914.

"Considering the difficulties of transportation, the shipment was taken through with comparatively small loss until the fall of 1913; but the success of the herd is not fully assured until it is certain that they can be controlled and prevented from stampeding at the time when the flies are most active. If matters go satisfactorily with them for another year, it may be advisable to consider increasing the number by a further shipment."

MOOSE

The European moose was formerly under domestication and proved valuable for transportation purposes in the cold northern countries. It is on record that it once hauled a sleigh 234 miles in one day. For divers reasons—the chief one being that exiles used it to effect their escape—it became unlawful to maintain the moose in captivity in some countries. Probably it would have developed into a valuable domestic animal for northern latitudes had this prohibition not been imposed.   It is possible also, that the Canadian moose, which is of greater size and strength, could be developed into a domestic animal of value.   Several cases are recorded of its being successfully used for draught purposes, in the first generation from the wild state. It is but just to add, however, that the moose has not yet been bred in captivity.

IV. Preparing Skins for Manufacture

MAMMALS which have a short, fine, soft coat of fur through which grows hair, usually of greater length, variously called over-fur, water-fur, guard-hair, are known as fur-bearers. To provide more warmth for the animal, the coat of fur and overhair is usually thicker and longer in the winter; hence, furs taken in winter, or when prime, are more valuable than those taken in warmer weather.

Pelt of a Fur-bearer
When the skin is unprime, it has a bluish appearance on the flesh side down the back and sides; when prime, it is of a whitish or creamy colour. An experienced furrier can, by the appearance of the skin and of the overhair, determine the season at which it was taken. It is desirable to capture fur-bearers when prime, because the fur and overhair are fuller and heavier and will not fall out easily, as commonly occurs in 'springy' pelts. It is also desirable to take skins shortly after becoming prime, which is usually about the first of December, immediately after the first winter weather. When taken then, the pelt is better coloured and less worn. In a climate like that of Prince Edward Island, where winter sets in about Christmas, the last week of the year is chosen for killing the fox. The pelts of the majority of animals become prime late in November.

The fur, or, as it is called in relation to the hair, the underfur, consists of soft, silky, downy, curly filaments. It is usually short and thick, and towards the skin it grows lighter in colour. It is barbed lengthwise and hence is capable of felting—a quality not possessed to so great a degree by wool or silk, which is best handled by spinning and weaving. In a prime pelt the underfur is hardly discernible unless the overhair is blown apart. Then the light colour of the underfur appears. If it were generally known that the undyed skin is whitish and that the underfur close to the skin is a light drab, or pale blue colour, it would not be so easy to sell dyed skins as natural.

The overhair is straight, smooth and, usually, comparatively rigid. It is scattered throughout the fur and, on the living animal, prevents the fur from felting. It serves as a protection against cold and storm as well as against injury. In the case of the fox, which lies out in the open, exposed to the coldest northern weather, the dense overhair, usually three, but sometimes over six inches in length, protects the body, while the toes and face are protected by the immense tail, which covers them when the fox lies down. The beauty of a pelt is due largely to the overhair. It is the glossy black or the amphimaculated silver-black

MICROCOPY RESOLUTION TEST CHART

(ANSI and ISO TEST CHART No. 2)

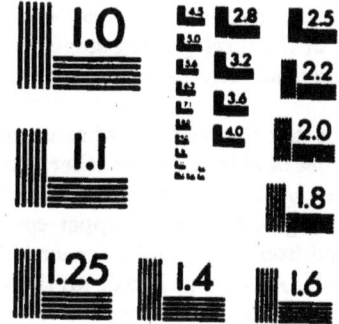

APPLIED IMAGE Inc

1653 East Main Street
Rochester, New York   14609   USA
(716) 482 - 0300 - Phone
(716) 288 - 5989 - Fax

overhair that makes the silver fox one hundred times more valuable than his red full-brother. Some kinds of animals, as, for example, the beaver and the otter, have overhair which is not always considered as beautiful as the underfur alone. Thus, they are put through a process of pulling and the manufactured skins are usually plucked.

Killing   Usually animals intended for slaughter are fed well and are carefully housed so that no injury can bo done the overhair, such as from rubbing, the attachment of burrs or from lying in dirt. The killing presents no difficulty except that it must be done so as not to alarm the breeding animals. Therefore, in most cases, the animals to be slaughtered should be removed to the finishing pens in the autumn. The fox is usually killed by crushing the chest with the foot, a man's weight applied just back of the foreleg being sufficient, or a blow with a stick on the snout, or the head may be forced back until the neck is broken.

The information available indicates that the adoption of some more humane method of killing, such as the use of chloroform or ether, would not injure the fur and, at the same time, be far more merciful. A small padded box with a wad of cotton batting in one of the upper corners upon which chloroform could be dropped from a hole in the corner of the box would be all that would be required. As soon as it is dead, the animal should be removed from the chamber. In the case of such a valuable animal as this, it is not too much to expect of ranchers that they provide one of these inexpensive lethal chambers.

Poisons that are available are: cyanide of potassium, prussic acid, strychnine and white arsenic. A very small quantity of cyanide or of prussic acid will kill the fox instantly, but, as these drugs are excessively poisonous, it is dangerous to have them in one's possession unless securely locked up. Strychnine and white arsenic do not kill immediately, and, if another animal ate the flesh of an animal poisoned by them, it would be poisoned in turn.

Skunk, on account of its liability to scent, presents the greatest problem. It can be removed from its regular pen, however, by a wire snare placed on the end of a long pole. It is then dispatched outside its pen by the usual method of clubbing. If scenting is feared, it may be drowned in a tub of water.

Skinning and Curing   There are two distinct methods of removing the skin. Some animals are opened down the belly, as in skinning a sheep, and the skins are stretched flat or 'open.' Others are slit up the hind legs to the vent and the skin is stripped off the rest of the body. These are stretched by a board wedged inside and are

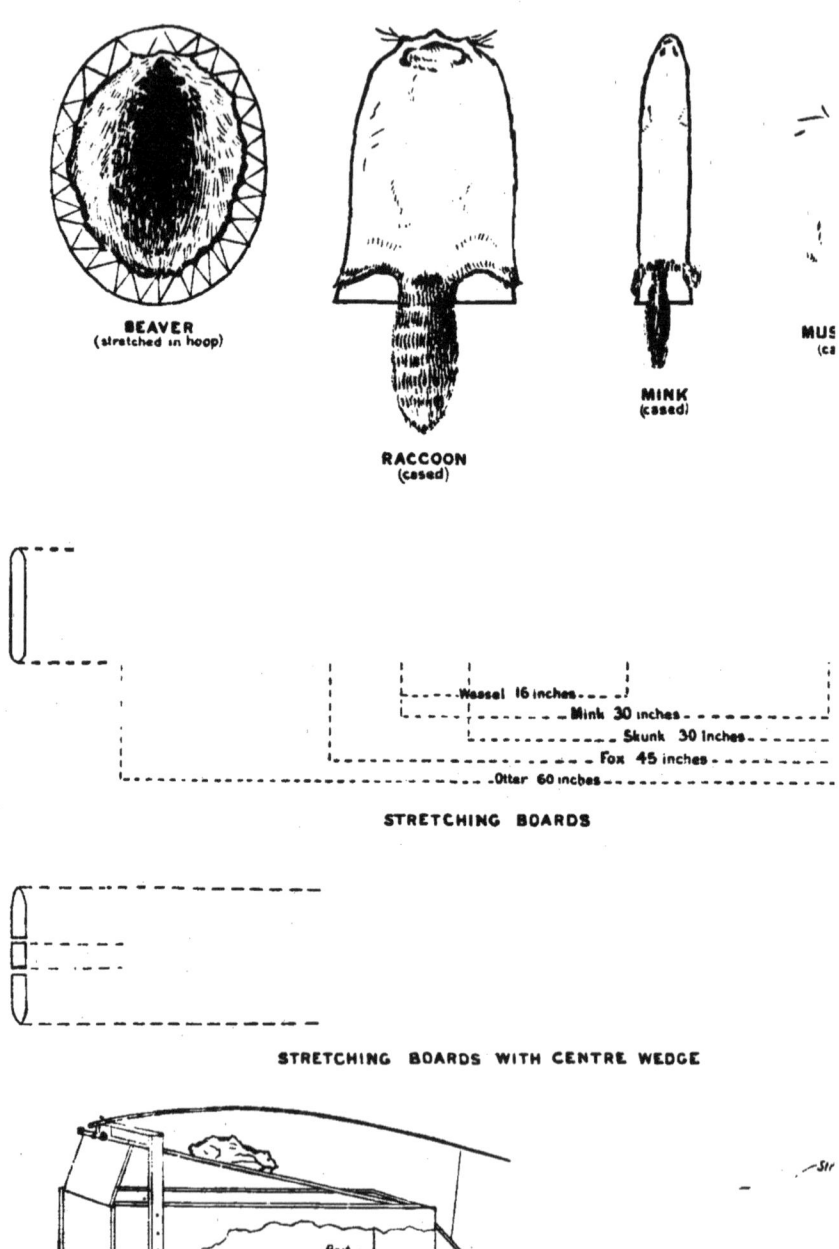

BEAVER
(stretched in hoop)

RACCOON
(cased)

MINK
(cased)

MUS
(ca

Weasel 16 inches
Mink 30 inches
Skunk 30 inches
Fox 45 inches
Otter 60 inches

STRETCHING BOARDS

STRETCHING BOARDS WITH CENTRE WEDGE

Bait

BOXES FOR CATCHING LIVE ANIMALS

said to be 'cased.'   The methods of skinning in use for common Canadian fur-bearers are as follows:

Cased—Fox, marten, fisher, weasel, otter, skunk, lynx, cat,
muskrat.
Either Cased or Open—Raccoon, wildcat.
Open—Wolverene, badger, beaver, wolf, bear.

The process of removing a cased skin is well described by the *Fur
News Magazine* as follows:

"Slit skin on both hind legs on the under side of animal from
the heel to the vent; skin out the legs to the feet, and in the case
of mink, skin out the toes and leave them and the claws on the
skin.   Skin around the tail, leaving the tail on the back of the
skin, and after loosening the tail bone at the base, take hold of it
with your forefinger and pull it out of the tail.   If the tail bone
is hard to remove, split a stock, insert the tail bone in split, and
with this to grip the bone, you should have no trouble to pull it
out.   "Now turn the skin back and carefully pull it off the body.
Use a knife to start the skin if it does not come off easily, but be
careful not to cut the pelt.   Skin so that as little flesh and fat
adhere to the skin as possible.   When the front legs are reached,
skin around them near the body and then push them backward
out of the skin—turn them inside out, as we might say.   Skin out
the legs to the paws in the case of mink, keeping them on the skin;
for the other animals cut off the legs at the first joint.   Skin carefully around the head, pushing the skull back through the skin
until the ears are reached; these should be cut off as near the skull
as possible, so that they remain attached to the skin.   Then carefully skin around the eyes, not cutting the eyelids, and when the
mouth and nose are reached use care also. Do not pull the skin
off the head, but remove carefully, for the heads of some animals are
used in manufacturing the furs, and all skins have a better appearance if the head is skinned out with care."

Skunks and raccoons present some special problems.   They fatten
in the fall and go to their dens in cold weather.   Therefore, those designed for slaughter must be segregated from the breeders before cold
weather sets in or they cannot be captured without disturbing the nest.
After skinning, also, a large quantity of fat adheres to the skin.   This
must be scraped off or it may heat and decompose the skin.   Skunk
fat should be kept and rendered into oil.   In baled shipments, also,
the grease of these skins is liable to injure other skins in the same

pack. They should be specially wrapped in burlap and, because of their odour, it may be advisable to box the skunk skins separately.

The flesh and fat are removed from skins by a dull knife or hatchet. The skin is slipped on a fleshing board with dulled corners, having one end in a grease pan and the other against the skinner's chest. The fat is pushed off the skin towards the tail. Much scraping of the skin is injurious, it being necessary to remove only the fat and loose flesh. The tail may give trouble if it is not split and scraped. Sometimes salt is dropped into it to prevent decomposition; but in no case is salt nor any other preservative, applied to any other part of the skin. Often the tip of the tail is cut off to allow circulation of air inside and to drain out the fat.

Open skinning presents no difficulty. The legs are cut off at the first joint and split up the inside to the slit which is cut along the belly from the lower jaw to the vent. The tail is cut open to extract the bone.

Stretching The cased skins are stretched on a wedge-shaped board, fur side inwards. The edges of the stretching board are along the sides of the pelt, the dorsal surface of the p' being wholly on one side of the board and the ventral on the other side. All skins except fox are marketed fur side inwards, fox being turned fur out after one day's drying, when the front legs are still pliable. Skins should be dried without artificial heat. A cool, dry place away from the sun's rays is best. Beaver skins are stretched within an elliptical hoop made of saplings. They are tied to the hoop with twine laced into the skin at intervals of two inches. Bear skins are usually laced similarly into a rectangular frame made from small sticks. Raccoon are nailed on a wall or board and stretched into a rectangular shape. The best nails are brass tacks or wire nails and they should be driven not more than two inches apart.

Otter tails are always split and stretched by nailing to the stretching board.

Stretching Boards Boards should be made of soft wood, like white pine, which permits easy driving and withdrawal of nails. For smaller animals, the stretching board should be about three-eighths of an inch thick, and for the larger—otter and fox—about five-eighths or three-quarters of an inch. It should be nicely rounded on the edges. Wedges are sometimes inserted down the sides of the board with advantage. They permit the circulation of air on the inside. A steel wire has served well in stretching muskrat on many occasions.

The best stretched skins are those that are extended very slightly in all directions. Mink and marten should be pulled slightly lengthwise and the lines of the sides should be only slightly converging. A stretching board may be split and a wedge inserted between the two sides will adjust it to any size of skin.

Marketing Skins   Valuable pelts are sewed up in muslin and expressed to destination. When shipped by express care should be taken to have the agent mark the full value of the skins on the receipt to ensure recovery of value if lost. When packing skins do not roll them; pack flat and then sew them up neatly in burlap. They should be wrapped in paper first. Label the package inside and outside to make identification certain. Skins must be packed dry and must be kept dry.

If all the pelts taken in Canada were prime and were properly stretched, dried and marketed, the increase in value would amount to millions. Nearly fifty per cent of the pelts of some species are blue, or (springy) or with hair rubbed off or falling out. The competition between trappers is producing more and more blue pelts, which cannot grade above No. 2. Conservation of fur would be achieved if it were illegal to kill except when the pelts are prime. It is probable, however, that only personal ownership of the fur-bearers would ensure nearly 100 per cent of the pelts marketed being prime.

The fur moth also causes immense losses. Modern refrigeration, however, has solved this problem by providing cold storage chambers for furs stored in the warm season.

Dyeing of Furs   All seal and Persian lamb skins go through a process of dyeing. Seal skin, after the water hair is plucked, is of a drab colour, but expert English dyers make it a dark, brownish black. As German dye excels in fastness of colour and in leaving the skins supple after treatment, the Persian lamb skins are mostly dyed in Germany. The French are very skillful in 'topping' where the overhair is made to imitate sable. Latterly, the Germans have developed a large trade in 'pointed fox,' which is an ordinary cheap fox dyed black, and afterwards 'pointed' by sewing in white hairs. The German dyed article is quite durable in colour; but it, again, is imitated by furriers in America, who colour with ordinary black dye and glue in badger hairs. In a few months the difference in the quality of the dye used is revealed. Good dyes—such as those developed in England for seals and in Germany for lambs—are likely to remain trade secrets.

The dressing d dyeing of furs in Canada is nearly all performed by one firm which handles about 2,000,000 skins annually. The workmen and experts are largely German and other Europeans and have received their training in the old world. The dressing and dyeing of furs in America is steadily improving and the proportion shipped to Europe is decreasing.

Esteemed Natural Colours The natural colours must be of a certain quality to be highly esteemed. Thus, pure white ermine is costlier than the gray or yellowish-white kinds. With white furs, it is the purest and, with black furs, it is the densest that are most desired. A brownish colour in a silver fox is very objectionable (although common in most districts), while a bluish cast is decidedly to be preferred. In fact, it is almost axiomatic that a bluish cast, instead of a rusty or brownish, is preferred. It is the brown cast of Hudson Bay marten that makes it inferior to the Russian sable, which often has a bluish-brown colour. The predominance on the market of brown or rusty coloured skins can be readily accounted for when it is remembered that most 'springy' skins are brownish, no matter how blue-black, or blue-brown, or blue-gray they were when prime.

Dressing Furs The modern art of dressing and dyeing furs is a great improvement on pioneer methods, especially in dyeing and finishing. For giving suppleness and durablity, the primitive methods are excellent; thus, the North American Indians and African Kaffirs are unrivalled dressers of leather.

Older Methods The older method of dressing furs, used universally until the introduction of machinery, is to "place the skins in a lye of alkali; when the pelt has become soft, the skins are tubbed, and then shaved by passing them over a large knife an[illegible] in an upright position; they are next buttered, and put in a la[illegible] w-dust by men half naked, who tread on them for some [illegible] heat of their bodies rendering the leather soft and supple; [illegible] en beaten out and finished."

Modern Methods Modern methods of dressing and dyeing are much different. The work is done in large factories where an expert handles every department and machinery does most of the tramping and beating. Invention has made possible the use of many commoner and cheaper skins which undergo many operations in the course of their preparation. They may be beamed, scraped, tramped, soaked, fleshed, tanned, dried, drummed, greased, kicked, drummed with sawdust, dyed, caged, shaved, pared and foot-tubbed before they are ready for the manufacturer. Most of this work is done by machinery, and the large numbers of skins put through at one time makes the product uniform and the cost much lower per unit than by the old-fashioned hand and foot process.

Apparatus Used Besides the engine or motor which supplies the power, the following apparatus is used:

Washing tanks, which are made of wire mesh and revolve in a tank of water;

Drying vats, which revolve very rapidly, to throw moisture out of the skins;

Cleaning drums, which, with an exhaust air arrangement, remove the sawdust or corn starch from the skins;

Polishing drums, which revolve the skins with sawdust to polish the fur and hair;

Wooden tanks, for dyeing;

Revolving stone cylinder, for beaming;

Kicking machine, for pounding the skins;

Sewing machine, built especially for joining fur;

Clipping machines, for shearing the underfur even.

There are chambers for drying skins, where the air is kept constantly in motion by exhaust fans, and many other tools or contrivances for hand-work, such as crescent-shaped sharp knives, for fleshing, rope for roping, tubs for tramping, knives, combs, boards for stretching, etc. As treatment varies so much, it is impossible to list the operations a given skin goes through. Marten, for instance, has a tender skin and has to be given hand treatment. Mink and fox are treated in a Canadian fur-dressing establishment about as follows:

Fox	Mink
Pounded	Pounded
Wet with wet sawdust	Soaked to soften head
Fleshed	Fleshed
Salt water put on skin	Flesh pickled
Dried	Dried
Broken in foot-tub	Drummed with sawdust
Buttered or greased	Greased and pounded
Tubbed	Stretched
Cleaned with sawdust in drum	Drummed (sawdust)
Dried	Stretched
Polished in drum with sawdust	Drummed (sawdust)
	Stretched and beaten
	Dyed

The Process of Manufacture* At 'the fur dressers' the skins are first dampened on the flesh side with salt water and left all night to soften. The following morning they are placed in a tramping machine, where they are tramped for eight or ten hours. The machine works about 2,000 pelts at a time.

The pelts are next covered with a mixture of sawdust and salt water, and remain so overnight. The following morning they are cut cpen down the front and are then fleshed, one man being able to flesh 200 to 300 in a day. The skins are next stretched and hung up to dry. When thoroughly dry, they are again moistened with salt water on the leather side, remaining so overnight. They are next brushed on the flesh side with animal fat—butter or fish oil and tallow—and laid in pairs, with fur side out. After remaining overnight they are placed in tramping machines and worked for six or eight hours, or until thoroughly soft and pliable. They are then stretched in every direction.

The next process is cleaning. The skins, to the number of 300 or 400, are placed with sawdust in revolving drums exposed to steam heat. They are revolved for about three hours, when the sawdust will have completely absorbed the grease. The skins are next incased in a beating drum, where they are revolved for two or three hours. On removal, they are beaten with rattans, and the fur is cleaned with a comb. The heavier pelts are fleshed down thin, thus completing the operation of dressing for the majority of skins.

Warmth and Weight of Furs Well-dressed furs afford a maximum of warmth for a minimum weight, while their suppleness lends an additional advantage to them for clothing purposes. The warmest garments of manufactured mate l are made from the stiff old-fashioned box cloth and, even where warmly lined, afford only two-thirds as much protection from the cold as fur, while being more than four ounces per square foot heavier than raccoon. The following table furnishes an approximate estimate of comparative weight and durability of the various furs when worn, fur outside, as body clothing:

---

*A summary from Chas. H. Stevenson's report in that of the United States Commission on Fish and Fisheries for 1902.

COMPARATIVE DURABILITY AND WEIGHT OF FURS

	Points of Durability	Weight in Ounces per sq. foot
The Costly Furs—Standard, Sea-otter		
Sea-otter	100	4½
Seal	75	3
Sable	60	2½
Silver or Black Fox	40	3
Ermine	25	1¼
Chinchilla	15	1½
The Less Valuable Furs—Standard, Unplucked Otter		
Otter (unplucked)	100	4
Otter (plucked)	95	3 15/16
Beaver (sheared)	90	4
Beaver (plucked)	85	3 15/16
Raccoon	75	4½
Skunk	70	2¾
Mink	70	3¼
Persian Lamb	65	3¼
Baum Marten (natural)	65	2¾
Sable	55	2½
Stone Marten	40	2¼
Northern Fox (natural)	40	3
Muskrat (natural)	37	3½
Opossum	37	3
Muskrat (plucked, sheared and dyed)	33	3¼
Nutria	27	3¼
Lynx (natural)	25	2¾
Squirrel	25	1¾
Fox (dyed black)	25	3
Lynx (dyed black)	20	2¾
Fox (dyed blue)	20	3
Broadtail	15	2¼
Marmot (dyed)	10	3
Moleskin	7	1¾
Hare	5	1¾
Rabbit	5	2¼

V. The Commerce in Raw Furs

THE chief operators in Canada are the Hudson's Bay Co. and Revillon Frères, and, in Labrador, the Harmony Co. During the past ten years a change has been taking place in marketing and many furs, particularly the more valuable ones, are consigned direct to German or to French fur houses. In the Old World, furs are collected at fairs at the following places:

Town	Time of Fair
Frankfort-on-the-Oder	January
Irbit, Siberia	February
Leipzig, Germany	Easter
Nijni-Novgorod, Russia	August
Ishim, Siberia	December

Many of the skins, particularly those of finer quality, are ultimately offered at the London sales where the majority of the world's fine furs are sold. In recent years, however, Germany and the United States have been purchasing a larger proportion.

Quantities of Skins The total sales in London are often utilized in estimating the quantities of furs at the world's disposal. Of the undressed skins not usually sold at London sales, there are the Persian lambs, broadtails and karakuls, of which Thorer estimates that 2,900,000 come to Leipzig alone. A United States consular report of 1911 estimated that Russia produces 4,525,000 squirrels, whose raw pelts are valued at $2,000,000. Of squirrel tails, Russia, in 1911, produced twenty-one tons, valued at $5.50 per pound. Owing to the growing popularity of muskrat or 'Hudson Bay seal,' the use of this skin has increased enormously and the sales now amount to over 9,000,000 annually, London selling 6,000,000, Leipzig, 1,000,000 and America retaining 2,000,000. Two hundred thousand ermine pelts, valued at $350,000, are sold annually in Russia. About 83,000,000 rabbit skins are imported into Great Britain annually, while immense quantities of skins are used in the felting industry in Australia.

Centres of the Fur Trade Leipzig, Germany, is the most important city for the dressing and dyeing of furs. Its raw supplies are drawn from all parts of the world but particularly from London and Moscow storehouses and the Nijni-Novgorod fair. Moscow is the largest storehouse for Russian and Asiatic furs, while New York, St. Louis and Montreal are important American centres which are rapidly increasing their facilities for fur-dressing and fur-dyeing. London is the largest selling centre and is still of great importance in the dressing, dyeing and manufacturing of furs.

THE LONDON FUR MARKET

The London Auction Sales Many skins are manufactured and used in the country of their origin, but the bulk of the world's fine furs are sold at auction in London. These sales are held in June, October, January and March, but most skins are sold at the winter sales, particularly the March sale, which attracts numerous buyers from a" parts of the world. A large proportion of the pelts are purchased by brokers on a commission basis. The Hudson's Bay Company's auction sales are held first and, as no reserve bids are placed on the skins offered, the results are taken to represent the state of the market. Messrs. C. M. Lampson and Co., Messrs. A. and W. Nesbitt and Frederick Huth and Co. are the chief firms selling American furs.

LONDON FUR SALES FOR THE YEAR ENDING MARCH 31st, 1906

Size in inches	Kind of Fur	No. of Pelts	Size in inches	Kind of Fur	No. of Pelts
24 x 12	Badger...........	28,634	27 x 13	Lamb, Tibet......	704,130
"	" Japanese....	6,026		Leopard..........	3,574
72 x 36	Bear............	18,576	45 x 20	Lynx............	88,822
36 x 24	Beaver..........	80,514	18 x 12	Marmot, linings and skins, equal to............	1,600,000
9 x 4½	Cat, civet........	157,915	16 x 5	Marten, Baum.....	4,573
18 x 9	" house........	126,703	16 x 5	" Japanese...	16,461
30 x 15	" wild.........	32,253	16 x 5	" Stone.....	12,939
9 x 4	Chinchilla, bastard.	43,578	16 x 5	Mink, American...	209,254
12 x 7	" finest...	5,603		" Japanese....	360,373
	Deer, Chinese......	124,355	30 x 15	Mouflon..........	23,594
12 x 2½	Ermine..........	40,641	12 x 8	Muskrat, brown...	5,126,330
				" black ...	41,788
30 x 12	Fisher or Pekan...	5,946	20 x 12	Nutria...........	82,474
12 x 3	Fitch...........	77,578	18 x 10	Opossum, American	902,065
20 x 7	Fox, Blue........	893	16 x 8	" Austral'n.	4,161,685
24 x 8	" Cross.......	276		Otter, land........	21,235
27 x 10	" Gray	61	50 x 25	" sea.........	522
	" Japanese....	19	20 x 12	Raccoon..........	310,712
	" Kit	4,023	17 x 5	Sable, American...	97,282
24 x 8	" Red......	158,961	14 x 4½	" Japanese....	556
24 x 8	" Silver.	2,510	15 x 5	" Russian....	26,309
20 x 7	" White... ...	27,463	40 x 20	Seal, fur..........	77,000
	Goats, Chinese....	261,190		" hair.........	31,943
			15 x 8	Skunk...........	1,068,408
24 x 9	Hares...........	41,256	10 x 5	Squirrel...........	194,596
	Kangaroo.........	7,115		" linings.....	1,982,736
	Kid, linings and skins, equal to..	5,080,047		Tiger.............	392
				Wallaby..........	60,956
12 x 2½	Kolinsky.........	114,251			
	Lambs, linings and skins, equal to...	214,072	50 x 25	Wolf.............	56,642
			16 x 18	Wolverene........	1,726
	Lamb, slink........	16,372	20 x 12	Wombat.........	193,625

Note.--The Persian lambs, astrakhans and Russian squirrels are sold and dressed in Russia and Germany.

A report made in the spring of 1911 by the United States commercial agent at London, Mr. J. D. Whelpley, to his government at Washington and published by the Bureau of Manufactures, Department of Commerce and Labor, gives considerable information on the London fur trade. The following extracts from it are informative:

"London is the fur market of the world, and the prices paid at its famous auctions are the determining factors in making prices the world over. A large portion cf the fur-skins gathered during the year is sold at one or other of its five auction sales. The first is held in January, the second in March (by far the largest and most important), another in June, and a fourth in October. In December is held the annual seal sale, at which nearly all the seal furs taken during the previous 12 months are offered. This selling of the furs in one market has its advantages, especially from the viewpoint of the sellers. With so many diverse interests, representing practically every country in the world, it is utterly impossible to form a dealers' 'ring,' as would almost inevitably result if the furs were offered in a smaller and more restricted market. That, probably, is one of the considerations that brings the furs over thousands of miles of land and water at considerable expense to be sold in London and returned for final disposal, perhaps, to places within a few miles of their capture.

"There was a time when only dealers bought furs at these great auctions. Now, however, several of the larger and richer wholesalers bid, eliminating the dealers' profit. The principal reason why this is not done to a larger extent is a financial one. Few of the wholesale houses wish to tie up capital for the long period necessary if they buy direct from the auctioneers. Buying for cash in January and March, it is in many cases close on to a year, and in some cases, when business is poor, two years before the wholesalers and manufacturers can hope to realize on their investment. On the other hand, the dealers extend liberal credit terms to their customers, and consequently the burden on the latter is not such a heavy one.

"There are no detailed figures as to British imports or exports, The only way in which the imports of any particular skin can be determined is to totalize the sales. This is difficult and unsatisfactory, as there are several small sales and some private offerings in addition to the great fur auctions. The English trade returns for 1910 give the imports of undressed fur skins as: 82,327,101 rabbit skins, value $3,675,-483; 333,033 seal skins, value $1,401,573; and 18,515,682 other skins, value $15,390,209. In 1909, when the total number of undressed rabbit skins imported was 66,135,374, valued at $2,548,537, the countries supplying the larger quantities were: Germany, 39,462; Belgium, 11,255,772; France, ⌣,845,158; Australia, 43,442,559; New Zealand,

7,379,960. Of the undressed seal skins imported'in that year the United States furnished 24,550; Russia, 27,980; Norway, 60,694; Japan (including Formosa), 11,398; Cape of Good Hope, 15,061; Newfoundland and Labrador, 126,796; the total imports amounting to 288,055 skins, valued at $1,328,219. Undressed, unclassified skins aggregated 17,960,661, and had an import value of $11,285,180; of these the United States supplied 6,426,851; Russia, 750,868; Germany, 3,370,525; China (exclusive of Hong Kong, Macao, and Wei-hai-wei), 507,637; Japan (including Formosa), 85,692; Chili, 46,558; France, 47,754; Australia, 5,499,814 and Canada, 987,321. Dressed rabbit skins numbering 537,051 and valued at $80,098; 18,608 dressed seal skins, value $400,339; and 4,856,818 dressed skins, not classified in the customs returns but having a value of $4,318,688, were also imported into the United Kingdom during 1909, as well as manufactures of skins and furs (including skin rugs) worth $5,005,122, thus giving a grand total for the 1909 imports of dressed and undressed furs and manufactures of furs and skins of $25,056,183.

French Competition "Of late years some big firms, notably one French house, with branches in London and the United States, and several American houses located in Philadelphia and elsewhere, have been dealing direct with the trappers, thus avoiding the London auction sales altogether. The French firm is a determined competitor of the great Hudson's Bay Co. in its own territory, and with ships and frontier stores is making a serious effort to obtain a portion of the Canadian fur trade. This firm does a wholesale and retail business, but offers no skins at auction. The Hudson's Bay Co. sells all

"Figures from the London sales are now not safe. Frequently of late years consignments of some sorts of skins have been either withdrawn from these sales or bought back by the owners, and offered again in the next sale. This feature was very noticeable in the January (1914) sales just held. I only wish some means could be devised for obtaining reliable statistics. Before 1845 there used to be a duty on all raw fur skins coming into Great Britain, and, as nearly the whole of the production of United States and Canada was shipped to London, the figures thus obtained were of great value. Subsequent to that year, the London sales formed a fair index. But for some years past the practices I have referred to, combined with the fact that many skins of certain kinds are either shipped to other European countries direct, without the intervention of the London sales, or are used by the American and Canadian fur trade without export, have made the London public sale quantities of little use in computing the total numbers produced.

"In the words of Mr. Mills (formerly Editor of the *Fur Trade Review* of New York), who wrote me a long letter on the subject of figures, and whose word I entirely endorse: he said, referring to a certain book on Furs and the Fur Trade: 'I have no patience with literature of that kind. Its errors are perpetuated and magnified through the ages.'

"The Provincial Game Warden of British Columbia writes me that he has succeeded in getting his government to introduce new measures, whereby a knowledge of the value of the fur trade there and the number of skins of each animal taken may be accurately obtained. Perhaps this may lead to useful statistics in the future."—*From Correspondence of Mr. Ernest Poland, 110 Queen Victoria Street, London, Eng., February 10, 1914.*

9

its furs at public auction in London.   The extensive buying of the American dealers in Siberia threatens to entirely nullify the importance of the Russian-Siberian fairs as fur marts.

"England maintains its position as the fur-seal skin dyeing and dressing centre of the world, despite many attempts that have been made to wrest away this supremacy.   The French, especially, were determined competitors and at one time had secured a fair share of the business. One of the leading dyers of Great Britain told me that five years ago the French business amounted to about 25 per cent of the whole, and its growth was a continual cause of alarm to those interested in the industry in England.   The superiority of the English work has been ascribed to various causes, notably to some peculiar and unique property of the water used and to some secret processes and methods of handling. The fact that for many years one man enjoyed a practical monopoly of seal dyeing in England would appear to lend weight to the latter assertion.

Lampson Sales, 1910   "The following table shows the Lampson sales for March, June, and October, 1910.   Prices are given in British pounds, shillings, and pence, the value in American money being approximately $4.86, 24 1-3 cents, and 2 cents, respectively.   The highest and lowest prices are per skin, except where indicated otherwise.

Other Offerings   "There were 476 silver fox skins sold at the March, 1910, auctions, which brought £540 as the highest and £1 as the lowest price.   In June, 64 of these skins were offered, the prices ranging from £230 down to £2, and at the October sales, 167 skins brought prices from £150 to £1.

"At the March Lampson sales, there were also offered 3,315 white hare skins, prices for which ranged from 5½d. to 4d.; 1,311 Persian lamb skins, prices 23s. to 3s.;   307 sea-otter skins, prices £350 to £4; 2 bales and 733 skins of North American rabbit skins, prices 8d. to 3d. per pound; 689 fur sealskins (dry), prices 13s. to 6d.; 2,124 hair seal skins (dry), prices 6s. 9d. to 1s.;   2,410 wombat skins, prices 2s. 11d. to 7d.; and 928 wolverene skins, prices 46s. to 4s.   At the June auctions 237 brown bear skins brought prices varying from 90s. to 9s., and 4,100 marmot skins from 3s. 1d. to 1s. 9d.

"At the December seal auctions, 13,584 Alaska skins were offered in 1910, against 14,350 in 1909, and brought from 240s. to 90s., which was somewhat lower than in the earlier year.   From the Northwest Coast came 12,586 skins, against 13,972 in 1909, the prices averaging a trifle higher in 1910 than the preceding year and ranging from 168s. to 35s.   Prices were 10 per cent lower for South Sea skins, the number sold being 1,060 in 1910, compared with 2,086 in 1909, and the returns being 182s. for the finest quality and 74s. for lower grades. Cape Horn skins numbered 1505 in 1910, compared with 611 in 1909.

"It will be realised that, in the valuation of furs, so much depends on size, condition, colour, age, district, etc., that a mere list of prices is no guide to the fluctuations of the auction-room value of the skins."

Skins	MARCH			JUNE			OCTOBER		
	Number of skins	Highest price	Lowest price	Number of skins	Highest price	Lowest price	Number of skins	Highest price	Lowest price
		s. d.	s. d.		s. d.	s. d.		s. d.	s. d.
Badger	4,830	22 0	6	4,793	19 0	0 3	2,259	19 0	0 3
Bear:									
Black	4,290	155 0	2 0	1,694	135 0	1 3	1,891	110 0	2 0
Brown	515	105 0	5 0	237	90 0	9 0	80	65 0	13 0
Grizzly	81	45 0	13 0	18	42 0	40 0	......		
" Russian	1,519	140 0	13 0	614	95 0	9 0	981	90 0	9 0
White	180	£32	£1	37	£8	£2	164	£16	£1
Beaver	8,768	56 0	10 0	2,353	44 0	7 0	2,719	33 0	8 0
Cat									
Civet	89,512	3 6	0 10	37,893	2 11	1 2	1,096	2 3	1 7
Horse	12,473	2 11	0 4	16,261	3 9	0 5	24,235	1 11	0 2
Wild	12,466	60 0	0 4	15,499	56 0	0 1	4,456	12 0	0 3
Chinchilla:									
Bastard	1,820	700 0a	18 0a	1,825	980 0a	90 0a	2,095	1,000 0a	140 0a
Real	5,294	780 0a	13 0a	2,468	400 0a	60 0a	1,474	800 0a	20 0a
Ermine	105,985	310 0b	13 0b	25,005	400 0b	10 0b	28,560	320 0b	1 0b
Fisher	679	175 0	8 0	412	90 0	2 0	46	90 0	17 0
Fitch	817	5 9	0 3	7,180	6 0	0 7	4,790	1 10	1 5
Fox:									
Blue	1,800	450 0	13 0	109	280 0	50 0	388	210 0	12 0
Cross	1,299	120 0	2 0	208	75 0	3 0	161	84 0	7 0
Gray	13,019	18 0	1 0	10,632	8 0	1 2	2,064	7 9	1 6
Jap	917	2 3	2 0	15,224	18 0	1 0	12,210	8 6	0 9
Red	28,459	80 0	2 9	14,831	70 0	1 2	12,278	62 0	0 9
Red Australian	3,883	10 0	0 3	11,174	10 0	0 4	24,341	11 0	0 1
White	2,697	90 0	10 0	2,561	80 0	0 8	4,221	70 0	3 0
Kangaroo	1,559	2 9	0 2	988	2 3	0 8	3,784	2 6	0 2
Kolinsky	47,172	6 0	1 3	25,710	4 3	0 3	37,934	5 3	0 6
Lynx	301	165 0	8 0	675	140 0	3 0	872	125 0	6 6
Marten	11,345	180 0	1 0	2,847	130 0	6 0	1,993	130 0	9 0
Baum	775	92 0	12 0	829	80 0	1 0	80	42 0	12 0
Japanese	1,167	20 0	5 6	9,373	20 0	3 6	2,247	16 6	6 0
Stone	2,854	28 0	4 6	2,046	32 0	2 0	1,012	22 0	3 6
Mink	82,987	66 0	0 8	23,460	46 0	0 8	12,513	35 0	0 10
Mole	169,618	27 0c	5 0c	324,828	40 0	4 0	308,711	30 0c	5 0c
Musquash	651,164	0 64	0 3½	627,440	0 50	0 2½	478,144	0 42	0 2
Black	14,920	0 58	0 13	14,015	0 50	0 18	12,380	0 41	0 18
Opossum:									
American	302,920	4 8	0 0½	77,302	4 4	0 4½	28,982	4 7	0 6
Australian	452,165	21 0	0 5	293,309	16 0	0 6	606 264	11 0	0 4
Otter	3,868	260 0	2 0	4,992	145 0	3 6	3,600	100 0	2 0
Raccoon	174,225	31 0	0 3	74,256	23 0	0 2	9,382	19 0	1 3
Sable, Russian	6,574	800 0	6 0	1,462	280 0	5 0	1,945	360 0	4 0
Skunk	362,216	27 0	0 3	146,700	21 0	0 2½	14,620	15 6	0 2
Squirrel	124,147	190 0c	17 0c	195,997	210 0c	34 0c	295,894	150 0c	5 0c
Wallaby	66,981	8 6	0 3	86,292	6 0	0 1	183,800	7 6	0 1
Wolf	22,617	65 0	0 3	17,871	50 0	0 6	3,728	80 0	0 5

aPer dozen. bPer "timber," or 40 skins. cPer 100.

PRICES OF SILVER FOX SKINS

Annual Production Emil Brass, a German commercial agent, who, for thirty-five years, has been engaged in collecting statistics of the fur trade, states that the average number of fox skins produced annually in the period from 1907 to 1909, was 2,042,300. The following figures are based on his estimates:

COMMON RED FOX
(*Vulpes vulpes*)

Red skins.................1,515,000
Cross skins...................18,000
Silver skins..................4,300

POLAR FOX   ⎫ White skins................105,000
  (*Vulpes lagopus*) ⎬ Blue   " 11,000
KIT-FOX   ⎪ 64,000
  (*Vulpes velox*)
GRAY FOX   ⎭
  (*Urocyon cinebrensargentatus*) 50,000

The Japan fox or Raccoon dog, and a few thousand skins of two South American species make up the balance.

Brass estimates the world's yearly production of the various species of foxes as follows:

FOX SKINS PRODUCED ANNUALLY

Continent	COMMON RED FOX			Kit-Fox	Gray Fox	POLAR FOX	
	Red	Cross	Silver			White	Blue
Europe ...	200,000	15,000	4,000	6,000	50,000	30,000	6,000
America ..	775,000					5,000	1,000
Asia	160,000	3,000	300	60,000		70,000	4,000
Australia..	30,000						

Geographical Classification The quotations published by fur-buyers make a geographical classification of furs, thus:

RED FOX No. 1, LARGE:*
Alaska, Northern and Western Canada....................... $12.00
Newfoundland and Labrador................................. 8.50
Minnesota, Wisconsin, Dakota, Missouri, Michigan.............. 7.50
Eastern Canada, Michigan, New York, and Northeastern states... 6.00
Pennsylvania, New Jersey, Ohio, Indiana, and Illinois.......... 5.00
Central and Southern states. 3.50

RED FOX No. 1, LARGE:†
Eastern Canada, Nova Scotia, Labrador.. .... 9.00
Maine, Vermont, Massachusetts, Ontario....................... 8.00
Northern New York, northern Michigan, Connecticut........... 7.00
Northern Pennsylvania, central New York, central Michigan.... 6.00
Central Pennsylvania, northern Ohio, W. Virginia, New York.... 5.00
Central Ohio, northern Indiana, Illinois...................... 4.75
South Pennsylvania, Delaware, Virginia, North Carolina, southern
    Ohio, northern Kentucky.............................. 4.50
Southern and Southwestern states........................... 4.25

The geographical classification reveals the fact that, in North America, the higher the altitude, or the lower the temperature, the heavier the pelt. Mink descends steadily in value from Labrador to Florida, Eastern Canada large No. 1 mink being quoted at $6.00 in March, 1914, and Florida at $4.00. A heavy pelt, if properly coloured, is usually the most valuable. Canada, therefore, produces the best fur in the New World as Russia does in the Old. It is quite possible, also, that the pelts

*Fur News Magazine, November, 1912.
†Fur Trade Review, December, 1912.

A COLLECTION OF 34 WILD SILVER-FOX SKINS, WOF   PWARDS OF $21,000

of raccoon, opossum, skunk and other animals not now found in northern Canada could be improved by domestication in colder regions. Ranch-bred animals properly kept will develop as heavy pelts as wild specimens, and they can always be killed when prime.

Average Prices of Silver Fox Skins The average price for all silver fox skins sold in London, including the wild stock and ranch stock, are as follows:

Year	Average Price
1905	$146.59
1906	166.93
1907	157.11
1908	168.91
1909	244.12
1910	414.37
1911	290.01

The high average price obtained for silver fox skins in 1910 is accounted for by the better market. More than one half of the skins selling for $500.00 or more were from Prince Edward Island ranches.

At the present time, the average price of wild silver fox skins in London is about $200.00 and, for ranch foxes such as are found with the best ranchers, $1,200.00.

Wild silver fox are not always prime and they are frequently shot, chewed, mangled and poorly dressed, while ranched foxes are usually killed when their fur is in primest condition. The highest price ever paid at the London sales for a silver fox skin was $2,900.00 It is said that this skin was sold by a Paris firm which had bought it at a previous sale for $1,950.00, and that it was from a ranched fox from Prince Edward Island.

The next highest price was $2,700.00, and a half dozen have sold for $2,500.00 or more, all being from Prince Edward Island ranches. A rather remarkable sale was made in March, 1912, when a pelt from a fox that died in James Rayner's ranch at Kildare, P.E.I., on October 12, 1911, brought the highest price, $2,050.00, although the skin would not have been fully prime before December.

Prices of P.E.I. Skins It is a difficult matter to obtain authentic records of sales of silver fox skins from Prince Edward Island; farmers, as a rule, do not give careful attention to correspondence and records. Many reports are alleged to have been lost and those examined gave evidence of having been filed in an inside coat pocket for a considerable period. Documentary proof of sales made in London was also difficult to obtain. Below are reproduced the sales reports of Charles Dalton and J. S. Gordon for the year 1910:

C. M. LAMPSON & Co.

64 Queen Street,
London, E.C., 7th April, 1910

Account sale of FURS received on consignment
for account of C. DALTON, Esq., Tignish, Prince Edward Island

C. D.	Invoice Quantity	Lot	Skins			£	s.	d.
		2105	. 1	Fox, Silver		310		
		2106	1			530		
Mail		2107	1			210		
5 pcls.		2110	1			160		
2 "		2120	1			46		
5 "		2149	1			280		
2 "		2150	1			540		
		2151	1			310		
		2152	2		220	440		
		2153	1			430		
		2166	2		125	250		
		2194	1			340		
		2195	1			340		
		2196	1			200		
		2197	1			370		
		2200	1			165		
		2230	1			500		
		2231	1			270		
		2232	1			200		
		2233	1			280		
		2234	1			290		
		2242	2		210	420		

C. M. LAMPSON & Co.

64 Queen Street,
London, E.C., 7th April, 1910

Account sale of FURS received on consignment
for account of J. S. GORDON, ESQ., Alberton, Prince Edward Island
Prompt 7th April, 1910

J.S.G.	Invoice Quantity	Lot	Skins			£	s.	d.
per mail 1 pcl. 1 "	2	2109 2156 —	1 1 — 2	Fox, Silver		490 180		

A discount of 2½ per cent off these prices is given and the selling commission of 6 per cent and the carriage and insurance charges bring the total cost of marketing furs in London up to about 9 per cent of the selling price.

Statistics for 1908 and 1909 are wholly lacking, the records being reported lost. Satisfactory proof was furnished that the following sales were made, although possibly not more than one-half the total quantity of skins sold in the period 1905-1912 are represented:

SALES OF P. E. I. SILVER FOX SKINS, 1905-1912

Year	No. of Skins	Total Value	Average Value
1905	11	$ 5,937.33	$ 539.76
1906	8	9,733.33	1,216.67
1907	28	22,892.80	817.60
1910	27	36,748.20	1,361.05
1911	10	10,852.67	1,085.27
1912	1	1,995 33	1,995.33
Total	85	$88,159.66	

The average for the last seven years would probably be slightly lower if reports of all sales were available. On the other hand, the price has advanced since 1905, most noticeably so in 1910 and in 1912.

On account of the demand for breeding animals, but few skins have been sold since 1910, and no ranches other than those on Prince Edward Island have furnished proofs of the prices obtained for them.

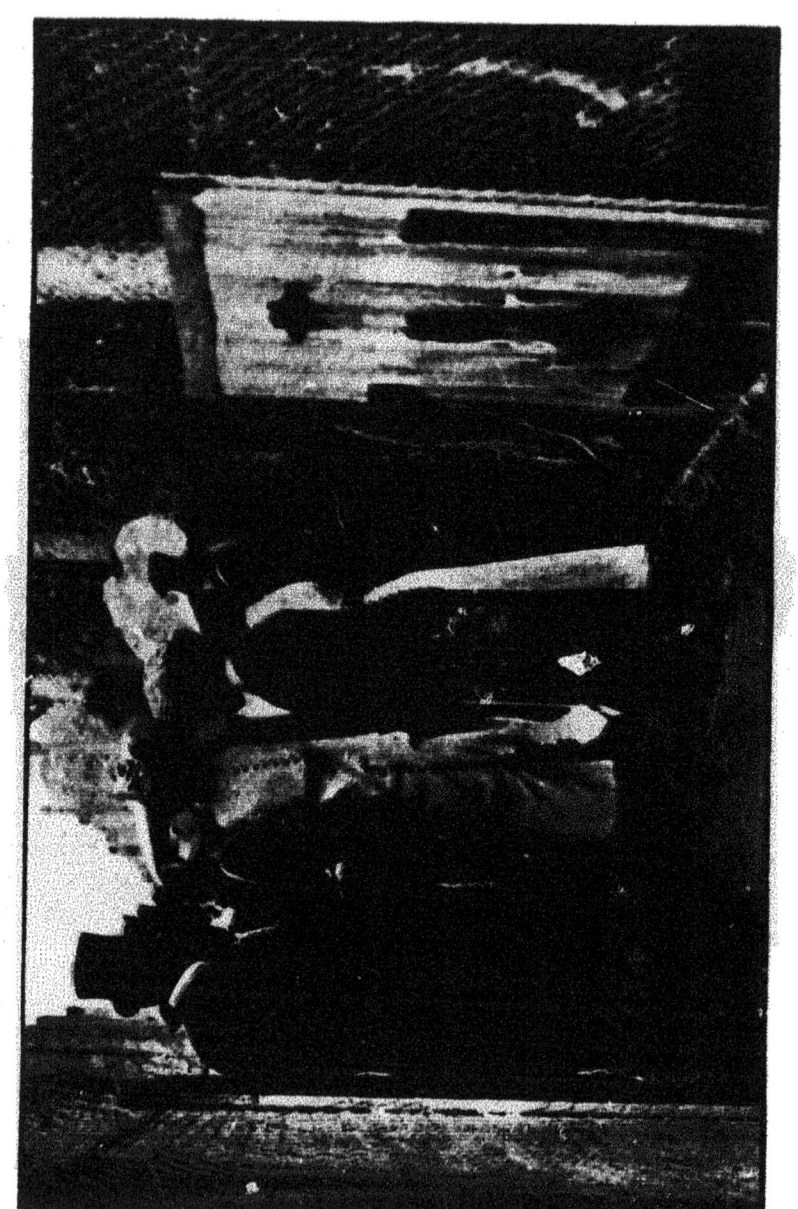

T. R. H. Duke of Connaught and Princess Patricia in Saint Patrick Ranch

Appendix I

Value of Wild Animals[*]

BY

C. D. RICHARDSON, WEST BROOKFIELD, MASS.

T'OSE beautiful wooded dells should be the haunts of the wild creatures, as when first discovered by the white man. Too long they, with their wild life, have been given over to the pot hunter and to him who would despoil them of their true charm. There is a growing recognition that the strain of modern life can be best endured by often fleeing to the wilds, which calls at times to all, but louder to some than others.

All over this great country of ours there are vast stretches of waste land, with their variety of woods, swamps, and hillside, which yield but little profit to the owner. Let us look a little into the future. Suppose we make something of this land, fence it in, reforest it, and stock it with game. It will require little care and the average farmer may realise from it more than he now does from his tilled acres. The fence problem is practically solved in the use of woven wire, and a large tract may be enclosed at a comparatively small expense.

The food problem, too, is a simple one, as grouse, pheasants, quail, etc., subsist almost wholly upon insects which, if unchecked, would destroy all vegetation, on noxious seeds, and on buds of unimportant trees, while the larger game animals, especially those of the deer family, feed almost wholly on twigs and leaves of vegetation which is of no real value, if not a menace to the farmer. In fact, the finest grazing ground for such animals is an old brush pasture in which the ordinary domestic animals would starve, but which furnishes to the wild creatures their most natural food.

The question of vermin—the fox, weasels, skunk, cat, etc., the natural enemies of the bird—must be considered and a systematic warfare waged against them. An English moor of from 100 to 500 acres often rents for £300 ($1,500) a season, just for the shooting privileges of the grouse alone. When the vermin is disposed of, the increase in bird life on such a tract is simply enormous.

There is a growing demand, at increasingly high prices, for live game to supply zoological parks, and for game as food. The revenue

[*]From American Breeders' Association Annual Report, 1911.

which may be derived from shooting privileges and from camping parties who would steal away to enjoy a season with nature, in all her fullness, may not be inconsiderable.

The national parks, whose value to the country cannot be over-estimated, are too far away for the average citizen to enjoy, but he may have that which will give much pleasure and profit nearer home. A tract of waste land of from 100 to 1,000 acres may be obtained in almost any section of the country, and especially in the hilly and mountainous regions, at a price within the reach of every alert farmer. The cost of fencing need not exceed $1 a rod for an 8-foot fence, and the game for stocking—birds and small game will rapidly multiply under protection—can be procured at a price no greater than that paid for domestic animals.

One of the secrets of the success of the English race is in the fact that they as a people have emphasized out-of-door life. The rugged physique and robust health of the average Englishman are due to the fact that he is able to dismiss all care and enjoy a day with rod and gun. His large landed estates, together with the climatic conditions, offer favourable opportunities for all out-door sports. While we believe that large landed estates are a menace to the best interests of any people, yet, with our large acreage of waste land and democratic ideals, there is no possible danger that we shall ever suffer by the establishment of game preserves in this country. These game preserves may not only be centres from which the surrounding covers will be stocked, but they may be object lessons in forestry, of which this country stands in vital need, to say nothing of making rural life more beautiful and attractive.

Appendix II

Experience in Raising Virginia Deer*

BY

C. H. ROSEBERRY, STELLA, MO.

I KNOW of no other branch of the live-stock industry that returns as great a profit in proportion to the time, labour and capital invested as that of deer raising.

My experience is limited to the Virginia white tailed deer (*Cariacus virginianus*) and covers a period of 19 years. Doubtless, the raising of elk or wapiti would be equally profitable—perhaps more so where raised for venison, owing to the greater size.

A tract of 10, 20, or 40 acres of rough brush land, enclosed with a 6½ or 7-feet woven wire fence, with provision for a constant supply of water, either natural or artificial, is the chief requisite. It is better if there be dense thickets of underbrush, coarse weeds, and trees of pin oak, white oak, pig hickory, chestnut, etc. The twigs, leaves, and mast of these afford an abundance of natural food as well as shelter and seclusion.

It is also desirable to have a plat of three or four acres of tillable land on which to sow rye or wheat for winter pasture.

As the underbrush is gradually killed out, as it will be as the herd increases in numbers, unless the range is quite extensive, white clover and orchard grass may be sown for summer forage.

In the latitude of southwestern Missouri, feeding is not necessary between April 1 and November 1. For the rest of the year a stack of cowpea or clover hay to which the deer have free access, supplemented by a light ration of corn and bran or other mill feed in severe weather, is sufficient.

Do not feed too heavily of shelled corn. If gorged with it, the results are often fatal.

If it is desired to raise venison it is, of course, not necessary that the fawns be accustomed to handling while young in order to tame them. But if raised for sale as breeding stock, requiring that they be handled and shipped alive, it is necessary to take the fawns from the does when they are ten days old and raise them by hand on cow's milk.

This, of course, involves a great deal more trouble and expense than to let the fawn run with the doe; hence the price received for breeding stock is proportionately greater than that received for the venison carcass. For example, a yearling dressed for market may weigh 60 pounds net, and could be profitably sold for 25 cents a pound, or $15; whereas

*From the American Breeders' Association Report, 1909.

the same raised by hand would be worth at least $30 for a buck, or $45 for a doe.

My method of raising by hand is as follows: A tract of 3 or 4 acres, free of underbrush, in which the fawns might hide, is fenced off from the main park. Early in May the does that are to drop fawns are confined in this small lot.

During the fawning time the lot is carefully searched at intervals of two or three days, and when a fawn a day or two old is found it is at once tagged by tying about its neck a strip of cloth—red if it is a buck or white if it is a doe—and allowed to remain with the doe ten days, when it is taken from the park and confined in a 5 ft. by 10 ft. cage made of one-inch poultry netting, lined inside with cloth and bedded with clean straw. A 5 by 10 cage will accommodate 12 fawns. The bedding must be kept dry and frequently changed for cleanliness. The cloth lining is necessary to prevent injury. The youngster is exceedingly wild at first and dashes himself against the sides of the cage in frantic efforts to escape.

If allowed to remain longer than ten days with the doe, it i ften impossible to capture the fawn except by a chase or by strategy. The latter consists in biding your time until the fawn found lying beside a log, stump, or clump of bushes, when it is very ealthily approached from the leeward to within springing distance and pounced upon before it can get to its feet. When other methods of capture fail, it may be run into a fish net in which it will become entangled.

The fawns remain in the cage for two weeks, during which time they learn to drink fresh milk from a bottle and become quite tame. They are then allowed the freedom of an enclosure 20 by 100 feet for two weeks longer, when they are given a still wider range. But they must not be returned to the park, else they will become wild again.

The adult Virginia buck, if raised by hand, often becomes vicious, especially during the rutting season, and should not be trusted until rendered comparatively harmless either by sawing off his antlers an inch above the burr or by bolting a 1 by 4 hardwood board 3 feet long across the tips of his antlers. The wild bucks never lose their fear of man sufficiently to attack him

I would not advise beginners with small means to go into the business of deer raising too heavily at first. It is better to begin on a small scale, say 10 acres, and a herd of vigorous stock and let the business increase along with the increase of knowledge gained by experience.

Thousands of acres of rough land unsuited for cultivation that now bring its owner no returns for his investments may, by converting it into small deer farms, be made to yield the owners a handsome profit, as well as much plea ure.

Appendix III

Selected Articles from the Annual Report of the American
Breeders' Association, 1908*

OBJECTS OF BREEDING WILD MAMMALS

EXPERIMENTS in breeding wild mammals need not necessarily be for their domestication. They may be bred in inclosures giving sufficient range and a habitat as nearly natural as circumstances will permit and the problem of ultimate domestication left for future determination. The chief objects to be sought by experiments in breeding wild animals are: (1) Preserving species; (2) Use in agriculture or transportation; (3) Use for hides and fur; (4) Use as food.

Perpetuating Species.—Extinction of species is a process of nature, and, from an economic point of view, is not necessarily a misfortune to the world. But when the rapacity of man is turned against a useful species until it is threatened with extermination, there is good reason for the intervention of organizations of men for its preservation. The imminence of extinction for the American bison, the African elephant, the eland, the walrus, the sea otter, and other species is not imaginary. Within recent times a considerable number of birds have been lost to the world. Of mammals, the quagga and the blaaubok (*Hippotragus leucophæus*), the latter a small relative of the roan antelope, have been exterminated from the South African fauna. Foresight might have preserved them; and foresight accompanied by governmental intervention will be needed to prevent the loss of many of the large game mammals of the world. The preservation of the best of them is a sufficient reason for advocating the expenditure of money in experiments in breeding them.

---

*The Committee on Breeding Wild Mammals of the American Breeders' Association is composed of the following members:—

Dr. E. Lantz, Washington, D.C., Chairman.

M. M. Boyd, Bobcaygeon, Ont.   W. M. Irwin, Wahington, D.C.
R. H. Harris, Clarksville, Tex.   C. J. Jones, Topeka, Kan.
Emory, E. Hoge, Baltimore, Md.   C. D. Richardson, Worcester, Mass.

Object: To investigate and report on the methods and technique of improving wild mammals; and to devise and suggest methods and plans of introducing, producing and improving such wild animals as may be useful for the production of food, skins, etc., or as aids to agriculture.

Agriculture and Transportation.—Our second object in breeding wild animals seems to be less important. The horse will never be surpassed in general usefulness and the other animals used in agriculture and transportation are excellent in their places. Two animals, however, both of the African fauna, are good subjects for experiments in breeding and domestication for these uses—the zebra and the elephant. The zebra is the only animal of its kind that is apparently immune to the fatal effects of being bitten by the tsetse fly. The zebra is easily domesticated, but seems to lack endurance. If it can be crossed with the horse so as to produce a hardy hybrid also immune to the tsetse fly, the problem of African transport would be partly solved. The domestication of the zebra and its improvements by judicious breeding are projects that are well worth the expenditure of money upon them. The African elephants have been domesticated and trained like their Asiatic relatives and have proved to be equally docile under careful management. There is little doubt that they could be made equally useful.

Breeding for Fur.—Investigation of the possibility of breeding fur-bearing animals profitably is especially desirable, in view of the failing supply of our better furs. As another committee has reported upon this subject, we do not take it up.

Breeding for Food.—From an economic standpoint we regard this as an important reason for attempting to breed wild mammals. Game of all kind is becoming scarcer from year to year, and sportsmen go farther and farther in search of it. Even after it is found, the laws upon the subject of sale and export of game often prevent the hunter from carrying to his home or disposing of game that has been lawfully killed. In our zeal to protect our vanishing game mammals and birds, we have in some cases, carelessly passed laws which, if not modified, will prevent the one movement that would do more for game preserving than any other agency that can be contrived. We refer to game propagation carried on not by the State alone, but by private enterprise as well.

EXOTIC SPECIES RECOMMENDED FOR BREEDING UNDER DOMESTICATION

The breeding of exotic species of the deer family is a promising field for experiment. The red deer and fallow deer of Europe have been successfully acclimatized in many parts of the world. It has been shown that the small Chinese water deer and the Indian muntjac are both suited to European deer parks and no doubt both would thrive in America. The water deer are noted for their fecundity, the female producing three or four young at a time. The muntjacs usually produce twins.

The flesh of both is said to be excellent. These small deer are less than 20 inches tall at the withers and, if domesticated in our Southern States, would furnish farmers a much needed form of meat which could be provided fresh every day or two as needed. Aside from fowls, most of our domestic animals are too large for immediate consumption by the ordinary farmer's family; and there is a distinct demand for a food animal of smaller size than the sheep for farm use. Some of the smaller African antelopes, as the red duiker, might perhaps be made to supply the demand.

In Africa there are nearly a hundred species of the antelope family, many of them hardy and some of them producing the best of venison. More than a dozen species would be promising subjects for experiments in acclimatizing and breeding in America. Some of them for instance, as the gazelle, undoubtedly would be found especially adapted for the arid range country of the Southwest and might be used to restock parts of the country from which the American antelope has disappeared.

The eland is the largest of the antelope family and is threatened with extermination in South Africa. The average weight of this animal is from 800 to 1,100 pounds and old males sometimes attain 1,400 to 1,500 pounds. The eland has often been recommended for experiments in domestication. It was first introduced into Holland in 1783 by the Prince of Orange. It was acclimatized in England by the Earl of Derby in 1842 and was bred successfully in his parks. At l' '-·'· bi·· herd passed into the possession of the London Zoological Socie _ _ ·i, and continued to increase in numbers for many years. In 1879, th·· Duke of Bedford had a fine herd of 14 elands in his park at Woburn Abbey. The flesh of the eland is highly eulogized by Harris, the African traveller, in these words: "Both in grain and colour it resembles beef, but it is far better tasted and more delicate, possessing a pure game flavour and exhibiting the most tempting looking layers of fat and lean, the surprising quantity of the former ingredient with which it is interlarded, exceeding that of any other game quadruped with which I am acquainted. The venison fairly melts in the mouth, and as for the brisket, that is absolutely a cut for a monarch."

Besides the eland, the sambar, the nilgai, and other foreign deer have given promising results when bred in enclosures. All told, there are perhaps 150 species of exotic *ungulata* useful for food, that might become promising subjects for experiments in acclimatizing and breeding in the United States. The cost of introducing and caring for ten or more of each species until acclimated would be small when compared with the important results that would follow success with even a very few species.

For those who would engage in growing deer for profit, however, we can recommend in preference to exotic species our native elk, or wapiti, and the Virginia deer. They need no acclimatizing and are, without question, adapted for propagation in this country.

BREEDING OF THE WAPITI OR AMERICAN ELK

Although our native wapiti is less prolific than the Virginia deer, and some other species that have been bred in parks, it makes up for this circumstance in hardiness and ease of management. It has been successfully acclimatized in England and on the Continent, where it has been crossed with both the Altai wapiti of Asia and the red deer of Europe. Both crosses with the American species have improved the stock in size and general stamina.

The wapiti has been successfully bred in many sections of the United States and affords one of the best subjects for experiments in breeding for profit. While the old males are apt to become dangerously vicious during the rutting season, making them somewhat undesirable for open parks, they are ordinarily docile and have often been trained to harness and driven in public. Under careful scientific management with, possibly, careful dehorning, the elk would in a very few generations develop into a gentle race of a true domesticity.

Judge John D. Caton, of Illinois, who during his lifetime contributed much to our knowledge of the deer family and of their susceptibility to domestication, was apparently unfortunate in having enclosures poorly adapted to deer. He believed that they contained some kind of vegetable food that was harmful to most of the species; but his herd of elk was always healthy. Writing in 1880, Judge Caton said:

"My elk continue to do well and are so prolific that I have had repeatedly to reduce their numbers and would be glad now to dispose of at least thirty. I have on an average about one old buck a year killed in battle and sometimes another by some casualty, but all appear healthy. Mine grow very large and of all the *cervidæ* they seem best adapted to domestication."

Your committee has recent reports from a number of breeders of elk, all of whom seem to confirm the opinion advanced by Judge Caton as to the success of breeding the elk in preserves.

Joshua Hill, of Pontiac, Mich., has a preserve of 300 acres in which he has been breeding elk and buffalo. Although not breeding animals for commercial purposes, he is of the opinion that elk, on account of their superior hardiness, could be more profitably handled than deer. He has heard of elk meat bringing from 50 cents a pound upwards, and thinks that the business of growing animals for market might be made to win if properly pushed.

Isaac Bonine, of Niles, Mich., breeds both elk and Virginia deer, and has had thirty years' experience. He prefers elk because they require less care than deer. Elk winter well on hay and corn fodder with a small amount of grain and thrive in summer on blue-grass pasture. While deer do reasonably well on the same food, they thrive better when fed vegetables and in that latitude require some sort of winter shelter. An elk requires no shelter. While Mr. Bonine has doubts as to the profit of growing deer and elk for the venison, he thinks that breeding them for park purposes can be made very remunerative. He has a number of elk for sale.

G. W. Russ, Eureka Springs, has a herd of 34 elk. They have abundant range in the Ozarks on rough lands covered with hardwood forest and abundant underbrush. He reports that the animals improve the forest by cleaning out part of the thicket. Fully 90 per cent of the females produce healthy young, and Mr. Russ thinks he could make the business of growing elk for market profitable, if the law would permit him to kill and export domesticated elk. He has an offer of 40 cents a pound for the dressed carcasses in St. Louis. He thinks that large areas now unutilized in the Alleghanies and Ozarks might be economically adapted to produce venison for sale and he regards the elk as especially suited for forest grazing. They should have about twice as much range as the same number of cattle.

J. W. Gilbert, of Friend, Neb., has been raising deer and elk for seventeen years. He has at present 30 deer and 16 elk on prairie pasture. He regards elk as the more profitable and has never had a barren cow elk.

T. J. Wilson of Lewisburg, Ohio, began raising deer and elk a few years ago, with three head of each at the start. He has not succeeded so well with deer as with elk. Deer require a higher fence and more care. Elk do well on hay, corn fodder and rough feed, and, if they escape from an enclosure, may be driven back like cattle. He originally paid $165 for two adult elk and a fawn. He has sold $300 worth of stock and has now a herd of 12, worth $1,000.

Your committee has the names and addresses of about a dozen other successful breeders of the American elk, but the time at our disposal did not permit our obtaining particulars of their experience.

BREEDING THE VIRGINIA DEER

Testimony as to the hardiness of the Virginia deer and the profits of breeding them is not so unanimous as it is concerning the wapiti; but the general opinion is that with suitable range, plenty of good water, and reasonable care in winter, the business of growing the animals for

10

stocking parks and for venison may be made as profitable as that of any other live-stock industry, and that untillable land may be utilized as preserves for the animals.

Mr. R. H. Harris, a member of this committee, who resides at Clarksville Texas, was requested to contribute his views upon the raising of deer as an industry. He writes as follows:

"Having been actively engaged in this business for some years, I feel qualified to speak on the subject with clearness and conviction. I find that the Virginia deer is adapted to almost every section of the United States. It fawns in May or June of each year, each doe usually bringing two young. The young mature rapidly. Virginia deer are the most beautiful, graceful and healthful animals known. No other meat is equal to venison as a diet for the sick, it being easily digested and agreeing with the most delicate stomachs. The demand for both venison and skins is unlimited. The flesh, being in wide demand in cities, especially in restaurants and cafés, is very high-priced.

"These deer are easily tamed; the wildest fawns, if taken from the herd when young, will, in a few hours, become as gentle as a pet dog. I have, for several years, been raising them in large numbers. They run at will in woodlands and fields, are never handled, but fed occasionally, and are as gentle as a herd of common cattle. They are easily and cheaply raised and seldom, if ever, die from natural causes. After years of practical experience, I unhesitatingly state that the raising of deer is in profitableness second only to the raising of cattle.

"The cost of feeding deer averages about one-half cent each per day. They feed on all kinds of vegetables, buds, and leaves of trees, growing wheat, clover, peas, barley, oats, etc, etc. Cotton seed is also a very cheap and satisfactory food for them. They also eat corn, bran, fruits and, in fact, anything that man or beast will eat, except dry hay. They live from twenty to twenty-five years. They are easily confined by a woven wire or barbed wire fence 6½ feet in height.

"I strongly urge this Association to appeal to our government to protect and encourage the industry of deer raising, believing it to be one of the most profitable and practicable industries now in prospect for our people. It is unnecessary to urge the need of quick and energetic action, for this noble animal is fast disappearing and is without adequate protection. Its extinction would eliminate from our continent what ought to be an industry equal in value to the raising of cattle, hogs, or sheep; and I would urge upon this Association the importance of securing legislation that will permit the marketing of domesticated venison at all seasons of the year.................."

In conclusion your committee would again urge upon this Association such action by resolution as will give emphasis to our desire that

State legislatures should so modify their laws as to permit the marketing, under needed regulations, of venison or live deer reared in preserves stocked and maintained at private expense.

REPORT OF THE COMMITTEE OF THE AMERICAN BREEDERS' ASSOCIATION ON BREEDING FUR-BEARING ANIMALS[*]

WHAT HAS BEEN DONE

The possibility of breeding many species for their fur has not been overlooked and spasmodic efforts along this line have been made in various parts of the country for generations. Almost every fur-bearing species has been the subject of experimentation. Fox and skunk farming has attracted most attention, but mink, marten, otter, beaver, and muskrat have come in for a fair share. The field has proved most alluring, as with pencil and paper any sanguine person can, in a few minutes, figure out a large fortune in fur at the market price and well-known normal rate of increase of a given species of mammal. Again and again, it has taken years of work and the expenditure of thousands of dollars to prove that important factors have been omitted in the computations. One well-organized company in Pennsylvania sank $25,000 in three years, only to prove that skunks would eat their young when in close confinement. Skunk farming, however, has, in some cases, proved a partial success, but "Why raise one-dollar skunks instead of thirty-dollar marten?" is a question asked by Mr. E. T. Seton, a member of the present committee.

The nearest approach to success in fur culture has been on the native range of species, where, owing to favourable conditions, protection could be afforded and the animals allowed to multiply until a profitable yield of fur was secured. This method has been especially applied to blue foxes, beavers, and muskrats, and with considerable success. It merits every possible encouragement; but, in most cases, there has been little attempt at domestication and nothing gained by way of permanent control of breeds of valuable fur-bearers. In fact, there seems to have been no systematic attempt to develop a domestic breed of fur-bearing animals. Most of the experiments have been in raising wild animals for fur, and these have usually ceased while the animals were still wild. The fur crop has been expected at once and has usually been the sole object of the experiment...................

[*] *Annual Report*, 1898. The objects of this committee are: To investigate and report on possibilities, methods and technique of breeding fur animals; and to encourage experiments in the production and breeding of fur animals.

PROMISING SPECIES

In spite of numerous failures there is no reason to doubt the entire practicability of successfully breeding in captivity almost any species of fur-bearing mammal. In most cases it will take considerable time to bring about the complete domestication and adaption desirable; but the object is of ample importance to warrant the necessary expenditure of time and money. It is not necessary nor advisable to start on a large scale, as the requirements of each species must be studied and worked out slowly.

In selecting species for breeding purposes the first important consideration should be to secure a permanently valuable fur. The fancy prices paid for sea otter and black and silver foxes, reaching $1,000 and even $2,000 for some choice skins, are based, in part, on the rarity of these animals, and would not be maintained if a large supply became available. Still, these skins will doubtless always be among the most valuable. Owing to their pelagic habits, however, the sea otter and fur seal need not be considered in the present connection.

The fur of each species varies greatly in colour, quality, and value in different parts of its range. The choicest natural strains should, if possible, be selected to start with; but these can doubtless be bred into later if a domestic breed be established.

The North American species promising most valuable results in fur culture are as follows, in sequence of greater permanent fur value: (1) black and silver foxes; (2) blue or Arctic fox; (3) otter; (4) marten, or American sable; (5) beaver; (6) mink; (7) fisher. Cheaper kinds of fur, such as skunk, muskrat, raccoon and opossum, may, under special conditions, yield paying returns, but need not be considered at present. Many exotic mammals are worthy of consideration, but in general they do not offer any advantages over our native species and have the disadvantage of not being acclimated.

BLACK AND SILVER FOXES

The black and the silver foxes are merely melanistic and partially melanistic individuals of the red fox. Both owe their value, in part, to their rarity; but it will be long before artificial production will seriously affect the price. In habits and requirements they are identical with the red fox, of which they are in some cases the offspring. Still, either the black or silver, if mated together, usually breed true. The cross fox is merely a dark form of the red with considerably more valuable fur. By selecting the darkest individuals to breed from and continuing the selection, an increasingly valuable strain doubtless could be obtained.

Foxes taken when young and carefully raised in captivity become tame and usually breed if properly paired. The red fox, as well as the Arctic or blue fox is evidently strictly monogamous . . . .

BLUE OR ARCTIC FOXES

Many of the islands in Alaska have been leased or taken possession of for fox farming. Some of these islands were already inhabited by blue foxes and other. were stocked with them, mainly from St. George island, where the best fur was found.

As shown by the report of the Harriman Alaska Expedition, Vol. II., p. 357, 1901, and by a more recent account in Forest and Stream for July 26, 1906, by T. E. Hofer, these foxes are thi ring and yielding considerable fur. On some islands they secure their own food and are merely guarded and trapped by those in charge. On most of the islands, however, they are fed for part or all the year, but their wild life has undergone little or no change. They appear to be naturally rather tame and with proper care could doubtless be thoroughly domesticated.

They breed when a year old, pair for breeding and have usually four to eight young at a litter. Prime skins are quoted at $20 to $25.

OTTER

Few wild animals thrive better in close confinement than otter. Given a small pen with a pool of water they seem comparatively contented and happy. They become very tame and are playful and intelligent. There are many accounts of their being so domesticated as to follow their master, come at his call and even catch fish and bring them out of the water for him. They are not easily trapped, and are quite able to hold their own against the encroachment of civilisation. They probably are as common to-day near the District of Columbia as they are over most of their range, which reaches from Florida to Alaska. They can be readily enclosed by a simple wire-mesh fence taking in a section of a stream. They do not climb or burrow to any extent. Their favourite food is fish and crustacea, and suitable places could be selected where these could be procured in abundance.

Prime otter skins from Eastern Canada, where the fur is at its best, are quoted in the January, 1908, Fur Trade Review at $15 to $20.

BEAVER

In spite of more than three hundred years of persistent trapping a

few beaver remain scattered here and there over a large part of the
United States and Canada, probably enough, could they be adequately
protected, to restock most of the streams. In many sections they are
protected locally and are becoming abundant again.

If unmolested for a few years, they lose their fear of man, work
on their dams and houses in the day time and become comparatively
tame. With such an animal, further domestication seems unnecessary.
Given a suitable pond or stream they find abundance of food and are
able to care for themselves in every way. They can be fenced in as
readily as a flock of sheep and their enemies, except man, can be fenced
out. Thousands of miles of forest, marsh and stream, fit for no other
purpose are lying idle and could be used to advantage as beaver farms.

Prime beaver skins from the northern United States and Canada
are quoted in the January, 1908, Fur Trade Review at $5 to $8.

By selecting breeding stock from the region where the fur is the
best and keeping only the choice individuals for breeding purposes, it
would doubtless be possible to steadily improve the standard and value
of the beaver fur.

MARTEN

The marten or American sable is a forest animal of the Boreal
zone. It comes into the United States along the Northern border and
extends south in mountainous sections as far as New York, New Mexico, and central California. It is a beautiful, soft-furred little animal
the size of a mink, but of much brighter appearance. It generally
inhabits coniferous forests, is an expert climber, but avoids the water.
Its food is mainly squirrels, rabbits, mice, birds, and such small game.
In the wild state it has the savage disposition of its family, but in
captivity is quiet and gentle.

The most valuable marten skins come from Labrador and eastern
Canada and are variously quoted at $20 to $40.

MINK

The mink is one of the most widely distributed fur-bearers of
North America and one of the few species able to hold its own against
persistent trapping. It is almost as common to-day in the thickly settled sections of the country as in the most remote wilderness. A half-
hour's run on a bicycle to the creeks in the suburbs of Washington will
enable one to find mink tracks.

Wild mink when taken young become perfectly tame and are gentle
and affectionate pets. They breed readily in captivity, are hardy,
easily enclosed and seem not to worry over confinement. They are

fond of the water, are export swimmers and divers and get much of their food from streams and lakes in the form of fish, frogs, and crustacea. They also climb trees and are at home in the forest.

There are numerous instances on record of "mink farms," or "minkeries," that have proved successful, but the low price of mink fur for many years has discouraged the industry. A few years ago mink skins sold at $1 to $2, but they are now quoted at $5 to $8. As other choice furs decrease in abundance there seems every probability that mink fur will hereafter increase rather than decrease in value.

With no other species is success in fur raising so simple and well tested. The value of mink fur varies greatly with different parts of the country, being least in the southern sections and greatest in the northeastern States and eastern Canada.

RULES FOR HANDLING FUR ANIMALS

A few general rules apply equally well to all species.

At first the animals should not be taken away from their native climatic conditions, at least not from their natural life zone. As a general rule the colder the climate the better the fur, and healthier the animals. This does not mean that all the fur raising should be in the far north. Mountain areas, extending south even into many of the Southern states, offer unusual advantages in the close proximity of sections with warm and cold climates.

A thorough knowledge of the native food and breeding habits of a species should be made the basis of care in captivity. This is of the greatest importance at the start, though later on the animals may be able to adapt themselves to greatly modified conditions.

Sufficient room is necessary for the animals to keep themselves clean and obtain exercise and healthy occupation. Quiet and freedom from excitement and nervous strain are essential. Also constant familiarity and association with one or more suitable keepers.

CONCLUSION

The committee believe (1) That, any experiments to be of value must be continuous for sufficient length of time to establish permanent and improved breeds of fur-bearing animals; (2) That, under proper management such experiments should result in developing an industry of great practical value to the people of North America; (3) That, to insure success those in charge of the experiments must be thoroughly familiar with the habits of wild animals, and the keepers, or those in daily intercourse with the animals, must have the rare quality of sympathetic understanding of animal natures.

Appendix IV

Reindeer Progress in Alaska*

BY

LILLIAN E. ZEH

THE herding and breeding of domesticated reindeer, introduced as an experiment a number of years ago with animals imported from Siberia by the Government, has now become the most prominent feature of the industrial education of the Eskimo and the main activity of many native villages of arctic Alaska. The progress in civilization that has been made by lifting up the natives formerly living as savages, and eking out a precarious existence by hunting with no other domestic animal than the dog, to the estate of civilized, self-supporting herdsmen, as accomplished through the reindeer industry, is a remarkable educational achievement. The Alaska Reindeer Service has now reached its most successful stage, as it marks the beginning of the period of full utilization of all the reindeer owned by the Government for the benefit of the native population.

At the present time there is hardly a surplus Government reindeer north of the Kuskokwim river. This has been made possible by the establishment of new reindeer stations, the employment of more natives as chief herders, by accepting the largest practical number of apprentices, and by transferring reindeer to both chief herders and apprentices in lieu of salary or supplies, the chief aim and fundamental policy of the Government being to turn the reindeer over to the natives as rapidly as they learn the industry and appreciate its value. The total number of reindeer in Alaska at the last census was nearly 23,000, and, of this number, over 11,000 are owned by the natives. One of the most striking and gratifying features is the large income which the natives derive from the sale of reindeer products, their share for the past fiscal year having been over $18,000. This amount does not include the value of the reindeer skins used for clothing, nor that of the meat consumed as food. These material benefits and the very considerable income thus derived demonstrate the fact that the reindeer industry has become one of the most prominent factors in the economic life of the Eskimo.

*American Forestry, January, 1913.

The total number of Alaskan reindeer is distributed in herds among twenty-eight stations, eighteen of these being owned by the Government and ten by church missions. The Lapps own over three thousand. The natives are very anxious to get deer and look upon them as a safe investment for their earnings, and usually take deer in preference to cash for services, when an opportunity is offered. The Government does not sell deer; this is done by natives and missions alone. The various missions are furnished a herd of one hundred deer on loan for a period of five years by the Government. At the end of this time, the original number must be returned. The mission keeps the increase of fawns, which amount to several hundred, derived from the Government loan. The Moravian mission of Bethel has one of the largest herds, nearly three thousand. Other missions having over one thousand deer, all in arctic Alaska, north of the Yukon, are located at Colovin, Kotzebue, Shishmerof, and cape Wales. At point Barrow, latitude 71°25', the most northern point on the American continent, there is a herd of 300. The total population here is about 400, men, women and children. One native, "Takpuk," is considered the richest man of that region as he owns a herd of 137 reindeer. The missions support and educate a number of young apprentice herders.

The native herders also take on apprentices and award them six deer a year in payment for their services. The Laplanders take a loan of deer for five years from the Government and give their services as instructors for that period. At the end of five years, the Lapp returns the 100 deer and becomes an independent herder himself with the large increase of reindeer he has obtained from the herd. The Lapp herders are not interested in the extension of the reindeer among the natives. Some of the largest owners of deer are Lapps, some half dozen of these men having accumulated herds of from five to nearly eight hundred.

In introducing the reindeer as a means to promote the industrial life and to provide a permanent livelihood for the Eskimo, it has been found necessary by the Government to put the young natives through a course of training. Those who get their deer directly from the Government serve an apprenticeship of five years. There are several hundred of these at present. They are bound by a written contract, the strict terms of which they cannot violate without peril of losing their annual allotment of reindeer and suffering discharge from the service. This caring for, training, and breeding the deer is an education in itself, and the best which the Government could give to the young natives. With careful training the Eskimo boys make excellent herders. They readily learn how to take care of the reindeer, to throw the lasso, to harness and drive the deer, and to watch the fawns. Siberian herders

were first imported to teach them; but, of late, the more intelligent and
efficient Laplanders, who have learned by centuries of experience the
breeding of reindeer, were secured.   The Eskimo boys take quickly to
some phases of the work, and, in some respects, excel the Lapps; they
can lasso better than the Lapps, and many become expert in making
harness and sleds.   The minding of the herd requires constant vigi-
lance, especially in the spring during the fawning season.   Then the
herders have to keep watch day and night by turns with rifle to protect
the herd from the ravages of the A: . tic wolf and the dogs.

In the ear of each Government deer a little aluminum button is
fastened securely, and all private owners and herders have a mark
which must be registered with a local Superintendent of the Reindeer
Station and also at Washington.   Besides being taught the art of deer-
manship, the apprentices are instructed in keeping accounts, the methods
of marketing reindeer, and in other practical matters connected with
the industry.   No apprentice can become a herder unless he is proficient
in the branches of elementary reading, arithmetic, and writing.   At the
end of his apprenticeship the young Eskimo native is allotted a number
of deer by the Government, and with the increase obtained during the
interval of his five years' service, each apprentice will have on an average, a herd of fifty reindeer.   As this herd will double itself every three
years, the graduate apprentice will have a herd which will afford and
assure a self-supporting income quite enough to satisfy the economic
wants of himself and family in the future.   He is thus established in
business by the Government and is given free pasturage thereafter.   The
reindeer produces one fawn in the spring each year for ten years.

Among the useful and profitable products of the reindeer are the
skins for clothing.*   Of these pelts most varied use is made.   From them
are fashioned the tight-fitting trousers and that wonderful outer garment, the 'parka,' universally worn in winter by both male and female
natives and by many whites.   The 'parka' extends to the knees and has
a close-fitting hood, which keeps the head and shoulders comfortably
warm even in the severest weather.   These reindeer garments are remarkable for their excellent qualities of resisting moisture and cold.   A
close examination of the hair of reindeer furnishes an explanation of its
peculiar value.   The hair is not merely a hollow tubular structure, with
a cavity extending throughout its entire length, but is divided, or par-
titioned off, into exceedingly numerous cells, like watertight compart-
ments.   These are filled with air, and their walls are so elastic and at

*"Buckskin is now worth $4.50 to $5.00 a pound and is steadily going up,
since nothing has been discovered to take its place.   A good-sized buckskin weighs
from one pound to one and a half pounds; so that the skin alone will pay for the
cost of raising the deer."—*Letter from E. Thompson Seton, April 9, 1914.*

the same time of such strong resistance that they are not broken up either during the process of manufacture or by swelling when wet. The cells expand in water, and thus it happens that a person clad completely in garments made of reindeer wool does not sink when in water, because he is buoyed up by the air contained in the hundreds of thousands of hair cells.

As a mineral industry continues to grow in Alaska the natives and graduate apprentices can earn high wages as teamsters, hauling supplies and furnishing fresh reindeer meat to mining camps in the interior, at points remote from railway and steamboat transportation. Well-trained sled deer have been used to carry the mail 650 miles from point Barrow, south to Kotzebue. This is the most northern mail route in the United States, and likewise the most perilous and desolate mail trip in the world. Two trips are made a year and $750 is paid for each journey. The average speed is about 40 to 50 miles per day, keeping up a steady trot.

One of the latest and quite remarkable feats showing the capacity of the reindeer for sledge driving was that accomplished by Mr. W. T. Lopp, the Superintendent of the Government Reindeer Service. During the recent winter's tour of inspection, Mr. Lopp travelled more than 2,500 miles with a reindeer sled over the frozen tundra and ice-bound rivers of the lower Bering Sea region from the middle Yukon to the coast of the North Pacific. Part of this route for several hundred miles lay through a country which had been so little traversed that not even native trails had been made. The Alaska Reindeer Service is under the direction of the United States Bureau of Education.

Appendix V

The Romance of Fur

LONDON THE MARKET OF THE WORLD

A VISIT TO THE WAREHOUSES
(From *The Times*, London, March 19, 1914)

LONDON is the chief fur market of the world, and the spring sales, the most important of the year, are now going on. They will continue daily for a fortnight yet at the public auction-room in College Hill, and in the course of the three weeks, it is probable that some 10,000,000 or 12,000,000 skins will be disposed of.

Yesterday, there were sold in the morning, 183,754 skunk skins; in the afternoon, 136,623 American opossum and 80,242 raccoons, as well as 3,602 civet cats. To-day, will be offered 430,401 skunks, and to-morrow 2,500,000 muskrats of various classes. In all there will be sold over 4,500,000 muskrat skins; and it is no wonder that the once familiar musk-rat "houses," which used to dot every lake and pond all over Canada and the United States, looking like great mole-hills sticking up among the rushes, are growing scarce.

VARIETIES OF SKINS

Muskrat, skunk, raccoon, American opossum, and the various foxes: these are the furs which are most in demand at the moment. Sable, seal, mink, chinchilla, otter, beaver, and other skins are, of course, always valuable; but, for the moment, they are "out of fashion," and the chief interest at these sales centres in the half-dozen creatures mentioned. The stock is unusually large; not so much because the supply has been exceptional, but because Germany has taken less than its usual share. None the less, prices are good—better, perhaps, than was expected— and the bidding in the sales-room goes on briskly from 10 o'clock in the morning until a late luncheon time, and again in the later hours of the afternoon. Besides the furs already mentioned, an extraordinary variety of items makes the sale catalogue a fascinating document. Among the lots sold this week there figured 208 grizzly bears, 141 black bears, eight brown bears, 16 polar or "white", 411 lynxes, 14 leopards, and 41 wolverenes. Among those still to come are 70 tigers, 1,100 leopards, 3,000 lynxes, 30 musk-ox, 18,000 wild cats, 658 emus, 181,943 wallaby, 40,000 wolves, and 8,592 kangaroo. It is a list to make the Roman Emperors envious. And so it runs day after day; 3,000 bears, we find in another column, 180,000 ermine, 5,600 Russian sable, 120,000 mink, 60 sea otter, 5,000 monkey, 1,000 grebe and 35,000 house cat! Again, we have 4,675 house cats, unkindly sandwiched in among badgers and marmots, leopards and Japanese foxes, and other agitating things. It may not be inherently any more sad to kill 39,675 house cats than an equal number of wallabies or foxes. But it comes nearer home to us, and the thought of it awakens personal griefs for pussies which have unaccountably "got lost."

IN THE AUCTION ROOM

In the sales-room itself one does not see any of these skins, but only a hundred or so gentlemen sitting on the curved tiers of seats which face the rostrum, each gentleman with a catalogue on the desk before him and keenly interested in the bidding. If you listen to the scraps of conversation you will hear all manner of tongues; for buyers from perhaps a dozen countries are here, and especially from Germany, France, and the United States. The bidding is very quick, the skins being put up in lots which may vary from a single silver fox or half a dozen sables to 400 or 500 skunks or 4,000 muskrats. The bids for these staple furs are commonly in shillings, and the values range very widely for the same kind of skin. A silver fox may fetch, as it has fetched, £440, and it may not be worth £50. Skunk vary from a shilling or two to 28s., muskrat from pence to half-a-crown, and house cats fetch about the same. House cats are not valued or graded as they are not on the show benches. They are not sold as long-haired or short-haired. Nor is any account taken of their qualities as cats, or their dispositions, which are immaterial by the time they reach the sale-room. They are simply "white" or "black" or—most unkind of all—"mottled."

BUSINESS AND SPORT

To see the skins themselves one must go to the warehouse of one of the great firms in whose names the sales are held, which are all grouped round the neighbourhood of the College of Heralds, in College Hill, Garlick Hill, or Queen Street. The interior of one of these warehouses is an extraordinary sight; a huge building, five storeys, perhaps, in height, and with each of the vast floors packed from floor to ceiling with skins. In one such building there are, literally, several millions. Science has now fairly succeeded in deodorizing the individual skin, even of our mephitic acquaintance the skunk. But in the aggregate—millions of

them together—they are far from odourless. Those who live always in
the atmosphere do not mind it; but it is a little "rich" to the accidental
visitor from the fresh air. And the skins are an amazing and humiliating
sight.

If, by any chance, the visitor has shot or hunted in wild places, he
remembers what the individual trophy meant to him—the all-day stalk;
the long, cramped vigil over the "kill" among the strange night noises
of the jungle; the hours of lying stretched uneasily and motionless by the
streamside as dusk fell and slowly it grew too dark to see the sights;
the moment when, breathless and quivering with exhaustion, until it was
impossible to hold a rifle steady, at last the hunter was face to face with
"it" among the forest trees. Then there was the triumph—and a
single skin, bullet-spoiled, to show for it. And here they are—1,100
leopards, 11,000 beavers, 208 grizzly bears!—better skins than the
visitor ever shot. Between the racks of packed skins, rising from the
floor to higher than a man's reach, narrow aisles run the length of these
huge rooms. In a dim corner, thrown down where there were a few feet
of spare floor space between racks which held hundreds of thousands of
raccoons, a shapeless tawny bundle had, as it seemed, been dumped and
overlooked. Big skins, evidently, and from one end protruded a great
yellow foot with huge claws. Just a few odd pumas (the label called it
"panther"), which, perhaps, will come under the catalogue item
"sundries."

BUYING BY SAMPLES

Just now, hanging on hooks around the racks, are the "sale bundles"
—generally 25 skins of such things as muskrat or skunk—which are
the samples by which the buyers estimate the value of the lots to be
offered in the sales-room. In the case of the more costly skins, as silver
fox (300 of them hanging in a row) or sable (a long, narrow room hung
with nothing else, every skin to delight a woman), the buyer can see the
whole "lot", whether one skin or half a dozen. But the cheaper skins
are thus shown in sample. And all day long just now the buyers are
here looking at the stock from the samples, they, as well as all the em-
ployees, being clad from head to feet in long white linen coats. It is
well for the visitor when he goes in to put on one of these garments.
Otherwise, when he emerges into the daylight of the street he may find
himself moderately furry. But to see it all is worth some inconvenience
—even the loss of conceit in one's poor individual trophies.

Appendix VI

The Muskrat

EXTRACTS FROM *Farmers' Bulletin* 396, U. S. DEPARTMENT OF
AGRICULTU. E, 1910

BY
D. E. LANTZ

PUBLISHED accounts of the muskrat's breeding disagree so widely
that the habits of the animals might be supposed to differ in
different sections of the country. Harlan states that the female brings
forth 5 or 6 young annually. Richardson, on the other hand, says:
"In latitude 55° the musquash has three litters in the course of the
season and from three to seven young in a litter".

W. Butler, writing of the muskrat in Indiana, states that he is
convinced that in his vicinity the animals breed but once a year, though
he admits the probability of exceptions. He gives the number of young
as 4 to 6 and the period of gestation as about six weeks. Roderick
MacFarlane, a chief factor of the Hudson's Bay Company, in writing of
the mammals of the Mackenzie River region, states that the female has
two litters the first season, and three each succeeding season, and that
the number of young at times varies from 8 to 20. His statements are
based on information obtained from the Company's Indian hunters,
who are keen observers....................

All this testimony shows that in their breeding habits muskrats
are not unlike field mice. This conclusion is further strengthened by
the remarkable way in which the marshes, depleted by vigorous winter
trapping, are replenished before the opening of another season. The
known facts may be thus summarised: Normally, the animals mate in
March and the first litter is born in April; a second litter is due in June
or early July, and a third in August or September. In favourable
seasons a fourth or even a fifth litter may be produced. The period of
gestation is possibly no longer than twenty-one days, as with the common rat and probably with the field mouse. The young are blind and
naked when born but develop rapidly. Outside of low marshes, muskrats are usually born in the underground burrows..............

Food.—Like nearly all rodents the muskrat is chiefly herbivorous,
but it sometimes indulges in animal food, a habit which it shares with
brown rats, house mice, field mice, lemmings, wood rats, squirrels, and
other gnawers.

In winter the chief food of muskrats consists of the roots of aquatic plants—pond lilies, arums, sedges, and the like—but in some localities the animals feed on mussels and also on carp and other sluggish fish that bury themselves in mud. When ponds are frozen over, muskrats are almost wholly restricted to food accessible under the ice, but in rare cases they have been known to leave the water and burrow under the snow in search of the crowns of grasses and sedges . . . .

In summer the muskrat's menu is far more extensive. It can then choose from many aquatic plants—roots, stems, leaves, and fruit— and in addition can obtain supplies from near-by fields or woods. . . . . .

Muskrat Furs.—In the raw state the fur of the muskrat is dense and soft and in general appearance much like that of the beaver. However, the pelage is shorter and less close and the pelt somewhat inferior in durability. The colour varies with season and locality. Northern skins are said to average lightest in colour, being often a light silver gray, sometimes nearly white on the underparts. This is probably because many are taken in summer pelage. Very dark skins, classed as black, come mainly from New Jersey, Delaware, and Maryland, but are found in limited numbers in other parts of the United States and in Canada.

Compared with most other furs of such small size, muskrat furs are of excellent quality and durability; their cheapness is chiefly the result of their abundance. The earliest demand for the fur was for the manufacture of so-called beaver hats, it making an excellent imitation. When silk replaced fur in hat manufacture, the demand for muskrat skins fell off greatly. They next became popular as imitations of seal-skin. Properly dyed and made up, they are difficult to distinguish from the genuine, but their wearing qualities are greatly inferior. The modern fur dresser and dyer have found means of imitating nearly all the more costly furs with that of this animal, and have thus created a continuous demand for the pelts.

Trade in Muskrat Furs.—The growth of the demand for muskrat furs is shown by the records of London importations and sales. From 1763 to 1800 (thirty-eight years) the total number of skins imported and sold in that market was 2,831,453, an average of less than 75,000 yearly. During the fifty years from 1801 to 1850 the total was 20,571,428, or an average of 411,000 yearly. From 1851 to 1890, inclusive, the importations were 99,893,591, a yearly average of 2,500,000. The average London sales in recent years have been over 4,000,000 per annum, and the entire output of skins for 1900 was 5,285,000. A large part of the total collection is sold through London, but in the last few years an increasing number are dressed and manufactured in America.

Notwithstanding that during the past century and a half, nearly a quarter billion of muskrats have been trapped, the supply has not greatly diminished. The total output of 1905, as indicated by London sales of 5,000,000 skins in 1906, was over 7,000,000. The sale of these was accompanied by an advance of 40 per cent in prices. The sales for 1907 showed a further advance of about 25 per cent, but a falling off in the offerings of fully 1,500,000 skins. The London sales for 1908 and 1909 showed a still further rise in prices, which were again advanced in the January and March sales of 1910. The total London sales for 1908 were 3,800,000; for 1909, 3,771,000.* . . . .

Information from dealers in raw furs in the Chesapeake region indicates that the supply of muskrat furs has been reasonably steady in spite of the prevailing high prices. Baltimore buyers paid 35 cents each for brown and 45 cents for black, ungraded, during the season of 1909. New York buyers offered higher prices, but the furs are graded in that market. On January 22, 1910, Baltimore buyers were paying 65 cents for brown and 70 cents for black skins, ungraded. Trade quotations in *The Trapper's World* for February, 1910, list No. 1 black muskrat skins at $1.00 each.† Prices are, of course, based on returns from the London auctions and must be low enough to permit a reasonable profit to dealers.

In order to dispose of furs to advantage, trappers should keep informed as to market values. Usually they can realise fair returns by selling to local buyers and at the same time run but slight risk of having the pelts graded too low. There has been much complaint of the practice of dealers in sending out circulars offering high prices for furs to induce shipments. Upon receipt of consignments, however, the furs are so much undergraded that the returns are far less than could have been realized in the local market.

Home Dressing of Furs.—Formerly many muskrat skins were home tanned and made into caps, collars, and other articles. At present the home utilization of skins is much less extensive, but knowledge of a good method of dressing the fur is still desirable. Most of the methods employed by amateurs involve the use of alum to fix the hair; but satisfactory results, so far as pliability of the pelts goes, depend largely upon the amount of labour bestowed on them.

A method in common use is the following: The skins are thoroughly cleaned in warm—not hot—water and all flesh and fat scraped off. They are then stretched on a board with the fur side down and covered with a mixture of two ounces each of salt and alum, 3 gills of water, and

* Statistics in the *Fur News Magazine* for April, 1914, show that the combined offerings of muskrat skins (except H. B. Co.) at London, in March, 1913, and in March, 1914, were respectively, 1,300,598 and 4,646,500 skins. The same magazine points out that the "offerings at London in March, 1914, made a new magnitude record that is not likely to be repeated," and indicate an accumulation from the previous year.

† The *Fur News Magazine*, for April, 1914, quotes black spring muskrat at 50 cents.

11

a drachm of sulphuric acid.   Thicken this with wheat bran or flour and allow it to dry on the skin.   When dry, the flour or bran should be scraped off, the skin removed from the board and rolled with the fur side in.   The folded skin is then drawn quickly many times through an iron ring.   It should be unfolded at intervals and re-rolled in another direction.   This is continued until the entire skin is soft and flexible.

The following method was recommended by the late William Hamilton Gibson:

> The skin should always be thoroughly cleaned in warm water and all fat and superfluous flesh removed.   It should then be immersed in a solution made of the following ingredients: Five gallons of cold soft water, 5 quarts wheat bran, 1 gill of salt, and 1 ounce of sulphuric acid.   Allow the skin to soak in the liquid for four or five hours.   If the hides have been previously salted, the salt should be excluded from the mixed solution.   The skins are now ready for the tanning liquor, which is made in the following way: Into 5 gallons of warm soft water stir 1 peck of wheat bran and allow the mixture to stand in a warm room until fermentation takes place.   Then add 3 pints of salt and stir until it is thoroughly dissolved.   A pint of sulphuric acid should then be poured in gradually, after which the liquor is ready.   Immerse the skins and let them soak for three or four hours.   The process of fleshing follows.   This consists of laying the skin, fur side down, over a smooth beam and working over the flesh side with a blunt fleshing tool.   An old chopping knife or a tin candlestick forms an excellent substitute for the ordinary fleshing knife, and the process of rubbing should be continued until the skin becomes dry, when it will be found to be soft and pliable........................

Manufactures of Muskrat furs.—Besides the considerable use of muskrat skins for manufacture into garments in imitation of high-grade furs, a good proportion of the poorer skins are used in the natural colour for lining overcoats and other outer garment   Garments made from skins of wolves, goats, or dogs partly supply this need, but cloth outer garments with linings of light furs are fully as warm and are less burdensome.   The growing popularity of the automobile for outdoor recreation in winter is another cause for the increased demand for fur-lined coats.

The better grades of muskrat furs, dressed in the natural colour, have a beautiful lustre, and make really handsome coats, boas, and muffs; and many smaller articles of apparel, as collars, gloves, caps, and the like, are made of muskrat fur.

Muskrat farming.—Fur farming has been a favorite topic for discussion in American newspapers.   While many fur-producing enterprises have been planned and some actually begun, few have prospered.   Various difficulties have discouraged the majority of persons who have engaged in raising minks, foxes, or skunks.* However, the possibilities of such enterprises have not really been tested, and present prices for these furs might well repay investment of capital in their production..................

Some Examples.—Muskrat farming is already a prosperous business. The Cedar Point Hunting Club, of Toledo, Ohio, controls 5,000 acres of marsh at the mouth of the Maumee river, near lake Erie. In the winter of 1903-4, after the muskrats had been undisturbed for two years, they were trapped for the benefit of the club. Five thousand were taken in a single month (January, 1904), and the skins were sold for 25 cents each. The carcasses also were sold at a dollar a dozen.

The muskrat industry has probably reached its highest present development on the eastern shore of Maryland. The extensive marshes of Dorchester county are a centre of muskrat fur production........

Formerly the owners of marshes in this vicinity paid little attention to them. The land was considered useless because subject to tidal overflow. Trappers were allowed to take muskrats wherever they chose, and a dozen years ago much of the marsh land could have been bought for less than 50 cents an acre. At the present time, some of the marshes are worth more, measured by the actual income from them, than cultivated farms of like acreage in the same vicinity. The increased values are due to the muskrat. Landowners now usually lease the trapping privilege, and trappers and owners unite to protect the marshes from poaching. The owner receives half the fur caught, while the trapper gets the other half and all he can realize from the sale of the meat. In the short season of seventy-four days, January 1 to March 15, during the last two years, trappers have easily made from $400 to $900 each.

A few specific examples will give a better idea of the value of these marsh lands. The owner of one tract of marsh informed the writer that he bought it three or four years ago for $2,700. It is leased for half the fur, and yielded him in 1909, $890, or about 33 per cent on the investment. The owner of a small piece of marsh—about 40 acres—bought it in 1905 for $150. Leased for half the fur, it has yielded the owner $30, $60, $70, and $100, respectively, for each of the four years, 1906 to 1909. Taxes are very light, and, on the basis of a 6 per cent income, the returns for 1909 would represent an approximate value of nearly $40 an acre for this land. The owner of a 1,300-acre tract of marsh trapped it this season, with the aid of his sons, and secured over 5,000 muskrats, which were sold for $2,300.

---

* Since this bulletin was written, fur-farming, especially with respect to the animals mentioned, has become an important industry in Canada.—*Ed.*

The furs sold in this region are seldom assorted before sale. They are separated into black and brown and then counted, a deduction of from 3 to 5 per cent being made for "kits." The skins sold throughout the present season at Baltimore prices, 35 cents for brown and 45 cents for black. The proportion of black skins varies on the different marshes from 10 to 60 per cent, the average being about 40 per cent.

The muskrat meat is an additional source of income to the trapper. It is bought by local buyers, who during the season, 1909, paid only 4 cents for each animal; it is shipped to outside markets or sold for local consumption. The demand for the meat is growing, and all of it is utilized. The Baltimore market takes about 30,000 animals during a season, the bulk of which comes from Dorchester county.

The editor of the *Cambridge Record*, a local newspaper, stated that the muskrat industry of Dorchester brings into the county about $100,000 annually. This would indicate that about a quarter million of the animals are trapped each season. The danger of exhausting the supply by continued close trapping has been discussed in Dorchester county, but trappers maintain that with the long closed season, March 15 to January 1, little ground for anxiety on this score exists.

Possibilities of the Business.—Muskrats require no feeding, since the plant life of ponds and marshes furnishes abundance of food. In many states the areas adapted to the muskrat are extensive, and doubtless the animals could be profitably introduced into sections from which they are now absent. As trapping is done in winter, the business of muskrat farming is peculiarly adapted to farmers and farmers' boys.

The improvement of the muskrat's pelage by selective breeding has never been attempted. Probably the black muskrat could be bred true to colour and greatly improved in the localities it now inhabits, and could be successfully introduced into other sections of the country. Indeed, to make the most of the muskrat industry requires that the possibilities of selective breeding be tested.

Appendix VII

PRINCE EDWARD ISLAND

An Act to Impose a Tax upon Foxes held in Captivity in this Province

3 Geo. V, Chap. 5

(Assented to April 24, 1913)

BE IT ENACTED by the Lieutenant Governor and Legislative Assembly of the Province of Prince Edward Island as follows:

1. This Act may be cited as "The Fox Tax Act."

2. From and after the passing of this Act there shall be charged, levied, collected and paid unto and for the use of His Majesty in his Government of Prince Edward Island the following tax upon the offspring in each year of all foxes kept, being or held in captivity in this Province, that is to say, at the rate of One dollar for each hundred dollars in value of such offspring.

3. The taxes imposed by this Act shall be payable on the first day of August in each year commencing on the first juridical day of August following the passage hereof on which day the first payment of the taxes aforesaid shall be due and payable to the Provincial Treasurer of the Province.

4. The Lieutenant Governor in Council shall nominate and appoint one or more collector or collectors whose duties shall be the enforcement of the provisions of this Act.

5. Such collector or collectors shall be allowed for his or their services a commission upon the taxes collected by him or them at such rate as shall from time to time be fixed by the Lieutenant Governor in Council.

6. The collector shall on or about the first day of June in each year cause a notice in Form "A" in the schedule hereto or to the like effect to be sent to or served upon each rancher requiring such rancher to declare on oath:

(a) The number of foxes in such ranch or in such rancher's possession or custody born previous to the year in which such affidavit is made and mentioning the number there is of each sex.

(b) The names and addresses of all the owners and part owners of each fox or pair of foxes in such ranch born previous to the year in which such affidavit is made so far as may be known to the rancher.

(c) Where such foxes or any of them are owned by any incorporated company the name of such company, the name and addresses of its President, Secretary and Manager, the number of foxes and pairs of foxes owned by such company and the amount of its paid up capital.

(d) The number of the offspring, born in the year in which such affidavit is made to each pair of foxes in such ranch.

(e) The value of the offspring of each of such pairs of foxes.

(f) The number of such offspring which may have been sold or agreed to be sold or upon which options for the purchase thereof have been given, stating the price of each animal or each pair as the case may be and describing the animals so sold or agreed to be sold or upon which options for sale have been given by reference to the parents of such animals and owners of same.

(g) The number of such offspring remaining unsold and the value of same.

7. The notices referred to in this Act may be either personally delivered to any rancher, owner or part owner as the case may be or left at his last or usual place of abode with some person apparently above the age of sixteen years or may be posted in His Majesty's post office in a registered letter postage prepaid addressed to such rancher, owner or part owner, at his last or usual place of abode.

8. Every rancher to whom the notice mentioned in section six has been sent or upon whom such notice has been served shall make an affidavit setting forth the facts as required by the sixth section, which affidavit shall be returned by him to the Collector or Provincial Treasurer within eight days after the service or mailing of the said notice.

9. The Collector may cause a notice in the Form "B" in the Schedule hereto or to the like effect to be sent to or served upon any owner or part owner of any fox or foxes, requiring such owner or part owner to declare upon oath:

(a) The number of foxes exclusive of the then year's offspring owned by such person or in which he has an interest.

(b) The name or names with the address or addresses of the person or persons in whose ranch, custody or possession such fox or foxes may be.

(c) The number of the offspring of each pair of foxes owned by such person or in which he has an interest, mentioning in whose ranch, custody or possession such offspring may be and the value of such offspring.

(d) The number of such offspring which may have been sold or agreed to be sold or upon which options for the purchase thereof have been given, stating the price of each animal or each pair as the case may be.

(e) The number of such offspring remaining unsold and the value of same.

10. Every owner or part owner to whom such notice referred to in Section 9 has been sent or upon whom such notice has been served shall make an affidavit setting forth the facts as required by the last mentioned section which affidavit shall be returned by him to the Provincial Treasurer or Collector within eight days after the service or mailing of the said notice.

11. In the event of any rancher or any owner or part owner of any foxes being an incorporated company, the notice or notices mentioned in this Act shall be sufficiently served upon such company by delivering such notice personally to any officer, manager or director of such company or by leaving the same at the last or usual place of abode of such officer, manager or director, with some person apparently above the age of sixteen years, or by posting the same in a registered letter in His Majesty's Post Office, postage prepaid, addressed to such officer, manager or director, at his usual place of abode. And it shall be the duty of such officer, manager or director, receiving such notice to make the affidavit required by this Act to be made by such company.

12. If any affidavit returned by any rancher, owner or part owner is not satisfactory to the Provincial Treasurer, or in case such rancher, owner or part owner does not return such affidavit as required by this Act, the Provincial Treasurer may cause a notice to be served upon, delivered or sent to the person in whose ranch, or in whose custody or possession any foxes are or are supposed to be, stating the time when any collector or collectors will attend at the ranch or premises of such person, in whose ranch, possession or custody, such foxes are or are supposed to be, for the purpose of examining such ranch and premises and inspecting such foxes. The time of attendance mentioned in such notice shall not be less than three clear days from the date of the mailing or service thereof, such notice may be in the Form "C" in the schedule hereto.

13. At the time appointed by the notice mentioned in the last preceding section, the collector named in such notice may attend with such assistant or assistants as he may deem necessary at the ranch or premises of the person named in such notice, for the purpose of examining any ranch, enclosure, or premises, and of inspecting any foxes kept therein.

. 14. It shall be the duty of every person receiving such notice to permit such Collector and his assistants at the time mentioned in such notice to enter into and examine all ranches, pens, enclosures and premises of such person and to inspect all foxes kept therein, to render such assistance by himself and by his servants and attendants as may be required by the Collector, and to give such information as to the num-

ber, value and ownership of any foxes in his ranch or on the premises
as may be required by the Collector.

15. If at the time mentioned in such notice the Collector attends
at the ranch or premises of the person receiving such notice, and such
last mentioned person refuses or neglects to allow the Collector or his
assistants to enter into and examine such ranches, pens, enclosures and
premises, or to render such assistance as may be necessary or required
by the Collector for the purposes of this Act, the Collector may break
and enter any ranch, pen, building, enclosure or premises of such person
and may do and perform all such acts and things as may be considered
necessary by such Collector for obtaining information as to the number
and value of foxes on such person's premises.

16. If the rancher to whom any notice is sent as provided by sectic
6, fails to return to the Provincial Secretary or collector, an affidavit a.
required by this Act, or if after receiving the notice referred to in Section
12 of this Act, the rancher does not attend at the time mentioned in
the last mentioned notice, or if attending he does not permit the Collector and his assistants to enter into and examine any ranch, pen,
enclosure or premises of such person, or to inspect any fox or foxes in
such person's custody or possession, or does not render such assistance
as may be necessary or required by the Collector for the purposes of
this Act, or does not give information as to the number, value and
ownership of any foxes in his ranch or on his premises that may be required by the Collector, the Provincial Treasurer in any of such cases
may from the best information he has, make up an estimate of the number of the increase in such year of the foxes in such rancher's possession,
or custody, and of the value thereof and shall notify such rancher of the
amount of such valuation, which shall be taken to be final and conclusive and shall be the amount upon which the tax shall be payable on
said foxes in said rancher's possession or custody. In any suit for the
recovery of the said tax, the production of a Provincial Treasurers'
certificate of his estimate shall be sufficient to entitle judgment to be
given against such rancher, for the amount of taxes mentioned therein
as being payable without any further evidence.

17. The Provincial Treasurer shall not be bound to accept the statements or the valuation contained in any affidavit which may be returned
to him by any rancher, owner or part owner, under the provisions of
this Act, but may by certificate signed by him increase the number and
value of the young foxes born in such year beyond that stated by such
rancher, owner or part owner, in such affidavit or affidavits, and may
sue for the same. In such action it shall only be necessary to produce
the certificate of such valuation signed by the Provincial Treasurer and
judgment shall be given for the amount of taxes payable upon such in-

creased valuation according to such certificate unless the rancher, owner, or part owner proves to the satisfaction of the Court, that the actual value of such increase is of a less amount, in which case judgment shall be given for the actual amount payable.

18. All taxes imposed under this Act may be sued for and recovered in the name of the Provincial Treasurer and suit therefor may be brought, either in the Supreme Court or in the County Court, and the County Court shall have jurisdiction, notwithstanding that the amount of the taxes claimed or payable exceeds One hundred and fifty dollars.

19. The rancher shall be liable to pay all taxes upon all foxes in his ranch or in his possession or cust   upon which taxes are made payable by this Act whether such foxes are owned by such rancher or not, and in the event of the rancher paying taxes upon any foxes not owned by him, he shall have a lien upon such foxes as against the owner or owners thereof for the amount so paid.

20. Every part owner of any fox or foxes shall be liable to pay the whole of the taxes in respect of such fox or foxes in which he is a part owner and any one or more of such part owners may be sued for the whole of such taxes without joining the other or others of such part owners. In the event of any part owner paying the taxes upon any fox or foxes in which he is a part owner he shall have a lien therefor upon such fox or foxes for the proportion of such taxes payable by his co-owners and shall also have the right to sue such co-owners for the proportion of taxes payable by them.

21. Proceedings for the recovery of the taxes imposed by this Act may be brought against the rancher alone or may be brought against him and any owner or any one or more of the joint owners of any foxes upon which taxes are payable.

22. Under any execution which may be issued upon any judgment recovered against any rancher, for taxes under this Act, the sheriff or officer enforcing such execution may, in addition to any other property of such rancher liable to be taken under such execution, seize and sell, any fox or foxes in such rancher's possession or custody whether the property of such rancher or not.

(2) In case the rancher pays any tax payable in pursuance of this Act upon any fox or foxes in which he has no interest as owner or part owner or if the rancher's property is sold under execution for taxes upon such fox or foxes the rancher shall be entitled to recover from the owner or owners of such fox or foxes, the amount or the proportionate part or parts of such taxes and costs as were payable by them.

23. Under any execution which may be issued upon any judgment recovered against any joint owner or part owner of any foxes, for taxes payable by him under this Act, the sheriff or officer enforcing such

execution may, in addition to any other property of such joint owner or part owner, liable to be taken under such execution, seize and sell any fox or foxes in which such joint or part owner has any share or interest,

(2) If the property of any part owner is taken and sold under execution pursuant to this Section, such part owner shall be entitled to recover from his co-owners their proportionate part of the taxes so collected together with the proportionate amount of the costs.

(3) The Provisions of the "Absent Debtor Act" shall apply to the collection of taxes on foxes from all owners or part owners thereof nonresident within this Province.

24. The Lieutenant Governor in Council, may from time to time, make such regulations not inconsistent with this Act as may be deemed necessary for the following purposes or any of them, that is to say:

(a) Providing where there is no provision in this Act or no sufficient provision in respect to any matter or thing necessary to give effect to this Act in what manner and form the deficiency shall be supplied.

(b) For any purpose whether general or to meet particular cases that may be desirable in order to carry out the object and purposes of this Act, or to give effect to anything for which regulations are contemplated or required by this Act.

(c) For extending or shortening the time for making any return required by this Act.

(d) For regulating the amount of tax in particular cases where special circumstances may call for adjustment.

25. In this Act, unless the context otherwise requires, the expression "Rancher" means every owner or manager of a fox ranch and every person having in his care, custody or possession any foxes. "Person," "Owner," "Rancher," and "Part Owner" each includes any Company or body corporate.

26. Any oath required to be taken under this Act may be administered by the Provincial Treasurer or any of his assistants in the Provincial Treasury, the Collector of taxes under this Act, a Notary Public, or any Commissioner authorized to take affidavits in the Supreme Court in this Province.

27. In the event of any rancher, owner or part owner of foxes not having paid in any year the tax on the full number of foxes upon which he was liable to pay tax in such year whether receiving any notice in respect to same or not, he shall be liable to pay in any succeeding year, the tax which he has so failed to pay, and such taxes may be sued for in the same manner as if they had become due and payable in such succeeding year.

28. In any action to recover taxes payable under this Act, the party suc·· eding shall be entitled to recover costs of suit according to the scale of costs in the Court in which such action is brought.

29. Notwithstanding anything in this Act contained, the Collector or Collectors may after three clear days' notice previously given to any rancher or owner or part owner, personally call upon such rancher or owner or part owner, and take from him a statement under oath, giving the information set out in forms "A" and "B" hereto or to the like effect with like remedies, in case of refusal to make such affidavits as are hereinbefore provided in the case of refusal to make a return or to make a return to the satisfaction of the Provincial Treasurer.

FORM A

(Sec. 6)
NOTICE TO RANCHERS
To A. B.   of

Sir:—
Take notice that under the provisions of "The Fox Tax Act" you are required to make an affidavit stating:

(a) The number of foxes in your ranch, or in your possession or custody, born previous to this year, mentioning the number thereof of each sex.

(b) The names and addresses of all the owners and part owners of each fox or pair of foxes in your ranch or in your custody or possession so far as the same may be known to you.

(c) Where such foxes or any of them are owned by any incorporated company, the name of such company, the names and addresses of its President, Secretary and Manager, the number of foxes and pairs of foxes owned by such Company and the amount of its paid up capital.

(d) The number of offspring born during this present year of each pair of foxes in your ranch or in your possession or custody.

(e) The value of the offspring of each of such pairs of foxes.

(f) The number of such offspring which may have been sold or agreed to be sold or upon which options, for the purchase thereof have been given, stating the price of each animal or each pair as the case may be and describing the animals so sold or agreed to be sold or upon which options for sale have been given by reference to the parents of such animals and owners of same.

(g) The number of such offspring remaining unsold and the value of same.

Such affidavit may be sworn to before the Provincial Treasurer or any of his assistants in the Provincial Treasury, the Collector of Taxes under the said Act, a Notary Public, or a Commissioner authorised to take affidavits in the Supreme Court in this Province and must be returned to the Collector or Provincial Treasurer within eight days from the date hereof.

And take notice that unless you make due return of such affidavit, the Provincial Treasurer may himself fix the amount of the taxes payable by you in respect of any foxes in your possession and may proceed for the recovery thereof as the law directs.

A form of affidavit is enclosed herewith.

Dated this   day of   19

                                    C.D.
                                    Collector.

———

FORM B

(Sec. 9)

NOTICE TO OWNER OR PART OWNER

To G. H. of

Sir:—

Take notice that under the provisions of "The Fox Tax Act" you are required to declare upon oath:

(a) The number of foxes exclusive of this year's offspring, owned by you or in which you have an interest.

(b) The name and address of the person or persons in whose ranch, custody or possession such fox or foxes may be.

(c) The number of the offspring of each pair of foxes owned by you or in which you have an interest mentioning in whose ranch, custody or possession such offspring may be and the value of such offspring.

(d) The number of such offspring which may have been sold or agreed to be sold, or upon which options for the purchase thereof have been given, stating the price of each animal or each pair as the case may be.

(e) The number of such offspring remaining unsold and the value of same.

Such affidavit may be sworn to before the Provincial Treasurer or any of his assistants in the Provincial Treasury, the Collector of Taxes under the said Act, a Notary Public, a Commissioner authorized to take affidavits in any Court in this Province or any Justice of the Peace and must be returned to the Collector or Provincial Treasurer within eight days from the date hereof.

And take notice that unless you make due return of such affidavit, the Provincial Treasurer may himself fix the amount of the taxes payable by you in respect of any foxes owned by you or in which you have any interest, and may proceed for the recovery thereof as the law directs.

A form of affidavit is enclosed herewith.

C.D.
Collector.

FORM C

(Sec. 12).
NOTICE OF COLLECTOR'S ATTENDANCE AT RANCH

To A. B. of
Sir:—

Take notice that on   day the   day of   A.D., 19   between the hours of
o'clock in the   noon, and
o'clock in the   noon, Mr.   a Collector appointed under the provisions of "The Fox Tax Act" will attend at your ranch or premises at   for the purpose of examining your ranch and premises and inspecting any foxes on said ranch or premises or in your possession or custody.

Dated this   day of
19
Provincial Treasurer.

FORM D

(Sec. 8)
AFFIDAVIT TO BE MADE BY RANCHER

I, A. B. of   in   County in Prince Edward Island make oath and say as follows:

1. That there are in my ranch at   or in my possession or custody at   ,   foxes of which   are males and   are females.

2. The names and addresses of all the owners and part owners of each fox or pair of foxes (exclusive of the offspring born during this present year) in my ranch or in my custody or possession so far as the same are known to me are as set out in schedule "A" hereto.

3. Of the above foxes   pairs are owned by an incorporated company by the name of   of which the name and address of the President is   of   and of the Secretary is   .   of   and of the manager is   of

The authorized capital of said company is $ and its paid up capital is $

4. The number of the offspring born during this present year of each pair of foxes in my ranch or in my possession or custody is as set out in Schedule "B" hereto.

5. The number of the offspring mentioned in the last preceding paragraph which have been sold or agreed to be sold or upon which options for the purchase thereof have been given, is as set out in Schedule "C" hereto.

6. The number of the offspring mentioned in Schedule "B" of this affidavit remaining unsold or on which no options have been given is   , which are of the value of $

Sworn to before me ⎫
at   in the County ⎪
of   this   day   ⎬
of   A.D.,   19   ⎭

———

FORM D

SCHEDULE A

Being a detailed list of foxes, exclusive of this year's offspring, with names and addresses of owners.

(a) Pair number one the owners of which are C. D. of   .
E. F. of   &c.

(b) Pair number two, the owners of which &c. (enumerate each pair, stating names and addresses of owners of each)

(c) A male fox of which the owner or owners are (state names and addresses) (Specify any other animals, giving names and addresses of owners).

FORM D

SCHEDULE B

Being a detailed list of the offspring of each pair of foxes mentioned in Schedule "A," and the present market value of same

(a)   offspring to pair number one of the value
of $ each.

(b)   offspring to pair number two of the value
of $ each.

&c., &c., &c.

FORM D

SCHEDULE C

Being particulars of such of the offspring mentioned in Schedule "B" as have been sold or agreed to be sold or upon which options for purchase have been given.

(a) One [or more] young foxes of the offspring or pair number three mentioned in the Schedule "B" at the price of $ each.

(b) A pair of young foxes, one being of the offspring of pair number   and the other of the offspring of pair number
at the price of $

&c., &c., &c.

PRINCE EDWARD ISLAND

An Act Relating to Foxes and Other Fur-bearing Animals Kept in Captivity

3 GEO. V, CHAP. 10

(Assented to April 24, 1913)

WHEREAS, certain persons in the Province of Prince Edward Island have engaged in the business of raising or breeding foxes and other fur-bearing animals kept in captivity, and it is desirable to protect the said animals from being disturbed by strangers or persons other than the owner or keeper of said animals.

BE IT THEREFORE ENACTED by the Lieutenant Governor and Legislative Assembly of the Province of Prince Edward Island as follows:

1. Every one is guilty of an offence and liable to the penalty hereinafter provided who, at any time hereafter, in any part of the Province without the consent of the owner or caretaker of a ranch or enclosure where foxes or other fur-bearing animals are kept in captivity for breeding purposes, shall enter upon the private grounds of the owner, or owners of the said animals within a distance of twenty-five yards from the outer fence or enclosures within which the pens or dens of the said animals are located and upon which said fence notices forbidding trespassing on the said premises are kept posted so as to be plainly discernible at the said distance of not less than twenty-five yards.

2. Any person convicted of an offence against Section 1 of the Act shall be liable to a fine of not exceeding one hundred dollars nor less than fifty dollars, or in default of payment of such fines, to imprisonment for a term of not exceeding three months nor less than one month.

3. Every one is guilty of an offence and liable to the penalty hereinafter provided who, at any time hereafter in any part of the province, without the consent of the owners or caretaker of any enclosure within which foxes or other fur-bearing animals are kept for breeding purposes, and on the outer fence of which enclosure are kept posted notices forbidding trespassing on the premises where the said animals are kept, and plainly discernible at a distance of not less than twenty-five yards therefrom, shall pass within the said fence of such enclosure or climb over, break or cut through the same for the purpose of entering the said enclosure.

4. Any person convicted of an offence against section 3 of this Act shall be liable to a fine of not exceeding five hundred dollars nor less than two hundred and fifty dollars and in default of payment of said fine to imprisonment for a term not exceeding six nor less than two months.

5. Every offence against this Act may be prosecuted and the penalties and punishments therefor enforced, in the manner directed by the Summary Convictions Act, contained in the Criminal Code, and the amendments thereto, so far as no provision is hereby made for any matter or thing which is required to be done with respect to such prosecution; and all the provisions contained in said Act and amendments shall be applicable to such prosecution, and to the judicial and other officers before whom the same are hereby authorized to be brought, in the same manner as if they were incorporated in this Act, and as if all such judicial and other officers were named in the said Act; provided always that in no instance shall a warrant to distrain, to levy the amount of the fine, imposed under this Act be issued, but on default of payment forthwith of the fine imposed, with costs, the offender shall be committed to jail.

NEW BRUNSWICK

An Act Relating to Foxes and Other Fur-bearing Animals Kept in Captivity

2 Geo. V, Chap. 10

(Assented to April 20, 1912)

WHEREAS, certain persons in the Province of New Brunswick have engaged in the business of raising or breeding foxes and other fur-bearing animals kept in captivity, and it is desirable to protect the said animals from being disturbed by strangers or persons other than the owner or keeper of said animals;

Be it therefore enacted by the Lieutenant-Governor and Legislative Assembly, as follows:

1. Every one is guilty of an offence and liable to the penalty hereinafter provided who at any time hereafter, in any part of the Province,

12

without the consent of the owner or caretaker of a ranch or enclosure where foxes or other fur-bearing animals are kept in captivity for breeding purposes, shall approach or enter upon the private grounds of the owner or owners of the said animals within a distance of twenty-five yards from the outer fence or enclosure within which the pens or dens of the said animals are located and upon which said fence, notices forbidding trespassing on the said premises are kept posted so as to be plainly discernible at the said distance of not less than twenty-five yards.

2. Any person convicted of an offence against Section 1 of this Act shall be liable to a fine of not exceeding $50.00, nor less than $5.00, and in default of payment of such fines to imprisonment for a term not exceeding three months, nor less than one month.

3. Every one is guilty of an offence and liable to the penalty hereinafter provided who at any time hereinafter, in any part of the Province, without the consent of the owner or caretaker of any enclosure within which foxes or other fur-bearing animals are kept for breeding purposes, and on the outer fence of which enclosure are kept posted notices forbidding trespassing on the premises where the said animals are kept, and plainly discernible at a distance of not less than twenty-five yards therefrom, shall pass within the said fence of such enclosure or climb over, break or cut through the same for the purpose of entering the said enclosure.

4. Any person convicted of an offence against Section 3 of this Act shall be liable to a fine not exceeding $100.00 nor less than $50.00, and in default of payment of said fine to a penalty not exceeding six nor less than two months.

5. Any person may kill any dog which he finds lurking about any enclosure in which are kept foxes or other fur-bearing animals for breeding purposes, and annoying or terrifying said animals, or any dog giving tongue and terrifying the animals so kept enclosed, or any dog which· he finds straying or being upon his or her property on which are kept enclosures of foxes or other fur-bearing animals of which he or she is the caretaker; provided, however, that no dog so straying, lurking or being on the premises above herein referred to, when muzzled or accompanied by the owner or person having charge or care of such dog, shall be so killed unless there is reasonable fear or apprehension that such dog, if not killed, is likely to annoy or terrify the said animals within the said enclosures.

6. The provisions of Chapter 123 of the Consolidated Statutes of New Brunswick, 1903, relating to Summary Convictions, shall so far as applicable and not inconsistent herewith, apply to all prosecutions and proceedings under this Act.

QUEBEC

An Act Relating to Foxes and Other Fur-bearing Animals Kept in Captivity

2 GEO. V, CHAP. 45

(Assented to Dec. 21, 1912)

WHEREAS certain persons in the Province of Quebec have engaged in the business of raising or breeding foxes and other fur-bearing animals kept in captivity;

Whereas it is desirable to encourage this industry, as well because of the diminishing supply of our most valuable furs, as of the rich source of profit which this industry has proved itself to be in some of the sister provinces;

Whereas it is essential to the successful breeding of these animals in captivity that they should be protected from disturbance by strangers, or persons other than the owner or keeper of the said animals;

Therefore, His Majesty, with the advice and consent of the Legislative Council and the Legislative Assembly of Quebec, enacts as follows:

1. Every one is guilty of an offence and liable to the penalty hereinafter provided who at any time hereafter, in any part of the Province, without the consent of the owner or caretaker of a ranch or enclosure where foxes or other fur-bearing animals are kept in captivity for breeding purposes, shall approach or enter upon the private grounds of the owner or owners of the said animals within a distance of twenty-five yards from the outer fence or enclosure within which the pens or dens of the said animals are located, and upon which said fence or enclosure notices forbidding trespassing on the said premises are kept posted, so as to be plainly discernible at the said distance of not less than twenty-five yards. No offence will be committed, however, by any neighbouring proprietor or occupant who approaches within such distance in the execution of work recognized or imposed by law or by municipal by-laws.

2. Any person convicted of an offence against Section 1 of this Act, shall be liable to a fine not exceeding fifty dollars nor less than five dollars and in default of payment of such fine and the costs to imprisonment for a term not exceeding three months nor less than one month.

3. Everyone is guilty of an offence and liable to the penalty hereafter provided who at any time hereafter, in any part of the Province, without the consent of the owner or caretaker of any enclosure within which foxes or other fur-bearing animals are kept for breeding purposes, and on the outer fence of which enclosure are kept posted notices for-

bidding trespassing on the premises where the said animals are kept, and plainly discernible at a distance of not less than twenty-five yards therefrom, shall pass within the said fence or such enclosure or climb over break or cut through the same for the purposes of entering the said enclosure, or for any other purpose whatever.

4. Any person convicted of an offence against Section 3 of this Act shall be liable to a fine not exceeding one hundred dollars, nor less than fifty dollars and in default of payment of said fine and the costs to a penalty not exceeding six nor less than two months.

5. Any caretaker may kill any dog wandering in the neighbourhood of any enclosure in which foxes or other fur-bearing animals are kept, and there giving tongue or otherwise terrifying such animals, provided, however, that the dog so killed is neither muzzled nor accompanied by the owner or by a person having charge or care of such dog.

6. Every infringement of any of the provisions of this Act is punishable summarily upon prosecution before a justice of the peace having jurisdiction in the district in which the offence was committed.

7. The provisions of Part XV of the Criminal Code respecting summary convictions shall, unless incompatible, apply to all prosecutions brought, tried and decided under this Section.

8. This Act shall come into force on the day of its sanction.

ONTARIO

Extracts from an Act Respecting Game, Fur-bearing Animals and Fisheries

3-4 GEO. V, CHAP. 69

40. (1) During the close season no person shall have in his possession, or in the possession of his servant or agent, or of any other person on his behalf, any game, wherever killed or procured, or any fish except that

(a) game lawfully killed or procured may be kept during the period between the end of the open season in any year and the 16th day of January in the following year; and

(b) skins of moose, deer, caribou and fur-bearing animals may be had in possession during the close season under the authority of a license issued not later than ten days after the end of the open season, and specifying the number and description of such skins.

(2) Except as expressly authorized by license, no person other than the actual owner for the use of himself and family, shall keep game in cold storage during the season in which the same may be so lawfully possessed. 7 Edw. VII, c. 49, s. 40; 8 Edw. VII. c. 65, s. 5.

(3) This section shall not apply to game animals, bred or *bona fide* procured for breeding purposes by persons *bona fide* engaged in the business of breeding game animals; and notwithstanding anything contained in this Act, such persons may at all times have in their possession such animals or any part thereof.

SASKATCHEWAN

Extracts from the Game Act

6. No persons shall hunt, trap, take, shoot at, wound or kill:

(5) Any fox at any time between the first day of May and the first day of September in any year.

. . . .

10. Except as provided in section 18, subsection (5) hereof, no person shall take out of, export or cause to be exported from Saskatchewan any big game or game bird or live fox without having obtained permission from the minister; the fees for such permit shall be $5 for each big game head, $100 for each live black or silver fox and $15 for each cross or red fox and $1 for each shipment of one dozen or less of game birds; and no person shall be entitled to export in one season more than five dozen such birds nor shall any permit be granted under this section for the export of any birds belonging to the grouse family. Substituted 1913, c. 58, s. 12.

. . . .

18. (5) A holder of a non-resident big game license shall be entitled to take with him out of the province as trophies the head, skin and hoofs of any big game which may have been legally killed by him and the meat of such big game; and the holder of a non-resident game bird license may take with him personally when leaving the province not more than one hundred game birds.

Appendix VIII

Notes Concerning the Conservation of Game in Quebec

By

JOHANN BEETZ,

Piastre Baie, Saguenay, Que.

THESE few notes are only suggestions made by a hunter, breeder and experienced observer towards the conservation of the fauna which represents one of the greatest resources of the Province of Quebec.

Hunting foxes out of season deprives the Province of Quebec of an enormous natural revenue; it will exterminate species particularly its own and ruin the fur-farming, for the following reasons:

(1) In the entire world, the territory between the strait of Belleisle and the Saguenay river produces the finest black, black-silver and silver foxes in the wild state.

(2) Eighteen years ago, when I arrived on the North shore of the gulf of St. Lawrence, the average catch of the choicest foxes, on the territory above mentioned was about 250 per year. To-day, under the same conditions, the catch averages 15 to 20, a demonstration that the animal is being exterminated and that it is better to protect it than to risk its extermination.

(3) Allowing the hunting of foxes out of season will inevitably result in, not only the useless and complete destruction of these valuable fur-bearers, but also in the destruction of all other fur-bearing animals living in that region as they will be unavoidably caught in traps not intended for them.

(4) As the fur of most foxes caught in traps or otherwise, out of season is valueless, they die without yielding the hunter any profit. Death will often be caused by a wound received in the trap during warm weather, by the absence of the mother because the captured animal is too young, or by the hunter not attending to it in a proper manner. Often also through an instinct of self-preservation, the fox brings forth its young in an inaccessible place. In such case the mother only, can be captured as, to provide food for the young, she must come out of the den. As young foxes

cannot provide for themselves before the end of July, capturing the mother condemns the young to death. This frequently happens on the rocky coast of the North Shore. Thus, as stated above, many foxes are uselessly destroyed to capture one, which, as often happens, may itself die after a few days.

(5) The North Shore is inhabited mostly by French Canadian families who until these last few years have obtained their living by fishing cod, etc. Now, the income which they obtain by fishing is totally insufficient, especially when considering the increasing cost of living. The winter hunting used to come at the proper time to compensate for the scarcity of fish. If hunting out of season is allowed the fox will disappear in about one year, and the inhabitants of that region will undoubtedly have to abandon their villages and go to other parts of the country.

(6) Where the fox is injurious to crops or poultry it should be destroyed, but, on the North Shore, that danger does not exist; consequently, it is better to conserve a natural resource of which other countries and the other provinces are envious.

(7) Everybody knows that every two or three years, the careful breeder of foxes needs new wild blood in order to strengthen and regenerate the stock. It has been demonstrated that in-breeding and captivity make the stock degenerate very quickly. In permitting hunting only in proper season in Zone No. Two, that is to say, from the 1st of November to the 15th of February (this latter date beginning the mating season for foxes) the hunters, *without any destruction* could put on the market enough living foxes to furnish the breeders with wild foxes, thus permitting the regeneration of those in captivity. Contrarily, if we allow hunting out of season in Zones One and Two (two unique territories in the Dominion for the production of wild black fox) in a year, the wild foxes will be exterminated and, in not more than six years, the breeder will be forced to cease breeding, his stock becoming rachitic and scrofulous by lack of new blood being introduced in breeding. Consequently, the result for the Province of Quebec and even for the other provinces of the Dominion will be marked by a net loss caused by the ruin of breeding and the gradual and accelerating diminution in the fur trade.

(8) The two classes, 4 and 5, of the measures that we suggest should be included in the proposed licenses, to prevent buyers of other provinces from taking foxes from the Province of Quebec out of season, which they will certainly do if no law prevents them.

Even now, Americans are preparing to settle in La Tuque and the neighbourhood of Pointe Bleue in order to buy all young and old foxes which will be caught in that region in the spring time. This will evidently happen in many other places. The only way to avoid all these regrettable consequences and especially to conserve our fine race of black foxes would be, as it seems to me, not to give such licenses in Zone No. Two (east of the Saguenay) which in this way would become a kind of National Park for the conservation of the black fox. Quebec is the only province in Eastern Canada which possesses wild black foxes. They are the finest in Canada and even in the whole world. No wonder that the other provinces are envious and would like to see us destroying that natural resource, which however, has served to form the basis of the breeding stock for which Prince Edward Island* and New Brunswick have become famous.

Let us try, for the pride and renown of our province, to conserve, and to increase this resource which we now possess.

If the basic reason for regulation by the province is to collect taxes for the animals taken alive, nothing prevents us from collecting such taxes for the foxes taken in winter or whose fur is sold. In this way, we will be able to collect that revenue for an unlimited number of years, while, otherwise, at the end of two years at most, the black fox will be destroyed and we will have, as it were, inconsiderately expended our capital in order to create temporary revenue.

SUGGESTIONS RESPECTING MEASURES TO BE TAKEN IMMEDIATELY AND BEFORE THE GRANTING OF LICENSES

(1) At present, as only four licenses have been granted in Zone No. Two (east of the Saguenay to Chateau bay) viz., to Mr. Fequet, Old Fort, Richard Joncas, Natashkwan, Peter Wright, Pigou, and to the undersigned, Johann Beetz, of Piastre Baie, all on the North shore of the Gulf, they should be cancelled immediately. Also, hunting the fur-bearing animals under any pretext in that zone, between the 15th of February and the 31st of October should be strictly forbidden.

(2) All licensees should be notified that, under the amended law, Zone No. Two is reserved by the Government.

(3) In Zone No. Two, notices of such law should be posted in conspicuous places and distributed by the game-wardens, game-keepers, fishery officials, postmasters and by the municipal councils.

---

* Prince Edward Islanders claim that the Island foxes are natives, and that they are the finest in the world. We do not express any opinion on the subject. (Ed.)

(4) To enact a law forbidding, the shipment of any living fur-bearing animal from the Province of Quebec (during the prohibited season from the 15th of February to the 31st of October) unless accompanied by a certificate by the authorities attesting that such animal came from a known fur-farm of the Province.

(5) Also a law prohibiting railway and other transportation companies accepting live foxes between the 15th of February and the 31st of October, intended for shipment out of the Province unless accompanied by the said permit or certificate.

Appendix IX

AVERAGE ANNUAL FUR PRODUCTION BY CONTINENTS*

By E. Brass

NORTH AMERICA

Lynx and Wildcat	$90,000
House Cat	80,000
Timber Wolf	8,000
Prairie Wolf	40,000
Red Fox	200,000
Silver Fox	4,000
Cross Fox	15,000
White Fox	30,000
Blue Fox	6,000
Gray Fox	50,000
Kit Fox	4,000
Hudson Bay Marten	120,000
Fisher	10,000
Mink	60,000
Weasel (Ermine)	400,000
Wolverene	3,000
Badger	30,000
Skunk	1,500,000
Civet Cat	100,000
Otter	30,000
Raccoon	600,000
White Bear	400
Black Bear	20,000
Brown Bear	3,000
Grizzly Bear	1,200
Marmot	30,000
Beaver	80,000
Muskrat or Musquash	8,000,000
Opossum	1,000,000
Hare	200,000
Musk-ox	500
Average production, about	$24,000,000

The average value of the fur produced annually in the other continents is estimated as follows:

South America	about	$ 2,000,000
Australia	"	6,000,000
Europe	"	24,000,000
Africa and Oceania	"	2,000,000
Asia	"	26,000,000

---

*Estimated on the basis of production of the three years, 1907–1909.

APPROXIMATE AVERAGE YEARLY PRODUCTION OF THE WORLD'S FURS IN THE THREE YEARS, 1907-1909

By E. Brass

The value of the world's production for each year amounts to 360,000,000 marks ($95,680,000), of which furs to the value of 160,000,000 marks come to Leipzig each year.

Skins used by the natives and hunters for supplying their own requirements are not included.

BEARS

White bear:
  Polar regions, Asia and Europe, 600; America, 400.
Grizzly bear:
  America, 1,200.
Brown bear:
  America, 2,000; Asia, 6,000.
Black bear:
  America, 20,000; Asia, 1,000.
Common brown bear:
  Asia, 3,000; Europe 2,000.

BEAVER
America, 80,000; Asia, 1,000; Europe, a few skins.

NUTRIA
South America, 1,000,000.

MUSKRAT OR MUSQUASH
America, about 8,000,000; Russia, 3,000.

CHINCHILLA
Peru, 600.

CHINCHILLINA
Peru and Bolivia, 12,000.

BASTARD CHINCHILLA
Bolivia, 3,000; Chili, 25,000.

BADGER
Europe, 100,000; America, 30,000; Asia, Japan and China, 30,000.

SQUIRREL
Siberia, 15,000,000; China, 500,000.

SQUIRREL-TAILS
Siberia, 73 tons; China, 2 tons.

Fox
Red fox:

    North America, 200,000; Siberia, 60,000; Russia, 150,000; Mongolia, China and Japan, 50,000; Australia, 30,000; Western and Central Asia, 50,000; Norway, 25,000; Germany, 250,000; other European countries, 350,000.

Karganer fox:

    Siberia and Central Asia, 150,000.

Cross fox:

    America, 15,000; Siberia, 3,000.

Gray fox:

    North America, 50,000.

Kit fox:

    North America, 4,000; Central Asia, 60,000.

White fox:

    Asia, 70,000; America, 30,000; Europe, 5,000.

Blue fox:

    America, 6,000; Siberia, 4,000; Northern Europe, 1,000.

Silver fox:

    America, 4,000; Siberia, 300.

Japan fox (raccoon dog):

    Japan, 80,000; China, 150,000; Korea, 30,000.

South American foxes:

    Pampas fox and Patagonian fox, total about 15,000.

HAMSTER
Germany, 2,000,000; Austria Hungary, 250,000.

HARES
Polar hares:

    Siberia, about 5,000,000; North America, 200,000.

WEASEL (Ermine)
America, 400,000; Siberia, 700,000; Europe, 10,000.

POLECAT
Germany, 60,000; Russia and Siberia, 150,000; other European countries, 80,000.

Fisher (Pekan)
America, 10,000.

Rabbit, Coney
France, 30,000,000; Belgium, 20,000,000; Germany, 500,000; Galicia and Russia, 1,000,000; Australia, 20,000,000.

Cats
Germany, 120,000; Holland, 200,000; Russia, 300,000; other European countries, 150,000; Asia, China and Japan, 150,000; America, 80,000.

Kolinsky
Siberia, 150,000; Manchuria, 50,000; China (weasel) 500,000; Japan (mink) 200,000.

Lynx, Gray Wildcat
America, 90,000; Asia, 30,000; Europe, 10,000.

Wildcat
South America, 10,000; Asia, 40,000; Europe and Western Asia, 10,000.

Marten
Baum marten:
Europe, 180,000; Northern Asia, 30,000.
Stone marten:
Europe, 350,000; Northern Asia, 30,000.

Sable and Hudson Bay Marten
America, 120,000; Siberia, 70,000; China, 20,000; Japan, 5,000.

Marmot
Asia, 4,550,000; America, 30,000.

Mink
North America, 600,000; Russia and Siberia, about 40,000; Europe, a few.

Otter (land)
America, 30,000; Asia, 55,000; Southern Asia, about 1,000; South America, about 5,000; Africa, about 500; Europe, 30,000.

Opossum
Australia, about 4,000,000; America, about 1,000,000

PERSIAN AND BLACK LAMBSKINS

Central Asia, Persians 1,500,000, Broadtails 100,000; Russia and Central Asia, Astrakhan 1,000,000; Crimean, 60,000; Schiras and salted skins, 200,000.

RACCOON

North America, 600,000.

FUR-SEALS

Alaska, northern waters and southern waters, 68,000.

SEA-OTTER

Northern Pacific, 400.

SKUNK

North America, 1,500,000; South America, 5,000.

CIVET CAT

North America, 100,000.

WOLVERENE

North America, 3,000; Siberia, 4,000; Europe, 1,000.

WOLF

America: timber wolf, 8,000; prairie wolf, 40,000; Asia: Siberia, 10,000; China, 5,000; Central Asia and Russia, 6,000; Europe, 1,000.

AMERICAN AND CANADIAN FURS SOLD BY A. & W. NESBITT AT PUBLIC AUCTION IN THE YEARS 1905-1912

Kind	1905	1906	1907	1908	1909	1910	1911	1912
Raccoon.......	37,424	26,833	8,471	49,990	60,028	58,323	48,531	60,869
Badger.........	3,720	2,393	1,165	1,264	2,652	3,934	5,229	5,954
Musquash.....	739,630	810,817	371,779	551,081	548,228	679,975	774,126	658,217
Skunk.........	124,357	162,015	130,213	190,298	239,145	239,573	352,313	326,845
Cat, Civet....	14,507	10,968	4,370	4,786	4,978	6,685	22,647	16,147
Beaver.......	919	10,780	13,577	3,232	6,402	6,122	2,097	2,438
Otter.........	2,614	2,203	1,476	3,831	3,141	2,496	1,429	1,325
Lynx.........	1,382	6,604	6,835	2,307	475	462	470	270
Cat, Wild.....	3,227	2,750	2,532	2,779	1,321	3,593	10,900	5,068
Wolf.........	8,614	12,548	4,580	14,854	10,074	19,223	21,930	30,173
Bear.........	1,164	1,235	1,473	1,890	2,297	3,662	1,960	1,908
Fisher........	238	726	1,030	768	264	167	300	57
Wolverene....	65	62	36	84	61	115	57	102
Ermine........	1,377	7,922	22,362	19,774	29,504	33,276	71,967	41,492
Fox, Silver....	60	94	243	94	111	102	70	50
Fox, Cross....	285	489	1,512	756	255	362	102	223
Fox, Red.....	3,974	16,536	6,550	8,034	9,612	8,808	9,574	4,283
Marten........	3,589	8,388	10,708	5,642	2,889	4,003	1,369	2,942
Mink.........	30,596	29,409	25,338	33,305	18,069	22,127	14,517	10,999
Opossum, Am..	146,328	292,231	30,382	98,397	95,187	77,507	136,417	256,759
Fox, Gray.....	9,966	14,527	3,597	3,724	3,151	7,082	6,613	7,258
Sea-otter.....	7	......	2	1	......	11	......	......
Musk-ox......	......	......	......	......	......	131		
Fox, Blue.....	......	62	39	25	95	280	48	255

IMPORTATION OF FURS TO LONDON, 1855

By E. Brass

Kind	From the Hudson's Bay Co's. Territory		Alaska, Oregon, Eastern and Southern Canada, etc., etc.,	
	Number	Value	Number	Value
Marten.........	136,513	£122,540	12,245	£11,540
Mink..........	55,740	38,540	171,083	12,305
Sea-otter.......	288	5,400	163	4,280
Beaver.........	69,376	25,480	6,078	4,780
Muskrat........	346,955	6,540	1,229,536	23,054
Otter..........	11,094	8,545	4,427	4,800
Fisher.........	4,911	6,840	3,174	2,256
Silver Fox... ...	480	6,840	218	4,580
Cross "	1,749	4,838	920	2,740
Red "	8,227	3,945	36,399	16,240
Blue "	86	172	5,086	12,758
Gray "	......	......	15,826	1,825
Kit "	4,646	485	5,086	1,025
White "	4,646	1,248	354	120
Wolf...........	15,392	4,975	......	....
Wolverene......	1,124	840	180	130
Lynx,..........	5,633	3,460	518	230
Wildcat........	374	120	6,989	2,005
Bear..........	8,961	22,480	3,206	8,425
Ermine.........	1,500	34	500	10
Skunk.........	5,945	6,743	200	40
Raccoon........	1,200	180	482,072	65,240
Badger........	1,084	228	......	......
Hare..........	83,757	1,025	2,095	50
Opossum........	......	......	12,745	1,875
Squirrel........	5,800	160	......	......
Others.........	28,000	,000	34,000	8,000

IMPORTATION OF FURS TO LONDON, 1875

By E. Brass

Kind	FROM THE HUDSON'S BAY CO'S TERRITORY		FROM ALASKA, EASTERN AND SOUTHERN CANADA, OREGON AND THE NORTHWESTERN UNITED STATES, SOLD BY RETAILERS AND IN THE LONDON SALES	
	Number	Value £	Number	Value £
Marten...........	131,154	173,500	37,712	38,563
Mink...........	72,400	73,840	39,245	33,
Sea-otter.......	223	5,480	3,653	102,580
Sea-otter (pup)...	......	......	520	3,280
Beaver...........	270,903	293,850	65,941	48,647
Muskrat.........	416,833	32,542	2,126,465	145,362
Otter (land)......	13,580	38,702	8,725	24,460
Fisher...........	3,558	11,200	1,868	3,780
Silver Fox.......	789	14,800	751	3,120
Cross "	786	3,870	1,451	6,587
Red "	8,945	6,325	75,365	28,956
Blue "	169	460	2,215	6,084
Gray "	......	......	25,602	6,850
Kit "	5,860	530	9,245	1,640
White "	6,026	2,100	2,072	850
Wolf.............	3,056	208	4,481	2,180
Wolverene.......	1,349	1,580	1,248	960
Lynx...........	13,242	11,480	2,504	1,800
Bear...........	6,880	23,500	6,796	22,540
Ermine or Weasel.	3,489	80	44,583	1,200
Skunk...........	2,789	1,860	275,943	81,540
Raccoon.........	7,154	1,240	341,077	58,650
Deer...........	15,005	300	......	......
Badger..........	8,386	3,000	12,522	4,540
Hare...........	60,520	5,680	429,474	10,402
Musk-ox........	23	50	5	10
Buffalo..........	108	560	200	580
Panther.........	......	......	165	183
Wildcat..........	......	......	2,197	2,650
Squirrel..........	......	......	8,146	100
Opossum........	......	......	143,653	2,253
Others..........	53,000	18,000	86,000	22,000

OFFERINGS OF FUR-SEALS AND SEA-OTTER AT THE LONDON AUCTION SALES

By P. R. Poland & Son, London

Year	Fur-seals	Sea-otter	Year	Fur-seals	Sea-otter
1850	13,915	....	1882	189,604	5,657
1851	9,348	....	1883	171,205	5,680
1852	16,193	....	1884	157,329	5,038
1853	9,714	....	1885	180,059	4,008
1854	18,199	....	1886	217,704	4,804
1855	29,464	....	1887	226,370	4,413
1856	20,641	....	1888	219,670	4,352
1857	9,423	....	1889	214,577	3,517
1858	19,504	....	1890	182,653	2,713
1859	14,476	....	1891	125,731	2,392
1860	13,231	....	1892	162,736	1,368
1861	24,341	....	1893	191,623	1,788
1862	31,949	....	1894	204,007	1,533
1863	27,086	....	1895	168,395	1,221
1864	20,326	....	1896	79,950	1,556
1865	17,259	....	1897	123,336	1,250
1866	19,844	....	1898	105,976	956
1867	15,697	....	1899	105,551	739
1868	83,941	....	1900	100,901	584
1869	149,808	....	1901	104,605	422
1870	153,654	....	1902	89,391	406
1871	154,939	3,824	1903	94,234	463
1872	168,672	4,307	1904	110,231	370
1873	170,678	5,095	1905	71,328	321
1874	161,291	4,920	1906	82,954	518
1875	174,107	4,564	1907	55,914	564
1876	167,141	5,059	1908	84,258	333
1877	142,671	5,420	1909	57,374	265
1878	169,497	5,258	1910	47,659	318
1879	175,119	5,176	1911	60,825	328
1880	205,240	5,583	1912	21,490	225
1881	210,745	5,647	1913	20,494*	81

*Not included in this total: 1898 "Alaska" sold at Seattle, U. S. A.

CATCH OF FUR-SEALS

Taken in Alaska, Copper Island, Lobos Island and the North West Coast for the years 1886-1911 inclusive

By Mr. Ernest Poland, 110 Queen Victoria St., London, Eng.

Year	Alaska	Copper	N.W.C.	Lobos Is.
1886	122,166	41,768	16,048	13,281
1887	104,059	54,584	39,629	10,863
1888	100,016	46,333	31,546	21,041
1889	100,037	47,416	42,025	10,245
1890	20,994	95,486	29,174	17,529
1891	17,652	17,025	47,207	13,635
1892	7,554	62,060	54,229	14,672
1893	7,500	32,857	129,820	13,624
1894	16,030	27,298	*144,691	13,437
1895	15,002	17,721	†110,449	16,450
1896	7,500	14,415	29,014	14,019
1897	22,504	......	68,893	19,250
1898	20,732	13,730	44,151	16,967
1899	26,434	9,487	39,277	15,381
1900	19,935	9,784	39,428	15,116
1901	22,276	13,372	29,851	12,882
1902	22,719	11,463	22,721	16,376
1903	15,295	7,733	22,426	11,070
1904	20,086	8,354	39,840	8,357
1905	22,400	8,313	22,677	......
1906	14,478	‡8,987	21,210	8,398
1907	......	7,069	14,363	4,529
1908	29,929	5,363	23,088	2,990
1909	14,350	3,145	16,455	......
1910	13,584	5,811	12,865	......
1911	......	3,322	......	2,997

*1894 should be 142,951 (see tables)
†1895 should be 109,301 (see tables)
‡4043 seized by Japanese (1904 catch) and 4944 (1905 catch)

QUANTITIES OF FUR-SEAL SKINS OFFERED ANNUALLY FOR PUBLIC SALE FROM THE YEAR 1886 TO 1910 INCLUSIVE

By Mr. Ernest Poland, 110 Queen Victoria St., London, Eng.

Year	Alaska	Copper Is.	Robben Is.	N.W.C. etc.	N.W.C. dry	Japanese	North Pacific	South Sea, etc.	Cape Horn	Falkland Is.	Lobos Is.	S. American	Chilian	Patagonian	Croset Is.	Amsterdam & St. Paul Is.	New Zealand	Australasian	Cape of Good Hope	Unclassified	Total
1886	122,166	41,768	1832	16,048	*	16,233			909		13,281								3,497	151	215,885
1887	104,059	54,584		39,629	*	9,512		200	2,705	212	10,863				51			200	2,389	189	225,471
1888	100,016	46,333		31,546	1,307	9,754		120	4,441	212	21,041	790			183			120	3,033	191	219,067
1889	100,037	47,416		42,025	1,130	5,683		315	2,670	93	10,245	1,476				905		315	1,877	416	213,886
1890	20,994	95,486		29,174	1,282	8,855		108	2,833	45	17,529							108	3,296	64	190,681
1891	17,632	17,025		47,207	1,177	8,117		136	3,048	140	13,635	84						136	4,906		113,103
1892	7,354	62,060		54,229	2,182	9,504		834	3,688	330	14,672	817		521				215	5,475	985	162,736
1893	7,500	32,857		129,820	2,069	242		88	2,199	517	13,624						386	217	1,141		191,622
1894	16,030	27,296		142,951	1,264		1,348	34	1,988		13,437			55				46	1,528		204,007
1895	15,002	17,721		109,301	1,607		1,272	584	2,802		16,450	873**	126					2,591	1,394	1,394	165,395
1896	7,500	14,415		29,014	1,171		1,148		2,069	698	14,019	2,001	51					2,747	2,531	144	79,950
1897	22,504			68,863	2,260	58	2,719	584	2,050	568	19,250†	5,319						1,223	457		122,326
1898	20,672	13,730		44,151	1,923	28	545		3,464	494	16,967	773						622	2,495		105,976
1899	26,434	9,487		39,277	2,716	860	583		6,431	766	15,381	2,845	452					932	651	99	105,681
1900	19,933	9,784		39,428	629	3,989			9,358	768	15,116							109	1,224		100,901
1901	22,276	13,372		29,851	83	7,028			11,737	819	12,882	827						193	4,786		104,605
1902	22,719	11,468		22,721	53	3,558		2,129	27,462	763	16,376	596				84		76	1,236		99,391
1903	15,295	7,733		22,426	601	87			27,462	8864**	11,070	68	32					640	5,802	116	94,234
1904	20,086	8,354		39,840	455				22,944	155	8,357	118						416	9,390		110,231
1905	22,409	8,313		22,677	549				11,387	97		400				358		161	5,345		71,126
1906	14,479	8,987		21,210	1,245			107	12,235	130	8,396	1,461						574	13,731		82,964
1907	29,929	7,059		14,363	78			58	15,648	110	4,529		53			198		397	12,701		85,914
1908	14,356	5,363		23,088	1,170			163	8,158	56	2,990	222					39	539	12,763		84,226
1909	14,356	3,145		16,455	46			5,304	4,953	160								39	12,013		57,374
1910	13,584	5,811		12,965	714			4,422	1,505	402		85				271			8,165		47,596

* N.W.C. dry for these years are included in tables of N.W.C. Seals, etc. From Fur-Seal Arbitration, in Appendix to Counter Case of H.M. Government Vol. II., 1893. **Includes 658 dry.

†13,481 of these were withdrawn and sold in 1866. They are not, however, included in the quantity for that year. †*Includes 680 black pups.

ABSTRACT OF CATALOGUES OF ALASKA SEAL PUBLIC SALES, SHOWING NUMBER OF DIFFERENT SIZES OFFERED ANNUALLY IN LONDON 1893-1910

By Mr. Ernest Poland, 110 Queen Victoria St., London, Eng.

Year	Date of Catalogue from which information is taken	Large Middlings	Middlings	Middlings and Smalls	Smalls	Large Pups	Middling Pups	Small Pups	Small Pups & Ex. Small Pups	Extra Small Pups	Extra Extra Small Pups	Odd Faulty, etc	Skins apart from rest of catalogue	Total for the year
1893	November 29th C. M. Lampson & Co.	20	118	1,337	3,276	1,788	859	104		17		1		7,600
1894	" 30th	12	902	3,625	6,405	3,560	1,350	149		10		5		16,080
1895	December 3rd		314	2,189	5,354	4,085	2,606	419		20		3		15,002
1896	" 9th		30	2,399	1,660	1,696	1,992	1,480		234				7,500
1897	" 9th		92	1,193	4,982	4,982	5,977	4,464	4	698		9		22,604
1898	" 15th		40	448	2,820	5,039	5,513	4,482		412		8		20,762
1899	" 15th		30	433	3,039	6,613	10,167	5,867		229		6		26,434
1900	December 14th "		10	183	1,370	4,011	7,223	5,797		781			560	19,935
1901	December 17th "		3	151	1,331	3,478	7,509	8,204		1,565	11	24		22,276
1902	December 17th "			131	1,180	2,848	7,145	8,676		2,169	50		520	22,719
1903	December 17th "		3	69	361	1,491	4,572	6,040		2,212	66	50	231	15,295
1904	December 16th		13	108	721	2,015	5,846	7,618		3,530	107	42	86	20,086

Skins apart from rest of catalogue:

1900 (560): Smalls 14; Large Pups 20; Middling Pups 95; Small Pups 180; Extra Small Pups 142; Ex. Ex. Sm. Pups 15; Faulty 74

1902 (520): Middlings & Smalls 12; Smalls 13; Large Pups 29; Middling Pups 123; Small Pups 143; Extra Small Pups 101; Ex. Ex. Sm. Pups 9; Faulty 80

1903 (231): Smalls 13; Large Pups 9; Middling Pups 40; Small Pups 95; Extra Small Pups 60; Ex. Ex. Sm. Pups 2

1904 (86): Smalls 12; Large Pups 18; Middling Pups 29; Small Pups 23; Extra Small Pups 4

(196)

ABSTRACT OF CATALOGUES ALASKA SEAL PUBLIC SALES (Continued)

Year	Date										Count	Details	Total
1905	December 15th	48	703	3,084	8,205	8,941	.....		1,288	1	79	100	5 Large Pups 33 Middling Pups 34 Small Pups 28 Extra Small Pups	22,409
1906	December 14th	11	200	1,590	5,740	6,272	.....		546	.....	33	86	3 Smalls 12 Large Pups 45 Middling Pups 22 Small Pups 2 Extra Small Pups 2 Faulty	14,478
1908	March 20th	2	141	939	3,218	2,788	.....		318	.....	18	76	6 Large Pups 28 Middling Pups 41 Small Pups 2 Extra Small Pups 2 Faulty	7,523
1908	December 17th	30	823	3,626	8,936	7,823	.....		1,109	4	58	.....		22,409
1909	December 17th	27	392	1,556	4,926	6,006	.....	1	1,255	11	40	136	5 Smalls 15 Large Pups 47 Middling Pups 58 Small Pups 11 Extra Small Pups	14,350
1909	December 16th	1	50	105	239	232	.....		36	.....	4			664
1910	December 16th		127	974	3,963	6,111	.....		1,510	11	38	186	1 Small 21 Large Pups 48 Middling Pups 98 Small Pups 18 Extra Small Pups	12,920

Seal Public Sales, Showing Number of Different Sizes Offered Annually in London, for the Years 1893-1898 Inclusive

By Mr. Ernest Poland, 110 Queen Victoria St., London, Eng.

Year	Date of Catalogue from which information is taken	Large Wigs	Wigs	Small Wigs	Middlings	Midgs & Smalls (mixed)	Mdgs and Smalls	Mdgs & Smalls & Smalls (mixed)	Smalls	Smalls & Large Pups	Large Pups	Large & Mdg Pups (mixed)	Mdg Pups	Mdg and Small Pups (mixed)	Small Pups	Sm. and Ex. Sm. Pups (mixed)	Extra Small Pups	Ex.Sm.& Ex.Ex. Sm. Pups (mixed)	Ex. Ex. Small Pups	Sm., Ex.Sm. & Ex.Ex.Sm. Pups (m)	Grey Pups	Black Pups	Odd, Faulty	Total	Total Yearly Quantities
1893	Hudson's Bay Co. ....23 Jan		2		9				130		106		42		42		13				90		30	403	
	C. M. Lampson & Co. ..27 Jan	21	114	20	220		2,782	31	8,750		8,184	50	7,711		6,417	24	3,901		927		175		427	39,854	
	C. M. Lampson & Co. ..21 Mar	2	10	2	4		26	20	91		133	15	114		[illegible]	11	35	21			1		11	875	
	C. M. Lampson & Co. ..29 Nov	140		238	698		5,438		14,345		12,385		11,705		10,973		7,764		2,365		375	3	217	66,617*	129,830-1893
	Hudson's Bay Co. ....29 Nov	43		35	189		441		1,345		1,447	160	1,157		1,531	171	1,044		500		14		10	8,088	
	Culverwell Brooks & Co. 30 Nov		88	275	316		1,631		2,333		2,901		2,257	71	2,146	12	1,461		441		226	3	92	14,253**	
1894	Hudson's Bay Co. ....15 Jan	1		6	22		164		943		1,289		1,053		977		508		990		1		10	5,191	
	C. M. Lampson & Co. ..15 Jan	2		15	44		499		1,461		1,506		1,536		1,223		893		227		26		9	7,453	
	Culverwell Brooks & Co. 15 Jan		24	3	18		255		384		576	57	502		434	26	363		90		17	11	19	2,687	
	C. M. Lampson & Co. ..15 Mar		1		2		20		186		426		607		428		406		234		25		9	2,344	142,951-1894
	Hudson's Bay Co. ....29 Nov	51		78	354		2,538		4,851		6,988		4,985		5,480		3,805		2,494		95		211	31,930	
	Culverwell Brooks & Co 29 Nov	21	78	44	179		1,850		6,706		7,305	69	6,017		6,142	76	6,290	34	5,760		2		221	40,794	
	C. M. Lampson & Co. ..30 Nov		186	1	375	5	4,122	211	10,558	4	9,739	359	9,070		8,016	101	6,089		3,427	101	562	22	504	52,548	
1895	Hudson's Bay Co. ....21 Jan	2		7	23		198		363		402		269		243		135		32				3	1,667	
	C. M. Lampson & Co. ..21 Jan			4	11		74		244		340		314		208		69		2				13	1,388	
	Culverwell Brooks & Co 21 Jan	21		10	7		23		67		212		227		224		179		58				2	1,030	
	C. M. Lampson & Co. ..20 Mar		39		75		508		1,617		2,048		1,780		1,036		581		90		11		343	8,137	
	Black, Chandler & Co. 14 Oct				3						21		62		26		25		2					139	
	C. M. Lampson & Co. ..3 Dec		440		685		4,990	22	10,850	12	10,444	70	9,359	17	8,033	7	4,523	48	1,416	25	228	31	349	51,549	109,301-1895
	Hudson's Bay Co. ....4 Dec	112		148	362		2,973		5,575		7,974		6,973		6,364		3,136		1,211		35		39	34,[illegible]	
	Culverwell Brooks & Co. 4 Dec		17		32		441		1,084		1,151	15	867		1,192	27	1,315		792					[illegible]	
	C. M. Lampson & Co. ..17 Dec		4		22		323		635		421		400		443		331		89		1			2,669	
	Hudson's Bay Co. ....17 Dec	8		4	12		118		214		260		136		131		60		17					955	
1896	Hudson's Bay Co. ....20 Jan	8		3	9		36		98		227		190		159		25		3					768	
	C. M. Lampson & Co. ..27 Mar		15		15		149		671	9	787	2	674		561	5	800		326		6		37	3,775	
	Culverwell Brooks & Co. 27 Mar		4		15		49		119		271		229		128		31		4					850	
	C. M. Lampson & Co. ..10 June						7		171		258		301		102		13							853	29,014-1896
	C. M. Lampson & Co. ..9 Dec	32	31	33	109		1,164	3	3,079		3,647	19	3,979		3,759		2,232		611		58	36	77	18,868	
	Culverwell Brooks & Co., 9 Dec		8	1	16		470		494		724		822		858		425		83					3,901	
1897	Hudson's Bay Co. ....18 Jan	15	288	9	490		3,050		5,593		8,066		8,058		8,132		3,363		1,176		51		161	38,453	
	Hudson's Bay Co. ....25 Mar	41		18	12		91		169		375		397		442		149						2	1,[illegible]	
	C. M. Lampson & Co. ..25 Mar		59	2	51		463		1,312		1,657		1,639		1,272		494	2	88		2		19	7,[illegible]	
	Culverwell Brooks & Co. 26 Mar		2	6	6		37		22		27		51		34		24		4					287	68,893-1897
	C. M. Lampson & Co. ..9 Dec		168		93		1,207	9	2,877		3,618	14	3,577	28	2,836	19	1,555	25	351		15		171	16,563	
	Culverwell Brooks & Co. 9 Dec		22	6	64		400		478		737		977		1,213		832		183		3			4,915	
1898	Hudson's Bay Co. ....17 Jan	104		73	215		1,244		2,642		3,991		3,789		3,605		1,354	84	350		10		75	17,536†	
	C. M. Lampson & Co. ..17 Mar		9	8	7		228		507		597		425		285	5	152		7				66	2,296	
	C. M. Lampson & Co. ..15 Dec	70	136	67	143		1,824	20	3,625		4,302	11	4,013		3,473	21	1,652		263		17		100	19,744	44,151-1898
	Hudson's Bay Co. ....15 Dec	17	1	11	29		322		691		1,030		1,074		933		[illegible]		83				34	4,575	

*[illegible] of this total were withdrawn and sold in January 1894.

**7008 withdrawn and sold Jan., 1894, but not included in that year's collection.

† Included in this total are the following quantities which were sold as under: 378 sold on 17/3/98, 3148 sold on 15/12/98, and 2367 sold on 16/1/99.

ABSTRACT OF CATALOGUES OF NORTH WEST COAST, ETC.

SEAL PUBLIC SALES, SHOWING NUMBER OF DIFFERENT SIZES OFFERED ANNUALLY IN LONDON, FOR THE YEARS 1899-1910 INCLUSIVE

By Mr. Ernest Poland, 110 Queen Victoria St., London, Eng.

Year	Date of Catalogue from which information is taken	Large Wigs	Wigs	Sm. Wigs	Middlings	Mdgs. and Smalls	Mdgs. & Sm. d. Smls. (mixed)	Smalls	Large Pups	L. P. and M. P. (mixed)	Mdle. Pups	M. P. and S. P. (mixed)	Small pups	Sm. p. and Ex. sm. p. (mixed)	Ex. Sm. pups	Ex. p. & Ex. f. r. sm. pups (mixed)	Ex. Fx. Sm. pups	(Gray pups)	Black pups	Faulty	Totals	Totals Yearly Quantities
1899	Hudson's Bay Co. ... 16 Jan	15			5	55		156	314		407		487		197		37			11	1,691	
	Hudson's Bay Co. ... 16 Mar	9			8	60		42	94		61		38		12					3	328	
	C. M. Lampson & Co. ... 16 Mar		21	1	15	115		245	253	8	201		115	11	14					44	1,049	
	C. M. Lampson & Co. ... 15 Dec		153		134		2,921	6,300	1,791		4,727		3,236		1,459		206	3		176	25,791	39,277—1899
	Hudson's Bay Co. ... 15 Dec	43		19	46	662		1,175			1,396		1,236		697		181			43	7,115	
	Culverwell, Brooks & Co. ... 15 Dec		3		37	143		232	486	2	865		1,032		434		69	6			3,303	
1900	C. M. Lampson & Co. ... 22 Jan		35		46	526		1,035	1,115		832		562		118		302			67	4,337	
	Hudson's Bay Co. ... 14 Dec	135		63	216	1,583		3,606	5,329		4,610		3,836		1,523		229	6		171	21,630	39,428—1900
	C. M. Lampson & Co. ... 14 Dec		88		64	1,273		2,399	2,632		2,435		2,568		1,632			16		131	13,461	
1901	Hudson's Bay Co. ... 21 Jan		3		3	20		50	113		103		81		17		1			4	395	
	C. M. Lampson & Co. ... 21 Jan		13	1	5	224		551	727		484		269		74		1	1		38	2,367	
	Culverwell, Brooks & Co. ... 21 Jan	2	9		60	308		614	1,272		761		389		162		19			6	3,594	29,851—1901
	C. M. Lampson & Co. ... 17 Dec		4		17	253		293	277		221		133		32			3		1	1,236	
	C. M. Lampson & Co. ... 17 Dec		76		98	1,399		2,423	2,728		2,654		1,395		1,122		156			173	13,696	
	Hudson's Bay Co. ... 17 Dec	35		13	40	466		945	1,748		1,993		2,021		959		292	4		127	8,643	
1902	Hudson's Bay Co. ... 13 Mar	27		7	28	214		549	1,109		1,110		710		181					77	4,033	
	C. M. Lampson & Co. ... 13 Mar	2		1	4	153		242	223		135		94		24		5			24	905	22,721—1902
	C. M. Lampson & Co. ... 17 Dec	30	33	30	243	1,987		3,062	3,114		2,858		3,024		1,680		364	96		148	16,668	
	Hudson's Bay Co. ... 17 Dec	9		2	12	222		598	641		567		374		199		10			41	2,885**	
1903	Hudson's Bay Co. ... 19 Jan	16		9	49	333		478	646		552		338		89		8			26	2,538	
	Hudson's Bay Co. ... 26 Mar	4	2		5	18		46	90		69		70		24					6	334	
	C. M. Lampson & Co. ... 26 Mar		9		13	309		569	785		624		446		139		2			223	3,110	22,426—1903
	C. M. Lampson & Co. ... 17 Dec		78		159	1,729		2,527	2,760		2,360		2,193		1,254		152	9		173	13,405	
	Hudson's Bay Co. ... 17 Dec	7		5	14	164		393	951		693		464		168					101	2,960	
	Culverwell, Brooks & Co. ... 17 Dec	1			2	2		21	17		16		9		1						79	

** 5 withdrawn—included in Total.

ABSTRACT OF CATALOGUES OF NORTH WEST COAST, ETC. (Continued)

Year	Date of Catalogue from which information is taken	Large Wigs	Wigs	Sm. Wigs	Middlings	Mdgs. and Small	Mdgs. & Sm. (mixed)	Smalls	Large Pups	L. P. and M. P. (mixed)	Mdlg. Pups	M. P. and S. P. (mixed)	Small Pups	Sm. p. and Ex. p. (mixed)	Ex. Sm. pups	Ex. S. p.'d Ex. Ex. Sm. pups (mixed)	Ex. Ex. Sm. pups	Gray pups	Black pups	Faulty	Totals	Total Yearly Quantities
1904	C. M. Lampson & Co.........25 Jan.	3	24	...	9	...	329	697	947	...	810	...	882	...	246	...	10	...	...	103	3,759	39,840—1904
	Hudson's Bay Co.........25 Jan.	...	...	3	17	...	325	704	1,384	...	1,023	...	470	...	112	...	...	4	...	70	4,164	
	Culverwell, Brooks & Co.........25 Jan.	...	1	...	...	...	14	74	235	...	200	...	60	...	9	...	...	...	...	31	563	
	C. M. Lampson & Co.........17 Mar.	...	8	...	5	...	164	381	453	...	268	...	167	...	45	...	10	...	...	409	1,552	
	C. M. Lampson & Co.........16 Dec.	2	92	...	287	...	4,021	6,921	6,539	...	4,300	...	2,992	3	1,242	...	242	...	...	27,038		
	Culverwell, Brooks & Co.........16 Dec.	...	...	2	5	...	28	66	50	...	82	...	76	...	27	...	5	...	...	374		
	Hudson's Bay Co.........16 Dec.	5	12	1	238	...	238	410	699	...	646	...	354	...	110	...	14	...	51	2,340		
1905	C. M. Lampson & Co.........23 Jan.	...	...	...	6	...	223	583	622	...	350	...	124	...	30	...	...	...	...	16	1,954	22,677—1905
	C. M. Lampson & Co.........30 Mar.	...	5	...	5	...	63	178	280	...	192	...	148	...	239	...	157	...	...	13	1,290	
	C. M. Lampson & Co.........16 Dec.	...	85	...	362	...	3,076	4,687	4,671	...	3,241	...	2,270	...	769	...	...	3	...	360	19,443	
1906	C. M. Lampson & Co.........23 Jan.	...	22	...	129	...	1,228	1,616	1,368	...	640	...	355	...	102	...	13	...	305	56	5,833	21,216—1906
	C. M. Lampson & Co.........14 Dec.	...	58	...	115	...	1,915	3,960	3,902	...	2,647	...	1,817	...	541	...	63	...	4	355	15,377	
1907	C. M. Lampson & Co.........24 Jan.	...	21	...	25	...	599	1,364	1,455	...	861	...	390	...	85	...	4	1	...	77	4,847	14,343—1907
	C. M. Lampson & Co.........21 Mar.	...	...	...	1	...	103	359	228	...	118	...	59	...	26	...	...	1	...	19	920	
	C. M. Lampson & Co.........	102	...	...	177	...	1,328	2,553	2,074	...	1,236	...	718	...	233	...	10	...	65	112	8,956	
1908	C. M. Lampson & Co.........24 Jan.	...	34	...	44	...	957	1,890	1,820	...	1,356	...	824	...	261	...	14	...	52	176	7,428	23,063—1908
	C. M. Lampson & Co.........17 Dec.	...	167	...	154	...	2,452	4,360	3,977	...	2,618	...	1,329	...	339	...	66	1	29	178	13,660	
1909	C. M. Lampson & Co.........28 Jan.	...	26	...	23	...	318	694	700	...	422	...	214	...	24	...	...	...	...	70	2,491	16,455—1909
	C. M. Lampson & Co.........17 Dec.	...	132	...	120	...	1,994	3,785	3,670	...	2,452	...	1,306	...	261	...	18	9	...	227	13,964	
1910	C. M. Lampson & Co.........27 Jan.	...	...	...	...	...	59	87	70	...	48	...	15	...	...	...	...	...	...	...	279	12,946—1910
	C. M. Lampson & Co.........16 Dec.	3	72	...	84	...	2,068	3,343	2,899	...	2,145	...	1,309	2	358	...	37	1	106	154	12,506	

QUANTITIES OF AMERICAN FURS (HUDSON'S BAY CO.)

(Figures for the years 1752 till 1849, inclusive, were obtained from Mr. Henry Poland's *Fur-bearing Animals in Nature and Commerce*)

Year	Coat Beaver	Parchment Beaver	Marten	Otter	Lynx	Fox	Wolverene	Bear	Wolf	Mink	Musk-rat	Raccoon	Elk and Deer	Rabbit, Amer.	Fisher
1752	10,143	33,675	24,639	1,296	4,009	913	670	350	968	233	553		534		
1753	9,061	29,041	25,725	1,338	7,179	1,015	712	375	1,820	88	285		410		
1754	7,295	22,270	10,787	1,123	4,198	638	721	250	1,071						
1755	7,441	27,755	9,671	1,191	1,444	753	868	414	1,450						
1756	9,825	25,042	6,050	1,192		1,222	847	333	1,927						
1757	9,846	26,388	5,352	1,339	836	572	761	340	1,621						
1758	8,000	22,886	7,882	1,305	917	352	652	387	1,452						
1759	7,000	20,110	20,295	1,250	1,881	2,445	934	434	4,006						
1760	9,900	23,126	22,465	1,514	3,842	4,755	871	621	3,395						
1761	13,300	30,446	18,547	2,232	5,338	4,820	952	585	4,718						
1762	13,000	36,265	13,389	2,557	6,820	2,057	1,221	641	3,212				1,072		
1763	9,353	24,881	17,332	1,478	6,000	2,207	1,322	648	2,731	147	2,789		1,927		
1764	10,600	23,068	11,814	1,553	2,005	2,892	843	494	4,073						
1765	14,450	30,450	7,558	1,935	1,771	1,536	755	706	3,461	120	1,269				534
1766	10,400	28,536	8,066	2,144	1,138	2,445	486	732	4,226	133	5,279	307	2,385		110
1767	10,500	17,950	20,768	1,752	1,088	3,323	885	409	5,905	362	1,458	300	4,010		116
1768	6,300	18,767	19,949	1,438	1,128	1,146	473	442	2,914	307	1,199	300	590		160
1769	6,750	18,767	15,897	1,171	2,508	1,952	461	373	3,080	174	622	416	2,274		120
1770	9,500	25,273	26,047	1,296	4,012	3,583	604	401	5,476	160	943	289	3,237		97
1771	9,900	22,427	22,496	1,605	4,225	2,126	933	275	3,565	129	2,323	300	3,944		67
1772	8,350	19,851	12,626	1,490	5,463	1,451	742	269	2,703	94	5,913	430	4,499		13
1773	9,700	17,689	9,891	1,579	2,301	1,552	570	250	4,293	116	4,909		3,127		30
1774	4,600	19,472	16,739	958	1,744	609	407	226	583	168	5,913		3,920		26
1775	4,050	16,668	19,742	1,698	705	911	451	243	1,955	163	5,626		3,206		36
1776	4,900	15,904	18,143	1,773	2,823	674	337	309	613	162	4,357		3,945		99
1777	5,700	25,597	17,798	2,144	2,476	867	434	314	375	290	3,700		1,252		46
1778	4,300	20,033	16,730	1,584	1,245	558	199	219	30	197	4,095		500		58
1779	2,900	17,320	17,484	1,343	3,168	988	193	300	2,644	263	4,750	540	6,421		95
1780	7,070	26,867	22,060	2,401	2,966	2,188	344	300	1,166	221	5,830	488	3,025		82
1781	6,360	35,763	18,277	2,306	1,553	2,149	396	310	375	218	5,500	401	516		59
1782	2,050	18,752	7,466	1,750	960	593	121	408	1,430	150	5,830	840	100		40
1783	1,500	13,100	13,420	1,400	980	540	87	350	480	200	4,040	660	700		74
1784	3,200	15,500	13,800	1,996	822	440	90	230	1,820	150	5,161	502	1,403		95
1785	3,950	24,350	16,322	2,145	1,090	515	218	196	2,393	188	5,700	406	2,379		80
1786	3,800	25,095	23,365	940	2,050	999	234	172	3,500	371	4,360	604	1,490		30
1787	2,900	37,100	27,990	2,674	1,550	1,440	250	177	2,580	380	5,147		3,665		181
1788	4,900	38,320	25,070	1,822	970	3,778	270	210	2,423	366	8,801	347	2,980	8,200	100
1789	3,600	41,530	23,901	1,701	1,603	2,290	242	384	3,038	464	9,004	644	3,430	4,445	182
1790	5,276	41,530	18,847	1,983	1,400	5,823	202	341	3,237	308	5,250	1,075	3,036	4,602	145
1791	3,600	49,738	20,954	2,338	1,546	6,000	300	479	3,450	567	12,776	733	4,040	9,294	148
1792	4,724	46,930	21,095	3,737	989	2,130	295	450	3,007	388	19,332	867	1,820		282
1793	4,024	42,242	11,639	4,667	1,102	1,837	296	372	2,619	323	10,390	910	2,923	842	344
1794	3,664	39,517	15,547	4,364	1,149	2,834	344	459	3,741	384	12,708	2,209	3,358	4,130	242
1795	2,516	51,123	25,787	4,151	1,625	2,683	312	629	4,734	876	9,309		4,217	17,470	457
1796	2,901	48,697	30,374	4,006	1,541	8,780	388	464	7,681	1,033	10,557		4,097	12,072	464
1797	2,595	44,516	18,488	3,097	11,754	549	410	526	8,264	1,145			3,938	9,646	585
1798	1,728	43,418	22,875		2,269	7,440	397	675	11,636	1,240				7,917	

(201)

	Cost Beaver	Parch't Beaver	Marten	Otter	Lynx	Fox	Wol- verene	Bear	Wolf	Mink	Musk- rat	Rac- coon	Elk and Deer	Rabbit Amer.	Fisher	Swan	Castor- eum	Badger Amer.
1800	1,668	35,037	30,053	3,694	3,708	10,164	495	605	5,693	1,344	15,272	970	5,185	21,825	572			
1801	1,406	33,253	22,949	3,486	3,495	32,754	466	672	3,122	1,073	15,894	2,329	2,642	24,600	208			
1802	2,150	37,187	18,265	3,911	3,658	17,165	377	683	4,646	923	8,334	2,635	3,354	18,009	418			
1803	642	32,127	9,893	3,897	2,083	7,624	368	607	4,035	678	10,751	1,322	3,556	10,613	762			
1804	1,668	31,737	17,182	4,160	1,091	3,100	358	560	3,252	847	16,153	800	4,314	9,856	228			
1805	1,802	38,083	22,318	4,548	1,052	8,322	356	529	3,199	1,399	31,100	1,062	4,902	28,048	211	166		
1806	1,011	20,732	40,182	3,447	1,588	13,284	313	566	4,260	1,880	21,046	1,500	4,441	24,746	417	435		
1807	1,050	29,759	40,476	4,320	1,588	3,052	401	759	4,181	2,662	14,886	1,013	4,059	54,338	502	266		
1808	1,684	32,884	33,706	5,077	2,788	3,741	163	1,060	3,704	3,185	24,660	1,173	5,339	25,914	714	1,192		
1809	1,425	32,025	2,350	866	277	2,700	37	162	97	706	21,167	1,152	45	34,210	164	1,067		
1810	1,274	28,720	51,807	8,206	7,029	7,114	401	1,560	16,330	4,499	32,564	1,071	4,352	101,072	980	1,652		
1811	1,060	15,524	11,339	3,044	2,593	2,019	155	425	3,162	690	25,296	101		15,003	614	4,631		
1812	1,525	41,873	24,425	6,492	1,884	5,273	314	1,036	5,933	398	44,144	168	3,884	2,506	570	517		
1813	672	18,066	9,990	3,425	167	2,363	163	684	1,290	641	80,341	98	141	2,105	317	588		
1814	462	17,356	23,106	3,947	122	8,802	116	846	505	1,066	138,772	46	324	19,835	550	4,305		
1815	666	17,380	21,787	2,908	131	1,923	166	446	1,520	1,324	18,963	70	48	19,835	228	3,384		
1816		11,243	16,628	2,297	116	1,923	34	151	20	633	18,963			19,437	61	3,635		
1817	661	27,815	56,648	5,837	847	3,704	182	1,044	2,190	2,475	154,070	22	35	77,052	395	25		
1818	651	35,493	65,493	7,753	845	2,970	291	1,568	5,077	3,667	63,857	87	772	14,268	962	3,670		
1819	480	17,356	65,851	4,211	1,533	3,811	257	763	2,994	1,638	63,431		49	16,055	802	2,463		
1820	281	16,683	62,411	3,747	2,901	2,964	247	260	627	1,722	65,286	300	258	19,682	779	279		
1821	297	20,565	69,995	5,394	4,128	3,847	18	1,511	3	2,647	113,914	350	300	16,650	870	713		
1822	210	59,847	87,834	7,371	8,966	8,048	778	2,700	285	4,067	164,270	290	992	9,661	1,805	48		
1823	708	46,202	62,961	8,769	7,173	5,119	579	2,312	384	4,549	217,646	64	678	970	1,299	447		
1824	1,290	76,060	61,216	10,528	6,456	3,309	631	2,153	727	5,929	206,801	51	3,221	530	1,588	1,507		
1825	800	64,600	61,520	9,635	5,104	3,730	694	2,139	1,141	5,559	225,000	78	712		1,588	1,605		
1826	1,652	61,400	88,539	7,895	5,161	10,011	560	2,118	1,087	6,982	397,497	183	1,633	2,330	1,440	3,811		
1827	472	61,125	105,681	9,061	7,254	2,787	513	2,600	1,269	11,119	473,266	138	1,000	5,444	1,321	3,817		
1828		57,200	83,417	10,552	11,680	7,708	402	2,999	1,261	16,862	859,088	79	2,779		1,482	5,082		
1829		66,614	73,960	11,192	20,858	4,122	454	1,941	2,106	7,672	1,062,813	107	3,340		974	4,207		
1830		25,718	25,524	18,705	24,611	4,434	652	1,583	2,140	22,700	396,300					3,734		
1831		87,000	96,450	18,100	16,347	4,453	1,242	3,490	6,371	9,900	728,000	177			3,000	2,589		
1832	lbs. 264	70,100	166,166	13,012	870	4,674	1,472	4,158	567	6,506	387,000	372		1,330	3,070	4,994	lbs. 2,707	
*1833	1,074	32,293	17,732	22,303	14,255	522	114	1,500		25,100	63,174	210	2,492		682	7,918	730	
†1834	860	96,298	64,190	15,487	6,990	9,937	522	1,087	8,494	17,860	664,492	713	2,130	293,677	5,296	4,705	3,462	
‡1835	960	78,906	61,000	10,208	4,440	15,904	1,571	7,451	3,722	16,049	711,046	822	3,700	20,000	2,479	12	3,029	
§1836	239	81,788	56,993	15,934	31,867	2,378	1,286	4,127	935	27,750	161,033	1,900	3,700	25,840	6,115	6,600	1,475	
1837	304	82,927	186,166	15,152	45,152	25,008	145	2,101	7,081	15,641	188,649	585	2,161	24,361	3,590	8,251	2,788	
1838	165	81,868	83,120	10,792	66,691	6,726	2,166	7,663	7,875	19,141	188,645	273	30F		4,042	2,704	2,030	
1839	198	56,298	63,129	9,465	45,143	8,626	944	4,161	6,869	22,190	573,600	1,115	3,518		6,401	2,129	1,520	
1840	220	55,431	56,860	8,636	45,860	12,681	1,328	1,077	8,185	17,680	196,226	1,034	1,971		5,293	2,002	1,667	
1841	322	50,900	57,848	7,153	45,143	8,407	1,986	4,923	9,550	17,088	100,440	1,175	3,700		4,040	1,940	1,492	
1842	372	40,305	63,529	5,940	10,034	7,115	2,034	5,409	8,694	17,780	540,577	1,820	3,700		4,397	2,456	1,161	
1843	184	39,086	70,532	6,820	8,247	9,061	1,647	5,576	10,733	25,382	543,155	1,908	2,385		4,404	2,574	773	
1844	409	38,252	71,954	6,971	7,173	11,104	1,230	6,040	13,204	24,855	265,117	1,763	653		4,504	2,670	1,055	
1845	484	41,111	103,621	6,398	10,339	16,312	1,075	5,700	10,191	32,031	295,617	1,467			4,678	2,433	2,000	883
1846	190	65,180	148,670	8,168	21,180	12,597	938	4,339	8,522	33,294	305,172	1,305			5,605	1,922	1,746	887 / 1,116
1847	211	26,892	146,137	6,648	31,062	10,759	965	5,630	10,725	36,621	248,710	1,140			5,269	1,573	1,657	1,226 / 728
1848	137	40,845	115,323	9,218	47,005	20,219	1,128	6,003	7,960	37,123	224,347	1,091			5,301	1,522	1,170	791
1849	135	32,502	65,558	11,310	43,253	15,977	1,465	6,342	12,045	34,712	179,075	1,280			7,505	1,510	1,709	1,140

*YF, MR not arrived this year.   †Including YF, MR of 1833.   ‡YF not arrived this year.   §including YF of 1836.

(202)

FUR SALES OF THE HUDSON'S BAY COMPANY

(Supplied to the High Commissioner for Canada for the Commission of Conservation)

Date		Bear (black)	Bear (brown)	Bear (white)	Wild-cat	Ermine	Fisher	Fox (blue)	Fox (cross)	Fox (red)	Fox (silver)	Fox (white)	Lynx
1850	No.		6,261		89	467	7,920	17	3,033	7,759	877	1,867	43,738
1851	No.		6,262		340	747	6,305	8	1,981	5,581	526	890	20,353
1852	No.		7,205		243	796	5,967	11	2,524	5,675	913	843	8,519
1853	No.		7,484		222	2,002	5,861	46	2,307	6,869	847	3,996	5,361
1854	No.		6,331		135	1,295	4,933	34	1,172	3,175	390	4,070	4,552
1855	No.		9,266		381	1,289	4,901	29	1,790	8,326	493	1,577	5,682
1856	No.		9,346		330	1,940	5,210	102	1,948	7,384	615	10,311	11,358
1857	No.		8,182		214	1,925	5,563	15	3,236	10,526	1,072	4,999	23,362
1857	Price		37/3				32/-		79/6	15/3	16/16/10	7/-	12/8
1858	No.		8,130		208	1,034	5,957	20	3,472	9,707	1,060	2,103	31,642
1858	Price		23/11				26/1		55/6	8/11	10/11/5	4/10	8/1
1859	No.		8,922		189	800	6,050	15	3,962	11,488	1,164	1,577	33,757
1859	Price		25/8				34/1		66/8	12/1	14/6/11	6/4	9/6
Average for decade (dollars)			7.00				7.30		16.40	2.95	67.75	1.46	2.45
1860	No.		8,144		143	1,206	7,197	3	4,030	11,031	1,177	3,395	23,226
1860	Price		23/9				32/11		60/-	12/4	12/13/5	6/10	10/-
1861	No.		7,474		134	1,267	5,853	42	3,407	8,897	1,066	5,069	15,178
1861	Price		28/2				32/10		59/10	11/8	14/11	5/10	8/1
1862	No.		8,214		115	912	5,980	23	2,248	7,782	632	2,805	7,272
1862	Price		30/9				26/8		41/-	9/9	10/14/11	5/8	8/6
1863	No.		7,571		164	1,175	6,053	29	1,946	6,402	588	3,365	4,448
1863	Price		35/7				26/3		39/-	11/-	10/14/3	6/-	12/3
1864	No.		7,878		75	899	5,424	82	1,963	5,719	612	12,242	4,926
1864	Price		31/5				28/2		34/1	12/2	10/16/3	5/11	14/6

(203)

FUR SALES OF HUDSON'S BAY COMPANY (Continued)

Date		Bear (black)	Bear (brown)	Bear (white)	Wild-cat	Ermine	Fisher	Fox (blue)	Fox (cross)	Fox (red)	Fox (silver)	Fox (white)	Lynx
1865	No.	7,337			63	2,094	4,953	33	1,800	8,760	459	4,821	5,437
	Price	32/3					30/4		30/9	10/11	8/17/-	6/7	12/7
1866	No.	8,931			117	1,514	4,605	36	1,912	7,660	579	5,919	16,498
	Price	27/3					30/10		33/5	9/11	6/19/2	11/6	11/7
1867	No.	7,603			83	3,526	4,864	42	2,712	20,824	888	5,401	35,971
	Price	23/5					36/2		35/5	7/-	7/16/-	7/11	8/2
1868	No.	6,920			94	3,869	6,311	13	5,080	26,822	1,253	2,541	76,556
	Price	27/1					33/5		22/3	6/-	6/11/6	11/9	6/10
1869	No.	8,661			89	1,979	7,477	124	5,174	20,267	1,490	12,082	68,392
	Price	26/9					32/11		22/4	7/9	5/10/10	8/-	6/1
Average for decade (dollars)		6.87					7.46		9.07	2.36	45.70	1.83	2.37
1870	No.	8,420			68	2,228	7,959	48	3,436	13,054	914	4,629	37,447
	Price	27/6					35/5	24/-	19/7	7/9	5/15/4	6/10	5/6
1871	No.	8,589			82	3,106	6,743	15	2,592	6,546	696	1,805	15,696
	Price	29/4			1/6		35/6		19/3	8/4	*/12/-	6/6	6/6
1872	No.	8,569			46	2,958	7,072	36	2,090	7,736	559	2,806	7,942
	Price	42/1			2/3	*32/9	49/3	27/-	27/9	9/6	9/9/8	10/6	11/10
1873	No.	8,172			24	4,012	3,639	90	2,315	8,339	694	7,325	5,123
	Price	41/-			2/3		48/1	45/3	27/9	10/-	9/11/9	8/-	19/10
1874	No.	7,431			28	4,477	3,539	60	1,645	7,428	416	5,315	7,106
	Price	41/9			2/3	*20/2	53/9	47/1	28/8	9/2	11/5/3	7/1	14/4
1875	No.	7,120			189	4,732	3,538	69	2,212	8,973	796	6,058	11,250
	Price	41/3			1/9	*13/-	51/2	57/9	46/6	9/3	14/6/7	8/3	14/2
1876	No.	7,804			83	6,369	3,265	58	2,455	9,538	687	4,323	18,774
	Price	38/2			2/09	*12/-	55/8	56/2	44/2	9/11	13/3/-	6/11	13/-

*Prices quoted for ermine are so much per timber of 40 skins.

(204)

FUR SALES OF THE HUDSON'S BAY COMPANY (Continued)

Date		Bear (black)	Bear (brown)	Bear (white)	Wild-cat	Ermine	Fisher	Fox (blue)	Fox (cross)	Fox (red)	Fox (silver)	Fox (white)	Lynx
1877	No.	....	7,543		40	5,338	3,338	48	3,550	11,233	971	5,299	30,508
	Price		25/5				37/-	48/4	27/6	6/11	7/18/3	5/9	8/3
1878	No.	....	7,415		10	5,838	5,461	239	4,291	16,791	1,063	24,402	42,834
	Price		24/3				30/1	44/8	22/6	6/4	8/4/6	4/6	7/5
1879	No.	....	7,796		10	4,956	6,132	60	3,493	13,038	914	5,938	27,345
	Price		27/11			*13/4	38/10	30/-	21/3	7/10	10/19/3	9/10	8/7
Average for decade (dollars)			8.13		.51	4.96	10.43	10.31	6.77	2.04	47.25	1.78	2.63
1880	No.	.....	5,951		2	2,324	4,216	24	3,289	12,401	830	2,311	17,834
	Price		32/-		3/6	*11/5	35/2	26/4	36/5	9/4	11/14/10	11/7	10/1
1881	No.	.....	8,531		24	3,695	5,059	50	3,224	9,126	912	4,362	15,386
	Price		36/2		3/9	*6/8	36/4	31/6	37/11	9/-	11/4/6	11/6	12/7
1882	No.	.....	8,021		6	4,561	5,143	55	2,214	6,035	668	5,722	9,443
	Price		39/-		4/-	*2/-	34/5	31/3	40/6	9/3	11/19/4	7/2	14/8
1883	No.	.....	11,188		19	5,112	4,640	37	1,762	5,869	506	5,896	7,599
	Price		45/1		3/6	*2/1	33/-	32/-	38/-	9/3	13/2/9	6/7	16/9
1884	No.	.....	5,515		10	3,912	3,820	76	1,489	4,696	336	6,461	8,061
	Price		64/9		2/-	*2/5	33/3	45/6	39/7	9/-	14/18/10	7/7	19/2
1885	No.	.....	10,765		24	7,042	4,200	18	2,192	10,090	622	2,801	27,187
	Price		63/-		2/3	*4/11	21/5	28/8	27/9	5/11	8/17/8	10/6	11/8
1886	No.	.....	8,386		10	4,780	1,041	18	3,237	11,526	874	3,280	51,511
	Price	62/5	56/4	45/6	2/-	*4/4	23/11	23/-	34/9	7/-	14/6/5	11/7	18/9
1887	No.	.....	8,270		2/-	4,166	4,510	35	3,221	11,830	836	4,152	74,050
	Price	79/8	104/10	40/9		*1/10	22/10	85/4	33/4	7/9	13/-/-	19/4	9/9

*Prices quoted for ermine are so much per timber of 40 skins.

(205)

MICROCOPY RESOLUTION TEST CHART

(ANSI and ISO TEST CHART No. 2)

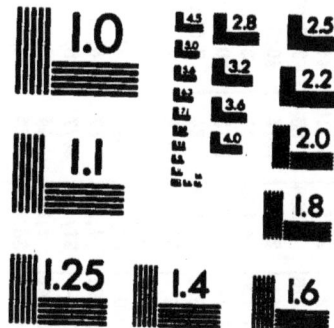

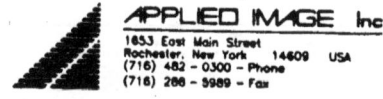

APPLIED IMAGE Inc

1853 East Main Street
Rochester, New York   14609   USA
(716) 482 - 0300 - Phone
(716) 288 - 5989 - Fax

FUR SALES OF HUDSON'S BAY COMPANY (Continued)

Date		Bear (black)	Bear (brown)	Bear (white)	Wild-cat	Ermine	Fisher	Fox (blue)	Fox (cross)	Fox (red)	Fox (silver)	Fox (white)	Lynx
1888	No.	......	10,080	......	33	8,933	6,165	73	3,877	17,228	954	13,170	78,773
	Price	58/9	94/1	36/8	2/-	*8/6	20/8	118/6	26/4	7/3	9/1;i0	10/7	9/4
1889	No.	......	9,606	......	18	3,592	5,408	77	2,935	14,503	739	9,551	33,899
	Price	87/3	114/2	51/7	5/7	*19/10	36/-	81/3	42/1	8/11	13/7/-	18/4	19/1
Average for decade (dollars)	No.	13.63	15.50	10.82	.76	*1.54	7.13	12.08	9.04	1.98	58.40	2.73	3.40
1890	No.	......	11,719	......	......	5,697	6,557	25	2,90	12,058	649	2,893	18,886
	Price	59/2	73/-	49/1	......	*11/2	25/6	44/6	36/98	7/2	11/16/9	12/4	13/79
1891	No.	8,960	1,411	83	14	5,417	5,683	38	2,518	14,134	565	3,725	11,52
	Price	77/7	98/10	71/4	3/1	*12/2	27/9	87/10	44/6	8/-	17/1/5	10/1	13/7
1892	No.	11,414	1,875	130	13	5,516	5,208	83	2,766	11,256	665	9,626	8,352
	Price	71/3	92/8	61/11	5/6	*13/4	25/8	65/5	40/2	9/1	14/8/11	7/5	19/4
1893	No.	9,683	1,390	90	5	9,120	4,828	51	2,673	11,964	615	4,708	8,660
	Price	80/4	120/-	60/-	3/-	*15/-	32/9	50/3	40/6	8/9	19/5/-	8/6	16/7
1894	No.	7,727	1,107	134	7	9,096	4,044	34	3,025	16,031	617	3,231	12,902
	Price	78/7	105/5	48/-	/10	*30/4	32/1	54/8	37/-	8/1	18/2/4	8/8	11/6
1895	No.	8,620	1,190	81	29	7,250	38,631	69	3,206	13,087	682	4,948	20,331
	Price	76/9	107/3	33/11	1/-	*19/6	32/1	49/4	38/9	8/3	16/-/3	19/6	12/1
1896	No.	8,467	1,090	128	15	9,302	4,169	67	5,044	20,311	981	6,68'	36,853
	Price	47/3	60/4	39/5	/4	*22/-	31/10	34/7	26/-	6/3	10/8/-	10/2	7/9
1897	No.	9,318	1,030	77	50	8,340	4,805	44	6,963	24,676	1,398	3,498	56,407
	Price	36/4	45/11	41/1	2/1	*35/1	36/3	32/3	22/9	6/-	9/2/7	10/6	6/2

*Prices quoted for ermine are so much per timber of 40 skins.

(206)

FUR SALES OF THE HUDSON'S BAY COMPANY (Continued)

Date		Bear (black)	Bear (brown)	Bear (white)	Wild-cat	Ermine	Fisher	Fox (blue)	Fox (cross)	Fox (red)	Fox (silver)	Fox (white)	Lynx
1898	No.	9,166	972	141	32	7,704	5,247	46	6,507	25,691	1,250	3,228	39,437
	Price	45/-	41/8	40/-	2/7	*36/-	32/10	28/2	22/9	7/2	11/6/11	13/2	7/1
1899	No.	8,993	910	130	27	9,788	4,964	61	5,358	20,399	1,018	6,681	26,761
	Price	46/10	36/-	48/6	1/6	*21/3	30/3	110/-	31/8	12/7	21/19/1	24/4	10/1
Average for decade (dollars)		14.86	18.75	11.84	.53	*5.18	7.37	13.37	8.18	1.87	71.80	3.00	2.83
1900	No.	9,137	897	118	67	14,075	5,042	19	3,742	11,533	608	3,623	15,185
	Price	47/-	45/2	43/10	5/9	*33/10	29/6	89/5	49/6	24/3	50/16/1	37/4	27/7
1901	No.	7,820	778	58	41	11,664	3,454	24	1,534	5,446	325	2,929	4,473
	Price	46/8	39/7	47/5	5/9	*43/6	22/10	39/8	34/5	13/7	17/11/3	21/1	17/3
1902	No.	7,087	788	170	5	16,374	3,716	68	1,460	6,992	283	8,515	5,781
	Price	54/5	52/9	99/2	7/6	*48/-	24/4	50/10	35/-	23/3	29/1/11	21/9	29/6
1903	No.	6,445	726	96	4	33,883	3,235	90	1,974	6,235	493	10,751	9,117
	Price	44/7	38/6	81/10		*81/8	30/7	40/9	38/6	23/3	33/15/7	23/7	45/8
1904	No.	6,085	640	55	5	15,902	2,590	43	2,212	6,216	422	5,579	19,267
	Price	26/11	22/6	89/9	2/6	*134/3	23/2	36/5	27/1	19/3	17/9/0	18/3	24/4
1905	No.	4,614	463	54		12,670	2,095	17	2,396	7,215	491	4,690	36,116
	Price	33/5	30/2	91/10		*182/1	29/-	55/-	25/8	17/8	30/2/14	17/7	27/-
1906	No.	5,041	495	149	2	21,704	3,020	44	5,011	12,204	942	6,394	58,850
	Price	31/9	31/2	149/11		*152/4	28/4	80/11	22/7	19/3	34/6/-	40/7	26/10
1907	No.	4,177	435	138	2	25,633	4,022	89	5,457	12,736	1,067	11,459	61,478
	Price	33/7	30/10	95/6		*122/1	40/-	77/3	22/2	23/1	32/5/8	28/7	27/3
1908	No.	4,100	388	60		27,821	4,701	64	3,194	7,537	663	6,785	36,3
	Price	26/7	28/1	75/1		*65/-	35/3	77/10	34/3	25/11	34/14/2	30/8	38/501

*Prices quoted for ermine are so much per timber of 40 skins.

(207)

FUR SALES OF THE HUDSON'S BAY COMPANY (Continued)

Date		Bear (black)	Bear (brown)	Bear (white)	Wild-cat	Ermine	Fisher	Fox (blue)	Fox (cross)	Fox (red)	Fox (silver)	Fox (white)	Lynx
1909	No.	4,042	397	93	1	26,872	3,600	14	1,782	3,641	397	2,068	9,704
	Price	44/8	41/2	95/9	....	*94/2	55/-	76/7	45/8	41/5	50/3/3	47/10	87/4
Average for decade (dolla)		9.37	8.76	21 17	1.29	*23.00	7.63	15.00	8.03	5.56	158.55	6.89	8.42
1910	No.	4,579	453	71	....	34,281	2,525	28	1,380	3,396	281	4,803	3,410
	Price	58/11	45/3	129/1	....	*109/2	68/4	82/11	58/2	48/3	85/2/11	60/9	123/1
1911	No.	4,964	384	82	2	49,963	2,310	113	2,067	4,558	382	14,692	3,774
	Price	47/9	36/6	69/-	10/-	*90/8	81/11	92/5	92/10	42/2	61/12/11	39/10	102/4
Average for decade (dollars)		12.80	9.81	23.80	2.42	23.98	18.04	21.04	18.12	10.85	352.30	12.07	27.05

*Prices quoted for ermine are so much per timber of 40 skins.

FUR SALES OF THE HUDSON'S BAY COMPANY (Continued)

Date		Marten	Mink	Musk-ox	Mus-quash or Muskrat	Otter (land)	Otter (sea)	Raccoon	Seal (fur)	Seal (hair)	Skunk	Wolf	Wolverene
1850	No.	65,051	20,610		175,472	11,050	138	1,338	7	814	1,272	12,088	1,424
1851	No.	64,495	21,151		194,682	8,928	79	1,847	11	340	1,136	9,747	1,491
1852	No.	88,412	24,859		292,530	8,959	229	1,255	24	858	1,452	7,813	1,773
1853	No.	73,055	25,152		493,952	8,991	214	1,695		1,425	1,619	8,508	1,302
1854	No.	91,882	42,375		512,291	12,079	236	1,193	13	2,021	4,474	6,788	1,090
1855	No.	137,009	50,839		345,626	11,141	338	1,676	15	2,842	5,959	15,419	1,154
1856	No.	179,736	61,581		258,906	13,802	319	1,798	38	5,267	11,320	7,588	1,145
1857	No.	171,022	61,951		302,267	11,577	187	1,895	79	8,649	7,750	9,572	693
	Price	17/5	8/6		1/-	19/6	17/6/9	2/1		2/7	9/5	11/11	16/4
1858	No.	138,535	76,231		313,502	12,511	343	2,295	39	13,112	8,213	7,728	1,06?
	Price	12/-	4/-		6d	15/7	8/11/8	2/2		2/3	5/7	5/3	8/9
1859	No.	139,124	63,264		254,246	13,165	174	1,273	116	12,77	8,529	12,659	1,129
	Price	14/5	7/7		10½d	26/4	10/2/7	2/1½		2/6	6/2	6/10	10/3
Average for decade (dollars)		3.55	1.62		.19	5.00	58.48	.51		.60	1.70	1.92	2.82
1860	No.	102,235	44,730		177,291	11,279	175	2,434	196	11,147	9,983	8,670	1,416
	Price	18/3	7/4		10d	24/3	10/16/10	1/2		2/8	2/4	5/4	10/1
1861	No.	74,738	31,094		206,020	13,199	129	3,397	186	18,104	3,758	6,051	1,410
	Price	19/5	6/9		9½d	20/5	16/11/9	1/3		2/-	2/3	4/9	10/2
1862	No.	80,484	49,452		335,385	14,158	84	3,640	176	13,726	3,315	4,087	1,529
	Price	19/8	6/7		7d	19/8	12/17/9	1/9½		1/9	3/10	4/11	10/2
1863	No.	79,979	43,961		357,060	13,331	106	3,883	403	16,933	1,969	3,932	1,426
	Price	20/1	9/2		7½d	19/2	12/16/6	1/5		1/6	5/11	6/10	10/11
1864	No.	112,396	61,727	23	509,760	15,443	189	1,794	655	15,297	2,966	8,035	1,328
	Price	17/8	8/7	32/6	7½d	16/9	14/19/6	1/7		1/5	3/-	8/3	13/3

14

FUR SALES OF THE HUDSON'S BAY COMPANY (Continued)

Date		Marten	Mink	Musk-ox	Mus-quash or Muskrat	Otter (Land)	Otter (sea)	Raccoon	Seal (fur)	Seal (hair)	Skunk	Wolf	Wolver-ene
1865	No.	124,830	60,334	8	418,370	13,600	167	3,335	977	14,500	1,617	5,717	1,230
	Price	16/4	8/10	......	8d	14/3	11/5/10	1/1	......	2/1	2/11	8/3	12/9
1866	No.	142,970	51,404	9	320,824	18,380	103	4,710	2,086	15,122	2,780	12,615	909
	Price	18/9	11/2	35/-	11¼d	18/11	6/15/9	1/4	......	1/9	3/2	8/9	13/7
1567	No.	126,616	58,451	......	412,164	15,271	182	11,678	2,314	21,458	2,779	6,340	768
	Price	16/3	9/5	28/10	11¼d	14/8	7/19/3	1/2	......	2/5	1/8	9/7	13/3
1868	No.	106,784	73,575	33	618,081	14,992	147	21,321	2,225	9,819	6,208	7,526	1,111
	Price	18/1	12/2	48/11	9¾d	22/1	9/13/6	1/10	......	1/10	2/2	10/6	15/1
1869	No.	81,706	74,343	14	404,173	12,545	242	4,894	1,727	7,927	6,679	9,318	1,457
	Price	19/-	10/-	63/-	9¼d	28/4	6/15/4	1/4	19/10	2/11	3/4	17/9	13/11
Average for decade (dollars)		4.46	2.19		.19	4.98	53.11	.33	4.76	.49	.74	4.04	2.96
1870	No.	52,308	27,708	72	232,251	10,973	89	1,696	688	9,917	9,606	5,856	1,421
	Price	24/8	8/8	30/10	7d	26/2	6/9/10	11d	13/5	2/8	4/2	9/7	12/-
1871	No.	55,453	31,985	4	443,999	13,105	107	3,341	7,944	15,740	3,286	5,399	1,848
	Price	27/6	10/9	30/-	8d	29/3	8/10/-	1/6	13/5	3/1	4/2	7/11	12/-
1872	No.	60,455	39,266	44	704,789	13,787	66	4,011	13,620	5,433	2,621	2,??2	1,656
	Price	28/11	15/3	45/1	10d	38/6	18/-/-	2/1	16/4	3/7	8/1	13/-	12/3
1873	No.	66,841	44,740	7	767,896	11,263	99	3,636	2,073	9,862	1,759	6,413	2,085
	Price	24/8	12/3		9¾d	44/6	11/15/-	1/5	45/9	3/7	3/7	12/9	14/7
1874	No.	66,750	60,429	54	671,982	9,016	96	3,152	2,354	3,259	1,322	3,724	1,765
	Price	19/9	10/6	79/-	11¼d	34/4	7/18/-	2/1	40/7	4/11	4/4	9/9	17/8
1875	No.	131,170	72,273	11	523,802	13,088	134	7,241	2,131	14,099	2,077	3,074	1,351
	Price	18/3	10/1	30/-	1/2	29/4	9/14/-	1/6	28/11	5/2	5/3	12/-	20/4
1876	No.	83,439	79,214	9	583,319	11,524	47	2,149	2,718	3,620	2,829	2,083	1,286
	Price	14/6	5/11	40/-	1/1	26/4	8/16/-	2/11	32/2	2/4	4/8	14/-	27/8

(210)

FUR SALES OF THE HUDSON'S BAY COMPANY (Continued)

Date		Marten	Mink	Musk-ox	Musquash or Muskrat	Otter (land)	Otter (sea)	Raccoon	Seal (fur)	Seal (hair)	Skunk	Wolf	Wolverene
1877	No.	81,174	79,000	127	437,121	9,926	127	1,042	1,588	7,564	3,928	1,865	1,136
	Price	11/5	5/5		8d	18/5	5/2/7	1/9	23/2	3/7	2/7	13/9	22/9
1878	No.	74,703	84,244	118	486,030	11,753	47	514	1,779	7,636	6,933	2,975	1,594
	Price	9/11	4/4		4½d	17/1	9/16/2	1/11	37/4	3/7	4/-	12/1	22/2
1879	No.	55,734	62,590	237	499,727	13,101	26	613	2,782	6,626	8,386	2,580	1,997
	Price	12/4	4/3	21/9	5½d	24/9	7/13/4	1/4	41/5	2/3	3/4	29/1	19/2
Average for decade (dollars)		4.61	2.10	9.59	.09	6.93	45.00	.42	7.02	.83	1.11	2.73	4.33
1880	No.	46,273	35,072	567	478,078	8,313	88	15	3,308	4,174	7,9	4,707	1,777
	Price	11/2	5/1	16/1	6d	31/11	13/15/10	3/-	57/8	3/3	4/3	7/-	17/-
1881	No.	46,030	36,160	655	829,034	10,177	22	830	3,085	4,287	6,818	3,136	2,471
	Price	10/11	4/2	25/6	5½d	34/9	13/16/8	2/7	43/4	2/2	4/3	10/9	14/3
1882	No.	52,631	45,609	564	1,029,296	10,191	77	538	5,005	5,442	5,40	1,450	1,614
	Price	10/6	3/2	24/6	7d	30/10	15/2/-	2/8	23/8	2/9	4/11	15/7	13/11
1883	No.	62,711	47,508	368	1,069,183	11,992	7	841	652	3,888	7,178	2,121	1,883
	Price	8/9	3/4	58/-	6d	26/10	12/17/-	2/8	40/-	2/11	5/1	12/5	15/6
1884	No.	71,116	52,280	235	1,083,067	9,246	26	354	560	2,713	6,473	1,580	1,583
	Price	12/-	4/3	61/4	6d	31/7	10/16/6	3/5	29/10	2/10	4/10	11/10	22/-
1885	No.	78,981	110,824	316	817,003	12,200	35	130	12	1,590	12,647	1,848	1,528
	Price	7/9	2/-	54/10	4d	17/6	12/9/-	2/11	10/-	2/6	3/5	10/1	24/6
1886	No.	79,027	76,503	395	317,050	10,875	10	124	2,077	6,965	21,249	1,334	1,203
	Price	11/4	3/3	79/4	4½d	30/9	21/4/-	3/7	14/9	2/4	4/9	11/7	24/-
1887	No.	51,151	64,303	222	380,132	8,326	10	325	1,846	1,279	11,009	1,180	1,245
	Price	9/6	2/9	79/3	4½d	31/10	25/12/-	2/11	36/6	2/-	3/10	18/7	30/6

Date		Marten	Mink	Musk-ox	Mus-quash or Muskrat	Otter (land)	Otter (sea)	Raccoon	Seal (fur)	Seal (hair)	Skunk	Wolf	Wolverene
1888	No.	73,259	83,023	514	344,878	11,613	11	250	179	2,590	16,390	4,706	2,452
	Price	7/6	2/3	6d	6d	32/8	17/13/4	3/8	15/9	1/9	3/6	7/3	20/3
1889	No.	64,558	40,748	505	223,614	8,771	11	217	737	672	11,334	3,404	2,031
	Price	11/4	F.	...	10½d	41/9	22/12/8	2/11	41/8	2/8	4/1	8/11	18/6
Average for decade (dollars)		2.42		.39	.12	7.45	79.68	.80	7.52	.60	1.03	2.74	4.81
1890	No.	73,123	35,-	.05	322,160	9,298	15	153	482	2,151	10,814	2,532	2,243
	Price	8/-	3/9	64/10	8½d	34/8	26/13/4	2/10	45/-	2/1	3/5	8/3	15/9
1891	No.	65,146	29,479	1,358	574,742	8,193	9	172	279	2,545	12,665	4,286	1,416
	Price	7/7	4/10	54/6	9d	38/2	33/2/2	2/11	64/8	3/2	3/9	6/2	13/2
1892	No.	73,850	42,264	1,935	806,103	9,798	6	171	932	2,604	10,646	1,725	1,147
	Price	8/7	5/8	53/7	5d	32/10	36/13/4	2/5	45/7	2/6	3/5	12/-	16/11
1893	No.	100,257	58,171	888	934,646	8,671	8	194	8,491	2,599	9,214	1,577	1,017
	Price	12/9	8/7	75/3	5½d	40/8	25/-/-	3/-	48/1	3/1	3/11	10/5	33/10
1894	No.	110,015	50,815	1,187	648,687	7,474	11	218	37,129	2,588	6,841	2,086	889
	Price	8/9	4/6	41/4	5½d	39/2	34/10/10	2/3	35/5	3/-	3/5	7/9	15/1
1895	No.	107,002	51,285	761	674,811	7,512	1	743	36,577	2,183	8,885	1,498	652
	Price	15/7	5/2	46/10	4½d	40/-	13/-/-	1/11	45/-	2/8	3/4	7/9	18/7
1896	No.	103,329	70,229	494	813,159	8,919	......	575	783	1,817	13,664	2,655	579
	Price	17/1	4/6	39/6	6½d	43/2	......	211	45/4	2/2	2/2	6/4	16/4
1897	No.	95,911	76,365	326	551,716	9,346	3	1,642	39,133	4,765	18,842	3,980	822
	Price	15/2	4/6	40/11	7d	37/6	3/15/-	2/-	30/6	1/7	1/7	4/6	13/5

FUR SALES OF THE HUDSON'S BAY COMPANY (Continued)

Date		Marten	Mink	Musk-ox	Mus-quash or Muskrat	Otter (land)	Otter (sea)	Raccoon	Seal (fur)	Seal (hair)	Skunk	Wolf	Wolver-ene
1898	No.	85,284	70,407	346	568,934	9,690	2	6,466	21,177	2,696	16,755	7,655	1,064
	Price	16/6	5/10	38/5	7d	37/3	3/15/-	1/9	47/3	1/10	1/11	4/8	10/3
1899	No.	67,738	41,839	453	701,487	10,016	1	2,916	8,821	2,791	9,874	3,575	904
	Price	27/1	9/7	44/10	6¼d	37/5		2/5	25/5	2/4	3/2	6/11	21/6
Average for decade (dollars)		3.29	1.27	12.00	1.3	9.14	86.57	.57	11.33	.64	.72	1.79	4.20
1900	No.	64,446	45,978	516	767,741	9,798	6	13,544	21,620	4,158	11,012	3,104	923
	Price	32/11	8/1	69/-	6d	45/2	74/11/8	2/4	64/8	3/9	4/3	16/-	20/7
1901	No.	55,777	47,813	574	928,199	9,198		9,177	9,039	2,599	6,172	2,643	776
	Price	28/4	7/-	97/7	5¼d	41/3	90/-/-	2/1	58/8	2/10	3/1	7/-	23/4
1902	No.	57,131	57,620	273	1,650,214	8,711		1,973	8,352	3,061	5,749	1,306	635
	Price	31/2	10/-	103/10	4¼d	49/-		3/1	58/2	2/10	2/11	19/4	27/3
1903	No.	79,147	66,549	256	1,488,287	10,296	1	1,024	5,832	2,508	5,207	1,805	695
	Price	30/6	11/3	64/7	7d	71/5	3/7/6	3/2	68/4	3/3	4/-	19/-	26/1
1904	No.	52,639	54,673	333	924,439	6,463		718	6,532	1,124	5,427	1,972	627
	Price	22/9	9/8	53/-	8¼d	52/2		2/11	72/6	3/11	2/10	15/11	16/5
1905	No.	35,752	55,906	100	1,056,253	4,892		404	35	762	6,090	1,246	412
	Price	34/2	17/-	86/9	7d	77/6		3/3	75/1	6/5	4/2	14/6	18/-
1906	No.	45,441	60,053	92	695,070	10,580		281	50	3,706	9,129	1,705	504
	Price	49/1	16/3	72/6	9¼d	72/4		2/11	102/-	3/11	4/7	13/-	19/2
1907	No.	47,494	39,109	45	407,472	7,726		602	65	1,152	11,581	2,798	730
	Price	49/6	23/10	118/8	1/-	74/6		3/8	94/-	3/7	2/11	11/3	19/1
1908	No.	34,874	21,534	113	172,418	6,137		243		1,522	5,235	4,510	894
	Price	43/6	21/2	82/1	1/4¼	85/9		2/4		3/9	3/8	13/-	18/7

FUR SALES OF THE HUDSON'S BAY COMPANY (Continued)

Date		Marten	Mink	Musk-	Mus-quash or Muskrat	Otter (land)	Otter (sea)	Raccoon	Seal (fur)	Seal (hair)	Skunk	Wolf	Wolver-ine
1909	No.	23,640	17,857	167	302,495	6,361	......	141	......	1,766	1,591	3,858	763
	Price	43/1	24/4	296/8	1/7	89/9		2/9		3/1	6/1	20/3	29/11
Average for decade (dollars)		8.76	3.57	25.31	.19	15.81	268.80	.73	14.21	.89	.92	3.58	5.36
1910	No.	28,979	21,788	76	749,112	5,487	......	266	......	1,517	1,613	3,149	807
	Price	11/3	20/6	188/10	2/7½	99/9		1/3		2/7	8/9	18/6	31/4
1911	No.	29,338	33,008	91	963,507	6,532	......	197	......	1,290	1,037	2,412	902
	Price	39/6	22/6	166/8	1/3½	71/-		6/5		3/7	6/3	18/1	20/9
Average for decade (dollars)		9.60	6.24	42.66	.47	20.19	......	1.26	......	.74	1.80	4.39	6.25

Appendix X

Statistics of Fur Prices

TYPICAL PRICES OF A FEW SKINS

By E. Brass

Australian Opossum, Adelaide prime blue, 1880, 16cts.; 1900, 28 cts.; 1908, 73 cts.; 1909, 97 cts.; 1910, $1.95.

Wallaby, 1880, 6 cts. to 10 cts.; 1900, 25 cts. to 75 cts.: 1910, 50 cts. to $1.70.

Kangaroo, 1880, 4 cts. to 12 cts.; 1900, 37 cts. to 60 cts.; 1910, 75 cts. to $1.45.

Wombats, 1880, 12 cts.; 1900, 36 cts.; 1910, 73 cts.

Native Cats, 1880, 4 cts.; 1900, 24 cts.; 1910, 49 cts.

Bastard Chinchilla, 1880, 73 cts.; 1890, 36 cts.; 1900, $2.92; 1905, $4.38; 1910, $9.73.

Japan Mink, 1900, 12 cts.; 1905, 19 cts.; 1910, 60 cts.

Chinese Weasel, 1900, 7 cts.; 1905, 16 cts.; 1910, 33 cts.
Japan Marten, 1890, 35 c's.; 1900, $1.43; 1905, $2.38; 1910, $3.81.

Japan Fox, 1890, 83 cts.; 1900, $1.43; 1910, $4.05.

Skunk, the best lot, 1900, $2.07; 1908, $3.30; 1909, $4.40; 1910, $7.06; 1911. $5.10.

Raw Persian, 1890, $2.06; 1900, $3.09; 1905, $4.12; 1908, $4.64; 1909, $5.15; 1910, $6.70.

Stone Marten, 1890, $1.43; 1895, $2.14; 1900 $2.86; 1905, $3.33; 1908, $5.23,; 1909, $6.19; 1910, $6.66.

Marmot, Orenburg, 1890, 10 cts.; 1900, 1   1904, 19 cts.; 1905, 43 cts.; 1906, 33 cts.; 1907, 37 cts.; 1908   1909, 43 cts.; 1910, 90 cts.

Black Fox, best skin, 1880, $632.70; 1890, $476.00; 1900, $2,822.66; 1905, $1,070.67; 1906, $1,557,33; 1907 $2,141.33; 1908, $2,238.67; 1909, $1,508. 67; 1910, $2,628.00.

Sea-otter, 1880, $584.00; 1890, $778.67; 1900, $62.67; 1905, $997.77; 1909, $1,849.33; 1910, $1,703.33.

TYPICAL PRICES OF A FEW STAPLE SKINS OF THE HUDSON'S BAY COMPANY ON THE LONDON FUR MARKET

By E. Brass

Year	Muskrat, YF, I	Mink, YF, II	Red Fox, YF, I, dark	Lynx, YF, I, large
	$	$	$	$
1882	.16	.73	3.11	4.87
1883	.15	.97	2.75	6.09
1884	.16	1.16	2.75	7.31
1885	.12	.59	2.07	4.51
1886	.16	.93	2.56	8.72
1887	.17	.89	2.60	4.70
1888	.19	.65	2.50	5.05
1889	.25	1.50	4.05	7.38
1890	.22	1.03	2.92	5.73
1891	.25	1.36	2.82	6.75
1892	.15	1.74	2.03	8.70
1893	.17	2.92	2.72	6.70
1894	.18	1.42	2.75	4.13
1895	.19	1.58	4.20	4.39
1896	.24	1.34	2.50	3.33
1897	.22	1.46	2.50	2.87
1898	.18	1.89	2.66	3.23
1899	.16	2.98	4.97	5.12
1900	.16	2.58	9.00	10.80
1901	.15	2.44	6.20	7.44
1902	.13	2.58	8.27	13.38
1903	.22	2.70	8.03	22.40
1904	.25	2.37	6.81	12.30
1905	.17	4.46	7.48	13.15
1906	.27	4.54	7.67	13.38
1907	.31	6.58	8.07	12.50
1908	.41	5.25	9.25	15.60
1909	.47	5.61	14.96	32.00
1910	.87	6.34	16.55	39.85

AVERAGE PRICE OF FUR-SEALS, 1886-1899

By Mr. Ernest Poland, 110 Queen Victoria St., London, Eng.

Year	Alaska Mid. Pups		Copper Island Large Pups		Lobos Island Large Pups	
1886	March / October / November	55/- / 67/- / 51/6	March	42/-	October	31/6
1887	November	75/6	March	43/6	November	25/9
1888	November	73/1	March	42/-	February / November	27/- / 31/6
1889	October	144/-	March	56/-	February	31/-
1890	October	128/-	March	96/-	October	32/6
1891	October	123/4	March / October	80/- / 93/-	January / October	34/10 / 48/9
1892	November	108/5	January / November	72/6 / 93/5	January / November	70/- / 51/6
1893	November	89/9	November	76/3	November	77/4 / 50/9
1894	November	85/5	November	61/11	November	46/7
1895	November	71/-	November	56/8	November	34/6
1896	December	69/1	December	46/-	December	33/3
1897	December	90/1	......		December	34/5
1898	December	172/-	March / September	57/10 / 60/11	March / December	26/-
1899	December		March	72/2	December	27/2 / 34/3 / 40/-

Year	N.W. Coast Large Pups	
1886	March / June / August	31/8 / 33/- / 34/-
1887	November / February / June	36/- / 30/3 / 31/11
1888	November / February	41/7 / 42/-
1889	October	46/-
1890	January / October	41/- / 17/3
1891	January / October	73/3 / 79/6
1892	January / November	54/- / 41/1
1893	January / November	64/6 / 64/-
1894	January / November	56/2 / 44/1
1895	November / March	47/5 / 54/2
1896	December / March	53/2 / 42/11
1897	December / January	57/4 / 42/5
1898	March / December	53/8 / 57/3
1899	January / December	56/6

AVERAGE PRICE OF FUR-SEALS, 1900-1911

By Mr. Ernest Poland, 110 Queen Victoria St., London, Eng.

Year	Alaska Mid-Pups		Copper Island Large Pups		Lobos Island Large Pups	
1900	116/8	December	134/10	March	55/9	December
1901	117/10	December	85/9	March	45/9	December
1902	144/10	December	104/3	March	63/5	December
1903	124/2	December	105/6	March	58/-	December
1904	155/3	December	75/4	March	60/3	December
1905	149/3	December	106/-	March	77/-	December
1906	134/3	December	115/3	March	76/6	January
					68/-	December
					75/-	December
1907	......		92/-	March		
1908	128/6	March	90/6	March	66/-	December
	125/-	December				
1909	168/6	December	106/3	March	....	
1910	161/3	December	135/6	March	....	
1911			122/-	March	82/9	January

Year	N.W. Coast Large Pups	
1900	55/-	January
	80/8	December
1901	70/8	January
	78/9	December
1902	76/-	January
	74/5	December
1903	74/6	March
	97/3	December
1904	92/6	January
	89/3	March
1905	80/10	December
	72/8	January
1906	87/-	December
	76/-	January
1907	134/7	December
	113/1	January
1908	108/3	December
	106/7	January
1909	107/9	December
	103/-	January
1910	102/11	December
	96/-	January
1911	144/-	December
	143/-	December

Dec. 29th 1897,—Bill passed by the U. S. Government forbidding imports of pelagic caught seals taken north of latitude 35° N., whether raw, dressed or dyed.

(218)

PRICES CURRENT

(From the *Fur News Magazine*, April, 1914)

NOTE.—The prices given below are for winter-caught skins, except as otherwise specified; springy and damaged skins will be graded and paid for according to value.

		No. 1 Large	Med.	Small	No. 2	No. 3	No. 4
Badger	Northern	2.00	1.25	.50	.40	.20	..
"	Southern and S.W.	1.00	.60	.30	.25	.10	..
Bear	Black, Northern	25.00	16.00	12.00	12.00	2.00	.50
"	Black, Central	20.00	12.00	8.00	8.00	1.50	.50
"	Black, Southern and S.W.	12.00	8.00	5.00	5.00	1.00	.25
"	Grizzly and Polar, according to size and quality						
Beaver	Far Western States and Eastern Canada	8.00	6.00	3.50	4.00	1.50	.50
"	Cent. and S.W. United States	6.00	4.00	2.50	3.00	1.00	.35
"	Cubs 1.00 @ 3.00						
Cat, Civet	Kans., Iowa, Mo. and similar	.60	.40	.20	.20	.10	.05
"	Tenn. and Pacific Coast	.50	.30	.15	.15	.10	.05
Cat, House	Black	.30	.20	.15	.15	.10	.05
"	Colours	.15	.10	.05	.05	..	..
Cat, Ringtail	Southwestern	.40	.25	.20	.20	.10	.05
Cat, Wild	Northern and N.W.	4.00	3.00	2.00	1.00	.50	.10
"	Southern and S.W.	1.00	.60	.40	.25	.15	.10
Fox, Blue	Alaska and similar	50.00	30.00	20.00	20.00	7.00	3.00
Fox, Cross	All Sections, Dark	40.00	25.00	15.00	10.00	5.00	1.50
"	All Sections, Pale	20.00	12.00	10.00	8.00	3.00	1.00
Fox, Gray	Central and Northern U.S.	1.75	1.25	.90	.90	.30	.15
"	Southern and S.W. United States	1.50	1.00	.75	.75	.25	.10
Fox, Red	Alaska, Northern and West. Can.	10.00	7.00	4.50	4.50	1.50	.25
"	Newfoundland and Labrador	10.00	7.00	4.50	4.00	1.50	.25
"	Minn., Wis., Daks. and Nor. Mich.	7.00	5.00	3.50	2.50	1.00	.25
	E. Can., Mich., N.Y. and N.E. States	6.00	4.50	3.00	2.50	1.00	.25
	Pa., N.J., Ohio, Ind. and Ill.	5.50	3.50	2.00	1.75	.75	.20
"	All Central and Southern States	4.00	2.50	1.75	1.50	.60	.20
Fox, Silver	As to Beauty				50.00 @ 600.00		

		No. 1 Large	Med.	Small	No. 2	No. 3	No. 4
Fox, White	Pure White	25.00	18.00	12.00	10.00	3.00	1.00
Lynx	N.W. Canada and Alaska	15.00	10.00	8.00	8.00	4.00	1.00
"	Eastern Canada and Northern U.S.	12.00	8.00	6.00	6.00	3.00	1.00
Marten	Alaska, Labrador and N.W., Dark	22.00	13.00	8.00	7.00	3.00	1.50
"	Alaska and N.W., Pale	9.00	6.00	4.00	3.00	2.50	.75
"	Eastern Canada and U.S., Dark	10.00	7.00	5.00	4.00	2.00	1.00
"	Eastern Canada and U.S., Pale	4.00	3.00	2.00	1.50	1.00	.50

PRICES CURRENT—*Continued*

		Dark	Brown	Pale
Fisher	E. United States and N. Canada.	20.00–40.00	10.00–20.00	5.00–10.00
"	Pacific Coast.................	18.00–25.00	8.00–15.00	4.00–8.00

		Spring	Winter	Large Fall	Small Fall	Kitts
Muskrat	N.Y., No. Pa., No. N.J., New England and East Canada..............	.46	.36	.25	.15	.05
"	Mich., So. Wis., No. Ohio, Ind. and Ill.	.45	.35	.25	.15	.05
	Cent. and S. Ohio, Ind., Ill., W. Va., Ky............................	.42	.33	.23	.15	.05
	Cent. and So. Pa., N.J., Del. and Md...	.40	.32	.22	.15	.05
	Va., Carolinas, Tenn.................	.36	.30	.22	.12	.05
	Mo., Ark., Kans. and Pacific Coast....	.36	.28	.20	.10	.05
"	La. and Texas......................	.20	.14	.10	.05	.02
	Wis., Minn., Iowa, Neb..............	.42	.33	.23	.15	.05
	Black.............................	.50	.40	.30	.20	.07

		No. 1 Large	Med.	Small	No. 2	No. 3	No. 4
Mink	East Can., New Eng. and No. N.Y.	6.00	4.50	3.00	2.75	1.00	.25
"	N.Y., No. Pa. and No. N.J......	5.50	3.75	2.75	2.50	.75	.25
"	Minn., No. Wis. and No. Mich...	5.50	3.75	2.75	2.50	.75	.25
"	Wis., No. Iowa and Dakotas....	5.00	3.50	2.50	2.50	.75	.25
"	Mich., No. O., No. Ind., No. Ill..	5.00	3.50	2.50	2.50	.75	.25
"	So. Pa., So. N.J., Del., Md. and W. Va..................	5.00	3.50	2.50	2.50	.75	.25
	Va. and No. Car...............	5.00	3.50	2.50	2.50	.75	.25
	B.C. and Alaska Coast..........	5.00	3.50	2.50	2.50	.75	.25
	So. O., So. Ind., Ill. and Ky.....	4.50	3.00	2.00	1.75	.65	.25

		No. 1 Large	Med.	Small	No. 2	No. 3	No. 4
Mink	So. Iowa, Neb., Kans. and No. Mo.	4.50	3.00	2.00	1.75	.65	.25
"	Pacific Coast and Rocky Mt. Sts.	4.50	3.00	2.00	1.75	.65	.25
"	So. Car., Tenn., Miss., Ala. and Ga.	4.50	3.00	2.00	1.75	.50	.25
"	So. Mo., Ark., Okla., Tex., La. and Fla......................	4.00	2.75	2.00	1.75	.50	.25
Opossum	N.Y., N.J., Pa., Ohio, Ind., Ill and W. V.................	.85	.55	.35	.20	.10	..
"	Ky., Tenn., Va., N. and S. Car...	.75	.50	.30	.15	.08	..
"	Georgia, Fla., Ala., Miss. and Tex.	.65	.40	.15	.10	.05	..
Otter	Eastern U.S. and Canada.......	20.00	15.00	10.00	10.00	5.00	1.50
"	Northwestern and Pacific Coast	15.00	10.00	7.00	7.00	3.00	1.00
"	Western and Southwestern......	13.00	9.00	6.00	5.50	3.00	1.00
	Virginia and No. Car...........	14.00	10.00	7.00	6.50	2.00	1.00
	Ga., Fla., Ala., La. and S. Car....	10.00	7.00	5.00	4.50	2.00	1.00

PRICES CURRENT—*Continued*

		No. 1			No. 2	No. 3	No. 4
		Large	Med.	Small			
Raccoon	Minn., Wis., Daks...............	3.00	2.00	1.00	1.00	.40	.20
"	N.Y., New England, Can. and Mich	2.50	1.50	1.00	1.00	.35	.10
"	Pa., N.J., Nor. Ohio, Ind. and Ill.	2.00	1.25	.75	.75	.30	.10
"	Iowa, Kans., Neb., and Nor. Mo.	2.00	1.25	.75	.75	.30	.10
"	So. Ohio, Ind., Ill., W. Va.......	1.75	1.00	.65	.65	.25	.10
	Ky., Tenn., Virginia, No. and So.						
	Car. and N. Ga.............	1.50	.90	.60	.60	.25	.10
	So. Ga., Fla., Ala., Miss., Tex. and						
	La......................	1.25	.75	.40	.40	.20	.10
	Extra Dark Colours...............	3.00	@	5.00			

		No. 1	No. 2	No. 3	No. 4
Skunk	N.Y., Pa., New Eng. and Canada..........	3.00	2.00	1.00	.50
"	N.J., No. Ohio, Mich., No. Ind. and Ill.......	3.00	2.00	1.00	.50
"	Kans., Neb., No. Mo......................	3.00	2.00	1.00	.50
"	Cent. O., Ind., Ill., W. Va. and Md.........	2.75	1.75	.90	.45
"	So. Ohio, Ind., Ill. and So. Mo..............	2.50	1.50	.80	.40
"	Ky., Tenn., Ark., Va. and N. C.............	2.25	1.25	.70	.35
"	Ga., Fla., Ala. and other Southern States.....	1.50	1.00	.60	.30
	Large Western, Long Narrow Stripe, prime...	1.50 @ 2.00			

		No. 1					
		Large	Med.	Small			
Weasels, White		.90	.50	.25			
Weasels, Stained	Gray, etc......................	.05 @ .25					
Wolf, Timber Northern, cased..............		4.00	3.00	2.00	2.00	1.00	.50
"	Western, cased................	3.50	2.50	1.50	1.50	.75	.25
Wolf, Prairie Canada.....................		4.00	3.00	2.00	2.00	.60	.20
"	N. Rocky Mts. and N. Prairie						
	States....................	3.75	2.75	1.75	1.75	.50	.20
"	Cent. Rocky Mt. & Cent. Prairie						
	States..................	3.00	2.25	1.50	1.50	.50	.20
"	Southwestern..................	1.50	1.10	.75	.75	.25	.10
Wolverene	Dark.........................	8.00	6.00	4.00	4.00	1.50	.50
"	Pale.........................	6.00	4.00	2.50	2.50	1.00	.50
Rabbits	Whole Skins....................						.01
Beaver Castors	Dry.....................................per lb. 7.00 to 9.00						

NOTE:—*For fur sales, March, 1914, see Appendix XII.*

Appendix XI

Fur-farming Companies and Fur-farmers in Canada

THE list of fur-farming companies and fur-farmers which follows, has been compiled from returns kindly supplied to the Commission of Conservation by provincial officials and by the Under Secretary of State for Canada. It includes fur-farming companies incorporated by special Acts of the legislatures and by letters patent in each of the several provinces, as well as those operating under Federal charters. The names of fur-farmers given are of those who reported to, or were otherwise known to provincial game officials. The whole list has been revised to April 1, 1914.

The names have been arranged alphabetically by provinces, the incorporated companies being grouped at the head of each provincial list.

PRINCE EDWARD ISLAND

Incorporated Fur-farming Companies

	Place of Business	Capitalization
Acme Silver Black Fox Co., Ltd.	Summerside	$170,000
Agnew, (John) Fur Farms, Ltd.	Charlottetown	500,000
Alberry Plains Blue Fox Co., Ltd.	Alberry Plains	5,000
Alberton Dark Silver Fox Co., Ltd.	Alberton	110,000
Alma Ideal Dark Silver Fox Co., Ltd.	Alma	40,000
Anglo-American Silver Black Fox Co., Ltd.	Charlottetown	80,000
Barkers Black Fox, Ltd.	Summerside	125,000
Bedeque Fur Farming Co., Ltd.	Bedeque	200,000
Beech Grove Black Silver Fox Co., Ltd.	Summerside	250,000
Beech Hill Fox Co., Ltd.	Charlottetown	20,000
Beechwood Silver Foxes, Ltd.	Charlottetown	75,000
Belfast Fox & Fur Farming Co., Ltd.	Kinross	50,000
Belmont Black Fox Co., Ltd.	Charlottetown	125,000
Bideford Fox Co., Ltd.	Ellerslie	24,000
Black Foxes, Ltd.	Charlottetown	20,000
Black Prince Fox Co., Ltd.	O'Leary Station	75,000

	Place of Business	Capital-ization
Bonanza Fox Breeding Co., Ltd.	Murray Harbour....	$150,000
Boston Silver Black Fox Co., Ltd.	Charlottetown......	50,000
Breeders Ranching Co., Ltd.	Charlottetown......	25,000
Brighton Black Fox Co., Ltd.	Charlottetown......	75,000
British American Silver Black Fox Co., Ltd.	Sherbrooke........	375,000
Brown (George E.) Fur Farming Co., Ltd.	Kensington........	50,000
Bunbury Black Fox Co., Ltd.	Charlottetown......	100,000
Canada Atlantic Fox & Fur Co., Ltd.	Charlottetown......	1,000,000
Canadian Silver Foxes, Ltd.	Alberton..........	100,000
Cardigan Silver Black Fox Co., Ltd.	Cardigan..........	50,000
Carruthers Silver Black Fox Co., Ltd.	New Perth........	175,000
Cascumpec Silver Black Fox Co., Ltd.	Cascumpeque......	100,000
Central Fox Co., Ltd.	Charlottetown......	22,000
Centreville Blue Fox Co., Ltd.	Centreville........	48,000
Charlottetown Silver Black Fox Co., Ltd.	Charlottetown......	150,000
Clow Silver Black Fox Co., Ltd.	Murray Harbour W.	50,000
Columbia Silver Black Fox Co., Ltd.	Montague..........	75,000
Connaught Pedigreed Black Foxes, Ltd.	Charlottetown......	300,000
Consolidated Silver Black Fox Co., Ltd.	Summerside........	500,000
Crapaud Fox Ranching Co., Ltd.	Crapaud..........	17,000
Crown Fur Farms, Ltd.	Charlottetown......	100,000
Crystal Silver Black Fox Co., Ltd.	Miscouche.........	42,000
Dalton (Chas.) Silver Black Fox Co., Ltd.	Charlottetown......	625,000
Delaney Smith Silver Black Foxes, Ltd.	Kinkora..........	65,000
Diamond Silver Black Fox Co., Ltd.	Central Bedeque....	60,000
Dinnis (John R.) Pedigreed Foxes, Ltd.	Charlottetown......	300,000
Dominion Fox Breeding Co., Ltd.	Murray Harbour....	20,000
Dunk River Black Silver Fox Co., Ltd.	Bedeque..........	95,000
East Bideford Silver Black Fox Co., Ltd.	Bideford..........	90,000
Eastern Bla. 'oxes, Ltd.	Charlottetown......	195,000
Eclipse Blu. : Co., Ltd.	Charlottetown......	15,000
Eldorado Fox Co., Ltd.	Charlottetown......	39,000
Ellis Silver & Black Beauty Fox Co., Ltd.	Travellers Rest.....	50,000
Empire Black Fox Co., Ltd.	Charlottetown......	150,000
Englewood Silver Fox Co., Ltd.	Graham Road......	99,000
Equitable Maritime Black Fox Co., Ltd.	O'Leary Station....	96,000

	Place of Business	Capitalisation
Eureka Fox Co., Ltd.................	Breadalbane........	$ 30,000
Excelsior Black Silver Fox Co., Ltd...	O'Leary Station....	40,000
Fidelity Silver Black Fox Co., Ltd......	Summerside........	49,900
Freeland Silver Fox Co., Ltd..........	Freeland..........	190,000
Freetown Fox Ranching Co., Ltd......	Freetown..........	30,000
French River Farming Co., Ltd.........	French River.......	20,000
Garden of the Gulf Silver Black Fox Co., Ltd..............................	Charlottetown......	100,000
Gem Silver Black Fox Co., Ltd.........	Freetown..........	150,000
General Fur Farms, Ltd..............	Charlottetown......	195,000
Georgetown Silver Black Co., Ltd......	Georgetown........	60,000
Glenaladale Silver Black Fox Co., Ltd....	Glenaladale........	60,000
Golden Pelt Silver Black Fox Co., Ltd...	Summerside........	524,000
Good Luck Fox Co., Ltd..............	Hazelbrook........	100,000
Hackett Silver Black Fox Co...........	Tignish............	90,000
Hamilton Silver Fox Co., Ltd..........	Hamilton..........	95,000
Hayes (W. B.) Silver Fox Co., Ltd.....	Bideford..........	90,000
H.B.M. Fox Co., Ltd.................	French River.......	45,000
Hilsborough Fox Breeding Association	Charlottetown......	50,000
Hillside Dark Silver & Cross Fox Co.,Ltd.	Tyne Valley........	63,000
Howatt Dalton Silver Black Fox Co., Ltd.	Coleman...........	165,000
Humber Silver Black Fox Co., Ltd......	Murray River......	100,000
Huntley Silver Fox Co., Ltd...........	Summerside........	50,000
Hygrade Black Foxes, Ltd.............	Charlottetown......	270,000
Ideal Silver Black Fox Co., Ltd......	Summerside........	49,900
Imperial Silver Black Fox Co., Ltd......	Montague..........	150,000
Inland Black Fox Co..................	Charlottetown......	75,000
Invincible Silver Black Fox Co., Ltd....	Northam...........	190,000
Ives Black and Silver Fox Co., Ltd.......	Montague..........	45,000
Judson, J. H., Fox Ranching Co., Ltd..	Charlottetown......	100,000
Kildare Cape Fox Co., Ltd............	Kildare............	45,000
Kinkora Silver Black Fox Co., Ltd......	Kinkora...........	95,000
Kodiak Blue Fox Co., Ltd.............	Charlottetown......	90,000
Laurentian Black Foxes, Ltd..........	Charlottetown.....	190,000
Lewis Dark Silver Fox Co., Ltd.........	Conway............	60,000
Long River Fox Ranch & Farm Land Co., Ltd.............................	Long River........	4,500

	Place of Business	Capitalisation
Mac Black and Silver Fox Co., Ltd......	Summerside........	$110,000
Macdonald Silver Black Fox Co., Ltd....	Montague..........	150,000
McNeil (R. J.) Black and Silver Fox Co., Ltd.............................	Tyne Valley.......	220,000
McLean (A.E.) Co., Ltd...............	Southwest, Lot 16..	190,000
Magic Silver Black Fox Co., Ltd........	Summerside........	190,000
Malpeque Silver Black Fox Co., Ltd.....	Hamilton..........	40,000
Maple Leaf Silver Black Fox Co., Ltd ..	Bedeque..........	80,000
Maritime Black & Silver Fox Co., Ltd...	Bedeque..........	40,000
Mason Pure Bred Silver Black Fox Co., Ltd.............................	Charlottetown......	170,000
Matchless Silver Black Fox Co., Ltd....	Charlottetown......	250,000
Medisshill Black Fox Co., Ltd..........	Cardigan..........	50,000
Mill River Fox Co., Ltd..............	Alberton...........	90,000
Milton Silver Patch Fox Co., Ltd.,.....	Milton............	35,000
Model Silver Fox Co., Ltd.............	Charlottetown......	56,000
Montague Black Fox Co., Ltd.........	Montague..........	90,000
Montrose Black and Silver Fox Co., Ltd.	Alberton..........	48,000
Mount Albion Fur Co., Ltd............	Charlottetown......	20,000
Mount Carmel Fox Ranch Co., Ltd......	Summerside........	45,000
Mount Edward Joint Stock Co., Ltd.....	Charlottetown.....	70,000
Mount Edward Silver Black Foxes, Ltd.	Charlottetown......	400,000
Murray River Black Fox Co., Ltd.......	Murray River......	150,000
Murray Harbour Black and Silver Fox Ranching Co., Ltd...............	Murray Harbour....	150,000
New Annan Black & Silver Fox Co., Ltd.	Summerside........	90,000
New Era Silver Black Fox Co., Ltd......	O'Leary...........	45,000
New Glasgow Silver Black Fox Co., Ltd..	New Glasgow.......	100,000
New Haven Fox Co., Ltd.............	Charlottetown......	50,000
New London Black Fox and Farm Land Co., Ltd.........................	Clifton............	5,000
New Perth Blue Fox Co., Ltd..........	New Perth........	24,000
North American Silver Black Fox Co., Ltd.	Montague..........	100,000
North River Blue Fox Co., Ltd........	Charlottetown......	50,000
North Shore Silver Black Fox Co., Ltd.	Darnley...........	100,000
North Tryon Silver Black Fox Co. of P.E.I., Ltd.................	North Tryon.......	100,000

15

	Place of Business	Capitalisation
Northumberland Silver Black Fox Co., Ltd..............................	Alberton...........	$ 99,000
Old Island Pedigreed Foxes, Ltd.......	Southwest, Lot 16..	195,000
O'Leary Silver Black Fox Co., Ltd.....	O'Leary..........	40,000
Orchard Black Silver & Cross Fox Ranching Co., Ltd.....................	Murray Harbour ...	30,000
Park Farm Co., Ltd..................	Summerside.......	4,500
Park Island Black Silver Foxes, Ltd.....	Summerside.......	125,000
Patricia Fox Co., Ltd.................	Summerside........	48,000
Peerless Black and Silver Fox Co., Ltd...	Summerside........	240,000
Perfect Silver Black Fox Co., Ltd.......	Charlottetown......	124,000
Permanent Silver Foxes, Ltd..........	Charlottetown......	500,000
Phoenix Fox & Fur Co., Ltd...........	Charlottetown......	100,000
Pioneer Blue Fox Co., Ltd.............	Charlottetown......	30,000
Pioneer Fox Farming Co., Ltd.........	Ellerslie..........	190,000
Prince Albert Black Fox Co., Ltd.......	Charlottetown......	190,000
Prince Edward Silver Black Fox Co., Ltd.	Summerside........	350,000
Prince Royal Black Foxes, Ltd........	Charlottetown......	75,000
Progressive Fox Breeding Association...	Summerside........	60,000
Proina Fox Co. of Prince Edward Island, Ltd.............................	O'Leary Station....	45,000
Prospect Silver Fox Co., Ltd..........	Kensington........	195,000
Provincial Silver Black Foxes, Ltd.....	Charlottetown......	150,000
Pure Canadian Silver Black Fox Co., Ltd.	Summerside........	160,000
Railway Mutual Fox and Fur Co., Ltd...	Charlottetown......	30,000
Rayner International Fur Co., Ltd.....	Summerside........	625,000
Record Fox & Fur Co., Ltd............	Charlottetown......	90,000
Regal Black and Silver Co., Ltd........	Summerside.......	240,000
Rexal Silver Black Fox Co., Ltd.......	Summerside........	10,000
Richmond Bay Black Fox Co., Ltd.....	Central Lot 16.....	120,000
Riverside Farming Co., Ltd............	Tryon............	50,000
Rogers-Farquharson Blue Fox Co., Ltd..	Charlottetown......	25,000
Rogers-Payton Silver Black Foxes, Ltd.	Charlottetown......	270,000
Rosemount Live Stock Co., Ltd........	Alberton..........	10,000
Royal Silver Black Fox Co., Ltd.......	Summerside........	25,000
Royal Strain Silver Black Foxes, Ltd....	Summerside........	524,000
Royalty Silver Black Fox Co., Ltd.....	Charlottetown......	90,000

	Place of Business	Capital- ization
St. Eleanor's Mink Ranching Co., Ltd...	St. Eleanor........	10,000
St. Georges Silver Black Fox Co., Ltd...	Summerside........	22,000
St. Lawrence Silver Blac ' Fox Co., Ltd..	Charlottetown......	195,000
St. Peter's Silver Black Fox Co., Ltd.....	Hd. St. Peter Bay..	100,000
Samson Silver Black Fox Co., Ltd......	Charlottetown......	100,000
Seal River Black Fox Co., Ltd..........	Charlottetown......	190,000
Silver Fox and Cup Oysters of Malpeque, Ltd.............................	Hamilton..........	95,000
Silver Foxes & Furs, Ltd..............	Charlottetown......	300,000
Silver Tip Black Fox Co., Ltd.........	Crapaud..........	25,000
Sirdar Silver Fox Co., Ltd.............	Summerside........	125,000
Smith Silver Black Fox Co., Ltd.......	Montague..........	150,000
Souris Silver Black Fox Co., Ltd..... ..	Souris............	50,000
Sovereign Silver Black Fox Co., Ltd....	St. Louis..........	750,000
Spring Park Black Fox Co., Ltd.......	Charlottetown......	90,000
Standard Silver Black Fox Co., Ltd....	Charlottetown......	60,000
Star Black Fox Co., Ltd..............	Charlottetown......	89,000
Sterling Silver Black Fox Co., Ltd......	Charlottetown......	99,000
Stewart (John) Fox Co., Ltd..........	Charlottetown......	48,000
Strathcora Silver Black Foxes, Ltd. ...	Charlottetown......	250,000
Summerside and Kensington Fur Farm- ing Co., Ltd...................	Kensington........	20,000
Superior Silver Black Fox Co., Ltd......	Kensington........	50,000
Sutherland Silver Black Fox Co., Ltd....	Montague..	85,000
Taylor's Silver Black Fox Co., Ltd.....	Montague..........	180,000
Thoroughbred Silver Black Foxes, Ltd.	Charlottetown......	195,000
Three Rivers Silver Black Fox Co., Ltd.	Montague..........	72,000
Tignish Silver Black Fox Co., Ltd......	Tignish............	90,000
Tracadie Cross Silver Black Fox Co., Ltd.	Tracadie Cross......	50,000
Trout River Silver Black Fox Co., Ltd....	Tyne Valley........	24,000
Tryon Black Diamond Fox Co., Ltd.....	Hampton..........	50,000
Tryon Mink and Fur Trading Co., Ltd.	Tryon.............	3,000
Tuplin Company, Ltd.................	Summerside........	4,500
Tyne Valley Black and Silver Fox Co., Ltd.............................	Tyne Valley........	75,000
Union Black Fox Co., Ltd.............	Charlottetown......	190,000
Union Vale Silver Black Fox Co., Ltd...	Union Vale........	48,000

	Place of Business	Capitalisation
United Silver Black Fox Co., Ltd........	Tryon............	$150,000
United States and Island Silver Black Fox Co., Ltd........................	Charlottetown......	99,000
Upton Black Fox Co., Ltd.............	Charlottetown......	70,000
Victoria Farm Silver Black Fox Co., Ltd.	Charlottetown......	250,000
Weeks Canada Silver Fox Furs, Ltd.....	Charlottetown......	0,000
Willow Hill Co., Ltd.................	Summerside........	11,400
Woodbine Silver Black Fox Co., Ltd. ..	Summerside........	48,000
Woodstock Black Silver Fox Co., Ltd.	Cascumpeque.......	78,000
Young (Dr. C.C.) Karakul Sheep Co., Ltd.	Charlottetown......	150,000

The following Fox Companies are not incorporated in Prince Edward Island but are doing business therein in connection with the breeding and raising of foxes.

Silver Ranching Company.............	Boston, Mass......	$350,000
Manager, F. L. Rogers, Alberton.		
Hartford Dark Silver Fox Co., Ltd... ...	Hartford, Conn.....	125,000
Manager, Walter M. Cahill, Alberton		
International Black Foxes, Ltd........	Sherbrooke, Que....	500,000
Manager, Jas. Warburton, Charlottetown.		
Massachusetts Silver Black Fox Co., 53 State Street.................	Boston, Mass.......	350,000
Manager, W. P. Purdy, Charlottetown		
Black Banks Corporation, Ltd.........		450,000
		$1,775,000

NOTE.—Probably not over sixty per cent of the authorized capital has been issued. It is also to be noted that a considerable number of companies failed to float.

J. W. J.

Fox, Mink and Karakul Sheep Ranchers in P.E. Island

Names	Addresses
Adams, David	Sea View
Agnew, John	Alberton
Agnew, John	Charlottetown
Allan, Gabriel S.	Lot 17
Arsenault, Hon. A. E.	Summerside
Arsenault, Ernest	East Bideford
Arsenault, Louis	Piusville
Ashley, Frederick B.	Alberton
Ashley, Lowden	Alberton
Bagnell, Rufus G.	Central Bedeque
Barbour, George	St. Anthony
Barnett, George	Elmsdale
Bearisto, Joseph	Alma
Bell, Wm. E.	Cape Traverse
Biggar, Joseph	Breadalbane
Birch, James E.	Alberton
Boulter, Wilfrid (mink)	Tryon
Bovyer, Franklin	Bunbury
Bowness, John	Montrose
Brooks, W. E.	Maddock, Lot 8
Brown, George E.	Margate
Brown, J. W.	Northam
Brown, J. W. (mink)	Tyne Valley
Buote, Paul	Tignish
Burke, Peter	Alma
Burleigh, Edmond S.	Ellerslie
Burleigh, William	Ellerslie
Burns, J. Roy	Freetown
Cahill, Walter M.	Alberton
Cail, James H. B.	Alberton
Callaghan, William B.	St. Louis
Campbell, David	O'Leary
Campbell, Neil	Sturgeon
Cannon, Samuel E.	St. Eleanor
Champion, Capt. John	Alberton
Champion, William	Alberton
Clark, Chester W.	Cascumpeque
Clark Frederick	Alberton

Names	Addresses
Clark, Frederick W	Cavendish
Clark, Ray	Bayview
Clark, William A	Alberton
Coffin, E. S	Charlottetown
Colwill, S. H	New Haven
Conroy, Fred	Tignish
Cousins, George	Long River
Cousins, James	Baltic
Craig, Lemuel	Brae
Craig, T. J	Orwell Cove
Crochett, John D	Elmsdale
Currie, Bruce	Elmsdale
Currie, Herbert	Elmsdale
Dalton, Charles, & Raynor	Tignish
Dalton, Daniel	Skinner Pond
Dalton, John E	Campbellton
Dennis, Wilbert	Margate
Dennis, William	Arlington
Dennis, Wm. H	O'Leary
DesRoche, Fred J	Miscouche
DesRoche, Stanley L	Miscouche
Dinnis, John R. (karakul sheep)	Charlottetown
Donalds, James	Indian River
Dunbar, Hugh B	Alma
Dunbar, Joseph A	Alma
Ellis, Foulton	O'Leary
Ellis, George	Maddock, Lot 8
Ellis, George B	Alberton
England, Elsworth	Travellers Rest
Evans, Philip M	O'Leary
FitzGerald, Gerald	Waterford, Lot 1
Foley, Alonzo	Bloomfield
Foley, Moses J	Kildare Cape
Foley, Richard	Kildare
Forbes, D. N	Tyne Valley
Forsythe, Albert E	Alberton
Found, Harlan	Clifton
Fraser, Daniel	Alberton
Gaffrey, Ernest T	Alma
Gallant, Joseph	Howlan

Names	Addresses
Gallant, Mrs. Meddie	Bloomfield
Gallant, S. T.	Piusville
Gard, Henry	Mill River
Getson, Albert	Kildare Cape
Gordon, Archibald S.	Lot 6
Gordon, George C.	Alberton
Gordon, Robert H.	Montrose
Gorrill, Walter	O'Leary
Graves, Andrew	Alberton
Grey, Wm. T.	Alberton
Hamill, Thomas B.	Greenmount, Lot 2
Handraham, Austin	Tignish
Harding, Gavin	Graham Road
Harding, Henry	Mill River
Hardy, George	Montrose
Hardy, Thomas M.	Hill River
Hayes, John T.	Searletown
Hayes, Wm. B.	Bideford
Haywood, George	Kildare
Haywood, Perley	Tignish
Henderson, Josiah	Freeland
Hillman, John	Bay View
Hinton, John S.	Summerside
Hogan, Henry	North Cape
Holland, A. E.	Clinton
Holmes, J. E.	Union Road
Hopgood, John	Mill Road
Horne, George	O'Leary
Horne, H. H.	Charlottetown
Howard, D. W.	Milton
Howard, Leigh	Cornwall
Howard, Pius	Cape Wolfe
Howard, Robert	Cape Wolfe
Howatt, Hubert	St. Eleanor
Hudson, David	Lot 4
Hudson, Thomas H.	Alberton
Hume, John D.	Murray River
Hunter, Allan	Bloomfield
Hunter, James	Georgetown

Names	Addresses
Hunter, James H.	Alberton
Hunter, J. E. C.	Alberton
Inman, F. J.	Central Bedeque
Inman, John	Alberton
Irving, James	Alberton
Ives, Isaac (foxes and mink)	Montague
Jardine, James	Kelvin
Jeffrey, Richard	Alma
Jenkins, Henry	Upton
Johnston, Charles	Alberton
Johnston, Edmond W.	Elmsdale
Jones, J. Walter (karakul sheep)	Charlottetown
Jordan, Simon	Murray Harbour
Judson, J. H.	Alexandra
Kearney, Wm.	Murray River
Keefe, Joseph	Alberton
Keefe, Thomas	Hill River
Kennedy, Murdoch	Breadalbane
Kennedy, Samuel	Breadalbane
Knight	Georgetown
Lackey, John	Bedeque
Laird, John	St. Anthony
Laird, J. M.	Kelvin
Langille, Frank	Howlan
Leard, L. B.	Alberton
Leonard, Wm. E.	Kildare Cape
Lewis, Charles	Alberton
Lewis, George B.	Charlottetown
Lewis, Henry	Lot 5
Lidstone, Edward I.	O'Leary
Lidstone, Merrill	Cape Wolfe
Lockerby, Fred. J.	Hamilton
Lovett, Austin	Alberton
McArthur, Spurgeon	Rosebank
McArthur, Wm. B.	Kensington
McAusland, Wm. G.	Bloomfield
McCaull, Patterson C.	Ellerslie
McDonald, Daniel F.	Montague
McDonald, George A. B.	Charlottetown

Names	Addresses
McDonald, Neil	Pinette
McDougall, James A.	Grand River West
McGuigan, Nathaniel	Indian River
McKendrick, J. C.	Charlottetown
McKinnon, Major C.	Glenaladale
McKinnon, Wallace	Fredericton
McLaurin, Arthur	Central, Lot 16
McLean, A. E.	Lot 16
McLean, Donald	Crapaud
McLean, John M.	New Perth
McLean, Wm. J.	Central, Lot 16
McLeod, Alex. N.	Tignish
McMillan, Charles L.	Bloomfield
McMillan, Hugh	Cornwall
McNeill, A. A.	O'Leary
McNeil, R. J.	Tyne Valley
McPhee, Patrick	Coleman
McRae, Curtis	Huntley
McRae, Frank B.	Hill River
McRae, F. B.	Vernon
Malone, John	Portage
Manson, Edward W.	Summerside
Marchbank, David	Montrose
Martin, John S.	Uig
Matthew, Waldo H.	Alberton
Matthews, Archibald	Alberton
Matthews, Jesse S.	Alberton
Matthews, Henry E.	Alberton
Megison, Wm.	Millvale
Metherall, Frank	Cape Wolfe
Metherall, James	Cape Wolfe
Metherall, Harry G.	Bloomfield
Mills, John	Clermont
Montgomery, W. Frank H.	Lower Bedeque
Moore, St. Clair	Eldon
Morrison, J. Andrew	Conway
Morrison, John C.	Ellerslie
Mountain, Wm. D.	Alma
Moyse, Thomas	Central Bedeque

Names	Addresses
Murphy, Richard	Lauretta
Murphy, Wm	China Point
Murray, George	Elmsdale
Murray, Major C	Breadalbane
Myers, George K	Brudenell
Nantes, John	Maplewood
Nicholson, Duncan A	Bedeque
Nicholson, N. J	Montague
Norton, H. V	West Royalty
O'Brien, A. D	Elmsdale
O'Brien, James	Elmsdale
O'Brien, J. Albert	Loretta
O'Brien, James E	Loretta
O'Brien, Harry	Elmsdale
Oliver, John I	Alberton
Oulton, Russell	Alberton
Peacock, John M	Bedeque
Perry, Romain	St. Edward
Peters, John P	Palmer Road
Peters, Joseph	Cascumpeque
Platts, Herbert	Kildare Cape
Platts, James	Howlan Road
Poole, W. L	Montague
Power, Patrick	Greenmount
Pridham, Charles N	Montrose
Prideham, Perry	Montrose
Profitt, John T	Alberton
Profitt, Lester	Bloomfield
Prowse, W. H	Murray Harbour
Purdy, W. B	Charlottetown
Ramsay, Austin A	Conway
Ramsay, Erwin	Rosebank
Rayner, Arch. H	Kildare
Rayner, Benjamin I	Alberton
Rayner, Silas, and Son	Greenmount
Ready, Michæl P	Palmer Road
Reeves, Calvin T	Freetown
Riley, William Thomas	Cape Wolfe
Robinson, George W	Summerside

Names	Addresses
Rogers, Fred J.	Alberton
Rogers, W. Russell	Coleman
Scales, Austin (minks)	St. Eleanor
Selkirk, Leigh J.	Cascumpeque
Sharbell, Khalil	Portage
Sharp, Williard J.	East Bideford
Shaw, Joseph	Haliburton
Shaw, McMillan	Alberry Plains
Shea, Frank	Waterford
Sheeham, Wm. (minks)	Port Hill
Simpson, Frank	Hamilton
Simpson, Jeremiah	Cavendish
Simpson, William George	Kensington
Skerry, John	Alberton
Smallman, John A.	Summerside
Smallman, J. F.	Alberton
Smith, Henry	Tryon
Smith, Arthur	Freeland
Sterns, Reginald H.	Charlottetown
Stetson, George S.	Freetown
Stetson, Henry J.	Unionvale
Taylor, Austin	Granville
Taylor, Robert A.	Montague
Thomas, Howard B.	Cascumpeque
Thompson, James P.	Campbellton
Thompson, Henry	Lot 14
Travers, Victor	Kildare
Tuplin, Frank F.	Summerside
Tuplin, James C.	Lot 11
Tuplin, Samuel B.	Lot 11
Tweedy, George	Alberton
Waite, B. D.	Little Tignish
Waldron, Nelson (minks)	Port Hill
Walker, David	New Annan
Wallace, William H.	Alberton
Warren, Benjamin	Alma
Warren, George B.	Mill River
Webb, James	O'Leary
Webster, John A.	Charlottetown

Names	Addresses
Weeks, William Frank.....................	Fredericton Station
Weeks, Carl..............................	Alberton
Wells, Andrew............................	Alberton
Wells, John A............................	Elmsdale
Whitten, John E..........................	Coleman
Wigmore, Thomas.........................	Breadalbane
Williams, Edward.........................	Tyne Valley
Williams, Thomas E.......................	Mt. Pleasant
Wood, Arthur C...........................	Alexandra
Woodman, Charles A.......................	Alberton
Woodman, Thomas B.......................	Charlottetown
Yeo, Robert..............................	Huntley
Yeo, Thomas..............................	South Kildare

NOVA SCOTIA

Incorporated Fur-farming Companies

	Place of Business	Capitalization
Acme Silver Black Fox Co., Ltd.........	Truro.............	$150,000
Amherst Foxes, Ltd....., ...	Amherst...........	40,000
Bedeque Black Silver Fox Co., Ltd......	Halifax............	25,000
Bout Island Fox Co., Ltd..............	Wolfville.	100,000
Brookline Fox Ranching Co., Ltd........	Amherst..........	40,000
Burgeo Co-operative Fox Breeding Co., Ltd............................	Halifax............	60,000
Canada Newfoundland Fox Farms Syndicate, Ltd.......................	North Sydney......	10,000
Carbonear Fox Company, Ltd..........	Amherst...........	20,000
Cumberland Fox and Fur Co., Ltd......	River Hebert.......	20,000
Diamond Black Skunk Co., Ltd........	Truro.............	30,000
Doctor's Pedigreed Silver Foxes, Ltd. ..	Truro.............	100,000
Dominion Fur Farms, Ltd.............	Sydney............	20,000
Dominion Karakul-Arabi Sheep & Fur Co., Ltd.........................	Bridgetown...	150,000
Eastern Canada Fur Farming Co., Ltd...	Halifax............	20,00,000

	Place of Business	Capitalisation
East River Fox and Fur Breeding Co., Ltd.		$ 25,000
Fur Producers, Ltd.	Halifax	2,000,000
Garia Bay Fox and Trapping Co., Ltd.	North Sydney	10,000
Haliburton Fox Co., Ltd.	Pictou	25,000
Hillside Fox Co., Ltd.	North Sydney	30,000
International Fox Breeding Co., Ltd.	Pictou	100,000
Island Silver Black Fox & Fur Co., Ltd.	Yarmouth	70,000
Laplanche Fox Co., Ltd.	Amherst	10,000
Lunenburg Silver Black Fox Co., Ltd.	Lunenburg	50,000
McConnell Silver Black Fox Co., Ltd.	Port Hillford	300,000
MacKenzie Black Foxes, Ltd.	Amherst	100,000
Middleton Wool and Fur Co., Ltd.	Middleton	30,000
Northumberland Foxes, Ltd.	Amherst	30,000
Nova Scotia Black Fox Co., Ltd.	Antigonish	50,000
Ohio Fur Co., Ltd.	Shelburne	10,000
Peerless Black Skunk Co., Ltd.	Sydney	20,000
Prince Edward Island Scotia Black Fox Co., Ltd.,	Truro	150,000
Prince Edward Silver Black Fox Co., Ltd.,	Bridgetown	75,000
Ramsay Black Skunk Sable Co., Ltd.	Truro	5,000
Ramsay's Fur Farm, Ltd.	Truro	20,000
Rayner (B. I.) Silver Fox Co., Ltd.	West Gore,	50,000
Rayner, Clarke and Harlow Black Fox Co., Ltd.,	Bridgetown	60,000
Riverside Fox and Fur Co., Ltd.	West New Annan	50,000
Seaside Fox Co., Ltd.	Lunenburg	10,000
Silver Black Fox Co. of Nova Scotia, Ltd.,	Kentville	100,000
Stellarton Silver Black Fox Co., Ltd.	Stellarton	25,000
Sydney Silver Black Fox Co., Ltd.	Sydney	100,000
Truro Black Skunk Co., Ltd.,	Truro	10,000
Truro Fox Farm Co., Ltd.	Truro	50,000
Tuplin Silver Black Fox Corporation, Ltd.	Halifax	300,000
Whycocomagh Black Foxes, Ltd.	Whycocomagh	50,000
Wilden Silver Black Fox Co., Ltd.	Halifax	2,000,000

Fur-farmers who have Taken out Permits in Nova Scotia

	Place of Business	Animals Farmed
Aikens, W. F. & R......	Guysboro Intervale...	Foxes
Allen, H. A.............	Arcadia..............	Foxes
Ambrose Albert.......	Stewiacke...........	Skunks
Archibald, J. B. & Sedge-wick, J. H...........	Middle Musquodoboit.	Foxes
Atkinson, E. P., M. D...	Northport...........	Foxes, Raccoons, Mink
Babcock, Clarence P....	Amherst.............	Skunks, Muskrats
Baird, Wellie..........	Little River..........	Foxes
Baltzer, T. P..........	Aylesford...........	Skunks
Banks, Chester, R......	West Inglisville......	Foxes
Banks, Percy G........	Brickton............	Minks
Bass River Fur Co., Ltd..	Bass River..........	Foxes
Beach, Edgar..........	Westfield...........	Minks
Beckwith, Andrew......	Bishopville..........	Foxes
Berwick Breeding & Fur Co.................	Berwick............	Skunks
Berwick Fur Farm Co..	Berwick............	Skunks
Betts, H. B.,..........	East Wentworth......	Foxes
Bishop Bros...........	Greenwich..........	Foxes
Boates, William, & Gam-mon Austin	Westville...........	Foxes
Bower, Edmund L......	Shelburne...........	Skunks
Bower, Geo. W.,.......	Lower Ohio.........	Foxes and Skunks
Bower, Howard.......	Upper Clyde	Foxes
Boylan, S. A..........	New Ross...........	Foxes
Brechin, J.............	Upper Nine Mile River	Minks
Brownell, H. W., & Carter, B. G.........	Amherst............	Foxes
Bruce, Alex. J........	Boyleston...........	Foxes
Burke, Phillip L.......	Minudie............	Foxes
Burke, J. S...........	Drum Head.........	Foxes
Burke, Whitfield.......	Port Hood..........	Foxes
Burns, Harding........	Ross Creek..........	Foxes and Skunks
Burrill, George H......	Brooklyn............	Foxes and Skunks
Cameron, Alex.,.......	Sunnybrae..........	Foxes
Cameron, Johnston.....	Stellarton...........	Foxes
Carter, F. A...........	Canso..............	Foxes

	Place of Business	Animals Farmed
Carty, William.........	Pubnico Head.......	Minks
Cavanagh, C. C. & Oscar,	Tusket.............	Minks
Charles, Joseph.........	Hectanooga.........	Minks
Chute, A. C.,..........	Clarence............	Foxes
Chute, A. T.,..........	Bridgetown.........	Foxes
Chute, J. N., & Ward, B.F.	Berwick............	Foxes
Clark, G. B............	Tatamagouche.......	Foxes
Clow, Lemuel.........	Shelburne...........	Foxes
Cole, G. A.............	Chester.............	Minks
Corbin, P. G...........	West Lahave.......	Minks
Cranton, G. W.,.......	Amherst............	Minks
Creighton, W. O.,......	Cen. West River.....	Foxes
Crowell, Robt. N.......	Kemptville..........	Skunks
Cruikshank, Howard S .	Truro...............	Skunks
Cummings, A. W........	Glenholm...........	Foxes
Deveau, John F.........	Meteghan...........	Minks
Doane, Stanley.........	Barrington..........	Minks
Doherty, Kamp........	Great Village........	Skunks and Minks
Doherty, R. Peel.......	Great Village........	Foxes
Doucett, Charles.......	Havelock...........	Foxes and Skunks
Drew, Frederick, D.,....	Yarmouth..........	Skunks
Durling, F. S.,.........	Paradise............	Foxes
Durno, Alex...........	Cambridge..........	Skunks
East River Fur & Fox Breeding Co..........	Pictou..............	Foxes
Eaton, P. H., & Corbett, E..................	Westville...........	Foxes
Edgewood Mink Ranch .	Shubenacadie........	Minks
Embree, Wasson L......	East Wentworth.....	Foxes
Feindal, A. B..........	New Germany.......	Foxes
Feindal, A B. & Norman	New Germany.......	Skunks and Minks
Feindell, C. E..........	Bridgetown.........	Foxes
Field, E. H............	Port Howe..........	Skunks and Raccoons
Field, M. A............	Oxford Junction......	Foxes
Field, S. M............	New Salem..........	Foxes
Filmore, W. A..........	Oxford Junction.....	Foxes
Forsyth, Ernest........	Kentville...........	Foxes and Minks
Fulmer, B. B........ ...	Shubenacadie........	Skunks

	Place of Business	Animals Farmed
Gardner, E. M.........	Brooklyn...........	Minks
Gillen Bros............	Wine Harbour.......	Foxes
Goodwin, Reginald.....	Lower Argyle........	Mink
Greeno, Martin T......	Newport...........	Raccoons.
Grimm, Ed. L.........	Parkdale..........	Skunks
Grimm, F. O'D........	Springfield..........	Skunks
Hall, Geo. B..........	Brooklyn..........	Foxes
Harding, D. D........	Berwick...........	Foxes
Harrington, John......	Coldbrook..........	Raccoons
Hemeon & Sheppard....	Liverpool..........	Minks
Hemeon, W. L........	East Ragged Islands..	Minks
Henley, J. M..........	Oxford............	Foxes
Hermann, Carl........	Yarmouth..........	Foxes & Skunks
Hicks E. A. & H. B....	Bridgetown.	Foxes, Minks & Skunks
Hill, Thomas E.......	Moose Brook........	Foxes
Hillside Fox Co., Ltd....	North Sydney.......	Foxes
Hingley, A. A.........	Hilden............	Foxes
Hiseler, Geo. J., & Slaughenwhite, John .	St. Margaret Bay.....	Minks
Hopkins, Chas. M......	Barrington..........	Foxes
Horne, John L.........	Enfield............	Foxes
Hurst, Geo. H.........	Port Hillford........	Minks.
Ingraham, J. W.......	North Sydney.......	Raccoons and Foxes
James, W. T. & McNintch, A. M......	Paradise...........	Foxes and Raccoons
Johnson, J. W.........	Truro.............	Foxes
Keith, Leander........	Coldboro..........	Foxes
King, Brenton S.......	Clyde River.........	Foxes
Lamb, Henry.........	Diligent River.......	Foxes, Raccoons
Langille, J. Walter.....	Tatamagouche.......	Foxes
Lantz, Avery L	New Germany.......	Skunks
Lantz, Howard........	Mahone Bay........	Minks
Larder, C. A..........	New Ross..........	Foxes
Lawler, C. F. & D. C....	Ogden............	Foxes
Lawson, E. R.........	Sherbrooke..........	Foxes
Lemard, E. S..........	Paradise...........	Foxes & Raccoons
Lent, William H.......	Tusket............	Foxes, Skunks, Mink
Lewis, Budd C........	Danvers...........	Skunks

	Place of Business	Animals Farmed
Linton & Co.	Truro	Foxes
Little, Frank	Truro	Skunks
Logan, Murdock & Petipas	Pictou	Foxes, Raccoons and Skunks
Lunenburg Mink & Skunk Ranch	Lunenburg	Minks
Lunenburg Silver Black Fox Co., Ltd.	Lunenburg	Foxes
Lynds, Wilbert	Wentworth	Foxes
Lyons, T. R.	Waterville	Foxes
MacDonald, Edmund S.	Halifax	Minks and Skunks
MacDougall, J. Munroe	West Gore	Raccoons
McCallum, Logan B. & E. S. McNutt	Truro	Foxes
McConnell, James & Sons	Port Hillford	Foxes
McDonald, David R.	Up-Nine Mile River	Skunks
McDonald, James	Lunenburg	Minks
McDonald, Sutherland	Lower Caledonia	Foxes
McDonnell, Berton	Renfrew Gold Mines	Minks
McElmon, E. H.	Dartmouth	Foxes
McGrath, E.	Tatamagouche	Foxes
McGrath, John D.	Sonora	Foxes
McGregor, Donald	St. Paul	Foxes
McGregor, Rev. Peter M.	Wolfville	Foxes
MacGregor, Murdoch	Hillside, Boulardarie	Foxes
MacKenzie & Bonyman, Black Skunk Co.	Bayhead	Skunks.
McKenzie, Angus	Cen. New Annan	Foxes, Skunks & Raccoons
McKenzie, Leonard D.	Truro	Foxes
McKinnon, Neil	Mount Thom	Foxes
McKinnon, James	Whycocomagh	Minks
McLellan, W. B.	Tatamagouche	Foxes
McLellen, C. K.	Tatamagouche	Foxes
McLeod, Alex	Whycocomagh Bay	Minks
McNintch, A. M. & W. T. J. & A.	Paradise	Foxes and Raccoons

16

	Place of Business	Animals Farmed
Macomber, John........	Maitland	Skunks
McPhail, Dr. Donald T..	Whycocomagh.......	Foxes & Minks
MacPherson, R. H.....	Port Hood..........	Minks
Mailman, E. W........	Hemford...........	Foxes
Matheson & Byers' Fur Farm..............	West New Annan.....	Raccoons
Mattatall, George......	Tatamagouche.......	Foxes
Mattinson, Lawson......	Great Village........	Skunks
Middleton Wool & Fur Co. Ltd.............	Middleton..........	Skunks
Miller, Rufus..........	South Oxford........	Foxes
Moland, David & Sons.	East Chester........	Minks
Moore, Robert M......	Shinimecas Bridge	Foxes
Morehouse, Reuben & Orie, Spechts........	Centreville..........	Minks
Morris, E. LaMont.....	Advocate...........	Foxes
Morse, J. E...........	Paradise............	Foxes
Mosher, John W.......	Victoria Vale........	Skunks
Mosher, Thomas A.....	Windsor............	Raccoons
Mossman, J. D........	Lower Rose Bay......	Raccoons
Muir, Alexander.......	Westville...........	Foxes
Muise, Lewis E........	Springhaven.........	Skunks
Mulhall, D. C. & Dr. C. S. Hennigan...........	Liverpool...........	Minks
Munro, Geo. A........	Truro..............	Minks
Munro, R. M..........	East Wentworth......	Mink, Foxes & Marten
Murray, Chas. B.......	Cove Road..........	Foxes & Raccoons
Neiley, B. L...........	New Glasgow........	Foxes
Nelson, W. K., & Crowe, E. P...............	Stewiacke...........	Skunks
Newcombe, R. W......	Ellershouse.........	Minks
Nova Scotia Black Fox Co. Ltd.............	Antigonish..........	Foxes
Nova Scotia Fox Co....	Yarmouth...........	Foxes
Nowe, Robert.........	Vogler Cove.........	Minks & Skunks
Ogilvie, Byard	Cross Roads.........	Skunks
Ogilvie, Loran S.......	Wentworth..........	Foxes
Ohio Fur Company Ltd.	Shelburne...........	Beavers, Muskrats & Skunks

	Place of Business	Animals Farmed
O'Regan, Thomas	Lakelands	Foxes
O'Rourke, Geo.	River Hebert	Foxes
Ozon, C. A., Jr.	Ingonish Ferry	Foxes
Parker, Frederick	Berwick	Minks
Patriquin, C. A.	Wolfville	Skunks & Raccoons
Pearson, G. L.	Paradise	Foxes & Raccoons
Peterkin, F.	Lunenburg	Minks
Piggott, E. S.	Bridgetown	Foxes
Pipes, Dixon	Northport	Raccoons
Polly, Dr. Geo. A.	Lunenburg	Minks & Foxes
Porter, Fred	Advocate Harbour	Minks
Powers, W. T.	Lunenburg	Minks & Skunks
Pride, Allen	Sonora	Foxes
P.E. Island Scotia Black Fox Company Ltd.	Truro	Foxes
Prime, Guy	New Tusket	Skunks
Pritchard & Bent	Oxford	Foxes
Purdy, C. O.	Maitland	Skunks
Purdy, William J.	Jackson	Mink & Raccoon
Rafuse, Joseph S.	Parkdale	Minks, Skunks & Foxes
Randall, Dr. E. A.	Truro	Foxes
Rayner, B.I., Silver Fox Co.	West Gore	Foxes
Rayner, Clark & Harlow Black Fox Co.	Bridgetown	Foxes
Read, John L.	Pictou	Minks
Reeves, F. H.	Oldham	Minks
Ritcey, Albert J.	Stanley Section	Minks
Riverside Fox & Fur Co.	West New Annan	Foxes
Robinson, A. B.	Nicholsville	Skunks
Rogers, Kenneth E.	Yarmouth	Skunks
Radcliffe, Royal	West Gore	Skunks
Ryerson, Percy O.	Lower Argyle	Foxes
Salt, William	Falmouth	Minks
Sanford, Sandie	Chester	Minks

	Place of Business	Animals farmed
Saunders, Charles O.	Clarence West	Foxes
Saunders, Otto M.	Clarence West	Foxes
Schurman, Fred B.	Truro	Foxes & Skunks
Scotia Silver B. Fox Co.	Lunenburg	Foxes
Sheridan, J.A. & Donaldson, James	Enfield	Foxes
Silver B. Fox Co., of Nova Scotia Ltd	Kentville	Foxes
Silver, Elbert	Bridgewater	Minks
Simpson, Noble	Five Islands	Foxes & Skunks
Slade, William D.	West Tatamagouche	Foxes & Skunks
Slaughenwhite, John	Tantallon	Minks
Smith, Alex. A.	Vogler Cove	Minks
Smith, D. M.	Springhill	Minks
Smith, Freeman	Pleasant River	Foxes
Smith, John	Shinimecas	Minks
Smith, J. D.	Clyde River	Minks
Sperry, A. H.	Petite Riviere	Minks
Stewart, Robert C.	Chester Basin	Minks
Stubbert, James A.	Pt. Aconi, Boulardarie.	Foxes
Sullivan, Eugene	Bedford	Foxes
Sutherland, John D.	Arichat	Foxes
Sutherland, S. W. & J. H.	Watervale	Foxes
Swan, Arthur	New Annan	Foxes
Swan, George W.	New Annan	Foxes
Sweeney, Heber M.	Lunenburg	Minks
Tallman, O. H. & O. E.	West Gore	Skunks
Teed Larkin Silver Fox Co.	Malagash	Foxes
Thompson, Clarence N.	Victoria	Foxes
Thornton & Bancroft	Joggins Bridge	Minks
Trenholm, Alfred R.	Northport	Foxes
Trueman, Osburn	Shinimecas	Minks
Truro Fox Farm Co., Ltd.	Truro	Foxes
Walsh, James H. & M.	Upper Prospect	Mink
Walton, E. F.	Kemptville	Mink and Foxes
Ward, Bruce	Weston	Skunks
Warren, W. A.	Bridgetown	Raccoons

	Place of Business	Animals Farmed
Waters, Albert E.	Whycocomagh	Minks
Wells, Clarence	Whitehead	Foxes
Welton, Malan H.	Kingston	Skunks
Wentzel, Chipman	Maplewood	Foxes and Skunks
Wentzell, Ira L.	Maplewood	Minks, Foxes & Skunks
Whidden, Charles G.	Antigonish	Foxes
White, John	Somerset	Minks
Whitman, Fred. L.	New Albany	Skunks
Whitman, L. R.	Central Clarence	Raccoons and Skunks
Wilniff, Wallace	Lunenburg	Minks
Whycocomagh Black Fox Co., Ltd.	Whycocomagh	Foxes
Wight, Jas. A. & Wm. H.	Eastern Points	Minks
Will, Thomas E.	Moose Brook	Foxes
Witham, Ira W., & Banks, Atwood R.	Clarence Centre	Skunks and Raccoons
Wood, Amos	Lake Killarney	Raccoons
Woodworth, Henry D.	LeRoy	Skunks
Woolaver, John R.	Hantsport	Foxes
York, Judson	Diligent River	Foxes
Zwicker, C., & Oakes, H.	New Albany	Skunks

NEW BRUNSWICK

Companies Incorporated by Letters Patent

	Place of Business	Capitalization
Alaskan Foxes, Ltd.	Botsford	$ 24,500
Bathurst Silver Black Fox Co., Ltd.	Bathurst	99,000
Canadian Karakul Arabi Sheep and Fur Co., Ltd.	Apohaqui	49,000
Chaleur Fox Co., Ltd.	Jacquet River	27,000
Coverdale Fox Farm, Ltd.	Coverdale	99,000
Crockett Fox Co., Ltd.	Moncton	49,000
Eastern Black Foxes, Ltd.	Port Elgin	150,000

	Place of Business	Capital- ization
Fundy Fox Co., Ltd.................	St. John........ ...	400,000
Grand Manan Silver Black Fox Co., Ltd.	North Hea⁴........	49,000
Great Canada Northern Black Fox Co., Ltd.............................	Loggieville	299,000
Gulquae Silver Black Fox Ranching Co., Ltd.............................	Woodstock........	30,000
Henderson's Silver Black Foxes, Ltd....	Shediac...........	39,000
Ideal Silver Fox, Ltd.................	Moncton..........	49,000
Little River Silver Black Fox Co., Ltd....	Moncton..........	49,000
Lutz Mountain Ranching Co., Ltd......	Lutz Mountain.....	24,950
Mapleton Fox and Fur Co., Ltd........	Moncton..........	49,000
Maritime Black Foxes Co., Ltd.........	Murray Corner.....	299,000
Melrose Black Fox Co., Ltd...........	Melrose...........	49,000
Millerton Silver Black Fox Co., Ltd....	Millerton..........	99,000
Miramichi Black Fox Co., Ltd.........	Douglastown.......	24,900
Moncton Black Foxes, Ltd............	Moncton..........	30,000
Mountain Park Silver Black, Foxes, Ltd.	Moncton..........	70,000
Murray Corner Black Fox., Ltd........	Murray Corner.....	248,000
New Brunswick Black Foxes, Ltd......	Salisbury..........	60,000
New Brunswick Black and Silver Fox Co., Ltd.............................	Renous...........	99,000
New Brunswick Taplin-Irving Black Foxes, Ltd........................	Buctouche........	100,000
Northern Foxes, Ltd.................	Blacks Harbour.....	35,000
Petiticodiac Black Fox Co., Ltd.......	Salisbury..........	90,000
Provincial Fox Co., Ltd..............	Renforth..........	99,000
Reade Fur Farms, Ltd...............	Moncton..........	49,000
Restigouche Fox Co., Ltd.............	Campbellton.......	20,000
Richmond Fox and Fur Co., Ltd......	Woodstock........	20,000
Riverbank Fox Co., Ltd..............	Renforth..........	99,000
Sackville Black Foxes, Ltd............	Sackville..........	39,400
St. John River Black Foxes, Ltd.......	Gagetown..........	49,000
St. Stephen Fox Ranching Co., Ltd.....	St. Stephen	75,000
Salisbury Black Fox and Fur Co., Ltd..	Salisbury..........	60,000

	Place of Busines	Capitalization
Scotch Settlement Black Fox Ranching Co., Ltd.	Moncton	49,000
Stanley Fur Ranching Co., Ltd.	Stanley	20,000
Sterling Silver Fox Co., Ltd.	Hampton	49,000
Timberdale Fur Farms, Ltd.	Dorchester	100,000
Williams, Barker, Ltd.	St. John	49,000

Permits issued to Capture Fur-bearing Animals in New Brunswick?

Connell, Dennis	Little Bartibog	4 Mink
Connell, Martin	Chatham	2 Sable
Connell, Michael	Little Bartibog	2 Beaver, 2 Sable
Cormier, Nazare	Rogersville	2 Beaver
Day, Thomas	Plaster Rock	2 Marten
Doak, James	Doaktown	1 Beaver
Dorcas, Keith	Harvey Station	1 Mink
Estabrooks, George B.	Cookville	2 Mink
Finigan, Joe	Rogersville	1 Beaver
Frauley, Geo. E.	St. George	5 Mink
Great Canada Black Fox Co., Ltd.	Loggieville	4 Mink, 2 Marten and 5 Fisher
Johnson, Wallace	Halcomb	4 Mink
Johnson, Wilbert	Lawrence Station	1 Mink
Kay, William C.	River Glade	1 Mink
Landry, D. V.	Buctouche	4 Mink, 20 Skunks, 20 Raccoons, 20 Foxes
Little, Clarence	York Mills	2 Mink
Little, M. George	York Mills	4 Mink
Martin, Enoch	Alma	1 Mink
Matheson, Henry E.	Bonny River	2 Mink
Murray, R. J.	Murray Road	4 Mink
Parkin, A. G.	Petitcodiac	4 Mink
Parkin, George R.	Parkindale	1 Mink
Richard, Antoine A.	McLeod Mills	4 Beaver
Short, Harry W.	McAdam Junction	1 Mink
Sullivan, William M.	Red Bank	4 Sable and 10 Mink
Sutherland, F. D.	Cassilis	2 Mink, 2 Sable
White, George E.	Narrows	2 Mink
Williston, H.	Newcastle	4 Mink

QUEBEC

Incorporated Fur-farming Companies

	Place of Business	Capitalization
Cascapedia Black Fox Co..............	Cascapedia.........	....
Compagnie et Ferme d'Animaux à Fourrure.............................	Eastman.............	....
Compagnie Zoologique Nationale (La)...	Montreal............	....
Dominion Fox Co...................	Montreal...........	....
Renard Noir Limitée, (Le)............	Marieville..........	....

Permits Issued for Taking and Keeping in Captivity, During the Close Season, Fur-bearing Animals for Breeding Purposes in Quebec

Bastien, T.............	Lorette.............	Foxes
Cascapedia Black Fox Co., Ltd., The.......	Cascapedia..........	Fur-bearing animals
Coffin, Walter.........	....	Mink
Compagnie Zoologique Nationale, La........	Montreal............	Fur-bearing animals
Elliot, A. J............	La Tuque...........	Foxes
Hadley, W. A..........	Rock Island.......	...es
Hardy & Pinault.......	La Tuque..........	...e
Holt, Renfrew & Co.....	Quebec.............	...es
Hyman & Sons, William.	Gaspe..............	Foxes
Joncas, Richard........	Natashquan.........	Foxes
Lacombe, Elie.........	Lavaltrie...........	Foxes
Malone, T.............	Three Rivers........	Foxes
Martin, Robert........	Armagh Sta., Co. Bellechasse...........	Mink
McNelly, A. R.........	Weymontachi.......	Foxes
McRea, Dr. H. A.......	North Hatley........	Fox
Rowley, George.......	Lake Edward........	Foxes
Stocks, T. J...........	....	Mink
Thompson, Howard E...	East Angus.........	Foxes
Tremblay, Alphide......	La Tuque...........	Foxes
Wright, Peter.........	Pigou, North Shore...	Foxes
Wright, William Henry..	Cowansville.........	Mink

ONTARIO
Names and Addresses of Fur-farmers

Bates, Bros................	Ridgetown
Beggs, T. J................	Heron Bay
Black, Alex. N............	Dutton
Burrowman, T. L..........	Wyoming
Clark, Rev. George........	St. Catharines
Croft, L. V...............	Middleville
Cross, Ernest..............	Silver Islet
Davies & Swain............	McIntosh *via* Sioux Lookout
Deagle, J. M..............	Orangeville
Deeks, C. A...............	Feronia
Downham, John...........	Strathroy
Edwards, Frank...........	Sioux Lookout
Foster, W. B..............	Trout Creek
Hamilton, R. E............	Grand Valley
Hubbell, E. S. & Sons......	Thamesville
Laliberte, Edgar...........	Raith
Logan, David..............	Wilsonville
Lucas, Samuel.............	Wyoming
McCune, T. M.............	Wako
McDonald, Angus..........	Big Lake
McMillan, Allan...........	Graham
Nuttall, A. W.............	Port Arthur
Reihe, Franz..............	Hearst
Reid, D. G................	Bothwell
Ryan, Leo.................	Rainy River
Troke, Edward............	Allan Water, *via* Superior Junction
Wells, H. C.	Mile 24, Bell's Residence, East Superior Junction
Whelehan.................	Chesterville
Wilson, Nelson G..........	Vittoria
Vanatter, Blake...........	Ballinafad

MANITOBA
Fur-farming Companies and Fur-farmers

Winnipeg Fur Co., Ltd......	Lac du Bonnet
Grenon, J. P..............	Winnipegosis

ALBERTA

Fox Companies Licensed in Alberta

Alberta Black and Silver Fox Co., Ltd.	$ 90,000
Athabasca Black and Silver Fox Co., Ltd.	50,000
Calgary Silver Black Fox Co., Ltd.	50,000
Edmonton Silver Black Fox Co., Ltd.	375,000
Lamont Silver Black Fox Co., Ltd.	50,000
Northern Fox Co., Ltd.	100,000
Pioneer Black Fox Co., Ltd.	100,000
Prince Edward Island Silver Black Fox Company of Alberta, Ltd.	20,000
Star Silver Black Fox Co., Ltd.	40,000

BRITISH COLUMBIA

Incorporated Fur-farming Companies

British Columbia Black Foxes, Ltd., Vancouver	$250,000
British Columbia and Yukon Fox Co. Ltd. .... Vancouver	

Fur-farming Companies Operating Under Dominion Charters

	Place of business	Capital-ization
Black Banks Pedigreed, P. E. I.		
British Canadian Fur and Trading Company, Limited	Montreal, Que.	100,000
Canada Fur Company, Limited.		
Cascapedia Silver Black F x Company, Limited	Grand Cascapedia	100,000
Dominion Black Foxes, Limited	Sackville, N. B.	250,000
Dominion Karakul-Arabi Sheep and Fur Company, Limited	Lawrencetown, N. S.	150,000
Gaspe Fur Farmers, Limited	St. John, N. B.	250,000

	Place of business	Capital-ization
Gulf Shore Silver Black Fox and Fur Company........................	Chatham, N. B.....	45,000
International Black Foxes, Limited.....	Sherbrooke, P. Q...	500,000
North Canadian Furs Company, Limited	Montreal, Que......	100,000
Sherbrooke Black Fox Company, Limited	Sherbrooke, P. Q...	150,000
Silver Black Fox Company, Limited....	Toronto, Ont.......	$450,000
Tantramar Black Foxes, Limited.......	Sackville, N. B.....	200,000
Westmorland Black Foxes, Limited. ...	Port Elgin, N. B....	200,000

Appendix XII

Report of Sale of Furs

By C. M. Lampson & Co.

64 Queen Street, E.C.,
London, 3rd April, 1914.

Compared with last January Sale

OPOSSUM, AUSTRALIAN........Realized Old Prices.
The Blue and Thirds sold comparatively better than the other kinds
OPOSSUM, RING TAIL..........Declined 10 Per Cent.
WOMBAT.......................Too small an offering to quote.
WALLABY.....................Declined 5 Per Cent.
The Victorian and Tasmanian kinds brought fully last sale's prices, as did also the Thirds and the Second quality Furriers Silvery Light sides, but the first quality of these latter show a reduction of about 10 per cent in values.
KANGAROO....................Realized Old Prices.
FOX, RED AUSTRALIAN........Declined 15 Per Cent.
The offering consisted of late caught skins, and the decline was most marked on the lower qualities.

Compared with last March Sale

SKUNK........................Declined 27½ Per Cent.
The Black and Short Striped sold at about 10 per cent below January, but the Long Striped and White realized nearly January prices.
The Southwestern kinds did not sell as well as those from the better sections.
MUSQUASH....................Declined 32½ Per Cent.
 " Southern................ " 45 " "
 " Black.................... " 15 " "
were maintained.
The few "Spring" contained in the Catalogue were mostly early-caught. The strong-pelted "Winter" were keenly competed for, and the Fall and Southern were somewhat higher.
Black met with good demand, and prices show a material improvement as compared with January.
SABLE RUSSIAN................Realized Old Prices.
The offering, which consisted almost exclusively of Kamschatka skins, met with good competition, and realised fully last March values.
OPOSSUM, AMERICAN..........Declined 20 Per Cent.
These barely brought January prices. The bidding was without animation, and it was evident that the unusually heavy offering had a depressing effect.
RACCOON......................Declined 35 Per Cent.
Mainly owing to the extremely large offering, January prices could not be maintained, and values show an average production of 15 per cent

as compared with that sale, the small selling better than the larger sizes. The "Dark" did not sell at all well. A noticeable feature of the Sale was the absence of the usual support from Canada and the United States.

CHINCHILLA...................DECLINED 35 PER CENT.

The offering, which consisted principally of Chinchillona, also contained several small parcels of Peruvian. The few Bastards show a decline of 10 per cent.

T' ER........................REALISED OLD PRICES.

LEOPARD......................SOLD WELL WITHOUT CHANGE.

SQUIRREL.....................REALISED OLD PRICES.

SACS, &c.....................REALISED OLD PRICES.

BEAVER.......................DECLINED 25 PER CENT.

The demand was poor, and prices receded from those of January.
The reduction was more especially noticeable in the pale kinds and in the small sizes.

OTTER........................DECLINED 30 PER CENT.

The Canada and United States kinds show a decline on the reduced prices of last January, this being particularly apparent in the paler sorts.
The South American, African and Chinese, on the other hand, realized full values.

SEA OTTER....................REALISED OLD PRICES.

Full March prices were obtained, the best Black realising relatively higher values than the Brown and poorer colours.

FOX, CROSS...................ADVANCED 20 PER CENT.

The heavy lecline in values which took place in January has been further accentuated; nevertheless, values are still 20 per cent above those of last March.
In sympathy with the strong demand for Silver Fox, the Silvery kinds of Cross Fox realised excellent prices, but the reddish pale and off-colour skins barely brought March rates.

FOX, SILVER..................ADVANCED 25 PER CENT.

These were in excellent request and, although not as high as in January, are distinctly higher than last March.
The fresh blue, slight silvery skins were keenly competed for at considerably enhanced prices, and there was a brisk demand even for the poorer sorts. A feature of the Sale was the entire absence of demand for the Black skins, which in many instances brought less than half former values.
This is a serious matter to the breeders of black foxes in Eastern Canada, as values will assuredly be lower when the supply of this class of skins is largely increased.

FOX, WHITE...................REALISED OLD PRICES.

There was keen competition at full March prices.

FOX, BLUE....................REALISED OLD PRICES.

The collection contained a good many Siberian and Arctic skins, and these, together with the Alaskas, brought full values.

LYNX.........................DECLINED 40 PER CENT.

Sold steadily at full January prices.

FISHER.......................DECLINED 30 PER CENT.

On the average, values are about the same as in January. The dark sold at an advance, whilst the pale show a corresponding decline.

WOLVERENE................... Declined 40 Per Cent.
> There was a further considerable decline on last January, which was special-
> ly marked in the good colours, whereas the pale sold relatively higher

MUSK OX....................... Too small an offering to quote.

MOLE   Show no recovery from the depression existing in January and prices are
> below those of last March.

MARMOT........................ Sold Badly.

MARTEN........................ Declined 40 Per Cent.
> Values receded considerably as compared with last March, especially for the
> pale.
> The Light Brown and best colours on the other hand realised full prices.

MARTEN, BAUM.................. Declined 10 Per Cent.

MARTEN, STONE................. Declined 15 Per Cent.

MARTEN, JAPANESE............. Realised Old Prices.

KOLINSKY { Chinese............. Declined 50 Per Cent.
           { Siberian............. Declined 10 Per Cent.

FITCH......................... Advanced 50 Per Cent.

ERMINE........................ Declined 40 Per Cent.
> Prices receded still further from January, especially so far as the Firsts and
> Seconds were concerned.

FOX, RED...................... Declined 5 Per Cent.
> The North American and Continental kinds were well competed for at a
> slight advance on last sale's prices, but the flat Chinese were considerably
> lower.

FOX, GRAY..................... Declined 25 Per Cent.

FOX, KITT..................... Declined 25 Per Cent.
> The best fine pelted large sized Patagonian skins, which are becoming
> scarce, realised an advance on January, but all the smaller sorts and the
> heavier pelted skins from further North were difficult to sell even at reduced
> prices

HAIR SEAL, DRY................ Realised Old Prices.

CAT, WILD..................... Declined 40 Per Cent.

CAT, HOUSE.................... Declined 40 Per Cent.
> The Black and Blue brought advanced prices, but other colours show a
> corresponding decline.

CAT, CIVET.................... Declined 30 Per Cent.

MINK.......................... Declined 40 Per Cent.
> Owing to the extremely large offering and the lack f support from the
> United States and Canada, prices show a further serious decline from
> January; the Northern and Eastern sold better than Western and South-
> western kinds.

FOX, JAPANESE................. Realised Old Prices.
> The few good skins sold at high prices.

BADGER........................ Sold at Very Low Prices.

BADGER, JAPANESE............. Realised Old Prices.

BEAR, BLACK & BROWN.......... Declined 25 Per Cent.

BEAR, GRIZZLY................. Declined 10 Per Cent.

WOLF.......................... Declined 10 Per Cent.
> In spite of the good demand which has existed during the past winter,
> this fur sold considerably lower than in January, mainly in consequence
> of the large quantity offered.

STATEMENT OF QUANTITIES OF FURS SOLD BY C. M. LAMPSON & CO.

	1913				Totals for 1913	1914	
	January	March	June	October		January	March
	Skins	Skins	Skins	Skins	Skins	Skins	Skins
RACCOON ..	70,914	140,611	54,966	36,229	302,720	84,116	206,657
MUSQUASH .	1,635,768	826,394	784,575	614,273	3,861,010	1,534,065	3,079,371
" Black	10,870	17,060	36,105	12,729	76,764	22,733	63,862
SKUNK......	314,783	334,379	155,038	59,438	863,638	314,870	540,432
CAT, Civet ...	37,102	37,349	19,894	13,823	108,168	23,117	101,149
OPOSSUM, Amer'n.	272,068	323,393	165,552	54,581	815,594	321,802	635,024
MINK........	32,620	51,125	12,203	24,671	120,619	18,119	95,558
MARTEN ...	6,428	8,879	5,997	6,257	27,561	6,724	12,331
FOX, Red ...	15,393	17,889	26,254	36,859	96,395	15,110	24,536
" Cross ..	539	2,030	502	1,041	4,112	441	1,986
" Silver..	77	553	118	213	961	102	544
" Gray...	5,720	13,418	7,290	6,593	33,022	11,086	32,306
" Kitt ..	17,806	5,893	8,146	31,443	63,288	29,736	18,835
" White .	5,196	2,279	1,018	4,250	12,743	2,361	2,836
" Blue...	248	2,388	88	787	3,511	173	985
OTTER......	5,003	4,426	2,403	2,571	14,403	4,892	4,539
SEA OTTER.		81			81		124
CAT, Wild, &c.	8,942	6,594	5,797	13,977	35,310	12,023	14,029
" House....	14,561	35,239	23,450	24,427	97,677	31,079	35,320
LYNX.......	1,571	717	2,651	3,161	8,100	2,721	3,331
FISHER	433	1,042	448	499	2,422	270	1,703
BADGER ...	1,887	3,529	4,438	2,904	12,758	2,572	8,673
BEAVER....	7,575	7,498	3,417	4,580	23,070	4,450	12,286
BEAR........	3,150	5,294	3,966	5,098	17,508	2,591	3,049
WOLF.......	18,036	20,380	8,312	6,487	53,215	9,306	34,167
WOLVERENE	250	692	190	609	1,741	253	764
HAIR SEAL, Dry	1,229	207	87	17	1,540	181	728
GREBE......	13,516	1,328	600		15,444	6,662	1,630
FUR SEAL, Dry		204	34		238	53	181
" " Salted	5,570	1,795	570	7,010	14,945	450	1,224
SABLE, Russian	1,670	8,294	59	1,487	11,510	1,461	5,557
KOLINSKY .	18,646	22,900	15,326	86,945	143,817	114,791	64,500
MARTEN, Baum	541	471	977	1,093	3,082	404	1,220
" Stone	1,033	2,596	1,939	2,052	7,620	1,678	1,575
FITCH.......	4,050	6,777	10,043	8,145	29,015	4,031	16,679
ERMINE.....	58,747	79,718	70,315	43,252	252,032	42,821	194,406

STATEMENT OF QUANTITIES OF FURS SOLD BY C. M. LAMPSON & CO.
(Continued)

	1913				Totals for 1913	1914	
	January	March	June	October		January	March
	Skins	Skins	Skins	Skins	Skins	Skins	Skins
SQUIRREL..	212,790	123,197	141,658	150,532	628,177	156,706	101,194
SACS, &c.....	7,919	4,932	4,314	5,906	23,071	1,859	2,494
CHINCHILLA							
Real	3,624	12,300	1,731	2,339	19,994	4,021	5,842
Bastard							
MINK,							
Japanese	23,283	28,026	16,442	16,856	84,607	10,597	725
MARTEN,							
Japanese	5,453	550	683	2,369	9,055	307	1,124
SABLE,							
Japanese			57	170	227		
FOX,							
Japanese	4,474	3,106	1,679	6,058	15,317	8,287	11,017
BADGER,							
Japanese	1,254	1,935	978	1,092	5,259	907	673
MOLE.......	203,985	312,449	447,164	491,526	1,455,124	544,431	404,825
OPOSSUM							
Austrin.	90,155	87,500	20,498	77,447	275,600	57,470	42,919
" Ring Tail	61,641	33,234	3,741	193,426	292,042	79,806	156,031
WALLABY,	331,017	171,117	152,702	225,654	880,490	202,239	181,943
Austrin.							
KANGAROO							
Austrin.	4,022	4,295	695	16,682	25,694	3,927	8,592
WOMBAT,							
Austrin.	1,106	...	1,622	1,696	4,676	843	261
FOX, RED,							
Austrin.	45,695	19,995	10,560	49,457	125,707	22,943	8,286

Index

A

17